ASPECTS OF EDUCATIONAL TECHNOLOGY

VOLUME VI

Edited for the Association for
Programmed Learning and
Educational Technology by

K. AUSTWICK

N. D. C. HARRIS

General Editor

JOHN LEEDHAM

PITMAN PUBLISHING

First published 1972

SIR ISAAC PITMAN AND SONS LTD.
Pitman House, Parker Street, Kingsway, London WC2B 5PB
P.O. Box 46038, Portal Street, Nairobi, Kenya

SIR ISAAC PITMAN (AUST.) PTY. LTD.
Pitman House, Bouverie Street, Carlton, Victoria 3053, Australia

PITMAN PUBLISHING COMPANY S.A. LTD.
P.O. Box 11231, Johannesburg, South Africa

PITMAN PUBLISHING CORPORATION
6 East 43rd Street, New York, N.Y. 10017, U.S.A.

SIR ISAAC PITMAN (CANADA) LTD.
495 Wellington Street West, Toronto 135, Canada

THE COPP CLARK PUBLISHING COMPANY
517 Wellington Street West, Toronto 135, Canada

ISBN: 0 273 31782 2

Printed by photo-lithography and made in Great Britain at
the Pitman Press, Bath
G2—(G.4677:15)

Foreword

Conference aim and organization

The organizing committee for the Conference felt that an attempt should be made to apply the present state of Educational Technology to the Conference. The structure of the Conference, both internally and externally, was an attempt to practise what we preach.

The overall aim of the Conference was to encourage delegates to start again in their thinking about Educational Technology. It was felt that it would be helpful to subdivide the Conference into four modules. These four modules represent four strategies involved in course or curriculum development. It is possible to subdivide in other ways and there is no pretence that these are in any way independent strategies or that four has any significance: it was the constraints of the Conference that produced four main modules.

During each module the delegates who participated were expected to become aware of work being done in this country and overseas. By use of study groups the delegates became involved in these developments. The objectives here were mainly in the affective domain. The cognitive objectives were related to the resource materials available in the Library which required delegates to carry out anything from analytical procedures to pure retention of knowledge.

In parallel with modules 3 and 4, two modules were organized on a different basis for Medical Education, modules 5 and 6.

Module organization

The resource materials for each module were available in the University Library throughout the Conference. These were presented in a variety of different ways, some using media, some being only printed materials. Many of the media presentations are represented in the proceedings by only a summary, for the full presentation, application should be made to the appropriate author (the method of presentation is included with the summary).

The modules were organized by asking a speaker to pose the problems he saw in the area. This speaker also had access, beforehand, to the presentations in the module. The delegates then had a further hour to return to the Resource Materials before joining a study group in a sub-area of the module (see Contents Table). At the study group a rapporteur picked out one or two salient points relating to the problems posed. After discussion with the chairman of the group, the rapporteur reported back to a final session, chaired by the original speaker.

The University site

The compact nature of the University site and the design of the University Library made it feasible to organize the Conference on this modular basis (see figure). The Library, with large open plan spaces including study carrels and studies with appropriate services, lent itself to a situation such as this.

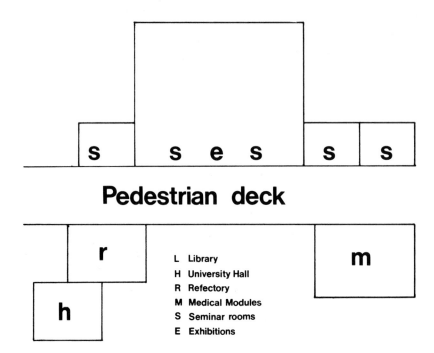

Pedestrian deck

L Library
H University Hall
R Refectory
M Medical Modules
S Seminar rooms
E Exhibitions

Layout of the Buildings used during the Conference

The medical modules

The medical modules were organized in association with Mr C Engel of the BMA Audio Visual Communications Unit. These were to emphasize objectives in medical education (Module 5) and the use of self-instructional material (Module 6). Papers were invited relating to innovations in these two areas, each paper being followed by a discussion. Each module consisted of a short introduction followed by a paper, discussion; second paper, etc. In addition, other papers were received which are included in the appropriate chapter; these were incorporated in a small exhibition in a concourse area specifically for the medical modules.

The organization of the papers and cross referencing system

The papers in these proceedings are shown in the section which the editors felt was most appropriate for the paper. Obviously many papers cover other modules too. At the end of each module in the Contents Table is listed the other papers which are also felt to be relevant to that module. Any responsibility for the papers being included in a particular module and section lies with the editors.

Acknowledgments

The editors wish to thank the authors for their cooperation in maintaining the schedules laid out for them. In addition the continual support and goodwill of Sir Isaac Pitman and Sons, and in particular the patience of Brenda Rowe and Betty Dickens helped us to achieve this publication. The diligence and initiative of Mr G Kirkby and the staff of the Centre for Adult Studies ensured the smooth running of the Conference. The computer print-outs on the study groups selected by delegates saved many tedious hours of work. Mr J Lamble, Director of Library Services, provided facilities and many hours of work in helping to organize the Conference and in particular the Exhibitions.

The chairmen and rapporteurs of the study groups made the modules function most efficiently. The chairmen were A Bano, J Barton, B Bolton, J Clarke, P R Crellin, J A Davies, W J K Davies, Wing Commander D R McCall, A P Mann, J T Mayes, E Phillips, Miss Phillips, J Pollock, A J Romiszowski, J K Sinclair, A Whitlock, R Willmore. The rapporteurs (from the University's School of Education) were C R Atthill, M Collard, R J Frost, H Hammond, F Healey, E Lewis, T McCombie, R Priest, D Roberts, B Simpson-Holley, J Smith, A Theunissen, M Walker, R Whitlow, J Williams.

The medical modules would not have been possible without the good offices of Mr C Engel of the BMA Audio Visual Communications Unit and the support of the following companies: Boehringer Ingelheim Ltd., Brocades (Great Britain) Ltd., Glaxo Ltd., May and Baker Ltd., Parke Davis & Co. Ltd. and G D Searle & Co. Ltd.

The directors of ESL Bristol, and in particular Mr Noel Whalley, gave considerable assistance in time and facilities to ensure the smooth running of the Conference.

The following papers were presented at the Conference, but for technical reasons are not included in this volume. It is hoped that they may appear in the Association's journal "Programmed Learning and Educational Technology":

The elements of social skills for young physically handicapped children, showing the use of programmed story material in the classroom.   D A Thompson

What, how and keypoints for training analysis.   Lieutenant Commander R E Hawkins, RN

Teaching algorithms and learning algorithms.   K Bung

Personality factors and self-instruction: a survey.   C Suchett-Kaye

'Mass' multi-media courses for adults.   N McIntosh and A W Bates

A curriculum designed to produce educational technologists.   P D Mitchell

The three c's in education: coding, control and communication.   A Karunanandan

ACKNOWLEDGMENTS

Parts of the Opening Address by Sir James Pitman (with appropriate revisions) were originally published in "New Approaches to Individualizing Instruction", A Report of a Conference on May 11, 1965, to mark the Dedication of Ben D Wood Hall, Educational Testing Service, Princeton, New Jersey, whose permission to republish it here is gratefully acknowledged.

Figure 2 in Michael Macdonald Ross's paper is from Richard Levins "Evolution in Changing Environments", #2, Monographs in Population Biology (copyright (c) 1968 by Princeton University Press), Fig.1.1, p.9. Reprinted by permission of Princeton University Press.

Contents

List of Contributors

Adams, M J	National Medical Audiovisual Center, Atlanta, USA
Austwick, K	University of Bath, Bath, Somerset, UK
Banks, B	32 Manor Road, Rusthall, Tunbridge Wells, Kent, UK
Bates, A W	Institute of Educational Technology, The Open University, UK
Bell, R D	Wye College (University of London), Nr Ashford, Kent, UK
Billing, D E	Thames Polytechnic Faculty of Science, Wellington Street, London, UK
Black, J	School of Engineering, University of Bath, Somerset, UK
Bolton, B	School of Electrical Engineering, University of Bath, Somerset, UK
Boyd, G M	Sir George Williams University, Montreal 107. PQ, Canada
Braham, M	Sir John Williams University, Montreal, Canada
Britton, R J	Eastbourne College of Education, Eastbourne, UK
Broderick, W R	The Royal Liberty School, Computer Dept., Romford, Essex, UK
Browaeys, R	CPTR de FPA, Route de labige, 31 Toulouse, France
Buckingham, D J	Department of Engineering Science, University of Exeter, UK
Budgett, R E B	HMS Collingwood, Fareham, Hampshire, UK
Clarke, J	Dundee College of Education, Park Place, Dundee DD1 4HP, UK
Clements, R	Group Sales Training Department, The Wellcome Foundation, The Wellcome Building, 183 Euston Road, London NW1 2BP, UK
Coldevin, G O	Sir George Williams University, Montreal, Canada
Cowan, J	Heriot-Watt University, Edinburgh, UK
Davies, W J K	St Albans Programmed Learning Centre, College of Further Education, St Albans, Herts, UK
Davis, Q V	Department of Electronic and Electrical Engineering, University of Surrey, UK
Draisma, T	formerly head Mathematics Department, Munali Secondary School, Lusaka
Edwards, R L	ESL (Bristol) Group, St Lawrence House, 29/31 Broad Street, Bristol, UK
Engel, C E	BMA AV Communication Unit, Tavistock Square, London, WC1H 9JP, UK
Eraut, M	University of Sussex, UK
Fleetwood-Walker, P	Technological Teaching Aids Centre, Faculty of Medicine, University of Birmingham, UK
Gilmore, S	Hamilton College of Education, Hamilton, ML3 0BD, UK
Glaser, D	BMA House, Tavistock Square, London, WC1H 9JP, UK
Hamer, J W	Enfield College of Technology, Queensway, Enfield, UK
Harding, J M D	ESL (Bristol), St Lawrence House, 29/31 Broad Street, Bristol, UK
Harris, N D C	University of Bath, Somerset, UK
Hills, P J	Leverhulme Research Fellow, Institute for Educational Technology, University of Surrey, UK
Howe, A	Enfield College of Technology, Queensway, Enfield, UK
Hubbard, G	National Council for Educational Technology, 160 Great Portland Street, London, W1N 5TB, UK
Hubert-White, G	35 Burrard Road, London, NW6 1DA, UK
Hull, E J	Luton and Dunstable Hospital, Luton, Bedfordshire, UK
Hutchison, I	Dundee College of Education, Park Place, Dundee DD1 4HP, UK
Hyde, G C	ESL (Bristol), St Lawrence House, 29/31 Broad Street, Bristol, UK
Isaacs, B J	Luton and Dunstable Hospital, Luton, Bedfordshire, UK
Iskander, K	University of Cairo
Jepson, J B	Middlesex Hospital Medical School, University of London, London, W1, UK
Leedham, J	College of Education, Loughborough, Leicestershire, UK
Leith, G O M	R M Phillips Research Unit, Sussex University, UK

Lenton, W	RAMC Training Centre, Aldershot, Hampshire, UK
McCormick, J	Portadown College, Portadown, Northern Ireland
Macdonald-Ross, M	Institute of Educational Technology, The Open University, UK
Mackie, A	Maths Learning System (now at City of Bath Technical College), Bath, Somerset, UK
Maclure, S	The Times Educational Supplement, Printing House Square, London, EC4, UK
Manwaring, G	Department of Education and Zoology, University of Glasgow, UK
Marson, S N	Programmed Instruction Centre for Industry, 32 Northumberland Road, Sheffield, UK
Millar, P H	Brain Sciences Information Project, Millbank Tower, Millbank, London, SW1P 4QS, UK
Mills, G M	University of Bradford, UK
Mills, J F	RAMC Training Centre, Aldershot, Hampshire, UK
Mitchell, P D	Sir George Williams University, Montreal, Canada
Moore, G A B	Sir George Williams University, Montreal, Canada
Moseley, D V	National Society for the Mentally Handicapped, 86 Newman Street, London, W1P 4AR, UK
Naeraa, N	Institute of Physiology, University of Aarhus, Denmark
Needham, M	St Albans Programmed Learning Centre, College of Further Education, St Albans, Hertfordshire, UK
Parsonage, J R	Thames Polytechnic Faculty of Science, Wellington Street, London, UK
Pitman, Sir James	ita Foundation, 154 Southampton Row, London, WC1B 5AX, UK
Raat, J H	Vrije Universiteit de Boelalaan, 1081 Amsterdam, Netherlands
Rees, D T	Inter-University Biology Teaching Project, School of Biological Sciences, University of Birmingham, UK
Reynolds, C	Stanbridge Earls School, Romsey, Hampshire, UK
Rogers, J	BMA AV Communication Unit, Tavistock Square, London, WC1H 9JP, UK
Romiszowski, A J	Enfield College of Technology, Queensway, Enfield, UK
Satanek, A	Department of Programmed Learning, Postgraduate Medical School, Praha, Czechoslovakia
Smith, A D	Middlesex Hospital Medical School, University of London, London W1, UK
Smith, J	School of Education, University of Bath, Bath, Somerset, UK
Sorbier, A	CPTR de FPA, Route de labige, 31 Toulouse, France
Sowter, D	National Society for the Mentally Handicapped, 86 Newman Street, London, W1P 4AR, UK
Sparrow, F R	Senior Research Officer, Schools Council, London, UK
Stenhouse, G	Department of Physiology, Glasgow University, UK
Taggart, G	Sir George Williams University, Montreal, Canada
Tinsley, J D	National Computing Centre Ltd., Quay House, Quay Street, Manchester M3 3HY, UK
Tribe, M	Inter-University Biology Teaching Project, Sussex University, UK
Tulloch, J	Ministry of Defence, Stanmore, Middlesex, UK
Vaughan, B W	Parochial School, Trowbridge, Wiltshire, UK
Verbrugh, H S	Department of Pathology II, Medical Faculty, Rotterdam, The Netherlands
Vries, M J de	Department of Pathology II, Medical Faculty, Rotterdam, The Netherlands
Wace, G H	ESL (Bristol), St Lawrence House, 29/31 Broad Street, Bristol BS1 2HF, UK
Walker, J T	Ministry of Defence, Stanmore, Middlesex, UK;
Walsh, J	RAF School of Education, Upwood, Huntingdon, UK
Womersley, J	Department of Physiology, Glasgow University, UK
Wyant, T G	Department of Educational Technology, Coventry Technical College, Butts, Coventry CV1 3GD, UK

Opening Address

SIR JAMES PITMAN, KBE

It may be a bromide to recall Thomson's dictum* that the ability to measure is the first step in the progress of science, but it is particularly apposite to do so when we meet to consider what needs to be done to open the eyes (and the minds) of Head Teachers — those with whom lies the action, and so the judgment and decision as to acceptance or rejection of those new ideas and new devices for improving the effectiveness of teaching and learning which Science — Social Science — has established as knowledge. Inherent in our meeting here today is the question: Does Development follow Research?

During the millennium since Pythagoras drew triangles in the dust, there has been very little advance in the devices to help the learner and the teacher. It was, after all, as recently as the reign of Queen Victoria that paper became cheap enough to permit the abandonment of the slate. Only then did the stick of wood give way to the stick of chalk, and a book came into the hands of the learners and not only those of the teacher.

We who at this Conference are aware of the great improvement in efficiency which the new ideas and devices here displayed at this Conference are offering, need to remind ourselves that notwithstanding that potential, there are, even today, not a few classrooms in which a Victorian teacher would find himself in a familiar atmosphere, and be made to feel very much at home by the attitude of his fellow teachers — that there are no ideas like old ideas, and no devices to match chalk and talk.

Possibly that negative attitude is not surprising after so many centuries of few new ideas and of fewer new devices. The present eruption, in a great diversity, of multitudes of new devices and new ideas, is probably in itself

---

*"I often say that when you can measure what you are speaking about, and express it in numbers, you know something about it; but when you cannot measure it, when you cannot express it in numbers, your knowledge is of a meagre and unsatisfactory kind: it may be the beginning of knowledge, but you have scarcely in your thoughts advanced to the stage of science, whatever the matter may be."

an explanation of, but not an excuse for, resistance to change, even when such changes have been shown incontrovertibly by research to be to the benefit of the teacher and learner.

This tendency to resist change is seen to be based on a too widespread unwillingness to study the evidence, on a contempt for the evidence and for research and for researchers, and on an unpardonable assumption that all is as well as it possibly could be, and always will be. Indeed, we must suppose that from the earliest days of history, the closed mind and a lethargic approach resisted novelty and described it as 'mere gimmickry'. Presumably that glib phrase "I, at least, don't fall for gimmicks" was spoken in Greek very long ago when there was first advanced the proposition that the square on the hypotenuse equalled the sum of the squares on the other two sides, and there then became available a device for demonstrating in the dust, the universality of the truth of that relationship. Presumably too a defence of any position once taken — one to be defended until death (literally, as I propose to show later) — has always been buttressed by complacency and moated in a false pride.

I cannot resist quoting from 'The Educational Obstacle Race: Factors that hinder Pupil Progress' by the late Dr Stephen Wiseman as Director of the National Foundation for Educational Research, when speaking of the resistance by Heads and class teachers in Nursery and Infant Schools to the innovative idea and the device of structuring the teaching of the mother tongue to pre-school children who lack the normal linguistic competence.

He was speaking of the particular device, The George Peabody Language Development kit and the NFER project in the EPA Schools in Slough — but what he said is clearly just as applicable to the resistance to all that for which this Conference stands, and for the resistance also to Sesame Street by the great majority of teachers in Infant and Nursery Schools, and by the 'acknowledged experts' on the Education Committees of the Television organizations.

This is what he said — from a long paper full of other most important truths:

> "It is true that much of the criticism" (of the Peabody Language Development kit) "derives from the fact that the programme in common use is American in origin, and that, apart from the chauvinistic reaction to an educational import, it is less than satisfactory in content and approach for British schools and British children. But it is also clear that here **we have a strong rejection by many teachers of any alteration in the traditional approach** to nursery education. The **strength** of feeling **and depth of emotional response** is often **more appropriate to religious controversy** than **to educational practice.** Educational philosophy has become educational dogma. Rachel McMillan and Susan Isaacs, both responsive to new ideas and concepts, both basing their teaching on the newest developments in educational thought, must be turning in their graves. **How can the training courses** of these teachers **have left them so inflexible, so unadaptable, so unresponsive to new insights? The educational world is changing around them, but they remain encapsulated within the shell of holy writ.** The function of our colleges

2

of education is to produce flexible professionals, adaptable to change and responsive to new demands. Some of them have clearly failed, producing instead missionaries preaching the one true doctrine, arrogantly repudiating any deviation from it. And this is all the more remarkable when one considers that a typical day's programme for nursery school children from deprived areas contains no more than 40 minutes or so of structured language teaching, with the rest of the day devoted to traditional free activity and play."

Is it to be unduly self-deprecatory to ask ourselves, particularly here and today, whether we moderns are not, as it were, emerging from the dark ages of knowledge and measurement rather than nearing perfection? Might it not be healthy to ask ourselves how far advanced we are as yet along that highway of measurement of knowledge and of progress based upon it? Have not the social sciences had a very poor start in developing a technique of testing and of measuring facts? After all, have not health and disease, property and poverty, knowledge and wisdom been from the beginning of time linked in men's minds with taboos, magic, morals, and religion? In those days, convention, no doubt because it is inevitably artificial, needed to be sanctified by mysticism — so much so that even today a ship, as well as a child, is never named save in an elaborate ritual.

We in the social sciences probably need to admit that we have inherently been less rapidly responsive to the disciplines of fact and of measurement than, shall we say, those in mechanical engineering. Even our colleages in mechanical engineering need to admit that, as in the Middle Ages, the 'generally accepted professional opinion' of their predecessors has, too often and too long, masqueraded as incontrovertible fact. Our mechanistic colleagues, however, have been more rudely faced than we have by the discipline that assumptions are **not** facts and that in a healthy tussle between those two, assumption **must** succumb to fact. We all need to recognize that the views of the experts of one generation have come to be rejected, and to be regarded with utter contempt, by the experts of succeeding generations.

In a historical setting in which the axioms of the past have thus generally been rejected contemptuously, may we be so complacent about all our rightness today, so sure that the tempo of change is even now not the slow tempo of science emerging from the Dark Ages? Are we so certain that all our current 'generally accepted professional opinions' are tenable because of fact and measurement rather than by the mere lethargy of continuity and traditions?

We know that medicine emerged only very slowly from the dark ages of 'generally accepted professional opinion' when it first experienced the shattering need to relate newly ascertained fact with existing tradition and opinion. George Washington was bled to death only because 'professional opinion' then agreed that bleeding was the therapeutic treatment for pneumonia — indeed, a panacea sufficient to make diagnosis virtually unncessary. Charles Dickens was writing of Victorian days, so short a time ago, when those two

3

medical students in the 'Pickwick Papers', Bob Sawyer and Benjamin Allen, held 'a hurried consultation on the advisability of bleeding the company generally as an improving little bit of professional practice'. Even as late as 1871, Queen Victoria wrote in her diary (3rd September) of her reluctant agreement to have applied to her the principles of aseptic surgery which Professor Lister had propounded as long before as 1858! It was to take very much longer before tradition was broken down and the benefit of ascertained facts could reach the operating table — so that a man need no longer enter a hospital for an operation, having made his will, justifiably fearing that his chances of coming out alive were less than one in ten.

We may perhaps ask ourselves whether the sad story of that overly slow change in medical opinion may not hold a warning, particularly to us experts in education even today. We may perhaps ask in what respect does conservatism of the status quo, invoked to protect the professional standing and collective infallibility of the expert and to respect the sacrosanctity of their 'generally accepted professional opinion', work any less strongly in education today.

It would come ill from me to suggest that the spirit of science is lacking in the field of education, seeing that I regard it as the greatest success of my lifetime, in a short span of no more than thirty years, to have brought to the acid test of measurement the proposition that for a teacher to continue initial or remedial teaching of reading and writing through traditional orthography is as grossly unprofessional as for a surgeon to operate on a patient with no antiseptic precautions, and so to question the most emotionally held of all existing value-judgments in education. Per contra, it has been a tribute of the highest honour to our educationists in the London University Institute of Education (Lionel Elvin) and in our National Foundation for Educational Research (Doctor Wall) that there were found experts not only willing but actually anxious to submit so sacrosanct a subject to the hard test of fact. Rather it has been in the rejection of their knowledge and in a failure to concede the consequences of facts so measured and numerated that we have lagged behind. The speed of acceptance of the lessons of facts and of consequent response in classroom action is the all-important test.

We need to concede that in education there has hitherto been no 'marriage' between Research and Development — no 'courting', and even very little 'walking out'.

If research be masculine and Development the essential female counterpart for conceiving and bringing to fruition the knowledge emitted by Research, we face, in a world still to be starved of Development, a sad present and most doubtful future for the survival of Research, and a 'dark age' in parturition by Development.

We in education cannot apparently be at all sanguine about the future of educational research as a fashioner of decisions. The closed mind, the authoritarian attitude which knows best, and refuses even to consider the evidence, is indeed to be deplored, but after all, the roots of conservatism run deep in human nature. A habit is something which saves us trouble. Just as 'the well-grooved golf swing' economizes effort, so a preconception saves thought. Thus we all tend to fight to preserve our habits, however bad they may be, and the scientist often tends to be as conservative as any other man.

It seems, however, that open-mindedness (and pre-judgment) vary as between one field and another. Indeed in the field of Social Science and in particular of education, the expert is at least as conservative and resistant to accepting any other point of view as anyone else is, particularly if the opposing view overthrows his accepted traditions and thus undermines his present theories and current practices. He tends to be more conservative in proportion to the extent that his assumptions are deeply entrenched and regarded as sacrosanct, and to the degree that his subject is vulnerable to the battery of facts. Even when, as in surgery, fact had incontrovertibly overwhelmed assumption, those surgeons who had devoted their lecturing lives to advising their young successors (incorrectly, as Lister's demon-strations had long ago shown), understandably found it hard to tear up their lecture notes and to admit, even to themselves, that their lives had been — albeit innocently — misdirected. Progress was achieved in the end, but at the cost of fifty years of mortality — and that mortality of patients was ended only by the mortality of the oldest surviving practising surgeon!

It would seem harder for the expert to forget than to remember, and harder to unlearn than to learn. Maybe experts in the Mechanical Sciences suffer less in this respect. Perhaps that is one reason why it is easier for the mechanical scientist to discard the old and accept the new.

At least the surgical expert does not find himself influenced by an addi-tional conservative pressure to which all of us in education are inherently prone. No medical expert, when viewing his own post-operative scar, would ever suggest not only that all other men should have a similar scar but also that they should have had it for the same reason, by the same surgeon, with the same anaesthetic, down to the same smallest detail of suture. Yet, we in education find it hard, when shaving in the morning, not to discover in the glass the solution to the greatest of all educational questions: how best to bring up the young. The conclusion is likely to be narcissistic:

Look at that fine chap reflected in the mirror. How did he become so? Ergo, conserve what is good: All cannot have been so wrong with what I had in my day. I will resist to the last gasp this particular piece of new-fangled gimmickry, this unwarranted reflection upon my own up-bringing. There must be some other explanation, which I may surely find, which will justify me in rejecting those purported facts.

We may ask ourselves whether it may not be true that **had** those, whose new ideas and new devices we are met together in this Conference to foster and develop, been operating in the mechanical rather than the educational field, acceptance would have been very much higher. Surely their contributions to knowledge would have been immediately accepted and forthwith applied. It is certainly true that a paper published on say a new alloy, having valuable properties hitherto not available, would lead forthwith to tests by replication – and to production in all the relevant metallurgical establishments.

Admittedly the mechanical sciences have had hitherto an important natural advantage over social sciences. The Social Sciences have hitherto, because assumptions are so subjective and hard to control, tended to lag behind the mechanical sciences in accepting the impact of measurement. All the same, will it be forever impossible to overcome this tendency? Can we not make absolutely clear in our minds the distinction between assumptions (and feeling) and the factual dimensions within which such assumptions may become **objective**? If so, there need surely be no limit to the precision of our measurement, nor to the objectivity of our decisions. Only then will we no longer need to admit that the social sciences do not parallel the mechanical sciences in building upon knowledge.

Meanwhile, what do we **know**? Do we really **know** what education is? Do we **know** even that education is good for the child? Or are we only stating the tautological — the good is good, the less good less good, and the bad bad? These questions need to be answered and generally accepted before we can hope that new ideas and new devices will be more readily accepted because those who form the judgments, take the decisions, and alone are able to act, will have done so as truly educated servants of knowledge.

If man's transcending excellence is his unique ability to be communicated with and to communicate to others by the medium of words, then it is of prime importance to develop that conceptualization and vocabulary which is the foundation of communication by language. If that ability in turn gives to man the opportunity to acquire further concepts and vocabulary from others, and to be stimulated by further thoughts which have come to the minds of others, then to an even greater extent the purpose of education must be so to perfect that verbal communicative system — first, in man's ability to be communicated with and to communicate, and, secondly, in the corpus of experience of that knowledge and of those thoughts which are so to be communicated and received. Thus, both second-hand and first-hand, experience and knowledge will come to be maximized. This second-hand experience received by verbal communication is of the greatest benefit and importance because it is added to first-hand experience and both may be, and often are, passed on to others. Such mutuality in the expansion of experience, knowledge, and thought, increases yet further the capability to develop creative verbal thought and verbal communication.

6

I wish to hazard what may be a rash suggestion: that it is in the communicative system that there is most still to be measured and learned educationally. I suggest that far too few English-speaking people adequately develop their own great potential to conceptualize and to communicate; and that they thus benefit too little from, and contribute too little to, their fellows.

If this conjecture were to be correct, we need to ask whether we are yet really able to measure communicative ability and, above all, whether we do so. We know whether a child is visually disabled and are able to measure the degree of his disability. Do we similarly know whether and to what extent a child is subnormal in communicative ability, or do we unwarrantedly assume that he is normal merely because he is seen to respond appropriately to what we may say to him? Do we not too often mislead ourselves that he is normally verbal because we are not aware that what he has received and comprehended has been only a **situational** message and not a **verbal** one — in the same way that a dog obeys his master, having been conditioned to his wishes rather than in responding to truly verbal stimuli? Even some apparently communicative adults not only do not understand all the words they hear or read, but will also even use such words imitatively, without possessing the concepts which they are supposedly communicating.

May we return to that question posed by Stephen Wiseman:

"How can the training courses of these teachers have left them so inflexible, so unadaptable, so unresponsive to new insights? The educational world is changing around them, but they remain encapsulated within the shell of holy writ."

and to the obvious fact that it is the Head Teachers, products of these Colleges of Education, in whom lies the judgment and decision as to the acceptance of new knowledge; that it is upon the lecturers in those Colleges upon whom lies the responsibility for initial training of those Head Teachers; upon the professed experts on the teaching of reading and writing among such lecturers lies the responsibility for subsequent advice to those Head Teachers. The circle has been self-perpetuating — first to school, then to Training College, then to school and back again to Training College. It may well be that there is little prospect of a true scientific attitude in the field of education, until our young children have been so taught that more and more of them become more and more facile masters of all four skills in language, and those who become lecturers can stop that circle being vicious. After all, Rhetoric (and P. E.) were the base of all the brilliantly new knowledge which has come to us so long ago through that wonderful flowering of the human mind in Greece. Speaking, Listening, Reading, Writing: success in all four of these skills is the necessary foundation for knowledge and for applying it, and of these the two emissive — speaking and writing — are the two most important. Would that a beginning were made to teach language in all four of its aspects, and that the teaching of reading should no longer be allowed virtually to exclude the deliberate teaching of the other three.

Conference Address

STUART MACLURE

I am not sure whether I really ought to begin — as is usual on these occasions — by thanking you for inviting me to take part in your conference.   I am an educational journalist, not an educational technologist. I find myself in that perennially unsatisfactory situation of being a layman among experts.   If I can claim to know anything about communication, my star is fixed firmly in the Guthenberg galaxy. I lack even the technique and the inventiveness to present my material in new and exciting ways as — I believe — is to be the rule throughout the rest of this conference. I stand, therefore, at every disadvantage in a professional conference of this kind. All I can do is to hope that as my ignorance is general rather than specialized I can try to start a few hares in those all important border areas where your expertise makes contact with the other skills of education and, in particular, with the teacher.

When I sat down to think what I was going to say, I began by ruminating on the brief which Professor Austwick gave me. He suggested that I should say something about the response of the schools to the prospects held out to them by what he called 'scientific or technological approaches to education'. Teachers have been, and largely remain, suspicious of educational technology: they sense that it threatens to change their traditional role and, if for no other reason, because most of us are apprehensive about change, they resist it. What can or should be done about this ? How can educational technology get rid of its cloven hoof and forked tail ?

There would be no point in standing up in this audience to argue that technology need not threaten the teacher with redundancy. You know, and I know, that this is a chestnut of an argument, and any way I have no taste for preaching to the converted. In fact, of course, if educational technology really did threaten to replace teachers (and, therefore, save a lot of money) we should have had a great deal more of it, a great deal quicker. I have always been amazed at the mealy-mouthed way in which exponents of your technology discuss this matter as if it were not quite decent to mention, or as if the tendency to pussy-foot around vested professional interests even

8

extends to those who have warmed themselves before the white heat of the technological age.

Of course one plausible explanation might be that there is little prospect of saving resources, only of getting better value for money, which would explain why the dividends have been expressed in the form of efficiency rather than cost saving. But the concepts with which the educational technologists have made us all familiar, emphasize that 'efficiency' is a quality which can only be considered in relation to some set of stated or unstated objectives. And as soon as you consider objectives and their efficient attainment you are squarely within the field of **curriculum development.**

It has now become a commonplace — in education at least — to regard educational technology and curriculum development as intertwined. If the content and objectives of education were already settled once and for all it might be possible to discuss a systematic approach to the learning of **this** content and the achievement of **these** objectives — as if, that is, the technology were neutral. But is the technology neutral? This is one of the critical questions in curriculum development which is receiving attention in Europe and the United States as well as here. Different styles of curriculum development have within them different social, educational, even political values. It makes no sense to talk about a teacher — or anyone else for that matter — being in favour of, or opposed to, curriculum development per se, as if it were a single entity: you can accept or reject different styles because of the values which they enshrine — and the same, as I see it, must logically go for educational technology interpreted broadly as 'scientific and technological approaches to education'.

However, let us begin by looking back to simpler times when some of these questions were asked and answered with disarming ease.

It has always seemed to me that Lancaster and Bell, in the early nineteenth century, were pioneers in the application of systematic thought to the solution of education problems and that the division of labour worked out in the monitorial system represented an impressive early example of a technological approach to education. One teacher, assisted by ten of his senior pupils using rote-learning methods could teach (after a fashion) 100 children. Without some such brilliantly simple innovation mass elementary education in the rapidly expanding cities could hardly have been considered as a practical possibility. It was the application of elementary factory procedures to elementary education and without ever achieving all that its inventors claimed that it would achieve, that made possible a real advance.

I suppose nobody would say this particular technological approach was neutral — it pre-determined the social and pedagogic role of the teacher and could only be used with an extremely limited curriculum and an extremely crude pedagogy. By the time the 1870 Act was on the horizon, pupil-teachers had replaced monitors and instead of the monster class gathered in ranks in an old warehouse or barn, class teaching in separate classrooms was about to be imported from Germany.

Elementary education was essentially conceived as something devised by the middle classes for other people's children. Perhaps this helped people to be objective about the limits which were set to what was to be taught. It was in no sense an open-ended operation but something which could be clearly defined in a set of standard examinations, reinforced by a code of grant regulations which related payments to managers and, therefore, in many cases, to teachers, strictly to the achievement of measurable results. Of course the standards were prescribed in cognitive terms, but my favourite proto-educational technologist is the Reverend James Fraser, later Bishop of Manchester, who, as you will recall, set out in a famous passage his objectives, in recognizably behavioural terms, in his evidence to the Newcastle Commission of 1861:

> ".... Even if it were possible, I doubt whether it would be desirable, with a view to the real interests of the peasant boy, to keep him at school till he was 14 or 15 years of age. But it is not possible. We must make up our minds to see the last of him, as far as the day school is concerned at 10 or 11. We must frame our system of education upon this hypothesis; and I venture to maintain that it is quite possible to teach a child soundly and thoroughly, in a way that he shall not forget it, all that is necessary for him to possess in the shape of intellectual attainment, by the time that he is 10 years old. If he has been properly looked after in the lower classes, he shall be able to spell correctly the words that he will ordinarily have to use: he shall read a common narrative — the paragraph in the newspaper that he cares to read — with sufficient ease to be a pleasure to himself and to convey information to listeners: if gone to live at a distance from home, he shall write his mother a letter that shall be both legible and intelligible; he knows enough of ciphering to make out, or test the correctness of, a common shop bill; if he hears talk of foreign countries he has some notions as to the part of the habitable globe in which they lie; and underlying all, and not without its influence, I trust, upon his life and conversation, he has acquaintance enough with the Holy Scriptures to follow the allusions and the arguments of a plain Saxon sermon, and a sufficient recollection of the truths taught him in his catechism, to know what are the duties required of him towards his Maker and his fellow man. I have no brighter view of the future or the possibilities of an English elementary education, floating before my eyes than this."

What we can see in retrospect, of course, is that the clear-cut definition of objectives — deliberately modest objectives — enforced by a rigid payment system was unpopular from the start and that teachers, school boards and inspectors alike campaigned against it. It was as though the system which educators like Mr Fraser, and financial controllers like Lingen and Cumin at the Education Department had devised to achieve specific and restricted goals, had an organic life of its own and refused to remain within predetermined limits. In the process of breaking out of the straitjacket, the schools and school boards also shed detailed curricular control by the

Éducation Department and later the Board of Education, and the peculiar pattern of non-control moderated by external examination which now characterizes English education, came into being over half a century and more.

Going back to payment by results is not a wholly fanciful exercise at a time when the Americans are experimenting with performance contracts on a 'no learn - no pay' basis. From the technological point of view, the learning system itself was primitive — all the emphasis was on teaching — and the learning materials which were employed did not constitute the basic resources for learning. But the experience of the early years certainly confirms the link with curriculum development — the pressure for change which penetrated even the rigidities of the urban elementary school. (When working on the history of London education, I was delighted to come across an early example of the Methods-Materials approach to curriculum development in elementary school science teaching in the year 1887. Dr J H Gladstone, FRS, a leading member of the London School Board, devised an inexpensive box of simple science apparatus for 'illustrating experimentally the elementary principles of chemistry and physics'. This was promptly linked with a programme of in-service training by the appointment of four science demonstrators to run courses for teachers on the basis of Professor Armstrong's 'heuristic' principles — and there you have it, discovery methods and all.)

As it happens, payment by results has lately been placed in a better light by historians of education — a rehabilitation exercise is taking place as a reaction to the traditional textbook acceptance of contemporary condemnation. There were pros to be set against the cons — as no doubt there will be in the United States — but the system lent itself to fraud as well as rigidity and even the retrospective objectivity of historical research cannot obscure its powerful unpopularity.

All this, however, amounts to little more than chasing embryos, and no doubt those who have looked into the subject more profoundly than I, could have found a good many more promising infants by delving into educational history. To all intents and purposes the 'scientific and technological approach to education' which concerns us now is a product of the past fifteen years or so, and in particular, of the application of systems analysis and the systems approach to patterns of learning.

This was largely contemporaneous with the upsurge in curriculum development in the United States in the immediate post-sputnik era. In the United States the Department of Defence, where the systems approach has paid off, was putting large sums into the reform of the science curriculum and many techniques — including the engineering model of the early curriculum development projects — were taken over into the educational field.

Since the early 1960s the processes of systematic curriculum development have changed and developed, because people have learnt more about how to achieve what they want and because they have come to want different things. They have also learnt that it is quite possible to achieve results which are quite different from those which are intended. Out of these changes have come, as I said earlier, a variety of developmental styles which carry with them basically different assumptions about children, teachers, society, the aims of education, the map of knowledge and so on.

In fact 'Styles of Curriculum Development' was the title of a short residential international conference held at Allerton Park in Southern Illinois last September, organized by the Centre for Educational Research and Innovation at OECD in Paris and as I have the unenviable task of writing the report of this meeting, I have had perforce to think about the way these styles have emerged and the competing ideas which they reflect. There were representatives at the conference from Canada and the United States and from Scandinavia, Germany, Belgium, Holland, France and Spain, as well as from the United Kingdom. I do not think even a determined rapporteur could produce concensus from the far-reaching discussions, which reflected, above all, the differences in the social and political context within which education systems (and curriculum development enterprises) operate. This, if nothing else, was a warning against any attempt to reduce curriculum development to a technocratic exercise, let alone sanction the emergence of an international technocracy of universal experts.

The idea of style can be used in various ways. You can have a period style or a national style or a style which emerges from a particular problem or a particular cult or theoretical belief. The assumption would be that if you could identify a style you could discover a set of related characteristics, reflecting a consensus about values, which interlock to form a coherent though not monolithic whole. For example, a particular style of curriculum development may make a particular assumption about the role of the teacher. It may assume a particular psychological theory of knowledge. It may assume a preference for one teaching method or another. It may assume a meritocratic ideal or an egalitarian one, it may emphasize competition or cooperation, it may be highly structured or barely structured at all. The permutations and combinations are numerous, but out of them it is possible to distil several different styles, each value-loaded in important ways.

Tony Becher of the Nuffield Foundation presented one of the key working papers at the conference, an elegant hypothesis about the evolution of developmental styles. Becher put forward a matrix as a means of describing the different styles — which he tentatively labelled 'instrumental', 'interactive' and 'individualistic' (Figure 1).

The matrix consisted of three vertical columns and some fifteen horizontal rows. You will see that he assumed that different approaches to curriculum development could cluster — not completely — but at least with

	Characteristic emphasis under:	Column 1 Cluster I	Column 2 Cluster II	Column 3 Cluster III
Row 1	Innovation model	Research, development and diffusion	Social interaction	Problem-solving
Row 2	Academic derivation	Behavioural psychology (learning theory)	Sociology (organization theory)	Philosophy (Deweyism/existentialism)
Row 3	Implicit values	Competition	Cooperation	Self-development
Row 4	Orientation and relevance	Manpower-oriented/utilitarian	Society-oriented/social	Individually oriented/personal
Row 5	Taxonomic domain	Cognitive	Affective	Evaluative/creative
Row 6	Teaching technique	Discovery methods/inductive-heuristic	Group projects/discussion	Self-instructional/practical tasks
Row 7	Teacher role	Dominating	Managing	Assisting
Row 8	Student assessment system	Conventional, but process-oriented	Continuous assessment	Self-checking
Row 9	Form of work organization	Conventional class groups	Varying-sized groups	'Cafeteria' study/practical working
Row 10	Institutional typology	Meritocratic	Comprehensive	De-institutionalized
Row 11	Subject-matter	'Linear' disciplines (maths, science, languages)	'Non-Linear' subjects (humanities, social studies)	Cross-disciplinary/wide-ranging options (arts-science mix, practical and creative skills
Row 12	Mode of materials	Highly-structured	Loosely-structured	Modular-based/non-structured
Row 13	Materials assessment systems/criteria	Objective testing/system engineered	Subjective expert appraisal/local adaptability	Consumer evaluation/success in take-up
Row 14	Forms of dissemination	Teacher handbooks, student workbooks, media back-up	Multi-media student packages, teacher guides	Complex resource banks, retrieval systems
Row 15	Means of implementation/principal clients	Rational persuasion and demonstration/institutional authorities	Changes in staff attitudes/teachers	Direct response to learner needs/students

Figure 1. A first-stage model of styles of curriculum development

some relationship to the suggested styles. Now this is more than a party game, though clearly the rules could be changed and if you chose to do so you could establish a matrix which used other criteria. Becher was suggesting, among other things, that as time has passed, styles have changed. After three days of discussions at Allerton Park, Tony Becher came up with a briefer alternative. Still using his three basic styles, this included only eight rows. For 'view of knowledge' he offered under column 1 'packages' — that is, subject disciplines. Column 2 turned this into 'problems' — that is, interdisciplinary inquiry, while Column 3 had 'personal exploration'. Among the other rows were 'teachers' classroom roles' which ranged from 'dominating' through 'managing' to 'assisting'. For 'view of humanity', there was a choice of 'people as things', ie manipulable, 'people as social animals', ie interactive, and 'people as individuals', ie idiosyncratic. The 'view of external reality' could be 'Terra firma' (the real world: with overtones of Newton), 'Sandbanks' (the changing world, with overtones of Einstein) or Terra Incognita (the unknowable), with the suggestion of Berkelean idealism.

The point about these, or similar formulations is that they represent at one and the same time, a progression of ideas, and ideas which are competing alongside one another. In one simple respect, the instrumental style represents the classic, engineering model, exemplified in the first science and mathematics projects on both sides of the Atlantic. The interactive style grew naturally out of this when the curriculum developers turned their attention to the social sciences and the humanities, and began to wrestle with quite different objectives such as those associated with the introduction of comprehensive education or compensatory education for socially disadvantaged children. The individualistic style is an evolution of the same process, taking into account the impact on curriculum development of libertarian ideas about personal development, coupled with a need for individualization which springs from the desire to postpone selection or streaming. Each style has its own set of values and sets out to tackle different, though overlapping problems.

It will be seen from all this that different styles of curriculum development make different demands on educational technology. They have had the effect of stretching almost beyond recognition the first narrow view of what this new scientific approach means. The educational technologists are being challenged to say what is the Ark of their Covenant. Is it the Systems Approach? Is it the central planning team, managing learning by objectives within a closed loop by which evaluation constantly feeds back the evidence for revision and renewal? Or is it just a systematic approach to learning instead of a disorganized approach to teaching? My point is that the attitude of the schools to educational technology is going to depend on the extent to which it can respond to the development of curricular thinking about the aims of education, without imposing its own technological values.

In the international context, the classic, engineering model, given ever increasing sophistication is still a powerful force. In Sweden where a holistic view is taken of educational reform, comprehending the notion both of curriculum reform and the reform of the organizational structure of the school, the educational planners remain deeply imbued with the systems approach. The elaborate procedures by which they translate the social and political goals laid down by the politicians into specific curriculum objectives for the schools is a model of its kind, even if it does cause the pragmatic English mind to boggle somewhat.

I came across a classic description of the systems approach in a Swedish research bulletin which appeared in 1967. This gave in outline, complete with flow chart, a description of the preparation of an instructional system through the production of a set of learning materials, from the original planning stage to its eventual implementation. The final comment made the point with concision: "All links in the chain" the bulletin concluded "must fit into each other and stand up to the demands made: if a pupil does not learn what is required of him, it is the fault of the system, not of the pupil."

I do not think — though I could well be wrong — that this would be stated with quite such confidence today. We owe to the Swedes the valuable experience of the IMU mathematics project, one of the most ambitious attempts to individualize and rationalize learning ever undertaken by any public system of education. I strongly recommend anyone who has not read Kim Taylor's draft evaluation of of the IMU project for CERI* — Independent Learning Systems: their production and international transfer — to get hold of a copy from the Paris office of that organization. the IMU maths course was largely self-instructional; each unit was available at three levels of difficulty with frequent diagnostic tests, intended to enable unstreamed groups to work together, while ensuring a high degree of individualization. It was also used as a means of testing different combinations of professional and ancillary staff, different sizes of working group, different periods of study.

What emerges from Taylor's evaluation is that the rigidity imposed by the original design and evaluation procedure were self-defeating — not because it was not largely successful when measured by its own objectives, but because it was unpalatable for the teachers and for the social relationships between the pupils and staff. Its reliance on teacher-free self instruction was excessive and intolerable, especially in an education system well-staffed by highly trained teachers. The main achievement of IMU was to pave the way for less systematic, less scientifically austere materials employing many of the same concepts, but which deliberately combined more class teaching with self-instruction. I saw for myself an IMU class in operation one morning at 9.00 am in a school at Malmö. It was an awe inspiring sight — 90 pupils working on their books in a gymnasium for 90 minutes attended by a squadron of teachers and a flotilla of secretaries.

It was even then — three years ago — obvious that if it were as successful as the sponsors hoped, and the technique was used for other subjects, either the children or the teachers or both would go mad, that there was a limit to the amount of individualization any pupil or teacher can live with.

Now let me try to draw this together. It seems to me that the schools

---

*CERI - Centre for Educational Research and Innovation, OECD, 2 rue Andre-Pascal, Paris XVIe

remain instinctively wedded to the ancient jest about education being what is left when you have forgotten everything you learnt at school. It is this which explains the obsession with **process** rather than **objectives** which can be traced through the progress of curriculum development in this country. It is not a question of rejecting objectives, behavioural or otherwise: it is a profound conviction that the business of defining objectives is just a great deal more complicated than has so far been made out. I do not suggest that this suspicion of objectives is always clearly articulated — nor yet that it is always rational. I am not suggesting that there is always any clear distinction between limited objectives which manifestly can be established and the bigger ones which may only be diminished by being pinned down, but the difference may be important, especially if for technical reasons those objectives which can be reliably evaluated have to be stressed at the expense of those which cannot. Philosophers and pedagogues can argue indefinitely about the structures of knowledge and of particular subjects — the experience of English curriculum development has certainly been that the more it has become involved in the humanities and social sciences the less people have been prepared to adopt the classic model and specify their objectives in behavioural terms or insist on rigorous evaluation procedures. Lawrence Stenhouse and the Nuffield Schools Council Humanities project have invested the 'process' model with a decent theoretical garment and articles now begin to appear with titles like 'Beyond Behavioural Objectives'.

What I am certainly **not** saying is that the objectives of secondary education as outlined for example in O-level examination syllabuses are adequate, or that they could not be much more clearly stated and analyzed. I **am** saying that 'a scientific and technological approach' has pinpointed the inadequacy of what now commonly pass for objectives. If you ask the O-level English teacher if the examination expresses his objectives, he will say that of course he must get his pupils through the exam, but that the objectives, the values, the experiences he is interested in go far beyond this, and that it may even be that the objectives for individual pupils will and should conflict with each other.

I suspect that we are moving into a period when it will be less possible than ever to establish the kind of centrally-established concensus which teams of experts armed with the systems approach can translate into reach-me down learning systems of the kind which we were once led to expect. There is much more sign that we are moving towards Becher's third, individualistic style, or even, to new community-based curriculum development of the kind pioneered in Eric Midwinter's e.p.a. project where the content of education is subordinated to the attempt to fan the dying embers of the inner-city community back to life.

It is also true that the large-scale R and D laboratory engaged in the systems-wide application of educational technology is in retreat in the only country rich enough to invest large sums in it. At the Allerton Park Conference I referred to earlier, the harshest critics of the classic model were the Americans.

In harsh caricature, the model came across as one which presupposed that scientists could make the initial discovery, engineers develop it, and at the bottom of the pile, teachers receive it ready-made. This caricature soon reflected a general suspicion of the military-industrial complex with short-term, specific and often materialistic aims. If pressed to extremes it meant "don't waste money educating teachers, or paying them much; they are very low level technicians who are happiest when they are doing what they're told".

It could mean a reductionist view of education — don't bother with mystical concepts like self-realization or something called 'understanding': say extremely simply what you want as, for instance, a list of specific words for children to be taught and examined on, and then write a contract for a commercial company, to be completed by a certain date.

In other words, the pressures which are associated with a particular technological approach may bear upon teachers and pupils in ways which the curriculum developer does not necessarily desire.

This, I think, brings me to the last but main point I want to make: that the acceptability of educational technology is dependent on the purpose to which it is put.

In this area of human affairs as in others there may be a clash between 'efficiency' and 'freedom'. Neither word can be used without begging a vast array of questions but I am for educational technology when it can enhance the freedom of the teacher and the freedom of the pupil. Very often increased efficiency is an element of this freedom. My own sympathy is with Kim Taylor in his ideal of resource-based learning as a means of liberating both teacher and learner from unnecessary constraint. But this means multiplying the points at which teachers and pupils can choose: it means many small packages not a few large ones. It means, perhaps, cottage industry educational technology, not the grand and glossy learning industry. It means using technology to achieve specific and limited tasks, not surrendering to the manipulative power of its large-scale application.

Taylor quotes the example of a Montessori secondary school in the Hague where resource-based learning includes the use of self-instructional programmed materials for 'quickly dealing with essential matters and allowing rest from constant teaching' in order to 'leave a child more time for his own private agenda'. In other words the aim and object is Montessorian while the tools are neo-Skinnerian and the divergence between the two approaches emerges not in the materials or the short-cycle operation but 'in the pervasive key and tone in the surrounding conditions of learning'. He contrasts the technologists' inclination (like that of the IMU designers) 'to persist until they have tooled their courses to the closest tolerance', and of the Montessorian desire to stop at the 'loosest acceptable fit'. And he concludes that 'in between those who want to leave as much as possible open, personal and unresolved, and those whose instinct is to Kinsey all creation there remains a final enmity'.*

There is a long way to go till the schools have the technological resources they need to reduce the chores of teaching and learning and free energy for deeper understanding and creative activity. The transformation of every library into a properly equipped resource centre is decades away at the present rate of progress, and because of the way in which local authority budgeting operates, there is a built-in tendency for books, stationery and equipment of all kinds to be skimped.

So much local education authority spending is made up of items over which the LEA has little or no effective control — loan charges, teachers' and other salaries, payments to the further education and teacher training pool and so on — that there is an inevitable squeeze on the residual items like books, stationery and equipment, when cuts must fall if any savings are to be made at all to shave a few pennies off the rate in a critical election year. The record of the past ten years shows how seriously this affects the schools in a matter which bears directly on innovation. But above all, what is needed is to tackle **the basic inflexibility which stems from a tacit assumption that schools will go on using teachers, equipment, books and other software in roughly the same proportions** which they now use them. It is this fundamentally conservative assumption which prevents enterprising schools and teachers from experimenting with quite different mixes and making a success of materials-based instruction at the secondary level. A few places like Leicestershire and Oxfordshire have made a start, but there is a long way to go — and till this mental and administrative blockage is removed, teachers will not have the conditions in which they can try, step by step, little by little, to come to terms with the resources which educational technology can put before them, and prove to their own satisfaction that it can enhance their freedom and opportunity to exercise a professional role.

Important as virement may be, however, there seems no reason to doubt that the resources which emerge at the end of the technological process **are** more expensive than those of the traditional kind, and this means that it is not just to spend money differently, but also more money which is needed.

Until there is **both** more money, and a willingness to spend it in different ways, the economic conditions will not exist to ensure a ready supply of new materials using all the techniques which science and technology can offer. I

---

* L C Taylor 'Resources for Learning, London' Penguin 1971

remain opposed as a matter of principle to the degree of centralization which could ensure by authoritarian edict the acceptance and implementation of any new course, however splendid its technological credentials. But unless the situation within the schools is changed and more cash is available there is no prospect of a vigorous exploitation of the possibilities of educational technology — possibilities which, given resolute and professional attitudes on the part of the teachers, mean better learning and more individual autonomy — more efficiency and a better chance to pursue that 'private agenda'.

And if educational technology and curriculum development are to be intertwined there must also be more money too for the production of self-instructional materials by teachers' groups at teachers' centres and elsewhere.

Educational technology, like curriculum development has passed through several phases from the first, highly programmatic stage, through a period when the cybernetic influence was paramount, to the present growing recognition that it must be co-extensive with educational innovation.

This is an important progression. It represents the feedback from some painful experience. It points to the need for sensitivity about the implicit values which a technological approach imports into educational thinking and it marks out the area in which real disagreement not just prejudice, can arise between the systems men and the teachers.

Current polemics about freedom and dignity suggest that if pushed into a corner the schools in our society must, of their nature, resist the extremes of mechanistic philosophy and in so doing pin their humanistic colours to the mast. So, too, I suspect must many educational technologists who see the techniques and mastery which they can offer as a means, not of cutting humanity down to size, but of realizing a little more of its true potential.

Module 1
Design of courses and curricula
Posing the Problems
F R SPARROW

Many years ago one of the problems which fascinated me was why it was that
a popular newspaper, of which I thought very little, was so clearly an enormous success in terms of circulation. When I mentioned my interest to a
group of adults, one of the reasons they put forward was that it was the policy
of the proprietors of this newspaper regularly to employ as contributors
people whose ideas, policies and views were not in line with the ideas, policies and views of the newspaper. This hypothesis led me to study the newspaper concerned with greater interest and I discovered that a large number
of the contributors were, in fact, expressing opinions very different from the
official opinion. Clearly, this is not the only reason for the commercial success of this paper, but it is an interesting possible contributory factor.

I began in that way quite deliberately. When the invitation came to the
Schools Council, to provide a speaker for this particular session, my first
reaction was one of pleasure. It was certainly an honour for the organization
and for me in particular to be invited.

Secondly, I felt that there was certain logic in the invitation. After all
the Schools Council has been in existence for nearly eight years, during the
whole of which time it has been continuously involved in devising curricula,
programmes and projects.

Thirdly, I realized from lots of things which I have heard from teachers
in the Schools Council that many, perhaps most of them, would have no hesitation in declaring themselves in favour of educational technology.

However, after these initial reactions came a certain nagging doubt. In
spite of what I have just said, I suggest to you that it is true to say that when
people in England hear the phrase 'Educational Technology' they do not immediately think of the Schools Council. There is a perfectly good reason for
this, in that of the one hundred and thirty odd projects that the Schools Council
has sponsored, very few have followed what might be defined as a 'systems
approach'. Very few been directly involved in programmed learning, or
the use of computers. Similarly, while a very large number of Council projects

make extensive use of virtually all the media, there has never been any tendency whatsoever to inflate this aspect of the project's work. There is, therefore, a sense in which I am different from everybody else here present. You, by definition, can be assumed all to be very strongly in favour of the advancement of the cause of Educational Technology as such; I am dedicated to developments in the curriculum and to improvements in examinations, and Educational Technology is almost parenthetic with me and with people like me. It therefore seems probable that my views and my opinions will not always harmonise completely with yours. I would hope, however, that just as the newspaper I mentioned seemed to get some benefit by employing people of divergent views, so this conference might get something of interest from the 'odd man out'.

In expressing this hope, I am sure you will all realize that I am not implying that I can give you the message as far as planning courses and curricula is concerned. Indeed, I am perfectly convinced in my own mind there is no such thing as 'the message'. The most that I can really hope to do is to provide you with a number of caveats, a number of cautions; the sort of doubts which come naturally to somebody like myself, who spends a great deal of time in the presence of practising teachers.

I would like to introduce these cautions by way of a true story. Some time ago I had the privilege of sitting with a group of teachers who had been asked to consider the possibilities of a programmed learning proposal aimed at teaching very young children to read. In the course of the discussion one very keen, and I am sure capable teacher, whom we will call Miss Jones, because that is not her name, said "I don't like this; the best teaching machine I can think of is my lap; I have taught hundreds of children to read while they have been sitting on my lap." At this juncture, I ventured the quiet comment "Yes, Miss Jones, but you have only one lap." This led to a certain amount of hilarity around the table. The interesting thing about this story is the end of it, for after the meeting finished she came to me and said: "Mr Sparrow, what did you mean when you said I had only one lap? Of course I have only one lap". Some of you might feel that in telling this story, I am deliberately denigrating a sincere teacher. Can I say that, my intention is precisely the opposite. I would suggest to you, and indeed, I know that others on previous occasions have passed on a similar message, that you cannot get anywhere at all without the full cooperation and involvement of teachers. This particular teacher revealed all the doubts, all the prejudices if you like, which are natural and which come naturally to teachers like her. You will also realize, I am sure, that Miss Jones was in no sense completely wrong — what she was really saying was that she was afraid of the depersonalized, mechanistic and potentially deadly dull aspect of the thing. "A machine", she was saying, "is no substitute for the warmth and friendliness of human contact, for that close rapport and relationship which exists between a good teacher and her/his pupils." What is wanted of course, is the best of all worlds. There has been some question as to whether somebody planning a course, in any particular area should be an expert in technology, in psychology, or in the subject matter. I have no easy answer to this question, but I say to you quite boldly, that if you can provide for all three, you will need something else. You still need a Miss Jones, somebody who is in day to day contact with the actual job, somebody who can make a unique contribution for that reason. In planning courses you must involve teachers, not for the crude reason that this enables technologists to sell their wares, but for the valid reason that teachers can make an invaluable contribution.

At this stage I want to consider very briefly the conservatism of teachers to which reference was made yesterday afternoon. I share Sir James Pitman's concern about teachers in whose classrooms their Victorian predecessors would feel completely at home. Even so, I often marvel at the progress which has been made in recent years. We do, of course, have some teachers who are only at home in the traditional rectangular box, teaching in the traditional way for the traditional 40/45 minutes. Equally, we have many teachers who never teach in this way at all. We have an even larger number who are not located at either pole: instead they try to adapt their methods to suit the perceived needs of their particular children at any particular time. It is also a fact that the trial stage of Schools Council projects would nearly always be over-subscribed if all applicants were admitted. It is another fact that thousands of teachers are working on the subject panels of Examination Boards planning new courses and devising new methods of assessment. Yet another fact is that there are some five hundred Teachers' Centres, all of which are engaged in varying degrees with curriculum innovation.

I marvel because of the many disincentives to change. Consider just a few:

1. The biggest single change associated with many innovations is a change in the teacher's role. The French have le mot juste here. The traditional teacher is 'en face de': the innovator is 'avec'. It would not be reasonable to expect teachers easily to accommodate themselves to so dramatic a change as this, especially over a short period of time!

2. A change such as this affects the authority structure of the school. The teacher is no longer the purveyor of wisdom. He is guide, counsellor, friend; he is no longer 'Sir' in the old sense.

3. Changes such as these can affect, or can appear to threaten to affect, not only the teacher's status but also his position in the salary structure.

The list could be extended.

Now what has this to do with the planning of courses? All planners aim at the perfect plan and their problem here is to try to involve teachers in at least the following three stages:

1. Can you — dare you — have a Miss Jones in at the first planning stage, partly because she is a sort of Devil's Advocate? You need to win her over and take note of her ideas.

2. As more teachers participate in your courses can you ensure that they are properly briefed, not by remote-control or through the media above, but by personal contact in training courses and subsequently?

3. As the work proceeds can you use the expertise of the teachers especially, perhaps in evaluation? It is not enough to make them the recipients of feed-back forms, necessary though these are for revision of courses. They have to feel committed and to come to realize that they are contributing. Can you, in fact, in your plan, help the teacher to realise that he is in a research situation as soon as he is involved in curriculum development? I have to say here that I am not convinced that research always paves the way for curriculum change. Indeed, Torsten Husen has said that in Sweden, the most research-oriented of European countries, changes arise from political, social and economic considerations, rather than from educational research. This must not be taken to imply that rigorous, fundamental research is unimportant. Its contribution to educational progress could and should be invaluable, especially if the researchers can successfully communicate their findings. It was a very long time ago that research first indicated that instruction in a Latinate Grammar superimposed on the English language was of little or no real value to children learning English. The message tends always to take a long time to get through. I believe, however, that the most fruitful research is that action research which is implicit in curriculum development. For this reason when I considered the interesting suggestion that research was the male and development the female, I was not sure whether I was unisex or hermaphrodite.

Can you provide for these things in your plan? If you cannot you will either fail or meet only limited success. Apart from the purely educational aspect, the vicious circle of the financial position is relevant. Many teachers are hesitant about using educational technology to the full. Because demand is low, the price of many of the machines on exhibition is high. Increase the demand and the price should drop, but you must first convince the teachers. You must therefore write them into your plans from the beginning.

I am fully conscious that by saying this I am not making the task of planning easier; indeed, as soon as practising teachers participate closely in this work all the well-known difficulties tend to be accentuated. I would argue that this is in itself a good thing. Let me illustrate: it is widely agreed that any educational course should have certain general aims, and many people at least think,clearly defined specific aims, or if you prefer it 'behavioural objectives'. My experience, and the experience of others of which I have heard, suggests that it is fairly easy for experts who share common views to draw up the most complete series of behavioural objectives.   I know beyond any shadow of doubt, however, that when large numbers of teachers are asked to participate in that exercise, there is a tendency to failure. The most infuriating thing that can be said about this is that it shows that the teachers are unused to doing it, that they need a course of training. Now I would suggest that this is not necessarily so; that when the teachers reveal difficulties the reason is that there really are great difficulties. If teachers eventually say that behavioural objectives are not the best method of approach, they are not automatically wrong; indeed, in certain cases, they might well be right. It would hardly be profitable here to rehearse all the well-known arguments for and against the specific statements of 'behavioural objectives'. I am quite prepared to do it in a discussion period at the end. All I wish to say here and now is that what some people assume to be an absolute truth ceases to be an absolute truth when challenged by teachers. So I would advise you to be exceedingly cautious when you actually write down the plan of your courses.

There are some phrases which jar upon sensitive minds. One example is 'the structure of knowledge'. I very much doubt that there is such a thing as 'The Structure of Knowledge'. We all know that certain subjects appear to lend themselves to a sequential approach and that they can be taught in a highly structured and, indeed, a logical order. Even here, however, I would advise you that I frequently hear such people as mathematicians stating their very strong reservations about any assumption that arbitrary closures can be put on certain stages of the learning process. Even if it is claimed that certain systematic approaches give apparently maximum rein to the individual to follow his own bent, I view such claims with some scepticism, for in a purely mechanical situation, nobody can conceive all the combinations of possibilities open to a child. If you have ever set a completion test, one where you have tried scrupulously hard to ensure absolute clarity of question and intended response, look at the thousands of variations you get that you did not expect. I dislike intensely assumptions about The Structure of Knowledge. One other example, there is a tendency for some people to talk of 'The Science of Learning'. If, of course, they mean an attempt to study learning in a scientific way, no one should complain, but constant reiteration of the phrase 'The Science of Learning' with never a mention at all of 'The Art of Teaching' does cause a certain dismay in the hearts and minds of teachers.

You will have noticed that when I use the phrase 'teachers' I tend to talk of 'teachers in schools'. A short while ago I was considerably disturbed at a meeting which was discussing the application of one particular form of educational technology, to hear one man whose job it is to advance educational technology, plead that the meeting should turn from schools and all their problems to Higher and Further education. What worried me was the possible assumption that it was easier to get away with things the further up the educational scale one went. I very much doubt if lecturers and teachers in Further and Higher education are different in essential ways from teachers in schools. Indeed, it could well be that the further up the educational ladder one goes, the more careful one should be in respect of the points that I have made. The reason is that it is much easier to programme learning, to arrange it in sequences and to arrange for periodic feed-back and evaluation when the subject under discussion is really one of **instruction**. The lower the level of the learning process the easier it is to design courses. We all know that in most subjects there are certain bases of factual knowledge and a large number of basic skills which have to be acquired, and perhaps the appropriate word for the acquisition of these skills is 'instruction'. However, as soon as one moves beyond this fairly rudimentary level towards the higher realms of 'education' it becomes much more difficult to plan programmes in a systematic way.

Equally, when a systematic approach to curriculum problems has been evolved, I believe that it should be subjected to continuous scrutiny and periodic revision, and that these should be written into the original plan. If this is not done there is a real danger, especially if the 'system' looks both neat and complete, that a new orthodoxy will result. This orthodoxy could gain strength from the apparent perfection of the diagrammatic representation of the system. It is common for curriculum developers to try to simplify problems of immense profundity by isolating elements into little boxes and showing interrelationships and interactions by means of arrows. The value of this procedure is beyond question; the hidden danger is that it might conceal or blur some of the fundamental issues. Again, I would illustrate with an anecdote. One day I showed a practising teacher a very good diagrammatic representation of a course. His first reaction was "It looks like an insect on roller skates" (you will realize that he, like most teachers, had only limited contact with social science methodology). He then asked me to explain the words in the boxes, thereby illustrating for the umpteenth time the problem of jargon. After my explanation he thought that each box should really be sub-divided, but realized that this would create 'a contortionist centipede on roller skates'. He even thought that if extensions were made, the really important thing when the system was actually in use with real children could well be the unforeseen 'hair on the centipede's foot'. I would not have you when you plan courses waste a lot of time looking for the hair:

all I would plead for is that flexibility of attitude which makes possible provision for the affect, perhaps the irritation, of the hair.

In everything that I have said I appear to have assumed a dichotomy: to have implied that teachers are teachers and educational technologists are educational technologists. I take this line because there could be a danger that a conference of specialists who have a strong common bond will stress this common interest at the expense of pedagogic aspects. In practice, I know, of course, that most of you play a double role: you are teachers, lecturers and instructors as well as specialists in educational technology. Those of us who do not share your expertise owe you a considerable debt in that you have always recognized common needs. So true is this that some statements of great importance now have an almost platitudinous ring. 'Educational Technology exists to serve and not to replace teachers' and 'Teachers should have available a wide range of choice of media' are typical examples. Perhaps, then, all is well, especially if teachers are brought in not just to use hardware and software but to play their part in the planning and development of courses, and if my other warnings are given such attention as you think they deserve.

However, I must end with one final note of anxiety, if not alarm. I take it as axiomatic that advances in educational technology, however complex and difficult they might be, are child's play compared to the successful application of these advances in the classroom. One of the main reasons for this is the age-old problem of communication. Let me illustrate with my last anecdote. I have recently attended two meetings of a Seminar Group on Computers in Education, thereby adding significantly to my own education. Thanks to papers carefully prepared in advance, I was able to follow most of the discussion with comparative ease. What worried those of us who know more of education than they do of computers was the realization that only a tiny handful of teachers would have understood more than a tiny fraction of what was said. This is partly due to the use of initial letters such as 'A.I.' and 'C.A.I.', but it is much more than that. The computer specialists were using premises, assumptions and language which struck me as totally different from those of teachers, or at least of appearing to be so. At this level there is no purpose in bringing in teachers to help in the planning of courses. What is needed first is to bring teachers and computer experts together for mutually helpful exchanges of information, attitudes and opinions. How many specialists in English Literature, for example, would have any confidence at all in the assertion that Computer Assisted Learning could play a real part in the planning of a course based on the general aim 'A response (to Literature) is personal or it is nothing'? The assertion was made by an expert in response to a challenge from me. I have only a small measure of confidence in his claim, but I think he should be given the opportunity to try.

26

He cannot try until he has help from teachers of literature and they have help from him. Is it too much to ask that in any implementation of the third cycle of the James Report or that in any other developments in in-service training, great attention should be paid to work of this kind?

I believe that the only way to progress in education is through that co-operation of all the interested parties on which the Schools Council itself is based. Educational Technology cannot — must not — be excluded.

That marks the end of what might be called my 'set piece'. I would like to add a postscript.

It has often been said, and I subscribe to the sentiment, that at conferences such as this people gain at least as much from informal contacts as they do from scheduled speakers. I spent much of yesterday listening to many of you who are now listening to me. One young man, to whom I immediately warmed, was talking with great enthusiasm about teaching and learning as enjoyable: he even used the word 'entertainment'. He obviously shared my view that a long period with students without a spontaneous belly-laugh or two is likely to be a failure.

Now I recognize that life is serious, life is earnest; that there is always a lot to do and time is always limited. I would nonetheless want to know how you can provide for the possibility of laughter when you plan courses based on the use of educational technology. As I see it you have serious problems here. Spontaneity by definition is not planned. The contrived joke repeated on video tape would be completely disastrous. There seems to me to be something about educational technology which minimizes, perhaps in some cases eliminates, humour. This could well be one reason for teacher-reluctance and — dare I say it? — for children and students sometimes to be less enthusiastic once the novelty has worn off. Does it have to be so?

I remember I was once at a conference addressed by Professor Elton, Professor of Educational Technology at the University of Surrey. At one stage of his talk he stressed an important point and then directed our attention to one of his hand-outs. This was a large sheet of paper in the middle of which the vital point was written in a circle. He explained that the reason was partly to focus attention but partly to give people who might want to make notes, but had not brought any paper, plenty of space. 'This', he added, 'is known as Educational Technology'. The immediate laughter which this provoked was the first and almost the only laughter I have heard on the subject of educational technology. I put it to you that an urgent problem in the planning of courses is always that of making it possible for the leaven of laughter to lighten the loaf.

Natural Organization and Education
MARK BRAHAM

A continuing problem for the theory and practice of education concerns the need to develop comprehensive schema or models that can be utilized to tie together the proliferating fund of information and knowledge about the nature of man. The rationale for this is at least three-fold: a) education, at base concerns human as bio-psycho-social beings, thus, b) any attempt to provide for the organization of human learning, and to establish a theoretical foundation to justify programmes and practices must take this three-fold nature into account, and c) the increase in information and knowledge about these discrete areas of human life has been so rapid and vast that we are lacking integrated concepts about the nature of man, and the role of education in human development.

As a consequence, educational programming and practice continues to be rather an ad hoc matter, with the individual worker resorting to whatever competencies he may have derived from a discrete field of enquiry and training, folk-wisdom and personal predilection in order to carry out his tasks. While this is problematic enough at the level of the individual teacher, whose actions involve a relatively small population of humans, it is compounded for the educational technologist who, through the development and use of hardware and software, film and television, systems analysis and design is liable to have a much wider spread of effect because of the larger population that comes into his sphere of influence.

Without even turning to the technological dimension of education we have such writers as Brameld asking for "graphic 'models' of integration" ...... for "systematized designs by which to draw together some of the specializations of knowledge and relate them to one another and to education" (Brameld, 1965). Reusch states that what we need is "a first approximation to a scheme that will enable us to represent physical, psychological and social events within one system of denotation" (Reusch, 1965). Writing more generally, Whyte has called for:

"... a universal method of thought, at once true to nature (so that the structure of all natural processes can be understood) and appro-

to present-day human nature (so that men and women everywhere can find a common ground in using it)"   (Whyte, 1950)

L von Bertalanffy, the instigator of 'General Systems Theory', has written of the necessity for "isomorphic laws in science..." or "general systems laws'" (Bertalanffy, 1953) to enable us to comprehend and integrate general principles of Nature in order to achieve a continuingly more comprehensive view of our world and its processes.

While what we may call general systems thinking has been gaining its adherents in scientific fields, it has scarcely begun to make any impression on Education. In this discussion, the bare outlines of a general systems model will be offered that may be of some value, particularly in the areas of curriculum development, course design and teaching. It is based on what we may call the **Principle of Natural Organization**, which may be stated as follows: every form tends to articulate its elements into functional structures; every whole is derived from the internal structuring of its parts. This principle is as applicable to conceptual and perceptual organization, as it is to organic organization generally.

THE PRINCIPLE OF ORGANIZATION

The Principle of Organization involves two major terms: **organizing** and **organization**. By 'organizing' we refer to the process through which an organization comes into being, tends towards optimal functioning and is maintained. By the term 'organization' we refer to the products of the organizational process, which appear as the vast range of organic and extra-organic (eg affective and cognitive) organizations that constitute the present order of Nature, viz: macro-molecules, macro-molecular aggregates, organelles, cells, tissues, organs and organ systems, individuals, communities, institutions, concepts, ideas and idea-systems.

The dual feature of **organizing** and **organization**, or organization as **process** and **product** expresses a basic duality in nature at large. On the one hand there is the process of organization that is constant over time and is recapitulated at successive stages of development. On the other hand there are the products of the process, the unique organizations that are emergent in time, that are a function of the intrinsic programme of the developing organization, the conditions of the environment, and of the organizational process itself.

In the discussion to follow our concern will primarily be with the process of organization, with examples drawn mainly from perceptual and conceptual data, as these are vital to educational activities.

CYCLES, STAGES AND PHASES OF ORGANIZATION

The process of organization as it is conceived here is cyclic. It involves two alternating periods: one of **divergence**, the other of **convergence**. The completion of a cycle leads to the attainment of a stage of complexity. The number of stages required for any organization to reach its optimum state will differ according to its nature and environing conditions. At the human level, no optimum state beyond the physiological can be inferred as there are no known limits to human affective and cognitive development.

An organization may, or may not, reach its optimum state. Although the tendency for optimization exists in all organizations, absolute determinism cannot be implied. Bertalanffy's statement for organic organizations, regarded here as applicable to extra-organic organizations as well, is that "so long as an organic system has not reached the maximum organization possible to it, it tends towards it" (Bertalanffy, 1962). The terminal point reached by an organization may indicate its maximum, more likely its optimum, or the limitations imposed upon it by its environing conditions and/or the restrictive factors arising within the organization itself. Stultification, distortion and death are the actual and potential restrictors in the organizational process.

Each stage of an organization is attained through a regular series of phases, or loci of dominant operations in the organizational cycle. The development of each phase depends upon a minimal state of development of stages, ie the development of a stage in an organization depends upon a minimal development of the preceeding stage.

Optimum development, whether of a phase or stage, may not come about, if at all, until after the development of later phases and stages. As organization proceeds there is always a 'filling out' behind, and an overall tendency to balance, symmetry and proportion. Several phases and stages may be developing simultaneously, although their genesis will have followed a strictly temporal order of succession.

THE PROCESS OF ORGANIZATION

Divergence

The first period in the organizational cycle is one of divergent activities, involving the development of structures and functions through the three phases of: initiation, differentiation and relation.

Initiation We may take it as axiomatic that every activity has an originating point in space-time. We may designate this as a phase-point to indicate that organization begins neither exnihilo, nor de novo but is the result of causally prior activities from which, at a critical point, a unique and somewhat amorphous and incipient organization begins to emerge. Objectively, we see this amorphousness in the early development of organisms, in the making of objects and in the creation of works of art. Subjectively, we encounter it in the organization of our percepts and concepts.

Hebb points out that a percept for newly sighted, but previously congenitally blinded patients is an amorphous, inchoate unity (Hebb, 1949a). Murphy says the same of the neonate's perceptions (Murphy, 1947), and Vygotsky writes of the young child's tendency to "merge the most diverse elements into one unarticulated image on the strength of some chance impressions" (Vygotsky, 1965).

Differentiation   The development of any organization involves the differentiation of parts having specific locations or functions, such that one may state the rule: **no differentiation, no organization.** "In all living things," says Waddington, "differentiation is a basic law of nature" (Waddington, 1953).

Differentiation is called for to bring an organization beyond a minimal state of activity, whether this concerns the development of an organism, or any act, object, process or idea. Werner, in discussing perceptual organization says:

> "the formation of percepts seems in general to go through an orderly sequence of stages. Perception is at first global, whole qualities are dominant. The next stage might be called analytic; perception is selectively directed towards parts" (Werner, 1957)

The same differentiating tendencies are required for the organization of concepts. According to Ausubel:

> "contemporaneously as a concept is acquired, certain characteristic changes take place .... It becomes increasingly less global, less impressionistic, and less diffuse ...; the learner focuses progressively on more salient critical attributes" (Ausubel, 1968)

Harvey et al say that "progressive development at every stage involves training conditions that induce openness of the conceptual system to differentiation" (Harvey et al, 1961), while Angyal points to some pedagogical implications:

> "The accumulation and organization of knowledge in a planned study may be compared to the process of biological differentiation. Developmental processes, as a rule from an initial diffuse state to a state of greater differentiation, in which parts become more distinct and gain more individuality" (Angyal, 1968)

Conceptual differentiation is the needed sorting procedure to give meaning to a message, whether it is sensorily, perceptually or conceptually derived. In the crudest terms, we speak of conceptual differentiation as 'trial-and-error' behaviour; Piaget speaks of it as "groping" (Flavell, 1963). In more sophisticated language we speak of 'discrimination', whether this concerns problem solving, discovery, or creative activity. Schroeder et al (1967a) define 'discrimination' as "the capacity of a conceptual structure to distinguish among stimuli".

While differentiation is essential for organizational development, over-differentiation (differentiation taken to the point of separateness or non-relatedness of elements, parts or aspects) is dangerous if not lethal. The result is a dissipation of energies and a breakdown in the organization's tendency towards a dynamic equilibrium.

Relation   The emergence of organization at any stage of development requires

31

the establishment of functional connection, or pathways of communication among and between differentia. These, when maintained over time become the basic structure of the developing organization. This is seen at the tissue level in the factor of junctional communication between cells. Writing of cortical organization, Hebb notes that "repeated stimulation of specific receptors leads slowly to the formation of association area cells" (Hebb, 1949b), which underlies the organization of a given percept or class of percepts.

Werner speaks of structuring, ie the establishment and maintenance of functional connections as "a basic tendency in perceptual organization" (Werner, 1957b), while Wolfe (1946), in writing of conceptual learning – and thus conceptual organization – says that "it consists not only of recall and retention of isolated objects and situations, but of relating objects and situations to each other".

Thus, unless thought and action is to be dispersive and fragmentary, to be subject to what Bruner has called "episodic empiricism", the establishment of functional relationships among and between differentia, and hence the establishment of a functional structure in cognitive organization is essential. Says Bruner:

"Episodic empiricism is illustrated by information gathering that is unbound by prior constraints, that lacks connectivity, and that is deficient in organizational persistence. The opposite extreme is illustrated by an approach that is characterized by constraint sensitivity, by connective manoeuvres, and by organized persistence." (Bruner, 1969)

With the fullness of differentiation, with the elaboration of a relational system and a structure, the divergent period of the organizational process at any given developmental stage is brought to a close. For pedagogical purposes, we have Ausubel's statement:

"Here it is hypothesized, two principles concerned with the efficient programming of content are applicable irrespective of the subject matter field — theprinciple of progressive differentiation and the principle of integrative reconciliation." (Ausubel, 1965)

The matter of integrative reconciliation will be taken up in the following section.

Convergence

There is a limiting condition that restricts the amount and kind of divergence that is possible for any organization at any stage of its development. This is the tendency for orderly and internally harmonious development, the tendency for "structuro-functional integrity and wholeness" (Russell, 1945), or "Holism" (Smuts, 1961a).

Functionally, holism is expressed in the tendency of every organization to move towards greater thermodynamic efficiency or 'good adaptiveness' with its environment. Structurally, holism is marked by the tendency of every organization towards increasing its symmetry, balance and proportion.

Overall holism is demonstrated in the articulation of elements, aspects or parts, that, emerging from minimally differentiated or inchoate beginnings become increasingly functionally-specific. In Smut's terms:

> "From the more or less homogeneous, to the heterogeneous multiplicity and again to greater, more advanced harmony, to a harmonious and cooperative structural unity; such a formula may serve as a rough-and-ready description of the holistic process." (Smuts, 1961b)

It may also serve as a rough-and-ready description of the process of organization.

The convergent period of organization, with which we shall now deal comprises three further phases: **integration, transition** and **concentration.**

Integration Integration, or to use Bennett's pithy phrase, "inner-togetherness" (Bennett, 1956), involves bringing the differentia of forming organization into a functional unity. It marks the transformation of the organizational process into a unique product at a given stage of its development. Lacking integration, there would be but an aggregate of elements without functional connections and organization would thus be impossible.

In physics, the factor of integration is translated into the notion of the 'steady state'. For some time biologists have used the term 'homeostasis' to indicate the organism's tendency to maintain its integrity or equilibrium. Clinical psychologists concern themselves with the integration of personality, or cognitivists in dealing with the integration of perceptual and conceptual phenomena speak of a **gestalt** to signify the equilibrium state. Thus, according to Gobar (1968) a percept "is a structure which consists of the synthesis of a set of elements into a whole — that is, a gestalt". The same may be said of a concept. Or, of cognitive organization generally we may note that with the phase of integration, the forming cognition becomes the formed cognition, and this is the case whether we are dealing with the acquisition or the generation of cognitive organization.

Transition As we have seen, in the course of its development an organization increasingly comes under the control of integrative forces. These enable it to both establish and maintain a new stage of form and function. Now, once an organization reaches its optimum state, no further development is expected. If, however, the optimum has not been reached such that further development is implied, and can be supported by the environment, a tension that appears between the achieved state and possibility; between the tendency to stasis and self-maintenance on the one hand and the tendency to optimization — or in Maslow's terms "fuller and fuller being" on the other (Maslow, 1962).

From the standpoint of perceptual organization, transition involves the individual's re-centring on the object of perception, a task that may be called for because of a change in the object, in the environment or in the perceiver. From the standpoint of conceptual organization, transition is

33

called for when a concept can be shown to be incomplete, to display inadequacies — for example, when its information-content is incomplete — or when its deductive implications are unclear, such that it is necessary that the individual seeks to press towards greater clarity, or to go beyond what has been attained for the sake of new possibilities.

This is somewhat of a critical matter. While we may have found a particular percept or concept to be adequate at one point, we may find that it is no longer so, yet be reluctant to go beyond the achieved state. We may prefer to cling stubbornly to old ideas in the face of contrary evidence or the inadequacy of our ideas. Everything that we have sought to understand unavoidably becomes a reference point for our activities and hence a limitation that we may need to overcome. The tension is unavoidable if development is to continue: "The system itself must generate conflict if it is to evolve beyond an adaption characterized by fixed rules" (Schroeder et al, 1967b).

This phase also has important pedagogical implications. Our general tendency in course design or teaching is to bring the student to the phase of integration, and thus to the completion of a stage of learning. Arrangements to assist the student to transit out of his achieved stage to a new one are seldom provided. He is usually left to his own devices to overcome the hiatus between the completion of one programme or the initiation of another. The position that is suggested here, is that with the completion of a set of learnings, provisions should be made to assist the student to overcome his achieved state, or prepare the way towards "a next step ahead".

Concentration Continued development requires a concentration of energies within the organization in order to overcome any restrictions which may be imposed upon it by the environment or the achieved organizational structure.

Should the energies for development be inadequate to overcome either internal or external restrictions, the immediate question is not of organizational development but of survival, for an organization that fails to develop its programme or potentialities tends to atrophy and die. Should the available energies be generally adequate for development, then three possibilities appear: a) the concentration of available energies will be sufficient to overcome all obstacles without distortion; b) the obstacles, whether organizational or environmental, will be overcome but with distortion; c) the concentration of energies, although potent, may be sufficiently blocked that it will become disruptive and damage or destroy the organization from within.

If the concentrated energies are successful in their thrust towards further development, they will, by their very intensity, yield a transformation of state and bring about a new level of organizational complexity, to the extent that we may state the rule: **concentration precedes emergence**. This rule seems to be as applicable to psychology as it does to physics and chemistry.

While organic organizations are internally, or self-organizing systems, that are capable of concentrating their energies for further development, this cannot be said — as far as we know — of perceptual or conceptual organizations. Rather, the individual must determine to press his percepts or concepts to further stages of development — to organize them from outside.

We do this with our percepts, when they strike us as incomplete, or as harbouring more information so that we feel impelled to intensify the very energies of our perceptual processes, until as a result of our concentrated attention, objects are seen 'in a new light'. And the case of conceptual concentration is similar. When we are no longer satisfied with our concepts; when we are trying to press towards new realizations; when we struggle to conceive, to have a 'mental breakthrough', conceptual concentration is called for — a concentration of energies that can take us across a threshold to a 'higher' stage of realization.

Transformation The transformation·of state — the metamorphosis — of organizational energies and activities that is derived from the phase of concentration becomes the phase-point of **origination** for the next stage in the development of an organization. The achieved organizational product gives rise to the organizational process; the convergent period of the old cycle is brought to its close and the divergent period for a new cycle begins.

With the developmental energies and activities freed from the constrictions of the phase of concentration and the prior organizational structure,

A MODEL OF NATURAL ORGANIZATION

NOTE: Fixation and Arrest is possible at any point.

35

they can expand into the environment and re-establish at a 'higher turn of the spiral': the further phases of **differentiation, relation, integration, transition, concentration,** and **transformation,** which may, in turn, lead to an additional stage or stages of development. It should be noted, of course, that development through one or more stages is by no means guaranteed for any kind of organization. Fixation and arrest is always possible at any point.

At each level of development (or of complexity), the organizational product is emergent and unique, the organizational process is continuous; a cycle of recurring activities.

Translated more concretely into educational terms, this model of natural organization may also be understood as a model for education; that is to say, it is regarded as fundamental to both a theory of learning, and of teaching or instruction. Hence, the periods of **divergence** and **convergence,** and the phases of organization are offered as normative criteria for educational programming and practice.

REFERENCES

Angyal, A . (1968) Foundations for a Science of Personality. Harvard University Press, Cambridge, Mass. Pages 7-8
Ausubel, D . (1965) in 'Readings in the Psychology of Cognition'. (Ed) R. C. Anderson and D. Ausubel. Holt, Rinehart and Winston, New York. Page 109
Ausubel, D. (1968) Educational Psychology. Holt, Rinehart and Winston, New York. Page 519
Bennett, J. G. (1956) The Dramatic Universe, Volume I (4 volumes). Hodder and Stoughton, London. Pages 59-60
Bertalanffy, L. von (1950) 'An outline of general system theory'. The British Journal of the Philosophy of Science, Vol.I, No.2
Bertalanffy, L. von (1962) Modern Theories of Development. Harper and Row, New York. Page 186
Brameld, T. (1965) The Use of Explosive Ideas in Education. University of Pittsburgh Press, Pittsburgh. Page 10
Bruner, J. (1969) The Nature of Teaching by L Nelson. Blaisdell, Waltham, Mass. Page 202
Flavell, J. (1963) The Developmental Psychology of Jean Piaget. Van Nostram, Princeton, NJ. Pages 75-76
Gobar, A . (1968) Philosophical Foundations of Genetic Psychology and Gestalt Psychology. Martinus Highoff, The Hague. Page 59
Harvey, O. J. et al (1961) Conceptual Systems and Personality Organization. Wiley, New York. Page 89
Hebb, D. O. (1949) The Organization of Behavior. Science Editions, New York. Page 29
Hebb, D. O. (1949b) op cit. Page 60
Maslow, A . (1962) Towards a Psychology of Being. Van Nostrand, Princeton, NJ. Page 151
Murphy, G. (1947) Personality. Harper, New York. Page 334
Reusch, J. (1956) in 'Towards a Unified Theory of Human Behavior'. (Ed) R. Grinker. Baric Books, New York. Page XI
Russell, E . S. (1945) The Directiveness of Organic Activities. Cambridge University Press, Cambridge. Page 11
Schroder, H. M. et al (1967a) Human Information Processing. Holt, Rinehart and Winston, New York. Pages 24 ff
Schroder, H. M. et al (1967b) op sit. Pages 17-18 ff
Smuts, J. C. (1961a) Holism and Evolution. Viking, New York. Page 232

Smuts, J. C. (1961b) Holism and Evolution. Viking, New York

Waddington, C. H. (1953) 'How do cells differentiate?'. In Scientific American. W. H. Freeman, San Francisco. Page 2

Werner, H. (1957a) in 'The Concept of Development'. (Ed) D. B. Harris. University of Minnesota Press, Minneapolis. Pages 128-129

Werner, H. (1957b) ibid

Whyte, L. L. (1950) The Next Development in Man. New American Library, New York. Page 10

Wolffe, W. (1946) The Personality of the Pre-School Child. Grune and Stratton, New York. Page 27

Vygotsky, L. (1965) Thought and Language. MIT Press, Cambridge, Mass. Page 60

Behavioural Objectives and the Structure of Knowledge
MICHAEL MACDONALD-ROSS

The idea of the behavioural objective has been, for a whole decade, the central concept of educational technology. The idea of defining what the student should do after learning (that he could not do before) is so attractive and powerful that some have claimed that complete educational specifications could be derived from such statements.

Behavioural objectives are seen as the starting point for the systematic approach to education, a type of rational planning believed by many to be the only acceptable approach to curriculum design. Gagné has said: "Once objectives have been defined, there is no step in curriculum design that can legitimately be entitled 'selecting content'." (Gagné, 1967). Many believe that the systematic approach provides a complete solution to the problems of providing effective learning (for example Davies, 1971; Popham & Baker, 1970). And, of course, there are those famous claims that we already have at hand a completely satisfactory technology of education (Gilbert, 1962; Skinner, 1968).

During the last few years there have been clear signs that these ideas are diffusing from their original base in programmed learning throughout the whole domain of curriculum design. One example is the development of behavioural objective banks, classified collections which allow teachers to select their lesson objectives from prepared lists. Another example is the growing demand for **effective** curriculum design, leading to the idea of funding by results (results, naturally, in terms of objectives achieved). And, most dramatic of all, we see in the United States that business organizations are contracting to operate whole school systems on a no results - no payment basis. Again, results are defined in behavioural terms.

There could be no more opportune moment for a critical re-examination of the behavioural objective, as part of the systematic approach to education.

A SECOND LOOK AT BEHAVIOURAL OBJECTIVES
Since we are all so familiar with the case for behavioural objectives, there

is little point in my repeating the persuasive arguments which have become part of the educational technologist's belief system (Gagné, 1967; Mager, 1961; Popham & Baker, 1970). But since much of what follows can only be understood in relation to the claims originally made, a summary may be useful. It is claimed that behavioural objectives are completely sufficient for the purpose of prescribing the **design** of the learning system; for the purpose of prescribing the way in which the student's success may be evaluated; and as a public system of communication.

It is important to realize that these claims were meant in a **strong** sense. Design is so prescribed that only one, or a few, precise schedule(s) of reinforcement will lead to the terminal behaviour; one and only one, or a small isomorphic set of, terminal test(s) is consistent with the objectives; and the objectives show the learner unambiguously what his goals are, and also act as an unambiguous public medium of communication between members of a design team. These are very important claims. If it could be shown that they are tenable in their strong sense, then they would indeed provide the basis of a completely sufficient technology of education.

But the claims are not tenable. Indeed, the system almost collapses like a house of cards when the question of **origins** is raised. Where do objectives come from? This is not much of a problem at operative-level industrial training, where the objectives do constitute behaviours that can be observed. The analyst can 'capture' the master performer by using a suitable notational scheme, to derive the objectives for the training programme. But it is not so simple in education, as the whole literature of curriculum design and educational philosophy testifies. If we wish to transmute the needs of the learner, or the structure of the subject-matter into a protocol of behaviours, then we certainly face deep problems. Do we get a fully specified prescription from the advocates of behavioural objectives? No, we do not. Indeed, some behaviourists have specifically disclaimed all responsibility for the origin of objectives (eg Gilbert, 1961).

This is quite a serious matter in the current climate of student unrest about the **relevance** of education. The 'deschooling movement' protests against the irrelevance of much of what passes as education in our institutions (Holt, 1964; Illich, 1971; Goodman, 1967; Postman & Weingartner, 1969). Radical thinkers of this school regard programmed learning as boring and irrelevant, and educational technology as a way of making pernicious education more efficient (and so even more objectionable). I cannot tackle these issues in the context of this short paper, except to point out that questions of origins and relevance are central to education, and maybe to our professional survival.

Now suppose the problem of origin is solved, and that we have our list of behaviours agreed. It is then claimed that the design procedure is strongly determined (or, completely prescribed) by the nature of the terminal performance. This has always seemed a bit optimistic, since the personal talents of the program writer can so radically affect the final product. But the claim can be demolished in other ways.

First, consider the implications of alternative learning pathways or concept sequences. Now, as long as it can be shown that there is one best sequence of frames (or concepts), it can be maintained that the sequence is determined by the character of the terminal performance. But it has long been known that this is not the case. In 1961 Mager carried out a series of experiments on learner-controlled sequencing (Mager, 1961; Mager & McCann, 1962). Not only did the learners perform effectively, but their chosen sequences bore little relationship to sequences in formal courses designed by experts. Recently, this idea has been made more precise in a series of experiments carried out by Gordon Pask to explore his notion of human learning as a form of information processing (Pask & Scott, 1971). Though space prevents a full account here, there is no doubt that an extraordinary number of alternative pathways are possible through any interconnected set of concepts: and consequently objectives do not specify one absolutely best sequence for all learners.

Second, consider the **interaction** between objectives and teaching material. A seemingly intelligent objective can be turned into rote learning by the nature of the teaching process. And this, in turn, reflects on the evaluation procedure: test items are not difficult or easy in themselves. They must be interpreted as part of an **interconnected system**. So objectives do not simply specify teaching materials in a feed-forward fashion. They are themselves just as much influenced by the resultant nature of the rest of the teaching system.

Now let us turn to the problems of evaluation. It has always been claimed that behavioural objectives provide the only objective basis for evaluation, and attempts to arrange evaluation 'after the event' suffer the sly insinuation that the target is being arranged after the shot has been fired! But it is common knowledge that one can devise both difficult and easy sets of test items, both relating to the **same** set of behavioural objectives. In fact, in some scandalous cases, this stratagem has been deliberately employed so as to make a program appear more effective than it really was. But I want to stress that this problem is not due simply to technical incompetence or dishonesty on the part of some programmers: it derives from the basic (and inerradicable) **ambiguity** of behavioural objectives.

Objectives are ambiguous: it is always possible to find more than one action (or test item, or whatever) to correspond to any one objective. This gives rise to problems of interpretation, and to the suggestion that ambiguity can be reduced if objectives are made more **specific**. But if objectives are made too specific, the lists become so unwieldy that they can hardly be comprehended, let alone used. On the other hand, if the list of objectives is kept brief, then their generality will cause all the problems of interpretation discussed above. There are, in fact, no satisfactory rules for deciding the appropriate level of specificity of behavioural objectives, despite the fact that some of the most prominent advocates of the method have worked on this very problem (for example, the work of Gagné and Mager on Project Plan).

I shall (mercifully) desist from commenting on the third major claim, that objectives act as an adequate medium of communication, because it is more essential to point out that most of the surface problems of behavioural objectives derive from two deep structural notions, both of which I believe to be fundamentally mistaken.

The first notion, or presupposition, is that an area of subject-matter (or knowledge, or skill) can be adequately represented as a **list structure**. It will be abundantly clear, by the end of this paper, that it is the interconnectedness of ideas that matters most; and this is precisely why a protocol of behaviours is so inadequate a representation of the structure of knowledge.

The second presupposition is the idea that theoretical concepts can be **reduced** to behaviours. This is a form of **operationalism**, Bridgeman's idea that, for example, 'The concept of length involves as much as, and nothing more than, the set of operations by which length is determined' (Bridgeman, 1927). Again I must plead lack of space to discuss this issue thoroughly, and suggest that the existing literature is consulted (Benjamin, 1955; Cronbach, 1971; Hempel, 1965). But it is fair to say that operationalism is not viable in its strong sense; and indeed, a healthy epistomology depends upon a willingness to recognize the value and necessity of hypothetical, theoretical and open-ended concepts which really constitute the growth points of knowledge.

This is enough to show the deficiency of the behavioural objective approach. The problems discussed are just a selection of those that have arisen in the course of the author's own work, mainly in higher education: but their significance is not limited to any specific subject-matter, nor to any particular educational level. Taken as a whole, these criticisms virtually destroy the 'sufficiency' case: the idea that behavioural objectives are completely **sufficient** for the purposes of curriculum design. If this is so, then claims that we already have a satisfactory technology of education must be unfounded.

THE STRUCTURE OF KNOWLEDGE

Yet demands for more relevant and effective education are perfectly well-founded, and must be met. How should we proceed, if our standard paradigm is not sufficient? Even if (for the moment) we think we know what may be relevant, can we effectively achieve our aims? The reaction of some, when realizing the inadequacies of the objectives approach, is to retreat to intuition.

In which case we shall be back where we started — surely no rational person could doubt that, whatever its defects, the behavioural objective paradigm is an improvement on purely intuitive methods.

The natural reaction of the pragmatist to these problems is to turn the systematic (feed-forward) approach into a cyclical (feed-back) system in which all parts of the system may be modified according to the performance of other parts. This is very similar to the way in which 'management by objectives' is seen by its advocates as a cyclical system (Odiorne, 1965,

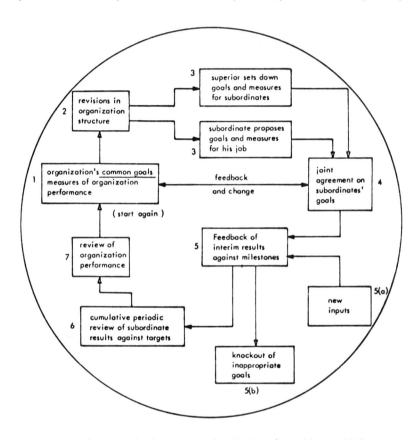

Figure 1. The cycle of management by objectives (from Odiorne, 1965)

Figure 1). Now, developmental testing can be used to improve the learning materials, and objectives and tests can be revised in the light of experience. If objectives are not sufficient, apparently all one needs to do is keep on cycling round the system until satisfied. But, this extreme empiricism is grossly inefficient, particularly if teaching materials are centrally produced, with consequent large investment. In such cases the system must work well first time. This puts our design system under extreme pressure. How should we respond?

We should respond by paying attention to the **structure** of the subject-matter. And all coherent subjects do certainly have a structure. For instance, in his celebrated attack on the Oxford school, Gellner describes linguistic philosophy as 'a system of interlocking, mutually supporting parts', a description that would suit many another subject area (Gellner, 1959). This provides a useful starting-point for our discussion. What is needed is a way of **representing publicly** a man's knowledge or point of view about the subject-matter. To do this we should need some agreed format or syntax, which specified how symbols were to be used, and what sort of operations were possible. Any system, to be satisfactory, would need to display the essential structure of the subject-matter in a way that could be understood and discussed. It would not (of itself) show how teaching and learning should proceed, but it would show what were the possibilities. We call such representations **knowledge structures**, and at the Open University we are actively investigating their design and use.

When my colleagues and I started this work we knew of no precedents. But we have since learnt that the idea of representing formally the structure of an area of knowledge has occurred a number of times during the last ten

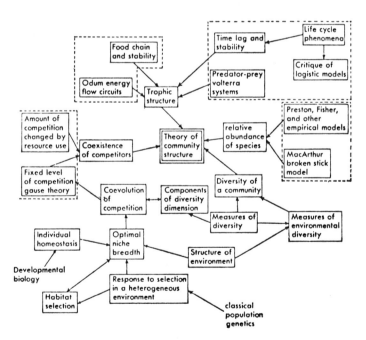

Figure 2. Relations among some of the components in evolutionary population biology theory (from Levins, 1968)

43

years, each occurrence being largely independent of the others. Examples can be found in the fields of philosophy, anthropology, biology, education, artificial intelligence, theory building, information science, and I daresay elsewhere. There is every reason to believe that the similarity between these efforts derives from a **basic functional need to develop ways of representing publicly a manipulable model of man's image of the world.**

Many of these examples are simply intuitive diagrams, of the kind shown by Levins to illustrate the cluster of models and concepts necessary for an adequate theory of population biology (Levins, 1968, Figure 2). Such diagrams have their uses, no doubt, but they are not 'well-formed'. The meaning of the various symbols are not prespecified; and too much is left unsaid. For example, the meaning of the arrows leading from one box to another is never specified, yet they represent the vital interrelationships which make the whole meaningful. The consequence is that such diagrams cannot function as a public medium of discussion.

To clarify some basic issues we shall consider the work of P H Winston, who has investigated how a machine may be taught to see and learn visual concepts (Winston, 1970). These computer programs work in the domain of three-dimensional structures made of bricks, wedges, and other simple objects: for our purpose the subject-matter is so simple that it does not obscure the problem of representation.

"From such visual images, the system builds a very coarse description (Figure 3) ..... analysis proceeds, inserting more detail ..... such descriptions enable one to compare and contrast scenes through

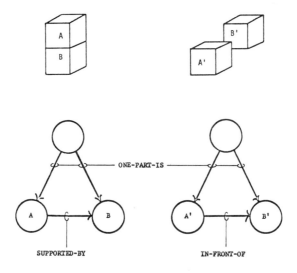

Figure 3. Descriptions of two simple visual scenes (from Winston, 1970)

programs that compare and contrast descriptions ..... there is further hope that the same machinery can be useful in situations ranging far from visual ones, giving the work a certain generality."
(Winston, 1970)

Notice first the critically important feature: the relations between concepts are relatively **well-defined.** Some are spacial relations (on-top-of, left-of, etc), some are logical relations (one-part-is, a-kind-of): but all are specified, and all are presented in ordinary language. This allows the machine to describe the world in terms conforming to human usage, so facilitating man-machine cooperation. One advantage is that humans can **teach** the machine: and the machine's performance can be evaluated in human terms.

Note also that the machine's descriptions have the structure of a network, not just because this is an economical way to store information (though this is so: Winston comments on the 'desperate inefficiency of list structures') but because the nodes or concepts can generally only be understood as relations between other nodes. For example, an **arch** entails the notion of a roof A 'supported by' pillars B and C (Figure 4).

The example of the arch gives me the opportunity to comment on the vexed question of depth **understanding.** For relational networks may be dense or sparse, and the extent and coherence of a net could provide a measure of understanding. If we truncated the net for 'arch', we could still say

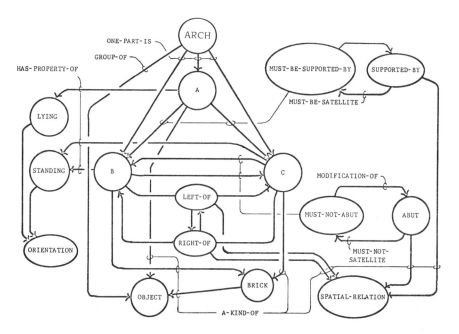

Figure 4. The complete net of relations entailed by the concept of an 'arch' (from Winston, 1970)

45

the machine understood the concept item arch: but its understanding would be more limited.

Perhaps the most extensive practical development of these ideas in education so far has been the work of Gordon Pask and his associates in the domain of probability theory (Pask, 1971). I shall try, as best I can, to avoid using Pask's arcane terminology whilst still retaining the sense of this elaborate system. The work starts with the construction of a gigantic network consisting of about 70 concept nodes and several hundred well-defined relations between the nodes. Very roughly, operations in the real world (like rolling dice) occupy one half of the net, whilst mathematical concepts (eg 'expectation') occupy the other half. Relationships of analogy link the two sides into a coherent whole. This structure was then made the basis of an elaborate computerized learning situation in which the learner was allowed to explore the network in his own fashion, though his progress was regulated by the need to pass tests of competence at every stage. In principle, the records of student progress and learning styles could then be used by a designer to provide a more rational basis for constructing the kinds of learning situations which are in more general use.

The point I am making is that the system **works**. It is possible to put the structure of knowledge into action, providing it is specified in a suitably well-formed syntax. Like Patrick Geddes' diagrams nearly a century ago (Boardman, 1944), knowledge structures are **thinking machines**.

Much more could be said on this subject, but this must suffice for now. Quite clearly the **idea** of representing the structure of knowledge is not sufficient by itself. We need exact procedures which would allow anyone who wished to build knowledge structures. And we must learn how best to put them to use to help tackle the design problems which were supposed to have been solved by behavioural objectives.

REFERENCES

Benjamin, A. C. (1955) Operationism. Thomas
Boardman, P. (1944) Patrick Geddes, maker of the future. Chapel Hill
Bridgeman, P. W. (1927) The logic of modern physics. Macmillan
Cronbach, L. J. (1971) Test Validation, in educational measurement.
   (Ed) R. L. Thorndike. American Council of Education
Davies, I. K. (1971) The management of learning. McGraw-Hill
Gagné, R. (1967) Curriculum research and the promotion of learning, in
   'Perspectives of curriculum evaluation'. AERA Monograph 1.
   Rand McNally
Gellner, E. (1959) Words and things. Gollancz
Gilbert, T. F. (1962) Mathetics. Reprinted in RECALL Supplement No.1,
   Longmac
Goodman, P. (1962) Compulsory miseducation. Penguin Books 1971
Hempel, C. (1965) Aspects of scientific explanation. Free Press
Holt, J. (1964) How children fail. Pelican Books 1969
Illich, I. (1971) Deschooling society
Levins, R. (1968) Evolution in changing environments. Princeton

Mager, R. F. (1961) Preparing instructional objectives. Fearon Press
Mager, R. F. (1961) On sequencing instructional content. Reprinted in
  Educational Technology. (Ed) DeCecco. Holt, Rinehart and Winston
Mager, R. F . and McCann, J. (1962) Learner-controlled instruction.
  Varian Associates
Odiorne, G. S . (1965) Management by objectives. Pitman
Pask, G. (1971) The CASTE system. System Research Ltd
Pask, G. and Scott, B. (1971) Learning strategies and individual competence.
  System Research Ltd
Popham, W. J. and Baker, E. (1970) Systematic instruction. Prentice-Hall
Postman, N. and Weingartner, C. (1969) Teaching as a subversive activity.
  Penguin Books
Skinner, B. F. (1966) The technology of teaching. Appleton-Century-Crofts
Winston, P. (1970) Learning structural descriptions from examples.
  MAC TR-76, Project MAC, MIT

The Sacramental Nature of Behavioural Objectives

P DAVID MITCHELL

Though the language of educational technology lacks religious or poetic symbolism it still may surround many a useful idea with a cloak of myth which must be examined if the field is to develop its greatest potential. One such verbal cult, that of the specification of terminal behaviour and guidance of students toward a predetermined state, is presently part of every educational technologist's repertoire. And this notion that precisely stated educational objectives can and should be divided into specific enabling and terminal objectives is so appealing in its concreteness and clarity that any proof of its limitations cannot help but suffer by comparison. Yet not all educational aims or desired changes in a student's capability — his capacity to behave — are amenable to such precise analysis, instructional regulation or even observation; the value of expressing all objectives as overt behaviour can be questioned as inadequate in principle and unrealistic in practice.

A FUNDAMENTAL MISCONCEPTION

Granted that explicit objectives are more likely than vague or badly-defined ones to achieve the intentional development of capability, the assumptions, language and tools of convergent instructional control must be questioned. There is a fundamental misconception in the cult of behavioural objectives, one which has had a deleterious affect on our thinking as educational technologists. This misconception derives from our failure to distinguish between isomorphic and homomorphic conceptualizations of capability. It is manifested by the assumption that instructional objectives and the student's terminal behaviour are, or should be, isomorphic (ie identical in all respects). In effect the objective is none other than the demonstrated behaviour.

Similarly, the paradigm of convergent instructional control is a simple feedback-regulated system whose output is sampled frequently or even monitored continuously and compared with a reference output, the desired terminal state. Such a system implies a precise delineation of both the reference capability and the student's monitored capability, so by its very nature the method is limited to those objectives and outcomes which can be clearly identified, articulated and measured. Therefore any statement of an intended terminal state implicitly identifies both the measuring instruments (including human observers) and the range of values of the events to be monitored (and the conditions necessary to produce the terminal behaviour repertoire). This interrelated sequence of component events extends back to the relevant input parameters so that the measured input anticipates the output. Any attempt to use this decomposition method to achieve broader objectives such as intellectual integrity, value clarification or developing a consistent philosophy of life must be tempered with caution — caveat emptor.

Because not all educational aims are amenable to the mechanistic language and underlying assumptions of convergent instructional control, expressing objectives explicitly as overt behaviour, facile princeps, is inadequate in principle. The practitioner of educational technology must recognize that although overt behaviour may bear witness to educational objectives they need not be coterminous. Overt behaviour provides evidence for covert cognitive and affective processes on the one hand; on the other, it samples aspects of intractable objectives or themes.

BEHAVIOURAL SYMBOLS

Behavioural objectives are appropriate at some stages of instruction and can be stated judiciously, but it is a gross over-simplification to think that stating or achieving instructional objectives in behavioural terms is desirable in its own right. For the criterion behaviour is simply a token of the student's capability — evidence of some presumed change inside the student which is sampled by an external indicator. That behavioural objectives function as symbols is indicated by the language in which they are frequently couched — language which includes terms such as identify, classify, predict, point to, circle or operate. In these cases the overt response signifies that the student has achieved a desired capability which is something more than the response from which it is inferred. This is not to deny that some capability may be sampled directly (eg solving three consecutive analysis of variance problems correctly) but even then the objective probably is not terminal but rudimentary.

OVERT SYMBOLS OF CAPABILITY

A problem arises when the absence of an overt demonstration of intended behaviour is taken as evidence that nothing was learned. An observer's statement of a student's capability is likely to be accepted as a reliable report even if he was the only observer present. But if his statement refers to his own capability, his report is likely to be suspect because the capability was not publicly observable. However, overt responses are not necessary in appraising instruction. As an observer, the student has access to internal events inaccessible to an external observer (as critics of B F Skinner frequently point out, blissfully unaware that Skinner himself has argued for the study of private events; cf Day, 1969). In school learning, often no overt response is needed in order for the student himself to know whether he can meet an established criterion provided he has a way to verify for himself that he has attained the requisite standard. However, when the student does not know the intended outcome of a particular instructional sequence an overt response is necessary so that the teacher or instructional system can assess and respond to his activity.

THEORETICAL CONSTRUCTS

I want to set forth several theoretical constructs that I feel would free the emerging technology of education from the limitations of the cult of behavioural objectives.

Usually the notion of 'learning' is invoked both to describe and explain change in strength of a specified behaviour as a function of observed or presumed interactions between the organism and his environment. I propose that 'capability' supercede such terms as 'learned behaviour', or 'behaviour change'. Capability may be understood to be the organism's demonstrated or potential capacity for acting, thinking, feeling or becoming. This implies something more than either the organized presentation of information or a carefully contrived behavioural curriculum both of which see the student displaying some knowledge or performing some activities thought to characterize a worthwhile field. However, it is important to recognize the difference between performing and participating.

R S Peters suggests the difference between capability and behaviour when he points out that an educated man's knowledge "must characterize his way of looking at things rather than be hived off ..... (Furthermore) It must involve the kind of commitment that comes from being on the inside of a form of thought and awareness" (Peters, 1966). Manifestations of the insider's commitment are inherent in such qualifiers as 'elegance', 'consistency', and 'coherence', but seldom in routine and stereotyped behaviour patterns the performance of which does not reflect inner experience or commitment.

Capability would seem to be a more appropriate concept than behaviour, learning or knowledge because it reflects (as I hope to demonstrate) the total process of participation rather than just terminal performance. And participation in itself results in capacities to behave in a certain way – capacities which may manifest themselves now, or which may be only a probability of appearing under conditions not currently present. In fact, if manifested later, a previously latent capability is evoked by its new circumstantial context, without the intervening conditions under which it was acquired; this lack of proximity has presented great difficulty to observers of human behaviour and students of learning.

LATENT CAPABILITY

That no proximal relationship need exist between a person's exposure to conditions of learning and demonstration of his capability is a fact that underlies formal education and mediated education (via ETV, etc). This helps to differentiate education from apprenticeship and from experience. Think of the change in a person's behavioural capacity attributed to formal instruction, reading, televiewing, thinking or imitation. Unless an overt demonstration is called for, passive or covert interplay with the environment need not produce immediate activity beyond that associated with information processing. Let us refer to a behavioural capability presumed to exist, but not demonstrated as **latent capability**. It may be inferred from what a person says about his capability or from a knowledge of antecedent events. Such latent capability is a hypothetical construct since it cannot be demonstrated per se but it has a de facto existence to the extent that it can be fostered intentionally or studied in the same way as other theoretical constructs. What evidence are we prepared to accept to infer the specified process or capability? This question of major concern will give rise to considerable research but the foundation has been laid in the taxonomies of educational objectives.

Tom Wyant's (1971) seminal research with a 'question-event network' may identify latent capability by asking a person if he knows the meaning of a topic or if he can answer a particular question. (His subjects were not required to state the meaning or answer the question.) Wyant showed that students can realistically assess their capability without demonstrating it. Thus in the absence of an overt demonstration of behaviour it is possible to consider the verbal report of a person's covert experience as evidence for the existence of latent (or other unobserved) capability. In this way we can avoid the verbal circumlocutions that usually accompany reports about one's past experience or present capacity.

DYNAMIC CAPABILITY

Once a capability has been evinced and confirmed it is no longer latent but is directly observable as **dynamic capability**. However, one must not assume that all latent capability will eventually become dynamic; its greatest importance to education may be its existence as such. Or a latent capability may be directly transformed into a higher order capability without ever appearing in its dynamic form. In this way a person's overt capability will depend upon prerequisite capabilities that may never have been exhibited. Indeed, fostering latent capabilities which will, in turn, facilitate the appropriation of dynamic capabilities should be an important educational concern.

For these important reasons the educational technologist should concern himself with producing latent capability that either may materialize at some future time or may remain latent. In fact the highest levels of both the cognitive and affective taxonomies seem to require various capabilities which may not be demonstrated during or immediately after the educational activities chosen to foster them. Some, such as the attitudes associated with one's

51

philosophy of life, must always be inferred from other events. For this reason precise specification of instructional objectives in behavioural terms, though usually appropriate when considering dynamic capability, is not necessary when latent capability is intended. Though we recognize the difference between teaching a student that something is so and his learning to do something, in what way is the currently popular shift from non-behavioural objectives (eg 'to understand') to the acquisition and demonstration of verbal behaviour verbatim et literatim an advancement in educational theory or practice? In fact, exclusive concern with publicly observable behaviour may improve skill training markedly without improving education.

Whether we are interested in its gross or refined patterns, demonstration of specific activity frequently permits inference of problem solving, a value judgment or some other cognitive or affective process. The described behaviour is merely a symbol of desired capability, seldom the desired outcome itself. In addition the desired capability normally would be more pervasive than a single episode.

DORMANT CAPABILITY

Once demonstrated, it is possible that a dynamic capability does not appear again. This lack of activity need not indicate that the capability no longer exists for it may be quiescent or replaced by another prepotent behaviour. Indeed, since only limited capability can be manifested at any given instant virtually all the organism's capability must be quiescent. If a dynamic capability does not continue to appear in appropriate circumstances, we may assume it to be dormant; on the other hand, a dynamic capability that is maintained in strength is called a habit. Thus most adults demonstrate a dynamic capability to perform simple arithmetic operations or to decide the day to day pattern of their lives but may have dormant (or no) capability to solve quadratic equations or formulate reasoned written arguments. Frequently only the student himself is in a position to assess readily his capacity to behave — the mark of the professional.

POTENTIAL CAPABILITY

Capability, therefore, must be demonstrated at least once under appropriate conditions to be considered dynamic or dormant. Latent capability may be inferred from a verbal report or from contact with an environment likely to produce it; in principle the inference should be stated as a probability that latent capability will become dynamic under appropriate circumstances. But it is possible that capability which does not yet exist as dynamic or even latent has a high probability of being generated under certain conditions (in the absence of intervention to arrest the process). Accordingly potential capability refers to the probability that specified behavioural outcomes will be demonstrated if a person who possesses prerequisite capabilities interacts with a properly designed instructional program. For instance potential capability would be taken into account if a properly programmed instruction system is characterized by the probability distribution that a person possessing stated prerequisite capabilities will achieve a certain standard as a function of time spent interacting with the system. However, such a probability statement may emerge from the student. Joseph Trenanman's (1967) important study of mediated communication and comprehension found a very high correlation (0.747) between viewers' subjective assessment of probable interest in a program and an objective measure of comprehension.

RUDIMENTARY, NOT TERMINAL OBJECTIVES

Defining instructional objectives in terms of precise and measurable behaviour implies that the specified behaviour is a terminal requirement of an instructional sequence. Yet while it might terminate one set of instructional activities it serves simultaneously as an initial requirement for subsequent instruction. Moreover a specified objective should indicate not merely that the student demonstrates certain behaviour but that in so doing he displays his capability to continue to do so under similar circumstances. Bert Masia (1969) transcends the means-ends language and value system of contemporary instruction by couching course objectives in such phrases as 'to develop skill in', 'to begin to form judgements about', or 'to begin to see that'. The criterion outcome is not a terminal achievement but a token of his achievement to date and an earnest of his potential to go on behaving in like manner or better. This more truly reflects the dynamic nature of education by anticipating achievement on a higher level.

In spite of current pressure to state behavioural objectives, teachers still prescribe activities rather than outcomes. Their injunctions to examine, evaluate, interpret or explore help initiate students into intrinsically and instrumentally worthwhile activities having many and unpredictable outcomes. Though they may be selected with certain ends in mind, these evocative activity-objectives are likely to produce diversity rather than uniformity of instructional outcomes. In this regard educational technologists have a great deal to learn from project-oriented approaches both of infant school teachers and of research centres (and even from conversation as it occurs in residential colleges).

By shifting to desired outcomes beyond the immediately obvious activity which only symbolizes dynamic capability, the educational technologist can resist specifying a linear instructional route to the token behaviour. Rather he must identify or generate a number of educational patterns (not necessarily confined to formal instruction or institutions) that allow not only for increments in latent as well as in dynamic capability but also for intrinsically worthwhile experiences (Mitchell, 1971). A number of these educational activities may contribute to coalescence of certain capabilities into a higher order of latent or dynamic capability. Even so, many outcomes will not be amenable to measurement or external observation.

It is appropriate to identify a network of rudimentary criterion behaviours and activity objectives to be used as a checklist for demonstration purposes and unlike prescriptive convergent objectives, to capitalize on the human capacity to learn more than one thing at a time. (Such a network may resemble superficially the networks of systems engineering (eg CPM, PERT) and other time-models.)

Specification of rudimentary objectives permits a student to direct his own learning activities to a considerable degree. It also makes possible instruction based less on convergent behavioural control and more on standards to be met and conditions for culturing which James Macdonald insisted upon in urging 'instruction characterized by beginnings rather than endings' (Macdonald, 1966).

STANDARDS AND STANDARDIZATION

Since standards are implicit in education certain standards of mastery must be met in order for a student to relate his latent or demonstrated capability to his educational goal. Normally an educational objective should include a standard of required behaviour with which a student may compare his own capability. While it is clear that a uniform standard of achievement is necessary in some instructional objectives and desirable for others, it does not follow that a standard product of the instruction system, as contrasted with the achievement of standards, is an optimal educational policy. Nor does it follow that the criterion (especially for rudimentary objectives) must be achieved by standardized techniques. Given a list of objectives, a variety of learning resources and the standards expected, students may select idiosyncratic ways of preparing themselves to meet the objectives.

It is probable that educational administrators will consider the preparation of alternative learning resources to be economically unfeasible — that standardization of procedures is less costly, more easily administered and more efficient. Nevertheless, unnecessary standardization of both means and ends allows little scope for a student to differentiate himself from his peers and is therefore antithetical to the achievement of cultural diversity. Yet if the overall education system is to support optimal cultural development, then diversity must be encouraged. Educational technologists committed to helping each person 'to inquire, to discover for himself, and in other ways to be original are enlarging the supply of mutations which contribute to the evolution of a culture' (Skinner, 1968).

DESTINATION OR DESTINY?

Lengrand has raised a critical issue. He asks:

"To what extent can education be defined as an intervention from outside, the transmission of know-how and technique? How far does education indicate a way of being in the world, a systematic directed effort by the individual to coordinate the facts of experience into a unified and harmonious personality?" (Lengrand, 1970)

If we conclude from Lengrand and Peters that education is directly related to the pattern of an individual's participation — that coordinated and unified forms of thought and awareness are indicative of the educated man, then the discrete interventions and isolated rituals characteristic of schooling, however valuable in themselves, may be far less educative than we expect. The type of intervention, whether informal or purposive, that may be most effective is that which produces a person who is more than the sum of all the instructional objectives he had demonstrated. (Recall that the classical method of developing the integrated outlook of an educated man has been conversation, not behavioural management.)

Since education is a way of life which may embrace, but is not limited to, instructional intervention, the value of the educational activity itself, as much as its outcomes or products, makes education worthwhile. As educators, practitioners of educational technology must not limit themselves to the production of predetermined, verifiable dynamic capability. They can serve their stewardship better by investigating those environments, those patterns of activity which will cultivate the seeds of an individual's total internal perspective. A developing, strengthening perspective may be the most effective dimension of the student's capability; it may encourage the enhancement and integration of capabilities, not performances, that is the mark of an educated person. Developing an educational ecology that will facilitate initiation into worthwhile activities demands a fundamental reappraisal of the nature and function of educational technology. This paper is intended to contribute to that reappraisal.

REFERENCES

Day, W. F. (1969) Journal of the Experimental Analysis of Behavior, **12**, 315
Henry, J. (1963) 'Culture Against Man'. Random House Inc., New York
Lengrand, P. (1970) 'Education put to the question'. Unesco Courier, Jan. 27-31
Macdonald, J. B. (1966) in 'Precedents and promise in the curriculum field'.
    (Ed) H. F. Robison. Teachers College Press, New York. Page 46
Masia, B. B. (1969) Personal communication
Mitchell, P. D. (1971) 'A proposal for programming research in training
    learners as educational technologists'. Paper presented to Canadian
    Educational Research Association, St. John's, Newfoundland, June
Peters, R. S. (1966) 'Ethics and Education'. Allen & Unwin, London. Page 31
Skinner, B. F. (1968) 'The Technology of Teaching'. Appleton-Century-
    Crofts, New York. Page 235
Trenaman, J. M. (1967) 'Communication and Comprehension'. Longmans,
    Green, London
Wyant, T. G. (1971) 'Network Analysis and its Use in Education'. University
    of Birmingham School of Education, Birmingham (unpublished dissertation)

The Application of the Operational Research Technique of Network Analysis to Primary Mathematics

B W VAUGHAN

Since the introduction of Program Evaluation and Review Technique (PERT) in 1957, it has been widely used in industry and has been found to be very valuable in planning, scheduling, and controlling complex projects.

PERT, or modifications, called Critical Path Analysis, or Critical Path Method, have been used in education mainly for school building projects (Werts, 1967; Stewart, 1969).

Platts and Wyant (1969) suggested that Network Analysis could also be used effectively in education for setting out a syllabus. Wood and Wyant (1970) have given an example of the manner in which Course 500 in Further Education can be set out in the form of a network diagram, and have listed the advantages which this layout would have over the conventional syllabus. Wyant (1969) has also drawn a critical path analysis of a course.

The technique of network analysis consists of the following stages:

1. A list of all the activities involved in the project is drawn up and checked.
2. The logical sequencing of the activities is decided and an arrow diagram is drawn and checked for logic.
3. Resources necessary to complete the project are allocated, including time, and the critical path identified.
4. Various methods are used to smooth out resource requirements, including tables of floats.

Of the above activities, all could be used in considering a primary mathematics syllabus except the allocation of time to an activity. Since the pupils will be proceeding along an individual course their individual times to complete an activity will depend upon the ability and motivation of each pupil.

A list of all the activities which recognized mathematics authorities have stated should be included was drawn up. This list was arranged in a logical order and critically examined and set out in the form of a network diagram (Figure 1).

The arrangement of the activities in the network diagram seems also to be in the series of hierarchies of learning postulated by several educational

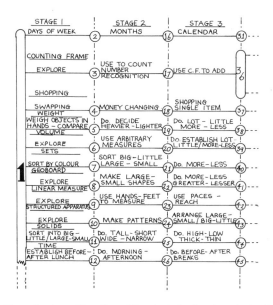

Figure 1. A small section of the start of network analysis of
primary mathematics showing division into 'stages'

psychologists (Bloom, 1956; Gagné, 1968; Leith, 1966). It would also seem to
lay out the material to be taught in a systematic framework which would meet
the needs of a pupil envisaged by Bruner (1966).

After including the modifications put forward in the critical examination,
the network was introduced into schools for evaluation in regard to the practicability of using this form of layout of a syllabus in schools. Head and class
teachers made many suggestions, including the use of network analysis as the
basis of an integrated scheme which would include the allocation of teaching
materials, and the design of a storage and retrieval system, and record
cards based on the node numbers of the network (Vaughan, 1971a and b).

AN INTEGRATED SCHEME BASED ON NETWORK ANALYSIS

Since each child should engage in each activity, and will not be working in
parallel as in industrial uses of network analysis, the network has been
used in a series of vertical columns, or 'stages' (Figure 2). When the entry
point of a pupil has been ascertained, he proceeds down the column of activities, or 'stage' until he reaches the foot of the column. At this point it is
intended that he will take a test to discover his mastery of the material in
that column (Vaughan, 1971c).

Teaching materials were allocated to the activities in the network and
numbered to correspond to the node numbers. These teaching materials consist at present of work cards and teaching programs in book format, Wiltshire

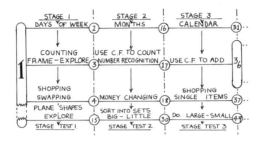

Figure 2. Diagram to show pupils progress down each column of activities (or stage)

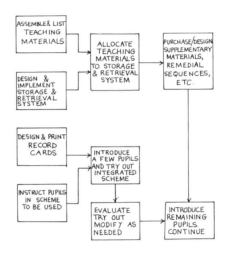

Figure 3. Flow chart of introduction of an integrated scheme for teaching mathematics in a primary school based on a network analysis of the syllabus

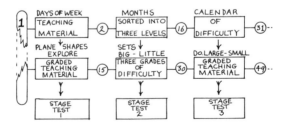

Figure 4. Diagrammatic explanation of allocation and grading of teaching materials according to node numbers of network analysis of primary mathematics

58

and Clearway in linear form, a Bingley Tutor machine and programs, and a Tutorpack machine on loan, with programs which have been donated (Figure 3).

When the teaching materials had been assembled and numbered, they were divided into three grades of difficulty. In the same way pupils were divided into three levels of ability. Thus each pupil could be guided into a course suited to his needs, and could be transferred to a higher or lower level of difficulty at any time. A pupil could also repeat any desired activity at a higher or lower level when this would meet his need (Figure 4).

Record cards were designed and printed. These were also based on the node numbers of the network. The columns of activities correspond to 'stages' mentioned earlier. These cards entail the minimum of clerical work by the teacher. A tick in a square shows the completion of an activity. The position of the square ticked shows the level of difficulty of that activity. The record card is also used by the teacher to guide the pupil to his next activity. This may be (1) to proceed to the next activity in that 'stage'; (2) to repeat the same activity, but at a higher or lower level of difficulty, or (3) to engage in a remedial sequence of activities based on a sub-network which splits up the material to be taught into simpler steps (Vaughan, 1971c).

In addition one copy of the record card is used by each teacher as a record of the teaching material which is available. There is a considerable shortfall, but a concerted effort is being made by teachers to remedy this.

Children have been introduced into the scheme a few at a time. Each teacher has instituted his own system based on the overall plan. Some have the whole class engaged in the activities in the network, others find that it is better to have half the class involved while the rest are engaged in a separate activity which does not require attention from the teacher. It is clear that a certain amount of class or large group teaching will be required for certain aspects of work, and this must be left to the teacher to decide.

THE OPERATION OF THE SCHEME

The overall plan of the present use being made of the integrated scheme is as follows:

The pupil is given simple instructions as to the way in which the scheme works, and how he is expected to use it.

He is tested, graded and placed at his starting point on the network.

He collects a card from the box file which tells him what to do.

He collects any apparatus or materials which he will need and carries out the required activity. When this has been done he returns any materials used to the correct place, and takes his completed work to the teacher. The teacher checks what has been done.

The teacher may ask supplementary questions to check mastery, or supply additional teaching.

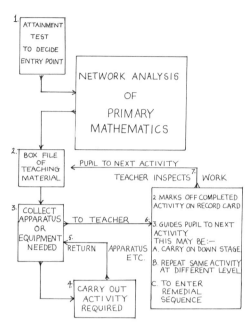

Figure 5. Flow diagram of classroom use of network
analysis based scheme for primary mathematics

The teacher marks off the completed activity on the pupil record card.
The teacher guides the pupil to the next relevant activity. This may be to go
on to the next activity in that 'stage', to enter a remedial sequence, or to
repeat the activity but at a different level of difficulty (Figure 5).

ADVANTAGES OF THE NETWORK ANALYSIS OF A SYLLABUS

1. A clear, visual, one page layout is possible.
2. The network layout enables all activities to be shown in the order in
   which they should be carried out.
3. The dependence of one activity upon another can be clearly seen.
4. New material can easily be incorporated, and modifications readily
   made.
5. The progress of individual children can be recorded in a simple manner.
6. After a period of use the records could be used to provide the data for
   evaluation of methods, media, and teaching materials.
7. Teachers find the scheme simple to operate, once the initial allocation
   of teaching materials has been completed.
8. Since the activities of the pupils are geared to their individual needs,
   learning should be facilitated.
9. Teachers are involved in the minimum of routine clerical work, and
   can devote their time to their role as course designer, guide, counsellor, and the motivation of pupils. They are also involved in designing additional teaching materials.

10. The need for remedial sequences, supplementary materials and apparatus can be decided in advance of need and can be ordered in good time.

11. Pupils like the scheme as it presents them with material suited to their needs, carefully graded. They find they are not being compared to other pupils, and can proceed at their own pace.

12. Movement from class to class is made easier, and there is the minimum of disruption of the pupils' work. Movement from school to school will also be made simpler as the record card will show the exact stage reached by each pupil, and the level of difficulty he is capable of attaining.

13. The research worker will be presented with data in a manageable form, readily adapted to use in a computer.

14. The teaching material designer will be presented with a tool which will enable him to break down any teaching sequence into logical steps of any required dimension.

15. The use of expensive audio-visual equipment can readily be incorporated into the scheme, and used with economy. After a period it should be possible to evaluate their worth, by using pupil records.

REFERENCES

Bloom, B. (1956) 'Taxonomy of educational objectives. Cognitive Domain. Longmans Green, London
Bruner, J. (1966) 'The process of education'. Harvard University Press
Gagné, R. M. (1968) Psychological Review, 75, 177
Leith, G. O. M. (1966) Visual Education, March 7
Platts, C. V. and Wyant, T. G. (1969) Educational Review, 21, February
Stewart, J. D. (1969) Local Government Chronicle, February
Vaughan, B. W. (1971a) Primary Mathematics, 9, 19
Vaughan, B. W. (1971b) Science Teacher, December, 32
Vaughan, B. W. (1971c) Primary Mathematics, 9, 157
Werts, C. E. (1967) National Merit Scholarship Reports 3
Wood, A. and Wyant, T. G. (1970) Industrial and Commercial Training, December
Wyant, T. G. (1969) Educational Review, 2, 2

Method of presentation: Tape/slide

Learning Systems Techniques Applied to a Large-Scale Educational Problem
W J K DAVIES and MARJORIE NEEDHAM

The starting point of this project was the identification, by the City of Birmingham Education Authority, of a potentially serious shortage of specialist mathematics teachers, especially in the non-selective secondary schools. The mathematics inspectorate realized that such a shortage would mean that much mathematics teaching would need to be done by non-specialists and decided to provide as much help for these as was possible.

The St Albans Programmed Learning Centre was initially approached in the Spring of 1970 to advise on the provision of suitable learning programs for issue to schools. The Centre was dubious as to whether the straightforward provision of commercial programs was an appropriate way of solving the problem and undertook instead to examine the situation and to suggest possible approaches. This paper describes the application of a learning systems analysis to define the educational problem and to indicate possible solutions within the constraints imposed. The chief ones were inevitably money — since no one was prepared to finance very expensive schemes; time — since the initial shortage was expected to occur in September 1970; and the urgent necessity to involve both mathematics teachers and non-specialists to ensure the sympathetic reception of any scheme.

(i) There was already a shortage of specialist mathematics teachers, but this was expected to intensify within the following few months to such an extent that some non-selective secondary schools might be without a mathematics specialist in September 1970.

(ii) That existing programs were unlikely to be sufficient in either quantity or approach to meet the needs of such schools and that in any case something more was needed. Specifically any help must:

    (a) as far as possible meet the requirements of specialist maths teachers in its content and approach, the more so because the work would not be directly under their control;

    (b) be strongly teacher-supportive to meet the hypothetical 'worst-case' a substitute teacher who knew little maths and regarded the allocation of maths teaching in addition to his normal timetable as an imposition;

(c) elicit a favourable response from teachers and pupils likely to be involved in it (ie the idea must be 'sold' to the teachers **before** work started; both teachers and pupils should be encouraged by their success);

(d) start to become available as soon as possible after September 1970 since the problem was a current one.

It was not to be expected that any considerable sums of money could be made available at short notice, especially as no saving in school staff could be envisaged — salaries were still being paid, even if their recipients were non-specialists or probationers.

The four constraints of finance, time, need to convince those involved, and necessity for operation by non-specialists ruled out all but one of the existing schemes investigated by Mr Moon and ourselves: the Surrey scheme involving autotutor classrooms was fully programmed, but still required guidance from maths teachers, and was in any case prohibitively expensive; the book schemes such as SMP or Maths for the Majority were largely at too high a level and designed for operation by knowledgeable specialists.   It became clear that any help must be quick, reasonably cheap and produced largely from local resources; it would also be desirable, because of the time element, to incorporate existing programmed material where this appeared compatible.

At the same time, one heavily structured mathematics scheme, that initiated by Bertram Banks in West Kent, appeared to have possible application in the situation. The main disadvantages foreseen were the need for some specialist help in compiling the 'matrices' of work that are an integral part of that scheme. A subsidiary project was therefore started to study the West Kent material in selected schools, but this is beyond the scope of this paper.

PROPOSALS

As a result of the analysis, the following proposals were put forward:

1. Groups of maths teachers to be formed, to try to draw up agreed schemes of work in the form of syllabi, and to examine existing programmed material for suitability of content and approach.

2. Selected maths teachers to be given a minimum training in the design and production of teachers' guide notes, test construction and production of student work material matched to learning objectives.

3. A small production facility to be provided, this to be extended if the scheme proved viable; either one full-time or two part-time

schools liaison officers to be provided to oversee the development
of the scheme, with provision for a full-time coordinator.

4. Material to be provided in the form of strongly teacher-supportive
   'tests' each containing three or four units of work material ('packages')
   to cover approximately six weeks' work on various aspects of mathematics.

MATERIAL

Inevitably much advice was received from various sources that 'Educational
Technology' (ie CCTV and/or slide tape-presentations) would provide the
best solution. These were eventually rejected in favour of paper-based material because:

1. cost would have been considerable both for equipment and for
   production of material. This would not have been insuperable,
   however, but for the other major disadvantages;

2. system had to be operated by non-enthusiasts — hence largely
   self-working which was incompatible with CCTV in particular;
   in addition, work material was envisaged as being individualized,
   as far as possible, rather than for class lessons;

3. system had to be mobile and portable: few of the affected schools
   had a specialist maths room and some 'set' classes for maths so
   that several parallel classes might be working at the same time;

4. material had to be flexible and capable of being produced quickly.
   Virtually no 'hardware based' material answering the scheme's
   requirements was available, although a number of Stillit programs
   with their associated Stillitrons were incorporated.

Indeed, the one piece of extraneous hardware that was introduced — a
simple 'program board' to take Tutorpack, Bingley and ITM programs —
has proved one of the few real mistakes made by the consultants. Schools
and children persist in using the programs in paper form with simple paper
sheets as 'sliders'. Part of this preference is probably because the packages have had to be carried about within schools much more than was anticipated.

COMPOSITION OF STAFF

There were plenty of arguments in favour of setting up a strong full-time
project directorate and training up a team of writers to be seconded full-time
to 'program-writing'. These were eventually turned down on the following
grounds:

(a) **Cost**: the project had no massive grant to cover the employment of such staff and, indeed, headmasters were at the time very reluctant to lose some of their best — and already scarce — teachers;

(b) **Philosophy**: it was felt strongly by mathematics teachers that writers should be in constant touch with children (ie teaching at least part-time in the schools: the selected teachers were also strongly of this opinion;

(c) **Material**: it was not envisaged that full programmed learning material was in many cases either necessary or desirable.

IMPLEMENTATION OF THE PROPOSALS

Briefly, Working Parties were constituted to examine proposals for:

(i) a five-year 'numeracy' course for non-examination pupils (NEX)
(ii) a three-year course for those likely to take examinations (EX)
(iii) 4-5th year course for CSE and GCE (CSE)
(iv) ways and means of implementing the project

A strong degree of commonalty was expected in the first year of NEX and EX to allow interchange of children between the courses.

Selected members then spent a fortnight at St Albans, examining available mathematics programs in detail, trying to define core syllabi and receiving an absolute minimum of initial training. These nine people formed the core of the writing teams which started work during the summer holidays of 1970. At the same time meetings were held to publicize the scheme and St Albans PL Centre designed a definite house-style so that the project had its own identity and everything connected with it was easily recognized. Two part-time liaison officers were appointed, followed early in 1971 by the secondment of a College of Education lecturer as full-time coordinator.

Problems of initial organization (teacher release, provision of clerical help) proved rather intractable so that the first material reached schools early in 1971, rather than in the Autumn of 1970 as had been hoped. By the end of the academic year, however, some 18 different packages had been produced, and this flow has been maintained during the current session. As had been predicted in the analysis, a lack of the right resources at the right time had led to set-backs, but this is probably inevitable in a pioneering operation of this type. The project has reached a state where it is now accepted, adequate administrative and clerical assistance is becoming available, and a long hard look is being taken at future development, so that full value can be obtained from what is being produced. There are problems, outlined below, but it is now possible to draw tentative conclusions about the design of a general model for such projects. The detail problems and their solutions — or rather ways of preventing their emergence — are also becoming clear and it should be possible to analyze these during the coming year.

PROBLEMS THAT HAVE ARISEN

The original concept had been of balanced 'kits' each containing three or four packages on related topics and providing about six weeks' work. Delays in writing and production, together with very tardy deliveries of commercial material, made this very difficult to achieve in the first instance, since packages came 'off the production line' in dribs and drabs, so that they had to be issued as they appeared.

The 'worst-case' teachers, too, tended to use packages end-on rather than in parallel, and it was found that children were taking too long to complete individual packages. Investigation showed the reasons for this to be two-fold: teachers were inexperienced in using individualized instruction, and did not maintain enough control over the learning situation; some packages were too long, mainly owing to the enthusiasm and determination of the writers to cover their topics very thoroughly. Nevertheless, there was also strong feed-back that the material was in general doing what had been hoped — relieving non-specialists of a severe problem and producing a favourable attitude to mathematics in both teachers and pupils — when we got reports of children **asking** to do work in the lunch hour or to take it home, everyone connected with the project felt considerably encouraged.

The other main problems have been basically administrative ones:

(i) the problem of controlling groups of part-time writers, ensuring that deadlines were met, that they did not allow enthusiasm to blind them to outside constraints, and ensuring that available commercial material was carefully considered;

(ii) the purely logistical problem of assembling and dispatching packages to schools; collecting them, checking them and restoring them to usable condition after they have been used;

(iii) the objective evaluation of various packages to allow for meaningful revision: it has so far been possible only to use a part-time evaluator so that this work is progressing much more slowly than is desirable.

The solutions to these problems are visible, but will take more resources than are at present available if they are to be fully implemented. More importantly, we can see how to avoid them in any future project.

CONCLUSIONS

It is possible to use systems training techniques to define a large scale learning problem and to suggest with a high degree of accuracy what will be needed to overcome it. Where this project has run into major problems of implementation it has been because outside constraints of finance and time proved even more intractable than had been envisaged: hence the resources required to cope with the initial stages according to the analysis were not available when needed and there were consequent effects on both quality and timing of the work. This is no criticism of the Birmingham LEA. Local authorities inevitably work to an annual fixed budget and are also unwilling to vote substantial backing for a project until some measure of success has been achieved — ie the idea has proved viable. This factor must be taken into account in the design of future models, as must the fact that partial success may ironically well hamper such projects. The usefulness of the material so far provided has helped to disguise the original lack of specialist teachers, and thus make it appear less serious: hence it is more difficult to persuade administrators to support it with resources.

As regards the detail design of such projects, we would generalize that it is possible quickly to train experienced teachers to produce strong teacher-support material and that on a large scale this appears more acceptable than learning-programs. On the whole, too, the idea of using part-time teacher-writers has been successful, although we would modify the concept somewhat in any future work. There are many lessons that have been learnt about improving the detail work in such projects, and we are currently codifying the the results for future use.

Method of presentation: This paper was intended to be read in conjunction with wall charts and other material at the conference

Individual learning in schools.
A course for GCE 'O' level chemistry.
C REYNOLDS

A CASE FOR INDIVIDUALIZED PROGRAMS IN SCHOOLS

Individualized learning schemes do not simply allow the teacher to opt out of his relationship with his class. Rather than his acting as information source and disciplinarian, seeking new ways to hold the class together, he communicates when one or a small group of his students cannot immediately cope. When he is discussing a point here, or directing a student's wandering attention there, the others are not disturbed. Each is working at his own pace, which, with the right atmosphere can be his optimum pace.

Perhaps the most important aspect is the motivation that is achieved. The students know that their progress is directly related to their effort, and that this is registered instantly. They see this progress as passage through a definite and evident syllabus towards a fixed goal. Assuming that the material they are working with is of at least average interest, how better can motivation and the self-discipline of mental effort be gained? Add to this the range of information sources in which the student is actively involved, the twenty-four hour availability of the material which allows a student to finish off in his time what he has started in class time, the ease of introducing new material and ideas with minimum course disruption, and one can anticipate a dynamic classroom atmosphere.

In turn, the teacher can handle multi-ability, multi-age and multi-course students simultaneously. In his class all are learning, rather than those who might listen. Since not more than two students need to be working on the same topic, his eighty book library carries two copies of forty titles rather than forty copies of two titles. He is immediately involved with the problems of each student, and can feel the reaction as they are resolved.

A COURSE FOR GCE 'O' LEVEL CHEMISTRY

THE SYLLABUS

The 'O' level syllabus is set out as a matrix, containing seven branches of the subject, to be studied at three standards. That part shaded in red is the General Science syllabus.

The student starts at the top lefthand corner of the chart, moving subsequently to a neighbouring topic. In this way he covers the course more or less on a diagonal front through to the lower right corner. Usually he can choose any adjoining topic from that previously, but there are occasions when one must be done first. These are shown on the Directive Cards.

DIRECTIVE CARDS

In order to cover a topic, the student seeks out the relevant directive card from the box. In the laboratory there are more copies of each card in more boxes, than on show here. The card directs him to a source of information which may be a publication, script or audio-visual arrangement.

The student covers the ground as directed, working in the main laboratory or adjoining rooms. Generally, those who require considerable contact with the teacher stay in the laboratory, while those who need less disperse to where they are visible but alone.

TESTS AND MARKING

After answering the topic to his satisfaction, and probably after discussion with the teacher, the student selects the relevant test card. As will be seen, this contains five numbered questions, as a test on fact and concept of the topic. There is also the Gold Star question, not included in the text he has just covered, but answerable if he has really understood it.

The objective of the test is not so much an accurate assessment, as to show the student (a) the most relevant sections of the material, and (b) how efficient his learning was. With this in view, after answering the test questions as far as he can, the student completes the process by reference to a standard textbook. Finally he selects the answer card, marking his own answers in accordance with the rules printed above the syllabus chart.

He keeps his own record card (a copy of the syllabus chart) up to date by colouring in the topic square in the colour relevant to his test score. A half yellow colour records that the Gold Star question was answered adequately on discussion with the teacher. Since the student must bring his test answers to the teacher for discussion of the Gold Star question, the teacher has the opportunity of checking the whole test for accuracy of marking, if he thinks fit.

RECORD KEEPING

In the laboratory the record cards for all students are displayed publicly. This allows the student and the teacher to follow progress at a glance, and compare it with that of others.

The usual mark book record of homework and practical accounts is also maintained.

RESULTS AND CONSEQUENCES

The question usually asked is 'Why do they not cheat?'. Although self marked tests are clearly open to abuse, if they are regarded as a necessary assessment by authority, such is not the case if this use is of secondary importance. The tests do show the student how well he has understood the material. The answer cards are the reinforcement to his efforts. Who else can he cheat except himself?

It is difficult to describe the atmosphere created, when a whole class really is working to the best of its individual's ability, with most of them enjoying doing just that. The consistent awakening to the realities of the subject, and consequent intellectual awareness is fuel for the teacher. It allows him to learn his subject afresh again as his students are. He discovers the meaning of a topic from the standpoint of the previous one, rather than look at it stalely from his far wider knowledge. He learns with his students, and in doing so improves that learning efficiency, and communicates.

Method of presentation: Chart, directive cards, tape/slide

Syllabuses and Methods for Computer Education in Schools

J D TINSLEY

THE CONCEPT OF COMPUTER APPRECIATION

The development of syllabuses for computer education in schools has been extremely rapid over the last two or three years following a gradual evolution in the previous decade. In the United Kingdom, two reports have had a significant impact on the formulation of working syllabuses: the document 'Computer Education for All' published in 1969 (revised in 1970) by the Schools Committee of the British Computer Society (BCS) and the Scottish Education Department (SED) curriculum report 'Computers and the Schools' (1969), often referred to as the 'Bellis Report' after the chairman of the drafting committee, Mr B T Bellis. Both of these reports stressed the need for **all** children to know something of the nature and uses of computers in modern society.

In Scotland, it was proposed that the **all** should refer to the 14-15 year old child who would subsequently consider the computer only where relevant to the subject under study, eg within mathematics, science, geography, economics etc. In the BCS document 'Computer Education for All' a broader approach was suggested, but it was emphasized that 'whenever any course of computer studies is being devised, not necessarily under the aegis of the mathematics department, all the topics from the appreciation course be included'. These topics were defined as:

INFORMATION PROCESSING

1) The history of languages and communication. The development of calculating and clerical aids. The influence of these aids on the development of scientific and commercial practice; 2) The organization and presentation of information, the communication of ideas in words and diagrams. The location, manipulation and adjustment of information. The concept of a file; 3) The formation of an algorithm.

THE STRUCTURE AND ORGANIZATION OF A DIGITAL COMPUTER

1) The basic requirements of an information processor; 2) The concept of a stored program computer; 3) The components of a digital computer — input

and output, storage, control and arithmetic units.

PROGRAMMING

1) The development of an algorithm into a computer program; 2) The writing and running of simple programs.

COMPUTERS, AUTOMATION AND THEIR SOCIAL IMPACT

1) Applications of computers in industry and commerce; 2) Data banks and information retrieval; 3) People who work with and use computers; 4) The social implications of computers.

CONCEPTS NOT TECHNIQUES

It will be noticed from the above topic list how **concepts** are stressed rather than **techniques**. Here lies the important change in emphasis which underlines the difference between **computer appreciation** and **computer science**. In the previous decade, the main influence on teaching about computers had come from University computer science departments where stress was placed on an understanding of hardware and where practical work involved mainly numerical methods within mathematics. This influence can still be felt strongly in recent syllabus submissions, particularly at CSE level, which show that the more generalized, conceptual approach has not yet been fully accepted. A syllabus report, developed by a working party of the BCS Schools Committee 'Computer Studies in the Certificate of Secondary Education (1971)' compares seven syllabus submissions from different schools in England and Wales with the guidelines given in 'Computer Education for All'.

CHANGING TECHNOLOGY

The main problem, when formulating syllabuses for computer studies, is that the technology of the computer itself is changing rapidly. If we fix a syllabus now which has a strong machine orientation rather than a conceptual basis for understanding the true nature of the computing tool, we will not help the child who will meet the effects of the computer in his later life in a form very different from that of today. In a guide for teacher training, prepared by a working party of the International Federation for Information Processing (IFIP) at the World Conference on Computer Education in Amsterdam (1971) the following statement is made:

> "Computer technology is in a state of continuous and rapid change and the machines which are used to process information now may be quite different from the ones that students will meet in the future. However, the concepts of information processing are fundamental and are independent of the actual machines which have been developed to apply these concepts. It follows that an introduction to the concept of a computer is an important and difficult section of any course: important because first impressions are often those which endure in a student's mind and difficult because the simplicity of the computer is often hidden behind the complexity of the equipment and the ingenuity with which man has applied his new tool."

INTERNATIONAL CONFERENCES

The Amsterdam World Conference was significant for workers in the United Kingdom for it showed how much further they had developed the concept of a computer appreciation course than workers in other countries. Notable exceptions were France and Canada, where in the former, a national teacher training course on 'Informatique' was being prepared, very much along conceptual lines, and in the latter, a fully developed series of computer courses had been planned for Ontario. Running parallel with the preparations for the Amsterdam conference were studies conducted by the Centre for Educational Research and Innovation (CERI) at OECD in Paris. A strong concensus of International opinion was developed at a seminar held in Sevres in the Spring of 1970 which led to a follow-up activity during the 1970/71 academic year. This activity led to the definition of a common course of computer appreciation for all children and the associated requirement for teacher training and the provision of suitable equipment.

THE NEED FOR TEACHER TRAINING

The CERI appreciation course (1971) follows closely that defined by the BCS and SED reports mentioned earlier, but the teacher training recommendations define three major requirements for all teachers, either in their in-service or pre-service training. It was recommended that all teachers be offered a course of computer appreciation, along the lines suggested for all pupils, whether or not they will themselves be responsible for teaching the subject to children.

Secondly, it was recommended that all teachers should consider the impact of the computer on educational technology, so that they can make the best use of techniques of CAL, scheduling and administrative data processing now that the computer is being applied to the total educational environment.

Thirdly, it is hoped that all teachers will learn of the relevance of the computer within individual subject disciplines.

The IFIP guide, revised in association with CERI at a joint meeting held in Paris during June, 1971, contains a section describing the developing importance of the computer and computer methods within school subjects. The following main headings are used:

A. The value of an algorithmic basis for a discipline
B. The availability of more data
C. Changes in the relative importance of various topics in the syllabus
D. Removal of drudgery from a topic
E. Illumination and understanding of a topic
F. Changes in the structure of careers

FUTURE INTERNATIONAL DEVELOPMENTS

The joint working party of IFIP and CERI are currently planning a fuller description of a teacher training course embodying the guidelines worked out in Paris. This work is to take place in Atlanta, Georgia, USA during the summer, 1972 and should give rise to a further publication with appendices which indicate examples of teacher training courses given in participating countries.

SIGNIFICANT DEVELOPMENTS IN THE UNITED KINGDOM

The development of suitable texts and teaching techniques for computer studies in school has not been easy. However, apart from the many books which are now available (BCS Booklist for Schools, 1971) five teaching schemes are worthy of mention.

1. In 1969 the IBM company embarked on the field trials of a computer specially designed for use in schools, incorporating an ordinary domestic TV and tape recorder as input/output and storage devices. A report on the work of the trials was published at the Amsterdam World Conference (1970). Although the basic concept of the machine as a teaching tool was sound, the computer was, in practice, used mainly as a calculator within a mathematical context. Very few teachers exploited the full computing capabilities of the machine to illustrate the broader concepts of record, file and general data handling. This was mainly as a result of the machine design, in which the character set was restricted to the digits 0-9, and implied for most users a numerical rather than general character handling approach.

2. The use of computing and calculating methods within mathematics has been covered in a recent report by the Mathematical Association (1971). An increasing dilemma felt by teachers, echoed by the work of the IBM schools computer field trials, is that many computing concepts within mathematics can be illustrated by the use of programmable calculators rather than computers. The justification for the purchase of a computer is difficult to accept if the **only** use to which the machine is put is within the calculating aspects of mathematical algorithms. If, however, a computer is available, then data processing, computer assisted learning and information retrieval methods can be developed which make effective use of available equipment. We are not yet in a position to make a full evaluation of the educational uses of computers within mathematics, but much work is in progress to compare various methods and means. The Schools Mathematics Project have played an important part in the development of suitable texts, especially through their new series of publications under the general title 'Computing in Mathematics' (1972).

3. Following the publication of the Bellis report computer education centres have been set up in Scotland to which all schools can send programs for processing and at which training courses for teachers, both in-service and pre-service, are provided. A curriculum development team has recently published a course for teachers and pupils under the general title 'The Computer: Yours Obediently' (1972). This course is supported by work books and 35 mm slides and constitutes approximately 100 hours of study for the 14-15 year old. It is hoped that the teacher's guides will adequately help those who may or may not have been on a training course. Pupils books give indications of games and class activities appropriate for these children.

4. The major British computer manufacturer, ICL, has developed two curriculum schemes for pupils: at 16+ level, a course with a computer science flavour, and at 16- level, materials to support courses for 15 and 16 year olds (ICL/CES Schemes). Both of these courses are linked to specific programming languages which are made available on ICL equipment.

5. Also, in 1969, a development of curriculum material was started by the National Computing Centre, with which the present author has been associated since 1970. This is described in more detail below.

THE WORK OF THE NATIONAL COMPUTING CENTRE (NCC)

The Centre is a unique partnership between Government and Industry and exists to promote the wider and more effective use of computers throughout the economy. Impartiality is its watchword and membership of the Centre is open to computer users, suppliers of computing facilities and services, educational establishments and others. Through its many contacts with the educational world the Centre is well placed to support the development of computer education at school level.

NCC and education

A major part of the Centre's work lies in education and training, for computer professionals, for computer users and for the public at large. The schools education activities of the Centre are now handled by three full-time consultants, two of whom are ex-schoolmasters, supported by an Education Information Officer. This year, three teachers are on secondment to the Centre from their local authorities in Essex, Herefordshire and Leicestershire.

The activities of the Schools Education consultants are divided into separate project areas, some concerned with advice and information and others devoted to curriculum development. Curriculum development is undertaken in response to requests from outside bodies and care is taken to avoid duplicating any existing projects or publications.

Curriculum development

The computer appreciation course 'Computers and their Impact on Business and Society' was developed within the Bristol area for use in sixth form general studies courses. Pilot teacher training courses were run by NCC itself in both Bristol and Manchester. Since this pilot stage, teacher training has been run on a local basis using guidelines published by the Centre. It has always been the Centre's policy to encourage the provision of local courses because they can be mounted with the help of experts from local education and industry at minimum cost to the teacher. The Lecturer's Guide, available from the Centre, enables advisers to plan their own courses. Successful courses have been arranged at local teacher's centres and colleges, with help on the choice of lecturers from NCC's many contacts throughout the country.

Practical programming

The sixth form appreciation course was planned at a time when programming was the staple and often exclusive diet of the majority of 'computer' courses in schools. The course has been criticized for its apparent lack of practical programming. The Centre did not, however, wish to abolish practical programming in school courses, but rather to place programming in its proper context, that is, as a tool to be used rather than as an end in itself. Many books already covered the practical aspects of computer programming and the Centre concentrated its attention on the uses and abuses of the computer in industry and commerce and on its effect on the individual within a changing society.

The COBOL project

The Centre has itself more recently developed a programming course for schools. This course, called Students COBOL, was again planned with the general studies sixth former in mind and enables these students to learn the elements of COBOL in a practical course lasting only 10 hours. This course forms a natural complement to the machine code exercises included within the sixth form package and provides an introduction to the most widely used computing language in industry. But why COBOL, when ALGOL and FORTRAN have held such sway for so many years in school programming courses? Simply because the language of COBOL has been developed so that literate, intelligent people, without necessarily having a mathematical or scientific background, can communicate their business data processing needs to the computing tool.

It has been very difficult, however, to persuade the non-mathematician to take an interest in the teaching of computer studies in school. So often the main effort in the development of computer courses has come from the mathematics department, following the mistaken belief that 'computers equal mathematics'. It is undoubtedly true that computers can be used as effective tools within mathematics, but computers serve so many disciplines that a true understanding of the nature of the modern computer requires a multi-disciplinary approach and an adaptable intelligence.

The multi-disciplinary approach

One must not, however, deny the fact that the computer is a most useful tool within mathematics. The study guides, developed for the sixth form appreciation course include details of the many other subjects within which the computer is playing an increasingly important role. What must be done is to persuade the non-mathematician that he can and should be prepared to teach about computers. Most existing courses do not appeal to the non-mathematician because of their preoccupation with programming, using examples drawn from mathematics, and with computer science. The NCC package and the COBOL language course break through this barrier at the sixth form level and make computers and programming relevant to the average non-mathematician. Some of the most successful courses based on the sixth form package have been run by a team of teachers, each contributing their own specialist interest to a multi-disciplinary subject. This is difficult to achieve, but a mathematics teacher with a narrow outlook on his subject is **bound to fail** with this package. If his interests are more programming or computer science oriented then the mathematician will be happier with a course such as that developed by ICL for the 16+ age group.

Pre-sixth form courses

But what of the lower school? The Centre is firmly of the opinion that all children should be given the opportunity to learn something of the nature and uses of computers in modern society. The sixth form course, now used by over 300 schools and colleges, has helped to meet this need, but there are many children who will not be able to follow a general studies sixth form course in computer work. It was decided last year that as nationally available courses were being planned as well as the many books which were on the market, the Centre should devote its efforts to the provision of advice and supporting aids rather than to duplicate these efforts.

Film package

To support the above activities, it was decided that the Centre should develop a set of films to assist with the presentation of support computer courses at all levels. A review was made of those films already available which had educational value and it was decided to compose a set of new films drawn from existing film sources, but without the 'selling' bias which many possessed. This project is now complete and the set of eight short films and one full length film are available as a package, accompanied by a set of teacher's guides which describe the films and give suggestions for class activity. The package is designed for use by local authority teacher's centres for local loan, thus avoiding the high cost of film hire by individual schools.

New developments

The Centre has now embarked on its two most recent development projects, a course for schools in the language BASIC and an experimental course of computer appreciation for those children who will be staying on at school until they are sixteen as a consequence of the raising of the school leaving age. The BASIC book will be going to press in April, ready for the September term and a limited first edition of the ROSLA Teacher's Guide should be ready at the same time. It is hoped that, in the long term, courses for teachers such as that planned by the Open University, with which the Centre is associated, will support a variety of courses at school level and the Centre will endeavour to coordinate these future developments wherever appropriate or possible.

REFERENCES

Computers and the Teaching of Numerical Mathematics in Upper Secondary Schools (1971) G. Bell & Sons Ltd., London
Computer Booklist for Schools (1971) British Computer Society, 29 Portland Place, London W1N 4AP
Computer Education for All (1970) British Computer Society, 29 Portland Place, London W1N 4AP
Computer Education for Teachers in Secondary Schools (1971) IFIP Secretariat, 3 rue du Marché, 1211 Geneva 11, Switzerland
Computer Studies in the Certificate of Secondary Education (1971) British Computer Society, 29 Portland Place, London W1N 4AP
Computing in Mathematics (1972) Cambridge University Press
Curriculum Report No. 8 'Computers and the Schools' (1969) HMSO, London
Guidelines for an Appreciation Course (1971) OECD/CERI 23, 2 rue André Pascal, Paris XVI
ICL/CES Schemes. Details from ICL/CES, Computer House, Euston Centre, London, W1
Proceedings of the World Conference on Computer Education, Amsterdam (1970) Wolters-Noordhoff Publishing, POB 58, Groningen, The Netherlands
The Computer: Yours Obediently (1972) W.R. Chambers & Sons, 11, Thistle Street, Edinburgh

Some of the materials mentioned in this paper, including the NCC film package for schools, were on display at the Conference.

Should the Programmer be a Subject Matter Expert?

MICHAEL MACDONALD-ROSS and
PATRICIA FLEETWOOD-WALKER

It has often been claimed that a program writer should be a generalist, simply using subject matter-experts (or 'master performers') as sources of guidance as to objectives. We are now suggesting a revision of this widely-held view, as a result of our work on the development of a self-instructional course 'The Growth and Structure of Flowering Plants', part of the Inter-University Biology Teaching Project at the University of Birmingham.

The broad range of expertise required for the creation of a self-instructional course in higher education is rarely found in any one person. This leads to the choice: **either** select a subject-matter expert and provide tuition in program writing, **or** select a programmer and provide tuition in the subject area. The latter solution, strongly influenced by behaviourist ideas, views the program writer as a generalist who operates at a meta-level (above the subject area) obtaining objectives from experts, devising schedules of reinforcement and tests. Successful programs have been produced in this way for industrial training, but we suggest that in higher education such an approach is liable to result in material that is naive, overly factual and lacking in depth of understanding.

THE RELATIONS BETWEEN TEACHING AND RESEARCH

A generalist programmer entering the subject area would soon find that the business of collecting objectives and defining content was far from simple. Consider using textbooks as possible sources. Texts tend to reprint 'facts' from previous texts, and even recent textbooks by well-known authors do present ideas that are supported only by tenuous and poorly documented evidence. This may be understandable, for to evaluate facts requires an examination of all the relevant research evidence. But if the specialists do not always do their homework, what hope has a newcomer of sifting the wheat from the chaff? We should also remember the lengthy background discussions at conferences and seminars which help the expert to reach judgments, but which are not so available to the generalist. Even an expert must make decisions as to how he should interpret the variety of (sometimes conflicting) experimental data that presents itself. In many disciplines there are alternative or even competitive schools of thought and the choice of a point of view can radically alter what data is searched for, and the way it is interpreted. For example, consider how a behaviourist and a cognitive psychologist differ in their approach to such concepts as learning, knowing and understanding.

But concepts cannot be taken for granted, even in more settled subject areas. As an example, consider how the terms 'cell division' and 'mitosis' are used in biology. They are often used interchangeably: when cells are in division, you can **see** the chromosomes (using suitable methods), and the process is called mitosis. This simple notion is the source of the most unbelievable confusion. For any adequate **explanation** of mitosis must start further back. Before cells are visibly dividing they are covertly active, busy synthesizing nuclear and cytoplasmic material. The act of division takes place when the conditions are set. A natural suggestion is to draw a distinction between **mitosis** (the visible act of division) and the **division cycle** (mitosis plus the covert preparatory stages). But confusion arises when some authors describe mitotic cells as dividing cells, when statistics for mitoses may be misinterpreted as including all cells in the division cycle. The above distinction avoids this problem, and explains discrepancies between figures given in research papers. To eliminate such confusion is a task requiring considerable **depth of understanding** of the subject matter.

So, even at first year level (for which this program is designed) subject matter is not a settled issue, and above all, facts and their interpretations are not 'given' to the programmer in any straightforward fashion. This is not simply an issue about teaching styles, nor about the difficulties of getting experts to define their objectives. It is a more fundamental comment on the nature of science as a human activity. What counts as a fact, and what counts as a satisfactory interpretation of that fact, is heavily **context-dependent**. It depends upon the pre-suppositions or the outlook of the scientist, or to make the same point, it depends upon the **structure** of the knowledge in a given area (Macdonald-Ross, 1972a).

This amounts to the rejection of any simple-minded empiricism. Science is not about 'stamp collecting' (even if the stamps of science were available 'ready made', which we have seen is not the case); instead, science is about explaining and understanding the external world.

THE GOAL OF AN INTEGRATED TEACHING SYSTEM

A really integrated teaching/learning system would contain many diverse elements whose interrelations would need careful definition. Deep information would be required about the learner, and about the structure of the subject matter; a viable and relevant model of the learning process would be used as a basis for specifying the learning possibilities — if we took the concept of integration seriously we should have a major research project on our hands. But for the present, two examples must suffice.

First, difficulties arise whenever attempts are made to integrate the subject matter area. For instance, although most schools of Biological Science are in principle working towards an integrated course structure, actually contributions come from isolated subject areas and are loosely stitched together. There are usually extensive areas of overlap and omission since the boundaries are not clearly recognised or specified.

Any attempt to design a total or all-embracing course from scratch would, of course, have to start with questions of relevance and need. In our experience one of the major contributions an educational adviser can make is to bring these issues to the forefront so they get a full hearing. Detailed discussions will also be necessary to clarify the unit boundaries; and here it is necessary to use design techniques such as concept networks in order to make precise the way in which the units relate to the course as a whole.

On the other hand, the problem posed by 'The Growth and Structure of Flowering Plants' was slightly different. It meant the integration of a self-instructional unit into an existing (traditional) teaching system. The advent of individual learning does bring administrative problems of timetabling and provision of resources, but these are sometimes more easily solved than the subject matter issues. The program content had been partly covered by traditionally structured courses, but some sections are novel, and others were treated differently in the existing courses. This means that the organizing committee of the first-year course could not simply replace an existing set of lectures and practicals with the program, nor could the program simply be added on to an already considerable burden of formal teaching. So issues of definition, negotiation and adjustment must be faced, and this all takes time and subject matter investigation. Very likely this would be the case wherever a self-instructional module was to be inserted into the structure of an already existing course.

Returning to the main theme of the paper, we can see that both educational expertise and subject matter expertise play essential roles. For it is often true that specialists usually do not raise these issues of their own accord; and also true that once raised their solution depends upon an understanding of the subject matter.

The second area for discussion is the integration of practical work and theory. It is a peculiar thing, as one of us has remarked elsewhere, that no satisfactory rationale for practical work in science exists (Macdonald-Ross, 1972b). As a matter of fact, the problem has been getting worse rather than better, for once it might have been possible to introduce a student to many of the practical situations he would face as a professional, but such a goal is now quite unrealistic. (Only in a few subjects such as microbiology might it be claimed that practicals meet present vocational needs; and even they cannot cater for the future.) Remembering how much time science students spend in the laboratory, one might expect this to be a widely discussed issue. But it is not, until with a sudden shock a department may come to realize that possibly half the students' laboratory time is being wasted, either because the work is not relevant or it is not effective. Naturally, some staff may have felt uneasy about this for some time: but institutional constraints on individual initiative can be quite severe.

Fundamentally important conflicts do lie unarticulated and unresolved in the structure of most science courses. Practical work is seen by some as a collection of existing techniques and methods to be passed on to the student, and by others as a means of introducing the students to the empirical basis of science (in biology, the animals and plants themselves). Still others see the student as a mini-scientist, solving problems by using the scientific method. The educationalist can at least raise these issues so that they can be publicly discussed.

But in a self-instructional course the programmer faces detailed design problems even when these questions of purpose and direction have been decided. A considerable amount of background research and experiment is necessary before the selection of material for practical exercises. Published experimental methods need trial and modification, and when at last a suitable task has been defined, still further hurdles must be overcome before the practical can be used by students. Availability of resources (for instance, can the plants be grown? do we have the apparatus?); student capabilities (do they have the prerequisite skills?), and the design of laboratory instructions must all be worked upon.

One example of the value of subject matter expertise occurred during the selection of material for the dissection of a flowering shoot apex. For this purpose the apex must be:

1. uncomplicated by secondary branching
2. free from obscuring hairs
3. large enough to see
4. cheap to grow
5. show clearly the structure of a developing flower.

It did not seem possible to meet all these conditions simultaneously until Wye Agricultural Research Station suggested Viscaria, a plant noticeably not in general use for this purpose, but which ideally meets the requirements.

Another example is the specially developed Shepherd's Purse practical. It so happens that it is possible to isolate embryos from this fruit in undamaged condition. This piece of knowledge required much development before it became a practical the students could do with much chance of success. This makes the important point that even the most intelligently conceived practical is likely to be counter-productive (to say the least) if students cannot actually do it successfully.

Of course, questions as to whether practicals should be open-ended or closed, and whether they should be well-structured or loosely structured, are really unresolved issues. In some cases they may be worth putting to an empirical test. The relative effectiveness of structured and unstructured laboratory instructions were tested in the Shepherd's Purse practical, and it turned out that using structured schedules students were much more successful and remembered more three weeks later. In addition, it appeared that colour transparencies of the embryos did provide for quicker working and better student retention. We have no desire, on this slender basis, to make sweeping claims about general rules for designing practicals; but we should like to stress the many dozens of hours that can go into designing just one or two straightforward exercises.

CONCLUSIONS

We have claimed that it is not possible to get an adequate set of objectives from any one source, and that the programmer himself needs depth understanding of the subject matter if he is to design a coherent course and evaluate and select the content on which the course is based. If a generalist were to attempt this kind of work, it is likely that deep confusions would lie unresolved, and that 'facts' would be presented out of context, as if in some conceptual vacuum. Preparations for this course involved an extensive collation of widely scattered information and illustrations, but more especially, a novel synthesis of research results.

Next we considered questions of integration. The first was the overall design of a course, and the definition of boundaries between units. The second was the relation between theory and practical work, and the subsequent design of practicals. Again we saw the need for detailed work at the subject matter level.

Underlying these points is a certain dissatisfaction with the generalists' rather poverty-stricken tool kit, consisting of the behavioural objective and the systematic approach to education. Behavioural objectives, though useful, provide only a weak guide for the process of design. What is needed (especially in higher education) is attention to the relevance and the structure of the subject matter. And this, in turn, places stress on the programmer's depth of understanding of the subject matter.

REFERENCES
Macdonald-Ross, M. (1972a) 'Behavioural objectives and the structure of knowledge'. APLET Conference 1972 (this volume)
Macdonald-Ross, M. (1972b) 'Towards a rationale for practical work'. In preparation, to be published in Journal of Biological Education

The Design of a University Service Course

MICHAEL MACDONALD-ROSS and
DAVID T REES

One of the most persistent unsolved problems in higher education is the design
and operation of service courses. In 'higher order' scientific subjects (such
as biology, psychology, geology) it is quite common for service courses in
basic subjects (such as statistics, mathematics, chemistry, etc) to be organized to supplement deficiencies in the students' academic background. But
one finds widespread dissatisfaction with the results of such courses. They
are often ineffective, even irrelevant, and tend to be unpopular with both staff
and students.

Partly because of this dissatisfaction service courses tend to be natural
candidates for conversion into self-instructional format. But such a conversion is apt to expose cruelly the lack of any rationale, without which there is
no hope of solving the problems of design. This paper is an attempt to lay the
foundations of such a rationale. The first section discusses those issues which
are general to all service courses; and the second section illustrates these
points by reference to the course 'Electricity for Biologists', part of the Inter-
University Biology Teaching Project at the University of Birmingham.

THE CONCEPT OF THE SERVICE COURSE

There are senses in which the design of a service course poses the same
issues as does the design of **any** course. We shall generally ignore this common ground so as to clarify the ways in which service courses pose **distinct**
issues. The first step is to clarify our use of basic concepts.

Any course which is studied either as an end in itself, or which constitutes
a major reason for the student attending college, can be designated a **main
course**. Typically main courses will occupy the major portion of the students'
timetable, and are operated by the main department or faculty to which the
student belongs. All main courses have prerequisites, and one can distinguish
between prerequisites in the same discipline from prerequisites in a different
discipline. The latter become candidates for a **service course**, for instance,
mathematics for physics students. The term 'service course' also covers a
number of instances where courses are closely ancillary to, but not absolutely

84

prerequisite for, the main subject. This means that the term does have quite a broad coverage, and no simple definition will cover all cases. One can usually identify service courses as being those courses which the main department prescribes **as a consequence** of the student choosing certain main subjects, but which have a different basic subject matter.

A whole spectrum of problems now follows on. How to ensure the course really is **relevant,** and that its relevance is understood by students? How to maintain student interest (almost the same issue)? How can the heterogeneous background knowledge of the students be handled? Should the course be defined by the main teaching department or the servicing department?

These must all be faced when designing a self-instructional course. But we should like to focus attention on one central issue which, in its turn, clarifies most of the other questions. It is the issue of subject matter **selection.** Of critical importance to a service course is the constraint on time. If, for example, a sociologist must learn some statistical method one cannot teach him the **whole** of statistics. And the selection of the right spectrum of goals will in itself largely determine whether the course is perceived as relevant by staff and students.

It is only within the context of the main course that the need for a service course arises, so the process of selection must start with a close look at the main course itself. But since few courses have their aims and objectives spelt out explicitly, ways have to be found to clarify these objectives. This task is made no easier by the fact that neither a traditional syllabus nor a list of behavioural objectives will count as a sufficient description of the main course (Macdonald-Ross, 1972). As an additional note of caution one must realize that the main course itself may be radically deficient. Service courses should not be used to prop up a rotten structure that would best be demolished and rebuilt from scratch. And even if the main course is satisfactory **now,** does it meet the needs of the future — these are difficult questions, but they may be solved to a certain extent. If they can, one has arrived at a sufficiently clearly analysis of a basically satisfactory main course.

As a consequence, the **boundary** of the service course can be defined. This will be done in the usual fashion, with an orthodox syllabus (for the benefit of orthodox staff!), behavioural objectives and concept networks, and sample test and examination papers. It is worth commenting (since one of us is launching an assault on behavioural objectives at this very conference) that the notion of terminal behaviour fits service courses rather better than main courses. Because often all that may be wanted is that the student should be able to **do** certain things so he can progress with his main education.

This leads naturally to determining student entry behaviour, or to put it less crudely, to discovering the relevant characteristics of the student population. It is really surprising how seldom this is ever done in a traditional teaching situation; for it conditions so much of what follows. The students may be so heterogeneous that diagnostic tests and different entry points, or even different courses, may be necessary. Or they may know enough to make much of the intended course redundant. Who knows unless he looks?

At this stage the constraints existing in the particular situation must be specified, for reasons which will soon be apparent. What sort of constraints are expected? Universally there is a shortage of **time**. This, as we mentioned earlier, is part and parcel of the service course situation where the whole subject can never be taught and some sort of selection must be made. Next comes available facilities. Laboratory space and equipment, access to a computer, library resources — they should all be noted. The third type of constraint comes from staff limitations. Even a self-instructional course may depend upon laboratory technicians or tutorial work, and these must be added to the list of constraints.

But why be so careful about constraints? Because it may actually be **impossible** to achieve the service course objectives given those constraints. And if **this** is the case then radical rethinking of the course objectives, and the whole teaching/learning situation is necessary before the service course is constructed.

Once the constraint hurdle is jumped, the main obstacles are over, and only one question remains, obvious but often overlooked; is there an existing course which satisfies these requirements? It is ridiculous to go to all the torment and expense of designing a service course if one exists off-the-shelf, as will increasingly be the case in future. But if those that exist do not reasonably fit your objectives, then the course must be constructed. And that is a story in itself: but it is common to all courses and so will not be discussed here.

We have suggested that there are at least six stages prior to the actual construction of a service course, and these stages are illustrated in Figure 1. But when reading this diagram, bear in mind that the system is really

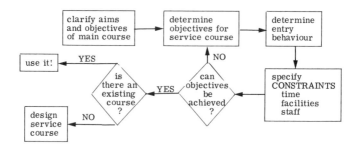

Figure 1. Preliminary stages in the design of a service course

more iterative (cyclical) than it seems, and also that some of these activities can be carried on in parallel. The proper representation of such processes is too complex an issue to consider here, so for the sake of simplicity the stages have been represented in the form of an algorithm.

ELECTRICITY FOR BIOLOGISTS

This course illustrates well the problems encountered when trying to decide upon the content of a service course. The basic reason for the course is easy enough to understand. These days biology is a fairly technical experimental science necessitating the use of sophisticated equipment, and concepts drawn from the physical sciences. At once you see the problems — it is not possible to teach a complete course in electrical theory and instrumentation, so what **do** biologists need, and how may it be supplied?

One sort of approach would be to teach the usual sort of physics-based electricity course. This would cover the basic concepts of the subject thoroughly, and would respect the 'internal logic' of the subject matter. But the danger would be that, after lengthy study, the student would have theoretical understanding, but would be unable to handle common laboratory equipment!

To counter this, one might advocate a task analysis approach: survey the whole range of electrical equipment used by biologists and construct the course around the most common tasks. But without some theoretical background could the student transfer easily to novel situations or instruments? And remember that electronics and electrical science is developing so rapidly that the risk of creating a redundant course is quite real.

The most fruitful starting point proved to be the examination of existing courses in biology at Birmingham University, and also the kinds of service courses that were already in use. By discussing with individual lecturers one got clear insights into areas where progress in biology was dependent on electricity: specific instances were cited, and these could be supplemented by looking at examination papers, text-books and other sources. With this as a basis the task analysis approach and the internal logic of the subject matter both influenced the content: but they were not allowed to dominate the clarification of major boundaries.

These surveys showed that biologists need two distinct but interconnected sets of skills in the electrical field. They need a knowledge of electric circuit terminology and the electrical properties of networks involving some quite sophisticated electrical concepts; and they must be able to operate equipment such as CROs, transducers, stimulators and amplifiers. These needs form the basis of the program objectives.

Any course which is published (as this one will be) has the additional problems raised by the differing aims of other institutions. These can never be totally resolved; and one must guard against grey compromises which leave the course structure demolished, resulting in a sort of porridge which suits neither one's own students nor anybody else's. But genuinely opposed viewpoints can be of great interest, and help force the designer to clarify his position. For example, we were advised by avant-garde electronics researchers that the advent of 'plug-in' modules meant that a biologist did not need to understand what went on inside the units. This we labelled the 'black box approach. But research biologists advocated more detailed constructive methods. This we labelled the 'string and sealing-wax' approach. Quite clearly one cannot satisfy both demands: we chose the latter.

The characteristics of the student population, the entry behaviour if you wish, were examined in great detail. We analysed the students' capabilities in handling practical electrical equipment, their grasp of basic physical concepts (especially electrical concepts), and we examined their mathematical ability, for so much electrical design work and operation is dependent on mathematics. We expected that they would not be too good at handling equipment (we were right), but we were a little alarmed to find how deficient their mathematics were, or rather, their translation of mathematical concepts into the domain of electrical science. Imagine, service courses having service courses, which on their back do bite 'em!

After a survey of existing courses we concluded that the construction of a tailor-made course was called for: so the remaining work was concerned with standard problems of design. One aspect is worth commenting on: the need for practical work made essential the development of special kits, for many biology departments do not have ready access to electronic laboratories or equipment for teaching purposes. Suck a kit should give reproducible results, be reliable, student-proof, relevant and flexible and cost-effective. Some of these are conflicting requirements, to say the least. Then further questions arise when practical work is integrated with theory, since theoretical concepts based on 'idealizations' meet the limitations of concrete reality.

These are exciting issues. Far from having at our fingertips a 'completely satisfactory technology of education' we neither have a rationale for service courses, nor for practical work. But the nature of the problems involved is now becoming clearer, partly as a result of this work.

REFERENCE

Macdonald-Ross, M. (1972) 'Behavioural objectives and the structure of knowledge'. APLET Conference 1972 (this volume)

A Self-Instructional Bridge Course in Biology at University Level

GAYE MANWARING

As part of the Inter-University Biology Teaching Project, our general aims were to provide an audio-visual self-instructional bridge course on Development Biology. First year University students would take this course to give them basic information, upon which later lectures and practicals could build.

Developmental biology provides the student with basic facts and principles (knowledge, comprehension, application), as well as providing insight into the approach of biologists to problems (analysis, synthesis, evaluation). It was also hoped that giving the students self-instructional programs would help them to begin to take more responsibility for their own learning.

The module was constructed as 15 programs, each representing about one hour's instruction. The student is provided with tape, slides or film-strip and a response sheet. He is asked questions and responds by writing on the response sheet which he retains for reference and revision. He works at his own pace and can repeat the program if desired.

The amount of previous knowledge of biology is very variable among our students. A great many students from Scotland do not take biology at school, but take a biology course in the first year at University. A diagnostic multi-choice test is administered to students when they first come up, to determine which students need which programs.

The actual administration of the programs is complex. There are 300 students in the first year biology class, and the majority need to do all 15 programs. We have only 12 sets of simple equipment (cassette player and filmstrip viewer or slide viewer) for individual use, and only one room available. This equipment is available from 9 a.m. to 5 p.m. Monday to Friday, and the students come whenever they have free time.

Biology is only one of the subjects being studied by each individual student and, since the other subjects vary widely, the students have different time-tables and can be free to do programs at different times. Advance booking is possible.

The self-instructional programs are a voluntary part of the course and, although the students are not compelled to attend, about 81% of the class took the programs.

The first four programs are very basic and the students are encouraged to do these as soon as possible, so that they could better understand the rest of the course. They were advised to complete programs 5-9 before the middle of the second term when lectures, based on the knowledge gained in these programs, began.

Attitude questionnaires have indicated that the students like this type of instruction and would welcome more programs on other topics.

Method of presentation: Summary information sheet and tape slide

Modular Multi-Media Materials for Movement Perception and Distance Perception

P H MILLAR

Rapid extension of programmed instruction techniques and educational technology depends upon acceptance by those directly responsible for teaching, of the expert assistance offered. Organizational factors influence both the resources which can be marshalled to assist given teaching units and the general acceptability of such 'outside' involvement. This paper considers the potential role of an organizational approach which has not yet been widely attempted in the British educational system. We are concerned with the provision of an educational technology consultancy service and teaching support materials by a central (international) unit which is specialized in the particular subject matter concerned — in this case, topics related to the study of the brain.

The financial case for establishing such a central facility is a strong one. Particularly in scientific subjects with a considerable body of well-established knowledge based on complex and expensive experimentation, it is wasteful to have individual local units duplicating their efforts to produce illustrative programs. Even in the brain sciences field, where there is a considerably less extensive body of accepted knowledge to be imparted to the student, there is great scope for the production of materials dealing with experimental situations not available in the majority of teaching establishments. It is easy enough to convince departments that modern audio-visual techniques can be of use in improving teaching about phenomena which cannot otherwise be presented to the students directly. The investment required to produce such materials is usually such as to give the departments concerned pause, and to make prima facie case for deeper consideration of teaching objectives and methods than is normal; the door is thus open for introducing programming techniques throughout the course in which the materials are to be used.

It is instructive to consider the extent to which the same considerations apply to materials produced by the local audio-visual aids or educational technology units now attached to many institutions. Although the cost of such teaching aids and the fact that they usually have to be produced outside the teaching department, are in this case two factors helping those who wish to press forward with new techniques, there are three major problems which make progress less speedy than might have been hoped when large investments in educational technology and audio-visual aids were made a few years ago.

The fact that teaching departments generally do not have to make any payment out of their own funds for programs made by the local A-V unit, tends to weaken the position of those arguing that such assistance ought to be matched by a preparedness to re-examine teaching methods and evaluation procedures. Although it is recognized that considerable expenditure of resources is involved, the impact is weakened by the decision to provide central finance for A-V production.

Secondly, the funds made available to the local unit for production have tended to be inadequate for the calls made upon them. This is particularly so in the case of funds needed for producing software as opposed to the funds for purchase of equipment. A predictable consequence of this is that a choice has to be made between a proper detailed involvement with a few departments to the exclusion of others, and the provision of such less substantial services — often little more than token involvement — to a more equitable selection of departments. In these circumstances it is inevitable that production is concentrated on areas where calls can be made on local personnel and resources to minimize costs. A consequence of this is that the help provided is much less impressive and attractive than it might be: location filming at distant sites is almost always out of the question, and the receiving department is under pressure to contribute staff time and effort much beyond the minimum needed for good production — such help keeps costs down. In short, lack of funds has tended to restrict the assistance which can be made available to a limited number of productions tied closely to existing locally available analyses and subjects.

Finally, the policy of establishing the suppliers of educational technology assistance within the existing institutions, and as separately funded entities, has exposed them to extra difficulties. Any new independent unit in an institution such as a university, where departments guard their independence with great ferocity and where emphasis is on academic rather than didactic excellence, will be treated with suspicion. The situation is worse when the new unit claims to be competent to make improvements in the performance of the existing departments. When the departments do accept the help offered they are faced with the further unpalatable consequence that a considerable amount of their staff time must be invested in familiarizing the educational technologists with the particular subject concerned, as well as in the actual detailed specification of the course objective and content. Thus, although the services of the local unit may be free, they need not appear attractive since they amount to incursions into the sovereignty of the department assisted and they are very expensive in terms of commitments upon that department's staff (in the short term at least).

A central unit like the Brain Sciences Information Project can, by contrast, be seen as an international version of the type of operation which an individual department might design for itself. Against a background of free materials provided by the local units and by various types of sponsor, such a central unit will have considerable difficulty in obtaining payment from recipient departments for the materials and services it provides. In the medium and longer term, however, payment by the participating departments offers the simplest form of control and assessment of the unit's performance. It has the further advantage that the psychological impact of the relationship is enhanced and there are better chances of introducing new educational techniques as part of the complex which contains much-desired teaching aids as its basic attraction for the traditional department.

It is an essential part of the concept of a central unit such as this that it uses its ability for widespread distribution as a means of financing relatively expensive software production without burdening any one software user excessively. This assumes that the materials produced are useful to a wide variety of departments. At the higher education level this is a difficult matter, since courses, emphasis and interpretations vary from department to department. It is only by concentrating upon the illustration and exposition of central ideas and facts which are discussed in almost all courses that one can hope to function effectively; further, one must arrange the material provided in such a way that individual recipient departments can make their own selections and, where necessary, reorganize the material. The consequence of these considerations is that the Project breaks courses down into modules and arranges its production so that the topic of each module (5-15 minutes lecturing time or equivalent) is covered with a minimum of explicit references to other material produced by the Project.

While there is naturally an emphasis on the production of materials which would be beyond the resources of individual departments, care is taken to assemble a range of materials giving a good basic coverage of a subject: such an approach ensures that the prospective user of the materials is guaranteed a comprehensive service rather than a dilettante assemblage of items whose relevance he must laboriously assess.

The fact that the Project limits itself to a particular range of topics greatly improves its ability to communicate with potential users. Since the position of the Project staff is not that of members of a 'rival' department in the institution, but that of individual's with a commitment to the subject concerned and with a basic stock of interesting material, the attitude of departments contacted is exceedingly open. Not only is contact easily established, but examination of the relevance of the materials for the courses in the department concerned and specification of new materials whose production would be worthwhile, can be done speedily and accurately — by contrast with the situation which arises when a local unit without experience of the subject matter has to be briefed.

Thus there are advantages in the organizational approach which the Project represents. First, although direct payment may be difficult to achieve in the short term, it offers a clear indicator of performance and helps emphasize the need to judge all teaching procedures with a view to increased effectiveness. Secondly, the central project can undertake production on a scale which would be beyond the resources of a local unit, and hence it can offer materials which are unambiguously superior to those which the user could have produced for himself. Finally, the subject expertise of the central unit assures it a more open reception, and helps to give it an identity distinct from any facet of the local institutional 'politics'.

In June 1971 the Brain Sciences Information Project embarked on the production of a set of materials for teaching Movement Perception and Distance Perception. These materials were made as a pilot project; the primary aims of this were to gain familiarity with the technical difficulties of production, and to produce a prototype collection which could serve to sharpen and refine the discussions with potential users which would have to precede production of any full-scale set of materials. Items of this pilot production can be used to illustrate the points made above. In all cases the materials have been made with a very modest budget in an existing Audio-Visual Aids unit; they therefore reflect the modular nature of the projected materials and the principle of providing coverage of a subject rather than simply isolated items, but they do not illustrate the further benefits which are to be expected from larger investment of resources with a view to spreading the cost of expensive production over a large number of users.

A Lecturer's Notes File would accompany materials supplied to a department. Differently coloured pages are used to state:

i) the range of points which it is felt might be raised under the topic (module) in question;

ii) detailed descriptions of the materials provided — slides, film, equipment and technical details of important background, are also included;

iii) bibliographical references;

iv) student activities, including small scale experiments and specimen test questions.

The book is loose-leaf and it is expected that the lecturer will add his own sheets giving the outline or text of his lecture. The book can only be made up after full consultation has determined which modules are required and which sequence of presentation is to be followed.

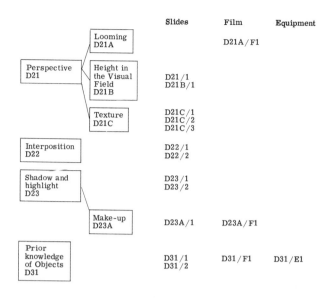

	Slides	Film	Equipment

Looming
D21A — D21A/F1

Perspective
D21

Height in
the Visual
Field
D21B — D21/1, D21B/1

Texture
D21C — D21C/1, D21C/2, D21C/3

Interposition
D22 — D22/1, D22/2

Shadow and
highlight
D23 — D23/1, D23/2

Make-up
D23A — D23A/1, D23A/F1

Prior
knowledge
of Objects
D31 — D31/1, D31/2, D31/F1, D31/E1

Figure 1. Conceptual map and related media

Discussions of the content of given courses can sometimes be simplified by the use of concise representations of the topics which might possibly be covered. While a simple list would suffice, a conceptual map upon which the topic names are displayed in spatial arrangements with connections shown by lines can also be of use. Figure 1 shows such a map; in this case the connecting lines represent only the relationship of 'relevant a propos' — they do not imply any theoretical relevance or explanatory significance, and indeed topics are related both to other topics of which they are examples and to topics to which they are definitely not theoretically allied (it being relevant to **deny** any supposed connection). Such lines are introduced to suggest sequences which might be worth following in an exposition, but they obviously cannot have any prescriptive force, and indeed the conceptual map is best regarded as a visual aid for the course planner.

As can be seen from the tabulation alongside the conceptual map, each topic may involve several different media. The materials involved may be alternative presentations of the same point (eg detailed presentation or alternatively recapitulation version) or they may be complementary. The film 'Make-up' is a reasonably leisurely presentation which can be used to illustrate the operation of light and dark pigments in make-up as cues for apparent depth thus leading to an illusory appearance of structure in the made up face. Time considerations or doubts about the relative importance of this point may lead to a desire to omit this film, and a single slide can be substituted. This slide can also be used for revision. The film 'Optokinetic

95

Nystagmus', however, is complementary to the slide of the eye movement recording labelled 'Optokinetic Nystagmus'. In this case we must assume that the naive student is unfamiliar with the details of eye movement recording, and it is therefore necessary to introduce the various pen recordings which he will have to study, by showing him the experimental situation, noting the need for calibration, and correlating an observable type of eye movement with one such pen recording trace. The film is intended to make this bridge from direct experience to interpretation of pen recordings, and naturally the slide of Optokinetic Nystagmus becomes the first of a series of slides, others of which relate to eye movements which would not be visible to the observer's unaided eye.

Certain basic topics are of almost universal relevance despite the diversity of course structure and emphasis (for example 'Looming' and 'Rotating random squares 1'). These items could be usefully integrated into most courses on visual perception. But for individual departments to produce the films or even to request their local A-V units to do so would probably be an unreasonable expenditure of time and effort relative to the resources available. A central unit can expect a demand which would justify pricing these items at a matter of a few pounds. An overall view of the sequence of operations leading to the production of materials by the Project is as follows:

1) A course has been selected and objectives stated at a general level. Subject experts are then commissioned to write 'archetypal lectures'. In these they give the coverage which an ideal course on the subject matter concerned would provide. There is at this stage no attempt to 'think in visual terms'; the only constraint is that the experts take **no** account of limitations which happen to inhibit their own teaching (eg lack of time, lack of demonstration equipment or space).

2) The archetypal lectures are analyzed to give a collection of concise 'topic specifications'. Each of these is as complete in itself as possible, and the few remaining cross-references are made explicit. This collection is seen as an encyclopaedia to be used during production thus avoiding any confusion as to what should and should not be covered in the individual modules (which may be being produced by different teams in different places). The conceptual maps are made at this stage and these serve as a visual aid facilitating discussion of the overall production task and the possible applications for the materials.

3) Selection of the media to be used is the next stage. In order to decide whether a given type of medium is suitable various factors have to be balanced, eg:

> difficulty and nature of topic (does it involve movement or three dimensions? Is it familiar or not?)

96

logistics of using the proposed material in the context of the course (is a film projector being used already?)

the balance of production cost against number of users likely to benefit (over how many people can we reasonably 'spread' the development costs?)

The proposed production schedules are checked with the subject experts and further advisers and collaborators brought in to help with specific modules. Production is generally contracted out to units within easy reach of locations where the main advisers are to be found. Continuity of style is ensured by means of detailed production instructions (tied in with the encyclopaedia items) and specimen materials which serve as examples.

4) The next stage is that of evaluation. This may be divided into qualitative and quantitative. Although the two types overlap in time, the initial tests are qualitative. Comments of staff engaged in the qualitative testing yield questions which can be examined more rigorously in the quantitative tests. Questions asked of students in the quantitative tests are aimed to indicate (i) general level achieved (topic by topic, since not all courses involve all topics), and (ii) comparison of alternative presentations of individual concepts (particularly arising out of comments by users in the qualitative tests).

5) The results of the evaluation reflect upon the adequacy of the archetypal lectures, the wisdom of the media selection, and the standard of production achieved. The loop has no exit; in practice all modifications must be further tested, and it is hoped that continuing evaluative feedback will be obtained from regular users once the material is on full scale distribution – hence the evaluation and improvement process continues indefinitely.

Given the need for continuous feedback on the adequacy and accuracy of the materials, there is a strong case for regular contact with users. The complexity of the ultimate catalogue, and the importance of encouraging staff to think through their requirements in terms of systematic course design, also make it advisable for a Project consultant to visit the user departments and undertake the final 'tailoring' of the materials to the local needs. It is therefore not the intention to offer the materials for sale on an 'over the counter' basis. By offering them as part of an educational technology consultancy service, the Project will be making a much greater contribution to education, ensuring a sensitive feedback mechanism leading to progressive improvement of the stock of materials, and creating a situation in which it becomes economic to keep the materials up to date and flexible.

Method of presentation: Visual materials referred to in the paper were presented at the Conference.

Designing an Introductory Programmed Course in Biology for Undergraduates
MICHAEL TRIBE

INTRODUCTION

At a series of meetings held at Nuffield Lodge during 1968, the University of Sussex, along with other universities, began to explore the possibility of using self-instructional materials for undergraduates studying Biological Sciences. The use of programmed materials and modules is comparatively recent in British Universities, although it has been a feature of teaching in some American Universities and Colleges for some time now, especially in first year courses (Postlethwait et al, 1969; Creager & Murray, 1971). The use of American materials in British Universities has obvious disadvantages because of the different level of academic attainment at entry and the courses subsequently followed by British students.

In 1969, with the help of a grant from the Nuffield Foundation, five Universities were each invited to explore different aspects (at different levels) of the Biological spectrum; further details about the project as a whole are discussed by Dowdeswell (1970, 1972). The team at Sussex comprised three individuals together with ancillary technical and secretarial help. The individuals involved were drawn from both Biology and Educational Technology on either a full-time or part-time basis. They were invited to design an introductory programmed course in Biology for undergraduates, which in the first place was aimed at those students coming up to study Biology with 'A' levels in Physical Sciences; such students usually represent between 20-30% of the first year intake.

Preliminary work on the project attempted to find out the conceptual difficulties and related problems experienced by students lacking a Biological background. Similar problem areas were also monitored for students with an 'A' level in Biology. The information in both cases was obtained in three ways: (i) from a short, written pre-knowledge test; (ii) from discussions with students and teaching faculty, and (iii) from several tape recorded seminars with those students lacking a biological background.

AIMS

The main aims of the course are as follows:

1. To design a course with the undergraduate specifically in mind and not to produce a 'crash course' in 'A' level Biology.

2. To teach important biological concepts and principles in an analytical and contemporary context, so that information and ideas are supported as far as possible by experimental evidence.

3. To concentrate on developing a conceptual structure on which the student can build his more advanced courses and to which he can attach more detailed information as and when he requires it.

4. To examine the ways in which a flexibly designed course of the self-instructional kind can be integrated into the existing patterns of teaching and learning in Universities.

CURRICULUM STRATEGY AND DESIGN

Decisions governing curriculum strategy resulted from team discussions about aims, objectives, time allowance for teaching, style of presentation, media used etc. A useful range of questions about curriculum analysis is summarized elsewhere (Stevens & Morrissett, 1967).

Before embarking on a Biology course of this kind it is also necessary to ask a number of key questions about the subject area.

Question 1
Why does a particular structure or behavioural function enable an organism to survive?

Question 2
How do the changes which occur in an organism bring about a response?

Question 3
How does the biologist investigate these problems?

To answer the first question, it is necessary to study whole organisms and groups of organisms in relation to their environment. To answer the second question, it is necessary to analyse the organism itself by examining its structure in relation to the physical and chemical changes taking place within it. The answer to the third question follows, since the techniques and methods of investigation used by biologists form an integral part of the answer to the first two questions.

With these questions in mind and the information available from preliminary studies, several blueprints were designed outlining conceptual diagrams of the course with its objectives and contents. Eventually one of the course plans was adopted, because it seemed to provide an easier access into Biology from first principles and also because it would be the best starting point for our target population, who in the main would have a good background in physical science. The five course units are shown in Figure 1.

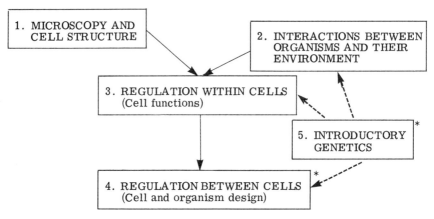

*Units planned but unfinished at present

Figure 1

The teaching time allowance for the course was tentatively put at 30 hours, but this has been found to be unrealistic and 50 hours would be a better estimate.

In designing this self-instructional course, it is first of all important to generate and maintain student interest and yet present challenging situations where possible. A real attempt, therefore, has been made to integrate theory with relevant practical work, as well as giving consideration to how tutorial back-up might be most usefully employed. Secondly, the course is designed so that course units become progressively more intellectually demanding. In units 2, 3 and 4 (Figure 1), for example, greater use is made of the switch between information, hypothesis, experimentation and deduction. Thirdly, very careful consideration is given to the mode of presentation in relation to the biological problems involved. Nevertheless, although the course incorporates programmed texts, tape/slide presentations, film loops, wall charts, review articles, back-up tutorials and tutor guides, every attempt has been made to avoid an unnecessary 'extravaganza' of audio-visual hardware, since consideration must be given to production costs when the materials are published by the Cambridge University Press during 1972-73.

EXAMPLES OF CURRICULUM STRATEGY AND DESIGN

The following samples taken from different units within the course are meant to illustrate the major points made above.

A. In the section on light microscopy, the choice of cells has been made on the basis of differences in size, shape and colour and because they are easily obtained and readily available. For example, cheek cells and blood cells from Man. Thumbnail sketches are used to show students how to obtain these cells and how to look at them under the microscope. See EXAMPLE A.

B. It is important in Biology to be able to deduce the correct three-dimensional structure of an object from two-dimensional pictures. This conceptual problem is illustrated by part of the programmed text taken from unit 1 (electron microscopy).
See EXAMPLE B.

C. Much of the first unit on microscopy involves the student in examining the structure of cells under 'static' conditions. It is also important to portray the cell in its 'dynamic' state. For this purpose, short film loop sequences with accompanying programmed text have been used, as illustrated by example C, showing the behaviour of fibroblasts in culture.
See EXAMPLE C.

D. In the same context, a short review article, written by Professor Abercrombie pointing out some of the differences in behaviour between normal and cancerous cells is also on view.
See EXAMPLE D.

E. Tape/slide presentations have been used for two different purposes in this course.
(i) to show the sequence of events involved in certain techniques; for example, the preparation of a specimen for use in the electron microscope;
(ii) to raise questions about experimentation.
The latter is illustrated by a sample from a tape/slide sequence showing the Hill reaction in photosynthesis. It is accompanied by questions (text).
See EXAMPLE E.

F. An important behavioural objective in most of the programs is the student's ability to interpret graphical data. A typical example is shown from the unit on 'Interactions', Ch.1 frames 23-24.
See EXAMPLE F.

G. The final example shows the way in which programs make use of the switch between information, hypothesis, experimentation and deduction. Two different sections have been chosen from unit 3 'Regulation within cells'.
EXAMPLE G_i from Photosynthesis frames 36-48
EXAMPLE G_{ii} from Mitochondria frames 10-15

The second example also provides us with one way of employing tutorial back-up, by selecting certain original papers as a basis for discussion and reasoning (Epstein, 1970). In this instance, four research papers outlining the historical developments which led to the first successful isolation of mitochondria are quite appropriate. *

EVALUATION

Within the course, each of the units is prefaced by a statement of objectives, which are pre- and post-tested. Evaluation is governed more by self-assessment (progress) and feed-back of information rather than grading. A more detailed analysis of the methods of evaluation and results are given in another paper at this conference (Eraut, 1972).

CONCLUSIONS

In conclusion, it should be stated that the effectiveness of the course depends upon feed-back from both experts and students alike. Consequently, there is considerable emphasis on trials at both Sussex University and in other centres of Higher Education, as well as scrutiny by subject experts.

Finally, testing with students of mixed backgrounds has upheld a belief that the first year's intake in most Universities is very heterogeneous indeed. It seems, therefore, that a greater range of pre-knowledge testing is necessary. When this is done, a flexibly designed course such as the one outlined here, will have a much wider application, because with only comparatively few modifications, individual units can stand in their own right to prime or reinforce existing lecture/tutorial courses.

REFERENCES

Creager, J. G. and Murray, D. L. (1971) 'The use of modules in college biology teaching'. CUEBS Publications, USA
Dowdeswell, W. H. (1970) 'Inter-university biology teaching project'. Journal of Biological Education, 4, 197
Dowdeswell, W. H. (1972) 'The Inter-university biology teaching project: a study in curriculum development' (in press)
Epstein, H. T . (1970) 'A strategy for education'. Oxford University Press
Eraut, M. R. (1972) 'Strategies for the evaluation of curriculum materials'. APLET Conference 1972 (this volume)
Postlethwait, S. N., Novak, J. and Murray, H. T. (1969) 'The audio-tutorial approach to learning' (Second Edition). Burgess Publishing Co., Minneapolis
Stevens, W . W. and Morrissett, I. (1967) 'A system for analyzing social science curricula'. EPIE Forum 1, No.4, 10

*Examples A, B, C, etc refer to material presented in the conference.

Learner Controlled Self Instruction
T G WYANT

At Coventry Technical College we are carrying out an experiment in Learner
Controlled Self Instruction. The course selected for the experiment is the
City and Guilds of London Institute Course No. 428 Programmed Learning.
The course's new approach has been designed by the College's Department
of Educational Technology.

As with all courses the first task was to analyze the contents of the
syllabus, for, as with all syllabuses, all that is given in the City and Guilds
handbook is a bare statement of the subjects and their topics. The tutor is
left to interpret the syllabus to the best of his ability, with his main objectives
being that the student:

a) learns and practices the subject matter;
b) successfuly passes the final examination

Very rarely in a syllabus is any indication given of:

a) the objectives to be achieved by the student;
b) the depth of learning, or expertise that the student is expected
   to achieve;
c) the relationship that exists between
   1. subjects within the syllabus
   2. topics within the subjects
   3. the relationship of the topics right across the subject bands
d) the time to be devoted to each topic or subject in the syllabus

Although most teachers appreciate this freedom of interpretation, where
they are allowed to make their own judgements of how and when topics and
subjects should be taught, when an attempt is made to apply Learner Controlled Self Instructional techniques there must be carefully defined parameters
for the student, or learner, such as:

a) the required depth of learning for each topic;
b) where, how and when topics may be dependent upon one another;

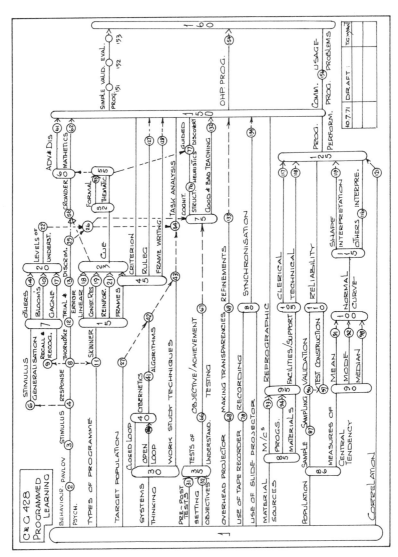

Figure 1

c) some indication of the importance of the various topics and subjects;

d) how he may proceed through the syllabus in the most meaningful and efficient manner;

e) how his present knowledge and experience may be utilized and incorporated to their best advantage

In the planning and construction of the course one of the most obvious first tasks was to compile and draw a network analysis of the syllabus (Figure 1). The network analysis was drawn following the disciplines of that technique, asking critically: what were the earliest and latest times that activities could start or finish. The network clearly showed that if this had been a normal teaching situation, the lecturer would have had a choice of twelve possible topics that he could have taught on the first evening of the course. These are shown on the lefthand side of the network as starting from node 1. The main virtues to be gained from drawing the syllabus in the network format is that it is:

a) a complete visual diagram of the syllabus;

b) it reveals the logical development of the topics and subjects within the syllabus;

c) it provides a ready made cross-referencing system;

d) it is a method of revealing the various strategies and routes that are available for the teacher or student to make progress through the syllabus;

e) it is tailor-made for input to computer facilities, and thus, has immediate access to the benefits that may be derived from computer usage

The terms of reference that were set for our Learner Controlled Self Instruction were:

a) the student must be able to freely choose those topics and subjects that he wished to study;

b) he may freely choose the order in which he wished to study the topics and subjects;

c) the student to be responsible for the depth to which he chooses to study any particular topic or subject

To help the student arrive at these decisions, use is made of the network and the other aids that have been designed.

The final system that was eventually installed was that on the first evening of the course the students were given a formal lecture on network analysis, so that they can interpret this novel presentation of the syllabus in the light of their particular requirements and individual differences.

Once familiar with the way in which the syllabus has been drawn, and

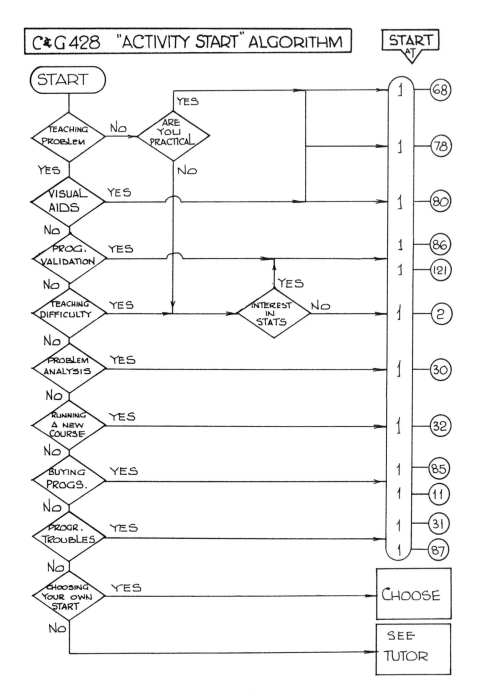

Figure 2

conversant with its possible implications, the student's usual first request is 'Where shall I start?' For indeed with this presentation he has a choice of twelve starting activities. To assist him in his selection an algorithm is provided (Figure 2). This tries to isolate or pinpoint the basic reasons for his attendance on the course. Once he has completed his route through the algorithm, he arrives at a point where he is given two reference numbers, which detail the activity that he is advised to start the course with.

For example, starting at the top lefthand side of the algorithm, the path can be followed to the first decision box, where the question is asked 'Have you a teaching problem?'. Let us assume, in this instance, that a teacher has joined the course purely out of interest, and he is that fortunate individual who has no teaching problem.

He follows the line marked 'NO' and is then posed another question in a decision box 'Are you a practical person?'. If the answer is 'YES' he is directed to the node reference numbers ①-⑥⑧ identifying these on the network shows that this is the activity 'Overhead Projector'.

Armed with these two reference numbers he approaches the tutor and states that he would like to commence with ①-⑥⑧ 'Overhead Projector'. The tutor, and if I may digress for a moment, the word 'tutor' has been cancelled by our present students and the title of 'Learning Leader' substituted instead.

C & G 428   ①————⑥⑧
Overhead Projector

Task Objectives:
1. What is an overhead projector.
2. Work through the programme on the use of the overhead projector.
3. Draw a transparency that will support one of your teaching topics.
4. Identify the main parts of the overhead projector, detailing the use of the various parts.
5. Design a use for the overhead projector so that it may be used with some other item of audio/visual equipment.
6. Carry out the use of either task 3 or 5, evaluate its uses, its advantages/disadvantages. Comment on any limitations with using the OHP.

Associated Areas:

Graphics - standard sizes of illustrations - photographic aids - montages - revelation and cover-up techniques - flip-a-tran -

Date on .... Date off ....

Next activity .... Event Nos ....

Previous activity .... Event Nos ....

Comments:

Figure 3

107

The Learning Leader then issues the student with the Task Objective sheet (Figure 3). This sheet carries the same identifying numbers in the top righthand corner. In the top lefthand corner, the course number and the activity description. Then follows what we have called 'Task Objectives'. Wherever possible these have been designed in six graduated stages or steps that roughly approximate to the hierarchy laid down by Bloom's Taxonomy of Educational Objectives. The student is free to select the particular stage or depth to which he intends to study the topic or activity.

The Task Objective sheet also contains under a heading of Associated Areas, other items that he may wish to consider during his study period. In an attempt to keep some record of the students progress and the sequence in which students tackled the course, spaces have been left for Date on - Date off - Next and Previous activities and their associated reference numbers.

Space is also provided for student comment as to the suitability of his selected strategy, or any other observation that he may wish to make.

To help the student tackle his learning commitment or study requirement, he may request from the Learning Leader the relevant Resource Data Bank package; this is in the form of a large envelope or wallet.

The packages also follow the referencing system, ie in our selected instance the numbers (1)—(68) appear in the top righthand corner of the package. The contents of the package, in no matter what form, also carry the identifying numbers to assist in refiling and easy identification when the student has finished with the package. The package may contain a variety of items, Tape/slide programs, OHP transparencies, algorithms, programmed texts, manufacturers catalogues, research papers, cuttings from periodicals, indeed, anything that may be of use to the student in achieving his self-elected task objectives. A further back-up occurs with the Reference Sheet Folder, again using the activity numbers he may, at any time, consult the folder of reference sheets which will direct him to further information or data possessed by the College library or other sources.

Having once completed his task objectives to their set level, he confers with the Learning Leader as to whether he has satisfactorily achieved his objectives. He may then choose again from any of the activities that lie open to him. For example, from the network it may be seen that once having completed activity (1)—(68) he could either proceed to 'Making Transparencies' or to a fresh activity altogether.

If during the course of working through any of the activities he acquires other reference material, data etc., or indeed, may even produce a small program of his own making, then this is copied or duplicated and fed into the Resource Data Bank or to the reference sheets.

Following this pattern the student is allowed to tackle and complete the whole syllabus using a Learner Controlled Self Instruction system.

Planning of Technical Courses for Agriculture in the Northern States of Nigeria

R D BELL

This paper describes the revision and expansion of training courses for Agricultural Technicians and Extension Workers in the six northern states of Nigeria.

Nigeria is the largest of the English speaking countries of West Africa, but it is believed that the principles and methods employed are applicable to other developing countries since many have similar characteristics, such as:

a) The economy is almost entirely dependent upon agriculture and the ancillary industries;

b) Agriculture is at present a peasant industry and therefore commands less prestige than many newer occupations;

c) There is a shortage of school leavers with good secondary education;

d) There is a shortage of adequately trained men to teach technical courses;

e) There is a shortage of money and physical resources;

f) The population is increasing rapidly and it is essential that there be a rapid increase in agricultural production to support these extra people;

g) There are few opportunities for employment for well trained men in commercial agriculture;

h) A further problem is that teachers and students often have different mother tongues and converse in a language foreign to both;

The subject is discussed under the following headings: 1) General conditions; 2) The Government Service; 3) Objectives; 4) Resources and Initial Planning; 5) Certificate Courses; 6) Diploma Courses; 7) Staff Development; 8) Future Possibilities.

GENERAL CONDITIONS

Nigeria is a federation of twelve states (Figure 1). It lies entirely within the tropics and most of the farmland is less than two thousand feet above sea level. The six northernmost states cover approximately twenty-six thousand square miles and have a population of about thirty-five million. These states have no mineral oil and little mining or engineering.

Natural vegetation varies from the Rain Forest of the Niger Valley to the dry Savannah of the north (Figure 2). There are few large farms in private

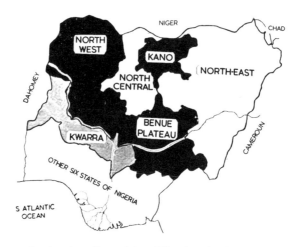

Figure 1. The six northern states of Nigeria. Population 35 million; area 26,400 square miles

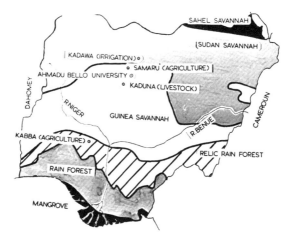

Figure 2. Vegetation map of Nigeria showing location of Ahmadu Bello University and its schools of Agricultural Technology

ownership and crop production is mainly in the hands of the small farmer. Nomadic Fulani tribesmen raise most of the cattle. Each of the states does provide elementary vocational training for youths who wish to become farmers but it is generally accepted that virtually all other agricultural training is intended to prepare staff for the Government service.

THE GOVERNMENT SERVICE

The Ministry of Agriculture in each State has a structure as in Figure 3. The

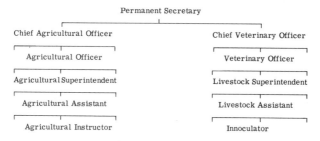

Figure 3. State agricultural services

service is headed by officers who are university graduates. These officers are assisted by senior technical staff termed 'superintendents'. The main grade of technical staff are termed 'Agricultural (or Livestock) Assistant'. It is this grade which is most effective in the introduction of new ideas and techniques to the farmers. The rate of national development is therefore largely dependent on the quality of these 'Assistants' and on the efficiency with which they are deployed.

There is at present a junior grade of extension worker known as 'Agricultural Instructor' who serve as aids to the 'Assistants', but these men only have practical training after a Primary school education and this grade will be phased out as soon as possible.

OBJECTIVES

a)   The broad aim of the programme is to improve and develop the agriculture of the country;

b)   More immediately the aim is to train technicians and extension staff for the Government service;

c)   All technical staff should have a sound practical experience and an adequate scientific education in order that they may understand current practices and assimilate new ideas and techniques as these are introduced by the research units;

d)   All extension workers should receive adequate training in communication and extension methods;

e)   All extension workers should have a good understanding of current mores, customs and practices of the area in which they work. This is especially important in Northern Nigeria where many ethnic groups, religions and languages are intermingled.

RESOURCES AND INITIAL PLANNING

The most important resources are human resources, ie potential students and teachers, but physical and financial resources may be limiting in some areas.

In order to utilize available resources to the best advantage it was agreed in 1969 that Ahmadu Bello University should train all technical staff for the

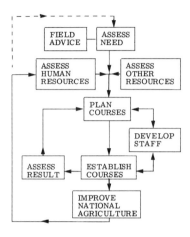

Figure 4. Course planning

Ministries of Agriculture of the six northern states of Nigeria. It was agreed that the University should utilize three schools of agriculture existing in different ecological zones and that a major revision of all courses should be made. The writer was actively concerned in this revision exercise.

The procedure adopted for the planning and revision of courses is illustrated in Figure 4.

'Field Advice' consisted of discussions with extension staff of all ranks to provide a 'job-analysis' of the duties of Superintendents and Assistants. At the same time an analysis was made of the projected personnel needs of the states in order that expansion of the schools of Agriculture might be phased to meet needs as they arise.

Next an assessment was made of available resources considering especially the standard of-secondary school leavers available.

Syllabi were then drafted and discussed in detail with the staff of the schools and potential employers. At this stage shortages of staff and facili-

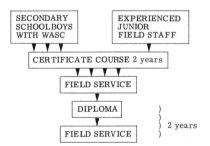

Figure 5. Training programme

ties became apparent and a subsidiary programme was prepared to develop these resources.

The courses were then introduced.

Since the object of the programme is to improve national agriculture success will affect both available resources and the need for particular courses. Improvements in secondary education should result in recruitment of better candidates. A consultative council has been set up (including state representatives) to keep the courses under continuous review.

Two levels of training are provided (Figure 5): (a) Certificate level for Assistant grade; (b) Diploma level for Superintendent grade.

The certificate course is entirely technical but the diploma course includes management studies. Candidates for certificate courses are mainly young men with West African School Certificate and they must be recruited in competition with other vocations. They are likely to be of moderate academic ability and to have little practical experience of agriculture. Some candidates with lower academic qualifications may be accepted if they have good practical experience as Junior Extension Staff. These men take a short pre-technical course to prepare them for certificate studies. Candidates for diploma courses are drawn from those who have completed a certificate course and a subsequent period of field service.

Certain broad principles may be applied to all courses at intermediate level:

a)   Subject matter and depth of coverage should be directly related to the future duties of the candidate;

b)   It is better to teach a reasonable amount of subject matter well rather than endeavour to cover too large a syllabus at a superficial level;

c)   The duration and intensity of any course should be related to the subsequent duties and career prospects of the candidates;

d)   All proposals for training should be feasible with the candidates, staff and physical facilities which may reasonably be made available

CERTIFICATE COURSES

The candidates for certificate courses are unlikely to be well adapted for much private study, even if adequate textbooks and journals are available, and this is rarely the case. It should, therefore, be assumed that certificate courses will be fully taught and that private study will be mainly revision of course work. Toward the end of the course effort should be made to encourage wider reading and private work. Programmed texts would be of great value to these students.

Structure of certificate course

The subjects may be divided into four groups:

a) Social subjects, eg Geography, Sociology, National Agriculture, Government Regulations

These subjects are to acquaint the student with the place of agriculture in the national economy and with his place and duties in agriculture. They are mainly taught by lecture.

b) Science subjects, eg Chemistry, Botany, Soil Science, etc

These subjects form a basis for the understanding of the applied sciences or husbandries and it is essential that they are taught by men familiar with and sympathetic to the needs of the husbandries. These subjects require both lectures and practical work: it is unnecessary to develop laboratory techniques which will not later be required.

c) Applied Sciences and Husbandries

Unless the student has a sound knowledge of the husbandries, he is unlikely to be of much use in the agricultural services. Because most of the students lack prior experience it is essential that there is a high proportion of practical work in which the student may become intimately familiar with the crops or animals with which he will later be concerned. Such practical work must be adequately supervised, explained and assessed. For the purpose of the practical work to be achieved the student must understand its relevance to his other course work and to his future duties.

d) Extension

In the early part of the course any work on Extension must be limited to theory but towards the end of the course the student should take part in adequately supervized extension projects so that he may become aware and learn to overcome many of the problems which he will encounter in his employment.

The duration of the courses is 2 years each of 3 terms of 12 weeks. This allows the students to see two full growing seasons, to proceed from school level to a maturity and technical ability acceptable to their employers and it provides a vacation period during which staff at the schools may be refreshed and brought up to date.

Specialization at certificate level

Strong arguments can be advanced against any specialization at certificate level on the grounds that the graduates may be too narrow in outlook and lack versatility. Even stronger argument can be advanced in favour of some specialization on the grounds that only in this way can the student acquire enough knowledge to be useful in **any** field, it enables students and staff to develop their special interests and so capitalizes their enthusiasm, and it may enable candidates with alternative prior qualifications to be accepted.

It is desirable that all students should take the first part of the course in common, in order that they should appreciate that 'Agriculture' is a whole of which the various disciplines or specialization are component parts. Later the subject matter of the courses will diverge, but both social and technical contact between students of different disciplines should be actively encouraged. If crop and livestock enterprises are to be integrated on settled farms then it is essential that there be close cooperation and understanding between the extension officers concerned. It is considered to be vitally important that the training in the husbandries takes place in an environment similar to that in which the candidate is to be employed. Environment in this context is intended to cover both ecological and social factors. In a region such as Northern Nigeria it is far more important for the school to be located in the right ecological zone than that it should be in any particular state.

Specialization at certificate level

Variants of the certificate course are: a) General Agriculture; b) Agronomy; c) Livestock Technology; d) Range Management; e) Home Economics (for women); f) Agricultural Mechanization.

DIPLOMA COURSES

The Diploma Courses prepare men for posts at the Superintendent level.

If a man proceeds direct to a Diploma course on completion of his Certificate course, recent work is fresh in his mind and he is attuned to classroom studies. If, however, he spends several years in field service he will gain experience and maturity and will have a sound understanding of the duties and problems of his juniors.

The prime duty of a Superintendent is to lead his team. To do this successfully he must demonstrate superior technical skill, imagination and initiative, and management ability.

The Diploma Courses extend over two years, of which approximately 15 months are spent in formal teaching and the remainder in 'in-service' training or probation in his Home State. The subjects are in three groups:

Group I	Management and Administration Topics	15%
Group II	Technical Subjects	65%
Group III	Project work and seminars	20%

It is intended that the first group would develop the man as a leader and organizer, the second should improve his technical competence and the third should help to develop his imagination and initiative in the solution of real problems.

If the aims of the Diploma courses are to be achieved it must be recognized by staff and students that these are mature students training for senior technical posts. In these circumstances emphasis should be placed on private study whenever suitable textbooks or journals can be made available. Formal teaching and private study should occupy about 50% of the total study time.

Care must be taken not to destroy the enthusiasm of candidates by excessive revision of certificate level work.

Specialization at diploma level

The need for specialization at diploma level is universally accepted. Variants of the diploma courses are: a) General Agriculture; b) Irrigation Agronomy; c) Livestock Technology; d) Home Economics; (e) Agricultural Mechanization.

In a developing country the changes in agriculture must be rapid. It must be accepted that syllabuses and training programmes will change frequently and that all extension staff will need frequent in-service training to keep abreast of new developments.

STAFF DEVELOPMENT

Provision of well qualified teachers for the Schools of Agriculture is a major problem. Staff are frequently ex-students of their own, or similar schools. Senior staff are usually graduates.

There is a need for instruction in teaching methods and, when possible, staff are granted study leave in Nigeria, UK or USA for this purpose. Expatriate teachers are still needed in the schools but their primary duty is to guide and develop their indigenous counterparts. The appointment of an expert to assist teachers in the preparation of programmed texts would be of great value since the discipline of preparing programmed texts would improve the quality of teaching, and at the same time the shortage of text books would be relieved.

REFERENCES

Bell, R. D. (1970) Recommendations for development of Certificate and Diploma courses at the Schools of Agricultural and Livestock Technology of Ahmadu Bello University. Mimeo - Ahmadu Bello University

Bell, R. D., Carpenter, F. and Prawl, W . (1969) Report of consultants on the non-degree schools of Kabba, Mando Road and Vom and their future relationship with Ahmadu Bello University. Mimeo - Ahmadu Bello University

CSNRD Report 1969. Strategies and Recommendations for Nigeria Rural Development 1969-85.
CSNRD - 11 Extension Priorities
CSNRD - 13 Improvement of Agricultural Extension Work and non-degree teaching. CSNRD, Michigan

Rowat, R . (1965) Report to the Federal and Regional Governments of Nigeria on the Development of Education and Training in the Field of Agriculture and Related Subjects. FAO, Rome

Spary, G. B. (1967) Education in the Six Northern States of Nigeria 1962-1973. Ministry of Education, Kaduna

World Conference on Agricultural Education and Training 1970 - Report Copenhagen. FAO, UNESCO, ILO (special reference to Volume 1)

Method of presentation: tape/slide

The Design of a Course for Royal Army Medical Corps Clerks in Special-to-Arm Clerical Procedures

J F MILLS and W LENTON

BACKGROUND

Clerks of the Royal Army Medical Corps (RAMC) are trained in both general clerical skills, applicable to any Army clerk, and also Special-to-Arm procedures. The latter are connected with general clerical work but are concerned specifically with the medical documentation and procedures used by the RAMC. In common with the rest of the Army, Clerks of the RAMC have three Classes which are related to proficiency and employment. The Class III standard is achieved after initial training while the Classes II and I are obtained as a result of relevant job experience and further instruction.

In 1970 it was agreed that, commencing in 1971, the Royal Army Ordnance Corps (RAOC) would train RAMC Clerks at the RAOC Clerks School in general clerical skills common to all Arms of the Service. This was in accordance with a policy that, as far as was practicable, all Army Clerks, irrespective of their Corps, would be trained centrally by the RAOC in general clerical duties. The training system used at the RAOC Clerks School has been described in detail (Edney, 1971) and is noteworthy for its extensive use of auto-instructional material and its completely individually paced nature. The RAOC system incorporated a further change in that theoretical instruction to the Class II standard was included in the initial course with formal classification dependent upon job experience and satisfactory performance instead of further instruction and examination.

These changes to the method of training RAMC Clerks, which also coincided with the move of the RAMC Clerks School to Aldershot, necessitated a complete reappraisal of the courses held since these would, in future, be limited to Special-to-Arm procedures. It was decided to begin with the initial course, which would now include theoretical instruction to the Class II standard, and redesign this, following the principles of a systems approach to training.

THE JOB ANALYSIS

Only a broad syllabus existed on which to base training and this was not written in terms of students' performance. It was decided, therefore, to conduct a job analysis of the Clerk Class III and II and derive from this training objectives for the Special-to-Arm procedures required by the actual job. Since job incumbents were located world wide and time prevented the extensive use of observation and interview, it was agreed that the main method of job analysis would be a postal questionnaire. This questionnaire would be based upon the Special-to-Arm procedures and tasks isolated by preliminary investigation.

Smith (1964) suggests many factors which can be usefully explored in a job analysis to determine training content. However, in order to keep the questionnaire simple it was decided that Clerks themselves should only be asked to indicate the frequency with which they performed tasks and the degree of difficulty they found with them. It was hoped that the former would give the basis for what should be taught while the latter would indicate where particular emphasis was needed during training.

It was also decided to approach the officers who employ Clerks (Employing Officers) since their expectations could be a major factor in determining the duties a Clerk performs and if his standard of work was satisfactory. In their questionnaire, therefore, Employing Officers were to be asked if they required the procedure to be performed by Clerks Class III and II and the standard of performance they expected, in three broad categories of 'Familiar', 'Trained' and 'Expert'. This information could then be used to identify any important but infrequently performed skills and the level to which the Clerk should be trained.

The tasks and procedures to be included in the questionnaires were developed from the existing syllabus, job observation and interviews and from discussions with experienced senior clerks and Employing Officers. During the course of this it was realized that, since training objectives were the ultimate goal of the job analysis, time and effort would be saved if these were produced in draft form and, in effect, validated by the questionnaires. This approach would also have had the added advantage of minimizing ambiguity since the questionnaires would be based upon precise statements of behaviour. This preliminary investigation also revealed that the job was not a single coherent one, but that particular skills and procedures were needed according to certain main types of employment. It was decided that replies to the questionnaires must, therefore, be strictly limited to the respondent's particular post. This would enable each type of employment to be analyzed separately to see if differential training was necessary and would ensure that replies were based on personal experience of a particular job and not on speculation.

Draft questionnaires for both Clerks and Employing Officers, together with appropriate instructions for their completion, were produced, validated and amended. These were sent by post to all Class III and II Clerks serving world wide and to a random sample of 75 Employing Officers representing all supervisory levels and the main types of employment. No problems were encountered in administering the questionnaire and a 95.5% response rate was achieved. Subsequent interview of selected respondents confirmed the accuracy of replies and revealed that no major problems were encountered in completing the questionnaires. However, it was found that frequency of performance was slightly over estimated since Clerks tended to regard the questionnaire as a form of test. They were reluctant, therefore, to confine their answers to their present unit if this would result in a response of 'never performed' to a task they had done in a previous unit.

TRAINING OBJECTIVES

It was decided to leave the training objectives at the fairly general level. Detailed standards of performance would not be specified in the training objectives but the three broad categories of 'Familiar', 'Trained' and 'Expert' would be retained. The use of these expressions subsequently proved to be confusing and, in the final objectives, Training levels 3,2 and 1 were substituted. For each category, however, overall pass marks would be laid down and also the minimum percentage of objectives in each category the student would need to achieve before graduating from the course. Thus, he would need to achieve all Training Level 1 objectives (Expert) but only 80% of those at Training Level 3 (Familiar). It was intended that this would provide a guide to the training and testing emphasis to be placed on each objective. Within this broad framework, precise standards for each objective would be developed and laid down in detailed test items.

Preliminary inspection of the results of the job analysis indicated that, while specific training for particular employments would be the ideal this was impracticable. Since the questionnaires already contained draft objectives, the job analysis data could be used directly to confirm their validity and determine the broad standards of performance required. To achieve this, decision rules were constructed based upon the concepts outlined by Smith. By these rules, draft objectives were omitted if they were not performed to a predetermined level of frequency or only a small percentage of Employing Officers required them. Similarly, the training standard was determined by considering the frequency and difficulty of the task, together with Employing Officers' expectations. It was recognized that, in the construction of these rules, some arbitrary decisions were made concerning the level of percentage response which should be regarded as significant. However, this weakness was accepted in view of the advantage the rules gave of providing a standard yardstick to apply to all data.

COURSE DESIGN

Once the final training objectives had been derived, the detailed design of a training course to achieve them was undertaken. The underlying concept in this was that the student should, wherever possible, actually perform the clerical procedures and skills required of them. For example, they would complete the specialized forms and returns using the actual documents which are available to them in the job. In this way, the emphasis would be on the practical application of skills, under simulated conditions, rather than upon the formal classroom teaching of knowledge which had been used previously.

Careful consideration was given to the production of a completely self paced course using programmes or other auto-instructional material. This would have been a natural extension of the system used by the RAOC and would have solved the administrative problem raised by students arriving individually from their general clerical training. However, it was decided that the administrative problems and production costs would outweigh the advantages, although it might be possible to develop such a system eventually.

The course was, therefore, to be basically group paced but with the following provisos:

a) the instructional material should be produced in a modular form and be capable of easy conversion to an auto-instructional system either for the course or as a basis for a correspondence course for Clerks of the TAVR;

b) the instructor's role in managing a training system, providing individual tuition and motivating students should be emphasized and the time spent on formal classroom teaching limited;

c) the form of the course should have sufficient flexibility to meet individual needs within the basic group-paced framework. Instructional material should be designed to facilitate this, no rigid timetable would be laid down and no fixed course length would be set.

The optimum sequence for instruction was determined by matrices similar to those used in writing programs (Kay et al, 1968) and detailed Lesson Plans were subsequently produced for each training objective. In these, the instructor is given guidance on how to introduce the subjects, provided with prepared visual aids, such as OHP transparencies or charts, and supplied with handouts for the students to retain and build into comprehensive notes. During the development of these parts of the Lesson Plans, the instructor was continually consulted to ensure his cooperation with the system. The Lesson Plans also give the instructor considerable discretion on how he approaches instruction to avoid enforcing a stereotype method.

The bulk of the Lesson Plans consist of specially prepared documents and material from which the student himself can undertake the procedure or skill being learned. Every attempt is made to make this realistic by using the actual books, forms and documents the Clerk will encounter in his job, building in the problems he will meet and compelling him to take appropriate and realistic action to solve them. The basis of the course is, therefore, a series of simulated situations where the student can learn for himself and also practise while the instructor provides individual tuition.

The nature of the work does not lend itself to the use of audio-visual presentation methods, except for the OHP in initial instruction. Limited use is, however, made of programs to teach certain topics where this approach seems appropriate and where suitable programs can be found.

Algorithms are, however, used extensively and have proved particularly valuable. Where complicated clerical procedures are involved an algorithm has often been found to be a successful way of guiding the individual student through it. Correct completion of an apparently complex and difficult task is highly motivating and the crutch of that algorithm is quite quickly discarded once the student has grasped the procedure as a complete entity. Algorithms are also used to assist the student in solving problems which involve consulting administrative instruction written in 'official' language. The use and value of this technique has been described by Lewis and Woolfenden (1969) and needs no further elaboration. As a result, however, it is proposed to publish the algorithm more widely to assist all RAMC Clerks in the interpretation of regulations.

Adjusting the course to individual learning needs is achieved in two ways. If the objective is essential to successful completion of the rest of the course provision is made for individual remedial instruction immediately. During this time other students practice specific skills, such as typing, where increased proficiency will be of personal advantage later. However, if the objective is unrelated to other work the student is retained at the end of the course for further instruction and practice. Since the initial selection of Clerks provides a comparatively homogeneous student population the spread of learning rates has not been found to be so great as to cause insuperable administrative problems.

ASSESSMENT OF TRAINING EFFECTIVENESS

While the course was being designed, attention was given to developing a comprehensive system whereby the effectiveness of training could be continuously monitored. This was considered essential to ensure the competence of students and that training weaknesses were quickly identified and remedied.

Achievement of the objectives themselves is measured by practical tests based on each objective. These tests, like the Lesson Plans, consist of all the necessary material for the student to perform the procedure in a simulated situation. Where the objective consists of separate routines which have to be mastered before total performance is achieved, similar test items have been constructed for each routine. Detailed marking schemes

121

have been laid down for each test so that precisely defined standards are available to amplify the training objectives. These marking schemes also reflect the criticality of each element in a procedure since they stipulate where complete accuracy is essential or where some latitude can be allowed. The practical test items are also supported by objective type tests which are used to examine the student in the knowledge components of the procedure.

Testing is progressive throughout the course. The instructor monitors the students' progress, using such test items as are relevant, and, as a result, will adjust his own teaching. Formal tests of each objective are given and the results recorded. These results are used to determine what remedial action, if any, is needed either for the group or for individuals. If there are a significant number of failures the validity of the test item and the instruction itself are examined to determine what adjustments are necessary. If an individual student were to consistently fall below the general level of the course, consideration would be given to his removal from training to avoid the uneconomical use of resources.

At the end of the course a final test is administered since it is believed that this provides a satisfying goal for students and ensures that objectives covered earlier have been retained. This test is not, however, used to make an absolute decision on whether students pass or fail and, if necessary, individual students or the whole course can be retained for further instruction. Since the final test is based on selected objectives a program has been drawn up to ensure that critical objectives are tested regularly, but that over a period of time all objectives will be included.

Formal assessment is also made of the students' attitudes to the course. To date, this has been done by interview, but a standardized questionnaire is being developed to aid comparison over successive courses. The questionnaire will give indices of global satisfaction with the training and obtain positive information on students' difficulties and distastes as an aid to remedial action.

After a suitable period of employment on the job, graduates from the course and their Employing Officers have been interviewed. The Clerks were asked about any difficulties they had with the job which could be overcome by adjusting the training, while Employing Officers gave their opinion on the satisfactoriness of the Clerk and what they thought the deficiencies in his training were. As a result of this minor modifications have been made to the course. While interviews were necessary during the developmental stage they are time consuming and questionnaires are to be constructed which can be sent by post to Clerks and Employing Officers. In this way it is hoped to ensure the continuing relevance of the objectives and the training to the job itself and identify where adjustments are needed to meet changing circumstances.

CONCLUSIONS

Only a few courses have been run under the new system so many of the conclusions concerning its effectiveness must be tentative, especially since the first ones were used to develop the system. It is also difficult to make valid comparisons with the old method of training because of the many fundamental changes which have been made.

However, it is considered that the standard of students' performance has been improved. The nature of the training is more orientated to practical performance and the job itself, the pass mark has been raised from 50% to at least 80% and the test items are more valid. The average failure rate under the old system was around 10% while, to date, there have been no failures on the revised course. Finally, both students and Employing Officers appear satisfied with the course and what it produces.

These higher standards are achieved in a shorter time despite the inclusion of the additional Class II material. The total training time has been reduced from sixteen weeks to an average of eight, when the training in general clerical work at the RAOC Clerks School is included. While it is sometimes difficult to isolate the Special-to-Arm procedures from the general work, training time for the latter has been cut down from approximately six weeks to an average of four.

No direct instructor savings can be shown, but the RAMC Clerks School is now able to take on other commitments. A correspondence course, based on the material in the Lesson Plans, is being produced for the training of Clerks of the TAVR. This will be administered by the Clerks School, thus reducing the training load on TAVR units and ensuring standardized instruction. Since the Clerks School is now part of the RAMC Training Centre it is also able to take on the training of other RAMC personnel in the clerical duties connected with their particular employment. This will free the instructors who were previously responsible and the reorganization of clerical training may be considered to have contributed, in a minor way, to the overall reduction of staff at the RAMC Training Centre.

REFERENCES

Edney, P. J. (1971) Royal Air Force Education Bulletin, 8, 17
Kay, H., Dodd, B. and Sime, M. (1968) Teaching Machines and Programmed Instruction
Lewis, B. N. and Woolfenden, P. J. (1969) Algorithms and Logical Trees
Smith, R. G. (1964) The Development of Training Objectives

A Report on the Redesign of a Trade Training Course for the Royal Corps of Transport.

J TULLOCH and J T WALKER

INTRODUCTION

The background to this study begins in the mid-1960s, when the Director of Army Training sponsored a major investigation into the conduct of trade training within the Army. The third report of this investigation proposed inter-alia a systematic procedure for designing and testing trade training courses. One of the outcomes of this was the establishment of Training Development Teams in most of the major Arms and Services of the Army, to apply the principles of the systematic approach to training and to examine special-to-arm problems.

In anticipation of the establishment of a Training Development Team for the Royal Corps of Transport (RCT), a Royal Army Educational Corps (RAEC) Major was attached to the Army School of Transport in 1966: he became the Training Development Adviser (TDA). The RCT Training Development Team, which was set up in early 1971, has four members; two officers and a warrant officer of the RCT, together with the TDA. The primary responsibility of the team is the planning and development of all RCT training, and in addition driver training for the whole Army.

The Royal Corps of Transport was formed in 1965, from elements of the Royal Army Service Corps and Royal Engineers. It is responsible for the operation of road, rail and sea transport services within the army. Part of the sea transport task is the running of a military port.

Two of the trades involved were Freight Handler and Heavy Crane Operator. In 1969 it was suggested that a study of these two trades be initiated, in order to prepare up to date job specifications, modify the trade structure if it seemed necessary, and redesign the training required to implement any changes resulting from the study.

CONDUCT OF THE STUDY

This study was conducted by a team of three officers – the TDA (co-author of this paper) an officer of the US Transportation Corps, on an exchange

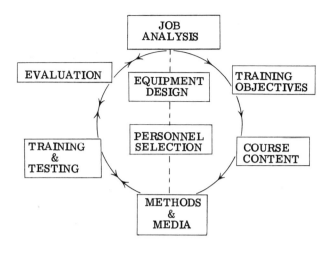

Figure 1

posting, and a RCT officer – and the experience gained has subsequently proved valuable to the present RCT Training Development Team. The team adopted a systematic approach which is diagrammatically expressed by Figure 1.

The first stage was to carry out a job analysis. This was not as simple a task as is sometimes the case in industry, where one man's range of tasks may be narrow. In the case of the RCT Port Trades, there were six grades to consider, three levels of Freight Handler and three of Heavy Crane Operator. One of the reasons for calling for the study was that at the higher, Class I, levels there was a degree of duplication between the two trades, ie at the senior non-commissioned officer (NCO), supervisory level. Additionally, operations on a quay were controlled by the senior Freight Handler – a group B trade in the Army classification system, who might have to supervise a higher paid class I Heavy Crane Operator – an A group trade.

The job analysis was made easier to some extent because the total number of men involved was comparatively small – less than 300. Another advantage was that most of these men were located in one area in the UK with a small proportion overseas.

Preliminary discussions were held with a sample of officers and NCO's currently engaged in either the operation of the Military Port, or the training of the Freight Handlers and Heavy Crane Operators. The aim was to draft a list of tasks which had to be performed by either or both of the two tradesmen, during the running of a military port, or in an operational situation with limited facilities. This list of tasks then formed the basis of a questionnaire, which was administered to 160 men in the two trades above the rank of Lance Corporal, and to a number of officers selected on the basis of their experience in Port operations.

The aim of the questionnaire was to ascertain which tasks had to be performed, by whom (ie by which ranks) and the degree of expertise required. Respondents had to indicate the level of skill required by both the driver and the Junior NCO for each task.

A note on the time scale is interesting. From the initiation of the study to the distribution of the questionnaire took about two and a half months. This included validation of a pilot questionnaire on a small sample. Completed questionnaires were returned, the analysis of replies carried out and the first report written in a further three months.

To return to the study, the next step was to analyze the questionnaire responses. These were collated, and converted to percentages so that a typical analysis sheet would appear as shown in Appendix A. Thus, 53% of respondents were of the opinion that drivers should be familiar at the skill of operating commercial fork lifts.

To enable job specifications to be prepared, a decision chart was designed which laid down the limit of the percentages which would determine who should be responsible for each task, and the degree of skill required. The decision chart is reproduced at Appendix B and if the example quoted above is taken, the chart indicates that the driver is required to perform this task and he should be trained to an attainment level 2. The M denotes that the skill is psychomotor, as opposed to being simply cognitive or practical. This method of analysis was based on an article by Sullivan (1969).

Following this procedure, job specifications were prepared for drivers and Junior NCO's. Certain additional tasks, also covered in the questionnaire, were identified as requirements for Senior NCO's. The tasks also appeared to fall into four groups and hence a revised trade structure linked to rank was proposed as shown in Figure 2.

Trade Level	Rank
BIII	Driver/L cpl
AIII	Driver/L cpl
AII	L cpl/Cpl
AI	Corporal/Sergeant

Figure 2

Eventually, some time after the submission of the initial report, the title Port Operator was selected for the new trade. Other points covered in the initial report were implications for the TAVR, which because of its nature has a number of different trades from the Regular Army; the financial consequences which would result from the adoption of the proposed trade structure; and the problem of retraining personnel at present qualified as

Freight Handlers and Heavy Crane Operators. It should be appreciated that the study dealt with these points in some considerable breadth and depth as the systematic approach to training demands.

TRAINING OBJECTIVES

In March 1971 approval in principle was given for the adoption of the new trade structure. The next stage of the study was then started, that is the production of Training Objectives based on the new Job Specifications. The authors of this paper had had some basic training in the writing of training objectives but no practical experience. Although the principles were well understood, the range and complexity of tasks in the job specifications for the four levels of the new trade, were a far cry from the straightforward examples we had followed through in training. The definition of Performance, Test Conditions and Test Standards for the task of tying a reef knot presented no great challenge. However, in the case of a junior NCO whose responsibilities included the organization and supervision of hatch operations in the process of stowing and discharging a ship, considerable problems arose.

Some discussion then took place concerning who should write the training objectives. It was argued that the trainers (the experts in the trades) were best qualified to write the objectives, taking advice from the team on the general approach. However, those responsible for instruction cannot normally devote enough time to this task, and are too closely associated with the details of the day to day training to be unbiased about the overall training requirements. Therefore, it was agreed, and the principle established the responsibility for determining training objectives should rest with the team, which by necessity would work very closely with the experts in the trade. In the event the process became a thoroughly joint effort, in which the team went considerably further than merely ensuring good presentation of the details in a new format.

The team and the instructional staff together examined all the skills involved in each of the tasks which comprised the job specifications of each of the four levels of the trade. For each skill the following factors were considered at length:

(1) Its relevance to the task and its significance to the total job,
(2) The practicalities of learning it in the current environment,
(3) The practicalities of testing it, particularly the conditions and standards vis a vis those desired,
(4) All administrative constraints acting upon the conditions of learning and testing.
(5) The choice of wording to make our meaning quite clear to everyone concerned with the results of our work.

There is one specific aspect of this study which is peculiar to a military situation. During the whole of our deliberations on the tasks we had to bear in mind that the majority of the training was for a possible operational situation, yet a large proportion of the tasks were executed in conditions of peace. Therefore a degree of overtraining had to be allowed for and the standard formula for applying the rule of relevancy to the job as practised daily could not be used as freely as we would have wished.

The format finally adopted for the training objectives was a result of trial and error. It is simple and easy to read, and by allotting one page for each objective, amendment is a straightforward process of page replacement. An example is given at Appendix C.

A fundamental aspect of writing training objectives is the question of the level of detail at which one defines the performance. The problem is to decide between having a few broad objectives which cover a large number of skills but which are difficult to quantify in terms of standards, and a large number of narrow objectives which are easier to specify in every way. Broad objectives are generally popular with those who have to implement them because they tend to allow some scope for subjective and arbitrary judgement, sometimes called the **human element**. They can also be popular with those who are responsible for defining the training requirement because they cover larger slices of the total task at one time. On the other hand if all the tasks in a job are broken down to their lowest level of activity, so that the performance required in each objective represents a very minor stage in the execution of the skill, the result will be a very long list of objectives which appear too trivial and are irksome to put into effect. We consider that in the objectives we have written we have chosen a level which, whilst facilitating accurate definition of performance, conditions and standards, does not offend the more inquiring mind. With regard to the test standards we had a particularly awkward problem with the basic level (BIII) of the Port Operator trade. A large proportion of the tasks at this level is achieved as part of a team using equipment which cannot be operated by individuals. Examples of such tasks are stowage and hatchwork and the problem was two-fold:

(1) Definition of the standard and
(2) Application of the standard to individuals in a team.

The definition we chose includes phrases such as **Without damage**, etc, and **Without causing injury or risk of injury**, and possibly they leave too wide a margin for error but there seems to be no feasible alternative. Application of the standard, we decided, can only be made by a continuous assessment of performance throughout a period of practical training, where the individual trainees in the team are closely observed by the experts.

Even so it is an extremely difficult task to decide upon the effectiveness of an individual in a team which is stowing or discharging a ship, except in extreme cases of poor performance.

After 12 months designing the training for the Port Operators we have almost completed the study cycle for the two operative levels. The remaining two higher levels are for junior and senior NCO's and because the majority of their tasks are supervisory the statement of the performance within the objectives must be in appropriate terms.

One has read and listened to doubts being expressed as to the feasibility of defining supervisory skills in suitably objective terms and much emphasis has been placed on the difficulties of defining accurate standards.

In the light of experience, we venture to suggest that the problem may have been overstated. Admittedly the performance required of a supervisor (or junior commander in military terms) cannot be described in the simple terms used for an operative's performance and therefore the test standards cannot be easily quantified. But this is not to say that a supervisor's performance and test standard cannot be assessed accurately – or at least accurately enough to ensure that he will be capable of doing his job well. To save lengthy discussion on the reasoning behind our work on the writing of training objectives for the AII level of Port Operators (normally a junior NCO) we have attached an example at Appendix D.

COURSE DESIGN

Having spent a great deal of time and effort on the objectives, the design of the courses was a relatively straightforward task. It was a question of allotting the correct amount of time for the attainment of each objective, and deciding upon a logical sequence for them. The methods and media to be used in the learning process had really been an integral part of the study and formulation of the objectives, therefore it only remained to state them formally in the various modules of the course.

We have so far designed two courses both basically for operatives. One course is designed for new entrants to the trade and on completion they are able to stow and discharge ordinary cargo, operate winches, tie a number of knots and make some splices, and demonstrate the very basic skills in the handling of barges. The other course is designed for those who have been in the trade for a minimum of six months. On completion they are able to operate and maintain one industrial and one rough terrain fork lift, and a quay crane. They are also able to interpret simple stowage plans, stow and discharge a heavy and awkward item of cargo and render first aid.

The length of the course has been reduced from 6 weeks to 3 and 13 weeks to 6 respectively. Only one of each has so far been held and no feed-back at this early stage has been received from the units to indicate the effectiveness of the training. Therefore, it is premature to comment on their degree of success. A 90% pass rate was obtained in both cases but of course this only tends to prove that, provided the test standards were applied rigidly by the examiners, the instruction was sufficient for the attainment of the objectives. One of the team's important recommendations has not been implemented for partly administrative, partly traditional reasons. We refer to the modules of time allotted for the learning of each objective. These vary with each objective and should be adhered to strictly, but for administrative convenience periods allotted for instruction of all subjects have been rounded to multiples of 30 minutes. This inevitably results in a degree of over training.

TESTING

The test standards are applied by a testing board consisting of a major and two warrant officers or NCOs, who are all experts in the trade. The tests fall into three categories, the first of which is the continuous assessment process mentioned earlier. The second is the formal practical tests which are set up at the end of the course and the third oral tests, all carried out before the testing board. There are no written tests at the two lower levels.

Having defined the training requirement as the absolute minimum necessary for the execution of the job of Port Operator, it would seem prima facie that in order to qualify, the trainee must attain all the objectives. On further examination however, this point is a little unreasonable, because not all the objectives are of equal importance. Therefore under a 100% attainment rule, it would be possible for a trainee to fail to qualify, because he gained 59% instead of 60% in one of the less important objectives. To forestall this potential weakness in the testing process, the objectives have been placed into two groups, one consisting of critical objectives and the other of the remainder, or desirable objectives. Failure in any one of the key objectives, or in more than 15% of the non-key objectives, constitutes overall failure to qualify.

CONCLUSION

It can thus be seen that the study followed the ideal pattern of a systematic approach, in that it was possible to start by looking at the job, and then allow the results of each stage to decide logically the content of the one subsequent to it. The study has resulted in a new trade structure and a considerable reduction in training time. A difficulty encountered throughout was the problem of overcoming resistance to change, and the reluctance to depart from traditional methods. Some time was spent in persuading those responsible for the planning and management of training that existing methods could be improved.

In the promulgation of these training modules, a package has been produced for each trade level, to include in one folder, a syllabus comprising a summary of the required training and a master program, a complete set of training objectives with explanatory notes, and rules for testing. It is at the testing stage that one can best judge the willingness and ability of the instructional staff to accept and put into practice the concept of really objective training.

An important lesson learnt was that a high degree of co-operation is required between those involved in course design, and the instructors who will implement the results of the study, and also the potential employees of the students. Not all course designers have the time or facilities to adopt this joint approach but the results of this study show that the time and effort expended on it have been justified.

REFERENCE

Sullivan (1969) Royal Air Force Education Bulletin, 6, 33

APPENDIX A

19. Operation of the following types of mechanical handling equipment:

	DRIVERS			
	Not required	Familiar	Expert	Derived Attainment Level
Commercial Fork Lifts	0	53	47	M2
Rough Terrain Fork Lifts	0	53	47	M2
Truck Mounted Cranes	6	42	52	M1
Rough Terrain Cranes	18	47	35	M3
Ships' Winches	0	47	53	M1
Ships' Cranes	6	53	41	M2
Quay Cranes	12	47	41	M2
Rail Mounted Cranes	23	53	24	C
Heavy Lift Cranes	23	53	24	C
Mobile Wheeled Cranes	12	53	35	C
Container Side Loader	12	65	23	M3
Others (specify below)				

APPENDIX B

ATTAINMENT LEVELS			QUESTIONNAIRE RESPONSES (percentages of total responses)		
Practical	Cognitive	Psychomotor	Not required	Familiar	Expert
Expert	Essential	Automatic	NA	NA 40%	60%+ 50%+
Effective	Important	Co-ordinated		71%+ 70%+ 65% 60% 50% 40%	20% 25% 30% 40% -50%
Trained	Background	Continuous		70% -65% -60% -50% -40%	-20% -25% -30% -40% -50%
	Not required		+50%		

131

APPENDIX C

TRAINING OBJECTIVES - PORT OPERATOR BIII BASIC TRAINING

1. **Training Objective No 8**

2. **Performance.** To operate a steam winch.

3. **Constraints and Test Conditions.** (a) In accordance with Instructor's Training Guide No 3. (b) Given a CLARKE and CHAPMAN steam winch. (c) In the process of stowing and discharging cargo. (d) By day.

4. **Test Standards.** (a) Without damage or loss to any part of the cargo, ship, gear or equipment. (b) Without causing injury or risk of injury to personnel. (c) The students must ensure that the runner does not become entangled on the drum. (d) Interpreting hand signals correctly.

INSTRUCTOR TRAINING GUIDE

Serial No 3	**Method** Demonstration and Practice		
Training Objective No 7 & 8	**Time**	Hrs	Mins
References	Theory		
Training Aids & Other Equipment	Practical	2	00
Steam Winch on landships	**Total**	2	00
Electric Winch landships			

Serial	Learning Points	References
1.	**Hand Signals** (a) Hoisting (b) Lowering	
2.	**Electric Winches** (a) Relevant Components: (1) Winch drum (2) Winch barrel (3) Foot brake (4) Control switch (5) Barrel release lever (b) Operation of control switch (c) Operation of foot brake to control winch speed (d) Attaching runner to winch and correct method of running on (e) Operation of hand release lever and its use (f) Safety precautions	
3.	**Steam Winch** (a) Relevant Components: (1) Winch drums (2) Winch barrel (3) Foot brake (4) Throttle (5) Reversing lever (6) Drain cocks (7) Gear change levers and pins (b) Draining winch (c) Single and double gear (d) Throttle control (e) Reversing (f) Attaching runner (g) Use of steam to ease back loads (h) Frost precautions (j) Safety precautions	
	Safety Rules (a) Always ensure that the control lever is returned to stop in the case of power failure. (b) When steam has been shut off and the winch drained, always ensure that the throttle is closed. (c) Never remove the guards from the winch gearing.	
	NOTE One hour fifteen minutes is allocated to formal training of winch driving. Further training will be received by students during practical stowage as indicated in Training Guide No 7.	

APPENDIX D

TRAINING OBJECTIVES - PORT OPERATOR AII

1. **Training Objective No 3**

2. **Performance**

   To organise and supervise the snatching of a Wheeled GS Scammel 20 ton 6 x 6.

3. **Constraints and Test Conditions**

   (a) In the Marchwood Freighter.
   (b) In accordance with Instructor's Training Guide No 3.
   (c) Given fellow students as available manpower.

4. **Test Standards**

   (a) The cargo must be moved through a distance of 10 feet from a position directly beneath the hatchway to a position in the corner of the hold.

   (b) This must be achieved without damage to the cargo, ship or gear, and without injury or risks of injury to personnel.

   (c) The task must be achieved within 30 mins.

   (d) The available manpower must be allocated as follows:
   (1) Winches (2) Runners (3) Snatch Block (4) Hatchman

   (e) The student must ensure by good supervision that the Rules of Safety as laid down in Instructor's Training Guide No 1 (Port Operator BIII) are observed by all.

The Use of Objectives in Course Design
G H WACE

A great deal is written and spoken about objectives in education and training — my excuse for adding to this literature is not to describe new ways of setting objectives, but to show how their use in running short courses can affect the design of the course and the methods of instruction.

There are two widely quoted authorities on this subject, namely B S Bloom, who has dealt with educational objectives, and Robert Mager, whose methods and ideas have a bias towards industrial and Armed Forces training. In this paper we are concerned with the application of Mager's methods to the training of adults in industry.

Mager remarks that if you don't know where you are going you are liable to end up some place else. Bloom, in more conventional phrasing, says that educational objectives are explicit formulations of the ways in which students are expected to be changed by the education process.

While in the courses that we designed we used Mager's techniques, Bloom's definition is at the heart of the reasons for using objectives as a method of designing courses.

Conventional teaching preparation has laid great stress on the organization of instructor behaviour — well prepared lesson notes will specify the headings for the instructor to talk to, the visual aids to be used, and the moment to use them. This preparation provides an almost complete description of the behaviour of the instructor.

But what of the behaviour of the student? Objectives, in Bloom's and Mager's sense, describe desired student or trainee behaviour.

Defining trainee behaviour immediately defines the type of course which is to be given, and, within reasonably close limits, the way in which it is to be run.

For instance, take this simple example, from a course on decimalisation training:

> "The trainee will be able to give the correct £p
> change when mixed £sd and £p coins are tendered."

Straightaway, the course becomes largely a question of role playing, in 'customer' and 'salesgirl' roles.

The behaviour of the trainee has been defined — as yet no mention or consideration of what the trainer does. The trainer is now free to give his imagination rein as to how he will organize and achieve the student behaviour — very different from the situation in which the instructor's behaviour is constrained, and the trainee's imagination is left free to roam, often not on the subject.

In fact, in the example quoted, the trainer first provided the course with a brief programmed text to study on £p and £sd conversion, and then provided the 'customers' with price slips and details of the mixed coinage they should offer, while he walked round checking results and acting as adviser and monitor in cases of difficulty.

Although this is a simple case, it makes the point which is very frequently neglected, namely the need to organize **all** the trainee's time and activities completely in accordance with the stated objective.

In the case quoted, the behaviour was clear and could be elicited fully. But what of situations, such as frequently occur in management training, where the behaviour is too complex to be fully elicited? Let us take a course of this kind.

The course lasts two days and is called 'An Introduction to the use of Programmed Learning'. The trainees are industrial training officers on a two month course, who may be expected to have some experience of training, though little or none of programmed learning.

The general aim of such a course (as part of a larger course) is stated by the organizer to be that the trainees shall be able to identify situations in their own firms when programmed learning could be used effectively and economically. Because of the wide range of companies represented on the course, and the very variable situations in which each trainee could find himself, to achieve this kind of behaviour in two days is clearly quite impossible.

At this stage the course designer must ask himself, with this target population, and within two days, what trainee behaviour consonant with the general aim can reasonably be expected to be achieved?

If the trainees are to be able to recognize situations when programmed learning can be applied, then clearly, they must know what programmed learning is. They can be expected, from what is learnt in the remainder of the course, and from their professional experience, to recognize the characteristics of a training situation.

Thus the objective is set:

"At the end of the course each member will, in syndicate, have set objectives, planned, written and successfully validated a short program."

The time and activities of the trainee are thus clearly defined — he will spend two days in writing and testing a program. The overall course design is set — syndicate work, obviously with assistance and discussion with the course tutor.

If the most economical course is to be designed then only that information needed to fulfil the objectives should be given to the trainee. How is the tutor to assess what information each trainee needs? All are different, with different information needs.

The tutor will 'prime the pump' by giving the trainees sufficient information to start the first step of the process, in this case setting objectives for pre-determined subjects for a program. Once objectives have been set and discussed with the tutor, the syndicates are told to plan their program.

At this stage they have not been given much detail on program planning, and the tutor has to be alert to the information needs of each syndicate for preparing their plans. He gives, at each stage, just the information that he is asked for, or that in his judgement the syndicate needs, to prepare the plan. The same tactic is pursued in frame writing. Each syndicate endeavours to write a frame — as they run into difficulties the tutor gives simple examples of a frame, with straightforward rules for writing one.

During the course of these tutorial activities, small group discussions will spring up spontaneously, directly related to the task in hand, but usually with a strong bias toward the syndicate members individual interests. These discussions are based on understanding of the process, as far as it has gone, and thus much more specific and meaningful than a large group discussion of the conventional kind following a lecture.

Finally, a short briefing describing the structure of a validation is given, and the syndicate left to devise their own validations (usually using members of other syndicates) and to report back results in full session.

Careful guidance and pacing by the tutor is essential to ensure that all syndicates are brought to a stage of success and to a success which they can see that their own efforts have brought about.

The course objectives are, of course, given out at the beginning of the course, and by this method all trainees can see that they have achieved the course objectives by their own efforts, and have at the same time, obtained an insight into the problems and techniques of the programmer.

No formal criterion test is necessary after such a course, as the whole course has been a working out of the criterion behaviour.

Because the overall aim of the course has been related to trainee's behaviour outside the course, it is necessary to ensure some way of checking that the attainment of the course objective does result in the desired behaviour change in the job itself. If it does not, then clearly the course objective needs reconsidering. At least one knows precisely what behaviour it is that is being reconsidered.

Method of presentation: Tape-slide

Summary of Discussions in Module 1

This module was concerned with curriculum analysis and development. It was felt that there was suspicion and unease about educational technology amongst both teachers and curriculum developers. This seemed to arise partly from a fear that curricula developed on the basis of a precise specification of objectives might be too restricted and not sufficiently open-ended. This led to discussions on the nature and origins of objectives and their relation to the context and form of subject matter, and there was a feeling that study and discussion of almost a philosophical nature was required to clarify thinking about objectives. This in turn high-lighted the problem of language. Educational technologists tend to develop a language with fairly precise definitions which is regarded by the 'grass roots' teacher as jargon, and the attempt to clarify and define one's meaning of terms thus becomes a barrier instead of an aid to communication.

Members expressed a commonly held view that increase use of educational technology could lead to a depersonalization of teaching, and that the progress from (teacher's) **lap** to (language) **lab** could strike at the roots of the teacher-pupil relationship. At the school level it was felt that some clarification of roles was needed between teachers, subject experts, educational technologists, programmers and so on.

The problem of roles and attitudes was also considered to be criticial in further education and in industrial training — must students be persuaded to use new aids and methods ? How can information be disseminated ? Do teachers and trainers need convincing of the value of defining objectives, analyzing skills, etc ? One area in which teachers' attitudes might be moulded — or modified — was in teacher-training.

At FE and industrial level there was a suggestion that management training is more difficult to define or specify than operator objectives, partly because of the problem of designing training for **future** as opposed to current activity.

The overall picture within this module was of a realization that the applications of educational technology to curriculum development posed a wide range of problems, from the meanings of words and the nature of objectives to the modification of attitudes of teachers and learners.

Module 2
Selection of methods and media
Posing the Problems*
R E B BUDGETT

It seems to be a common experience that to achieve success with the innovation of educational technology you must solve a learning problem; preferably
someone else's rather than your own, so that knowledge of educational technology can be spread. It therefore seems appropriate to open this session
by raising a few problems in that area of our technology which concerns the
selection of methods and media.

For me this is a relatively easy task. There are plenty of problems and
I am not expected to provide solutions, nor even to discuss them fully. That
is your task in the group discussions that follow. All that I hope to achieve
is to stimulate some thought about the papers that have been selected for this
module and to give some leads from which the discussions can start.

All good educational technologists have a model of the system to which
they work and in these models the selection of methods and media usually
takes its place in the sequence after the terminal objectives have been defined
and the test procedures established. Professor Reid, when writing on this
subject for those in Higher Education (Reid, 1969) has said that "Educational
Technology proper must be based on the behavioural sciences ..... not on
equipment". Therefore it behoves us to have a form of analysis based on
such a science which will enable us to select the right method and device for
a specific learning objective.

Romiszowski has described methods for doing this and reported success
with teachers' courses (Romiszowski, 1970). But a question which seems to
be in many people's minds is 'Does it work in practice, in the classroom or
the workshop?'.

In an interim report on the work with which he is currently engaged at
Glasgow University, Mr Dunn has provided me with a statement that is appropriate for discussion in this session. It would seem to question all that I

---

*The views expressed in this paper are those of the author and are not
  necessarily shared by the Ministry of Defence)

have said so far, for it reads "In the design of courses and the selection of media, it is a naive view that the objectives are developed independently of the selection of the instructional medium". It is suggested that we cycle this part of the system making better approximations each time, but, since we must exploit the instructional medium to the maximum, the instructional objectives will be affected.

A similar view was expressed to me recently by a colleague engaged in course design, who conscientiously applies the principles of educational technology in a systematic manner. He admitted that, as much as he wanted to select his methods and media by paying due regard to behavioural analysis, in the end he had to be content with using educational technology to make the best use of the resources already available.

This statement highlights one of the major problems of putting a systematic approach to course design into practice. There are other systems with which it has to interact and their time scales are different. So that, though our design shows that a particular resource is required, our budget or our supply system will not allow us to obtain it. Is this not everybody's problem? It is certainly so with naval course design teams. Using such staff as we can make available for design tasks, we find that we cannot start on a specific project until about two years before the course is to be run. Yet, like all public departments, decisions about supplies of some equipment, which will certainly affect the methods and media to be used in the course, and also the instructional objectives, have to be made about three years before the course is run. (This is to allow training devices to be produced in parallel with operational equipment.) Thus some decisions on methods and media must be made well before the analysis.

At least we know that we are not alone in the problem of applying systematic methods to course design. The recent descriptions of the design and production methods of the Open University given by Professor Lewis (1971) show that attempts to be systematic are often thwarted by human factors as well as by the shortcomings of other systems.

Evaluation is an essential part of educational technology and a model for an instructional system should show the need to test the course design. Yet we all know the difficulties that we encounter if we have to change any part of the design as a result of unfavourable feedback during testing. To this end it is salutary to read the recent account by Connors (1972) of the testing of the Open University's course design. In this he described the constraints of the system, which are such that the television component of a course has often to be recorded long before the correspondence unit, with which it is associated, has gone to press. These differences in production methods for each medium must surely influence the instructional objectives assigned to each.

Taking into account the peculiarities of a television company and a publishing house is probably not what Professor Reid meant by "basing our methods on behavioural science", so perhaps it is right, as Mr Dunn has suggested to me, that the selection of the medium is just as likely to affect the instructional objectives as the objectives affect the selection of the medium. It would be interesting to know the affect on the course design of the constraints of radio in an educational series such as those broadcast by the BBC. Perhaps there are some members of this conference with experience in radio, who will be able to contribute to the group discussions which follow and thus enlighten us.

However, there must be many at this conference to whom the matter of course design is much more personal than to the teams designing an Open University course, a BBC Education series, or the training course for the maintenance of a future naval weapon system. For them the papers of interest will be those submitted by practising teachers, like Mr Draisma working with rural African children in Mathematics, or Dr Buckingham with university students in Engineering Science.

This is not the first occasion on which at an APLET conference we have gathered to consider the problems of fitting the right methods and media into a learning system. The previous gathering, however, was much smaller; one of the working groups that met during the London conference of 1969. This group was considering the use of audio-visual aids in Programmed Learning, for in 1969 our field of view was only just widening to a system of Educational Technology encompassing all media and methods. Nevertheless it is perhaps worth looking at this group's report in order to judge if any progress has been made in the last three years (Aspects of Educational Technology III, 1969).

The report contained three main statements of which the first referred to the difficulties of communication between the research and operational fields. This resulted in teachers and course designers having to make decisions based largely on economic and practical factors, rather than on research findings. The group hoped that something would be done to bridge this gap. Has something been done in the last three years, at least within this conference? I leave you to judge from the discussions which follow.

You may also care to consider the other statements from this working group. The second was that the control of future trends (in audio-visual aids) would still lie in the hands of manufacturers, who were influenced by needs broader than those of learning. When we come to select a particular audio-visual device, are we still too dependent on those designed for the leisure rather than for the learning industry?

The third statement was that the situation would not improve until more guidance on the selection of methods and media was given to teachers and instructors during their training. Perhaps there has been this improvement already; at least there appear to be more departments of educational technology at Colleges of Education in 1972 than there were in 1969. The papers by Clarke and Leedham in this section are indicative of the developments that have taken place, so perhaps at the end of this session we will reach conclusions which will show some of the improvements desired by the 1969 working group.

For me one of the biggest problems has been that of innovation. One must select a method or medium which is acceptable to the students and, often more important, to the management. Let me conclude with a brief example. At the 1969 conference we described an application of audio-programming to Marine Engineering training (Budgett & Moore, 1969), in which tape-recorders were used in ships' engine rooms. Three years later the program is still in use, but it is now presented in text form with equal results. This change of medium was caused partly by the disorientation experienced by the trainees when moving in a ship's engine room while wearing muffed head phones, and partly by the difficulty experienced by the management in replicating and updating tapes.

In this field of learning duplicated texts are easier to manage and furthermore the trainees like a 'book' to take away for reference. However, I am sure that if we had tried to start the project with texts rather than tapes, we would have had difficulties in having the scheme accepted.

Here then are some of the problems, which you may care to discuss during the next part of this session, concerning the selection of methods and media in relation to aims and objectives:

a) Is enough attention being paid to the results of research in this field?
b) Is it practicable to base the selection purely on behavioural analysis?
c) Should we be content to use Educational Technology simply to make best use of the resources already available?
d) Can the objectives be developed independently of the instructional medium? (Dunn)
e) Are we justified in using an acceptable method in the first instance rather than the best?

It was suggested to me recently that many educational technologists are not sufficiently 'hardware-orientated'. I found this comment both disturbing and refreshing. Disturbing because in my experience many are content to deal with the intricacies of audio-visual devices rather than consider the broader aspects of the system; refreshing because it suggested that there are other places where the tide has changed. I hope that if I now stop this dissertation the ensuing discussion will provide the answer to this and other problems.

REFERENCES

Budgett, R. E. and Moore, J. D. S. (1969) 'Audio-programming for Marine
Engineering Training in the Royal Navy'. Aspects of Educational Techno-
logy III (Ed) A. P. Mann and C. K. Brunstrom. Pitman, London
Connors, B. (1972) 'Testing innovations in course design'. British Journal
of Educational Technology, **3**, No.1
Lewis, B. N. (1971) 'Course production at the Open University'. British
Journal of Educational Technology, **2**, No.3
Reid, R. L. (1969) 'Educational Technology: the background and the need'.
In 'Media and Methods' (Ed) Unwin. McGraw-Hill
Report of working group in the use of audio-visual aids in programmed
learning. Aspects of Educational Technology III (Ed) A. P. Mann and
C. K. Brunstrom. Pitman, London. Page 394
Romiszowski, A. J. (1970) 'The use of classifications, algorithms and
checklists as aids to the selection of instructional methods and media'.
Aspects of Educational Technology IV (Ed) A. C. Bajpai and J. F. Leedham.
Pitman, London

The Derivation of Programmed Lessons from Recorded Protocols

GARY M BOYD

In the next decade we can look forward to the widespread availability of audio-visual teaching machines (eg Sintra's MITSI or BASF's system 3400) and the less expensive (£300) forms of computer terminals for CAI (eg KSR33 teletype or any one of a number of acoustic coupled keyboard units which use regular TV sets for display purposes — LEK111, Lektromedia Co., Montreal).

A large proportion of the programs for these machines will have to be modified or made by the user-institutions, since universal standardization is both politically impossible and pedogogically undesirable.

The main problems to be faced lie not with the hardware, but in the provision of properly validated study materials suited to the particular students at hand. An elementary school library of less than four thousand volumes would be considered inadequate today; in a few years a library of instructional programs of fewer than several thousand cassettes will seem equally inadequate.

Already in the instructional film and television fields the lack of adequate quantities of suitable program material is acute. In particular, animated film is probably the most satisfactory way to present many concepts in science, engineering and mathematics. Unfortunately, animated film is rather expensive to produce, and instructional programs frequently make do instead with videotapes of someone talking at a flip-chart.

If we turn to the field of programmed instruction, CAI, and teaching machines, again the bottleneck turns out to be lack of properly validated well produced programs.

An hour of instruction — whether it be PI, television A-V language lab, or CAI seems to require between one hundred and four hundred hours of professional time to produce and validate, just to start with — all the other usual commercial production and distribution costs also apply.

Can a computer based system be developed to reduce the media production problem to manageable size while still turning out good material? There are a number of research projects relevant to this question: the SDC language

PLANIT (Feingold, 1968) when used in the author mode, does provide sub-stantial help for the production of CAI lessons by permitting and facilitating interactive dialogue between lesson designer and students during the course of lesson development. Similar modes of operation, but with less assistance from the computer are available in some other extant CAI research systems.

The work of Helmar Frank and Klaus-Dieter Graf (Graf, 1970) in Berlin is noteworthy in that they have used a computer based interactive system to develop programmed instruction materials for use in simple teaching machines. The lesson designer can try out his work on a group of 'typical' students in the course of preparing it; moreover, the system provides built-in guidance in the construction of sequences.

One may move in at least two directions from here: (a) Rouellette Smith (1969) of the University of California, Santa Barbara has recorded protocols from some hundreds of lessons conducted by (live) tutors with individual students (in the field of logic and predicate calculus) and is using these as the basis for computer simulation of tutor and student behaviour. The simulations will in turn provide a basis for the development of instructional programs. (b) at Sir George Williams we are recording protocols of tutorials and then using computer editing capabilities to produce programmed instruction and CAI lessons directly from portions of the recorded transcripts.

The next step in developing such systems is to add a video capability. With such a capability, graphics and film clips can be edited and worked into the program in the same manner that alpha-numerics are handled by PLANIT.

Direct digital editing of video and audio signals is not really feasible at present, as the required hardware is still in the research stage, and the memory requirements are vast. (A single video frame is about 10 million bits, and there are 30 frames per second.) Moreover, if the job is to be done in a real time with students on line, the problem is vastly magnified. The only feasible solution is a hybrid system with separate audio and video channels, which are, however, controlled by the digital system.

In my system at present the video and audio-visual equipment is not under direct computer control, but directions to the student such as 'go to footage 3201' on the videotape or 'go to slide three' can easily be presented where needed.

Ultimately the software of the system should incorporate some of the knowledge of the educational psychologist regarding instructional sequencing, reinforcement etc and most of the knowledge of the technical producer regard-ing continuity, graphics production, typography, audio and video signal quality control, and the digital logic and memory capability of the intended distribu-tion system (teaching machine, computer, or interactive TV).

Such a system would be suitable for producing instructional materials ranging upward from simple PI exercise books to CAI with audio-visual as well as alpha-numeric channels. It would, of course, also be suitable for research on cognitive and affective learning processes. The establishment of computer based instructional media development facilities has another advantage: it should help to close the gap between research findings and educational practice. By incorporating the results of research on learning into the operating software of the system, it should be possible to ensure reasonably well structured lessons.

The ultimate extension of this system might be one in which the software modifies itself to take into account the system's experience with learners and with different classes of subject matter, thus dispensing with the lesson design researcher altogether!

At present, freely constructed student responses and other capricious aspects of student behaviour require that a human tutor be in control — although not in any authoritarian sense; the whole point of the interactive system being to bring real students into the development picture so that their actual queries and difficulties may shape the production, and help shape future productions (Boyd, 1971a).

The system configuration which we settled on is shown schematically in Figure 1.

There are two rooms: in one the tutor is located together with his resource materials for the lesson, in the other a sample student works through the lesson. Two-way communication is by way of typewriter-like keyboards and television sets. In addition the tutor has a one-way CCTV link which enables him to show the student drawings, slides or films, and a one-way audio link for giving verbal instructions. Whatever transpires on the two-way link is recorded in a computer file. Whatever the tutor shows the student on the CCTV is recorded on videotape. Any spoken remarks made by the tutor are recorded on the audio track of the video tape.

The computer terminal used for the protocol recording generates a standard television signal and this is also recorded on the videotape in 20 second segments alternating with 20 second segments from the CCTV link.

Lessons are recorded in computer files using a control program 'SCRIBE' which records the actual times when the tutor and student start and stop each of their messages to each other. The computer is a CDC 6400 with the KRONOS time sharing operating system. SCRIBE is written in Fortran IV.

After a group of tutorials have been recorded (usually about five) the researcher-lesson designer looks over the files in the computer and identifies blocks of discourse common to all the tutorials. These are merged to form a core sequence of blocks for the tutorial program. Then attention is turned to the peculiarities of each tutorial and these are classified as to their relevance to the main objectives of the tutorial and to the characteristics of the student.

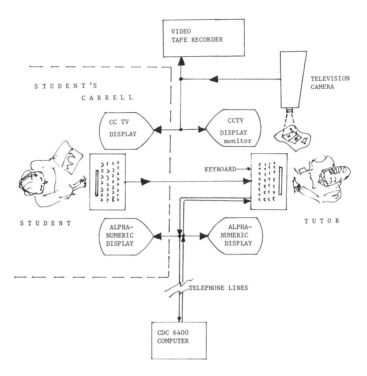

Figure 1. Protocol recording tutorial laboratory

Finally the editing facilities of the computer and of the television studio are used to prepare an instructional program from the protocols. The resultant program may be a CAI program, a program for the MITSI teaching machine, a programmed videotape, a tape-slide program or even a programmed text. To date, however, only CAI programs are being produced.

The theoretical basis for the analysis of the transcriptions of tutorials involves the four fundamental levels of control (ACTIONS or MOVES, TACTICS or PLAYS, STRATEGIES and META-STRATEGIES) identified by Boyd (1971b) and the eight types of ventures identified by Smith, Meux et al (1971).

Student characteristics relating to cognitive style as well as levels of entering knowledge and skills will be estimated from types of answers made, the response times, and number of mistakes and remediations required.

Subject matter characteristics and their relation to tactics and to modes of presentation — graphic, video, audio, alpha-numeric — are also being studied.

One of the problems in this approach is to ensure that enough variety in student characteristics and enough variety in lesson material and strategies is introduced in the sample tutorials. Eventually when some of the merging

146

is automated this problem will be partly solved by simply holding more tutorials with several different tutors dealing with the same topic (instructional objective set).

At present we are simply choosing sample students with widely variant academic records in the subject area concerned and covering a wide age range. To date the sample students are first or second year college students in 'Humanities of Science' (Science for Artsmen) or English as a second language (grammar) or Physics.

The tutors prepare a set of instructional objectives, a rough scenario for the tutorial, a collection of illustrative material and a collection of questions or problems which they deem appropriate. The students are chosen from those volunteering on the basis of the stated objectives of the tutorial and a statement that the tutorial will be transcribed for research and development work. They are usually drawn from large classes for whom the tutor normally conducts seminars or lectures.

The tutor and student complete tutorial evaluation forms similar to those used by project PLAN (Rahmlow, 1969). These are also employed by the lesson designer to aid in the merging and editing process.

At the time of writing (February 1972) it is too early to be able to give results on the comparative effectiveness of instructional programs produced by computer based transaction recording versus those produced in the usual a-priori manner. However, comparison programs are being produced in order to make an evaluation of this sort. It is also intended to use the system to design programs for MITSI or a similar teaching machine.

This project is supported by a DIGES research grant from the Government of Quebec, Canada

REFERENCES

Boyd, G.M. (1971a) In 'Fortschritte und Ergebnisse der Unterrichtstechnologie'. (Ed) B. Rollett and K Weltner. Ehrenwirth, Munich. Pages 66-68
Boyd, G.M. (1971b) In 'Aspects of Educational Technology V'. (Ed) D. Packham, A. Cleary and T. Mayes. Pitman, London. Pages 449-455
Feingold, S. (1968) Datamation, September, 41-47
Graf, K.D. (1970) In 'Zeitschrift für ersiehungswissenschaftliche Forschung, 4, 18-36
Rahmlow, H.F. (1969) In 'Developmental Efforts in Individualized Learning'. (Ed) R.A. Weissgerber. F.E. Peacock, Itasca, Illinois. Pages 53-70
Smith, B.O., Meux, M., Coombs, J., Nuthall, G. and Precians, R. (1967) 'A study of the strategies of teaching'. Bureau of Educational Research, College of Education, University of Illinois, Urbana
Smith, R.W. (1970) 'Computer simulation of teaching processes' - private communication. UC Santa Barbara, California 93106, USA

147

A System for Computer Managed Instruction

W R BRODERICK

The Royal Liberty School Computer Department is conducting a research project in the field of Computer Managed Instruction. This project is being supported by the Social Science Research Council and the Council of the London Borough of Havering. The original scheme for the Research Project was described in Broderick (1968).

Work on the Research Project started in January 1970. The present status of the work is that the first half of the teaching material has been written and tested independently of the computing system and that the computer programs are undergoing final testing independently of the teaching system. The first live runs for using both systems together are scheduled to take place in September 1972.

It is important to note that whilst the Research Team has selected Biology as the teaching topic, the system being developed is expected to be sufficiently general to enable it to handle a variety of other disciplines. In fact, Biology is an interesting subject to choose, because it is midway in the spectrum between a highly structured subject (eg Mathematics or Computing Science) and a very much less structured subject (eg Geography or Economics). It is anticipated that the techniques used for structuring the material in Biology will be equally applicable in other subject areas of this spectrum.

Teachers work with the Research Team by helping design a system to meet the real educational needs of teachers and children. Experiments are currently being conducted to find out if an experienced analyst can draw up the detailed objectives of the course (in consultation with teachers) so that teachers can themselves write material to meet these objectives. The teachers feel that it is important that a scheme should be devised whereby they can write teaching material to be used in a computer aided learning environment for it is only by doing this that the very considerable day to day experience of teachers can be brought to bear on the production of teaching material for CAI systems.

THE SYSTEM BEING DEVELOPED

The system being developed relies upon the computer to select for each individual student a work assignment from an analysis of stored information and of data about the student's abilities and attainments. The student works on this task and returns to the computer a completed questionnaire relating to the task he has completed. This is analyzed by the computer system and the most appropriate next assignment is selected for the student. Information about the student's progress is collected for the benefit of the teacher as also is information about the effectiveness of specific sections of the learning course. The student's work assignments are in fact modules of a completely structured course of instruction.

The use of the computer to control the student's path through a series of programmed tasks allows the logic of the system to be flexible, whereas with conventional teaching machines or programmed learning texts logic has to be defined from the outset and the conventional system is less adaptive therefore to individual circumstances. Further, the more passive systems are less capable (for practical reasons) of continuous updating and modification, whereas any particular learning task in a computer based course can be revised as necessary.

In practice a fully developed system is expected to work along the following lines:

1) All students will be given an initial booklet defining a structured lesson, including instruction, practical work and diagnostic tests.

2) Students will work through this booklet, record on a form or Mark Sensed Card their responses to particular questions as soon as they have finished the booklet.

3) At the end of each lesson, these response forms or cards will be collected and transmitted to the computer centre by a courier or other rapid means.

4) Upon arrival at the computer centre, the information received from the students will be processed and analyzed, then, and depending upon an analysis of these responses, the computer system will produce for the student the most suitable selection from its library of possible lessons for that student.

5) This information will be transmitted to the school and the student during his next lesson will proceed with that material. Thus repeating steps 2, 3 and 4 above.

RELATIONSHIP BETWEEN COMPUTER PROGRAMS AND TEACHING MATERIAL

In order that the educational material and the computer system could be developed independently it was necessary to define an interface between the two so that there was unambiguous understanding of the interrelationship between the computing system and the educational material. The design of this interface was one of the first tasks undertaken on the Research Project. Its design was based on an analysis of normal classroom practice and the types of responses and behaviours that a flexible computer aided learning system would be expected to use. The design of the interface is such that the interface operates on a teaching module. This teaching module is described by the designer of the educational material on a special set of forms which are capable of being directly input into the computing system. The teaching module is considered to have three parts, these parts being:

1) **The pre-requisites**: the list of behaviours which the student should have demonstrated before he tackles the learning task.

2) **The teaching material**: that is the material which will be used by the student during the learning activity; along with this there is the information which concerns Laboratory Assistants, the teachers and preparation of the lesson.

3) **Responses and Routing Information**: this section describes the responses that will be expected from the student having worked through the learning material and the information that will be required to route the student to the next most suitable learning activity.

This description of the teaching material is entered in a slightly codified manner into the computing system, which will build up the pattern of the various courses that can be taken through the network of the learning material available.

THE COMPUTER'S FILES

The computer system needs a number of files to enable it to administer the teaching system. It needs a file on the students, giving a profile of each student and a record of his or her learning history. It needs a file which describes the learning material available for the particular course in hand. This file contains all the description of the teaching material and associated information relating to interrelationships between various lessons, the responses which can be expected and the administrative information involved. The last of the files which the system keeps are files on its own behaviour. This is important during the research stage for it enables careful analysis to be made of the behaviour of various parts of the computer system during the trials. It remains to be seen whether or not this will be preserved in the final version of the system.

The computing system must firstly set up all the files required; the procedures adopted are as follows:

1) The Text Writer, who has produced the educational material prepares codified descriptions of the learning material for input into the computer. These are stored in the computer to provide the description of the learning material that will be used by the computer.

2) A description of the students, including name, school, class etc, which will enable the computer to keep a record of each individual student's learning history. From this record of the student's learning history the computer will guide the student along the most satisfactory path through the learning material.

3) Finally, the system must set up its own system's profile, so that it can record its own behaviour. Once this process has been completed the use of the system with that particular group of students and that particular learning material can start.

THE OPERATION OF THE SYSTEM

Initially the system issues the student with the pre-course test. This is a test which enables the student to start work at the most appropriate place in the learning material. Then the student answers this test and indicates his responses to the questions on a form which is converted into paper tape and input to the computer. The computer takes the student responses, analyzes his marks and scores him for each particular item in the learning material. Once this is done, the system then updates the student profile and updates the system profile. The next task is for the computer to select the most suitable work task for the student. The algorithm used for this purpose searches for an ideally suited task for the student. If one is found it is allocated, the student's record is again updated showing the new work allocated and a note is printed out for the teacher and the student showing what work is involved for the next lesson.

If the routing section cannot find an ideally suited lesson from the main stream it looks to see if there is any remedial work, which should be brought in to help the student join the main stream. The computer then allocates this and makes up the remedial lesson with a further suitable lesson to ensure that the student is occupied for the full duration of his lesson or homework.

The system may be unable to find suitable teaching material for a particular student. Under these circumstances, the teacher is notified and the student's profile and systems profile are again updated. The search for suitable teaching material is made from that which is stored in the file of teaching lessons. The teacher is automatically given information to help him or her plan his/her own lesson to enable the Laboratory Assistant to prepare apparatus etc that is needed for the lesson and to indicate to each student the results of his or her last lesson and the work that has been allocated for the next lesson. More detailed information can be requested by the teacher at any stage. For the research team, comprehensive summaries of statistics are produced and these are used to evaluate various elements of the system.

THE TYPE OF COMPUTER REQUIRED

The computer system required to run this suite of programs is typically like that used by Local Education Authorities for their normal data processing tasks. This implies that the system could be implemented by Local Education Authorities without the need to purchase expensive hardware. Furthermore, the system lends itself to being run at night. To aid the translation of the computer programs from one manufacturer's computer to another the programs are being written in a high level language (Algol 60). Resort to the use of machine language is kept to the minimum (for example on the Hewlett Packard computer less than 125 instructions are in machine code). It is hoped that the imposition of this constraint on the design of the system will help in the ultimate implementation of the system, should the research indicate that this is a worthwhile course of action.

The system appears as if it will fulfil its design objectives and also enables the teacher to run truly individualized learning projects in mixed ability classrooms.

ACKNOWLEDGMENTS

The Research Team wishes to acknowledge the support of the Social Science Research Council and the Council of the London Borough of Havering who fund this Project.

The team also wish to express their gratitude to the Biology Teachers in Havering without whose help and cooperation their work would be impossible.

REFERENCE

Broderick, W. R. (1968) An approach to Computer Aided Learning. In 'Aspects of Educational Technology' Volume 2. (Ed) Dunn and Holroyd. Methuen, London

The Development of Procedures for the Production and Distribution of Learning Resources in a College of Education

JOHN CLARKE and IAIN HUTCHISON

In late autumn 1973 the College of Education, Dundee, will be housed in new buildings if the timetable for the erection can be maintained. The original planning for the development of the new site assumed that the instructional methods would rely heavily on the conventional lecture, but that much greater weight would be placed on small tutorial group discussion. To facilitate this, each lecturer is to be provided with his own room spacious enough to accommodate a half section of students, ie a group of ten in number.

Following discussion among the College staff during the following two years, in which R H Richardson, the Principal Lecturer in Psychology played a prominent part, the possibility of placing greater emphasis on self-instruction was explored. The advisability of this latter approach eventually receive a general acceptance and modifications were made to the plan to allow the installation within the Library of approximately one hundred and fifty individual carrels. All of these study units were to have a power point and a variety of modes was to be installed so that all the media would be available to the students within the control of the individual.

The revised plan was submitted to the Scottish Education Department in February 1971. General agreement was reached on the implementation of the revised plan and the need to appoint a Co-ordinator of Learning Resources whose first task would be to carry out a detailed Feasibility Study of the venture.

My appointment took effect on 1 July 1971, and the first draft of the Feasibility Study was ready for the middle of September. It was based on the following premises:

1. The likelihood is that the demand by academic staff for the services which will speed the production of learning units will increase rapidly throughout the next five years.

2. That the enthusiasm of staff for educational technology, now aroused, will suffer a serious setback if immediate provision is not made to meet basic production requirements.

3. That the production of 'software' (programs/films etc) must go ahead

with all speed during the next two years to ensure its availability when we take over the new building and its built-in 'hardware' (technical equipment).

4. That all the learning units in 1 above are likely to contain printed and, possibly, photographic elements and most will use audio tapes.

5. That access to the learning units is likely to demand increasingly de-centralized technical facilities.

6. That control of the learning units ideally must be with the individual student or group and not with some distant operator.

7. That positive attitudes of students and staff towards educational technology will depend greatly on the ready availability and continuous serviceability of the technical equipment.

8. That a course on educational technology will eventually form a part of the College course for at least all three-year diploma students and for a percentage of all other students.

9. That such a course (8) will necessitate the provision of work areas for students which will be continuously available for preparatory activities.

10. That CCTV will be used increasingly to provide inserts for learning units and that many (if not most) of these will be produced away from the College site, quite possibly on film stock.

11. That most CCTV equipment to be purchased must be colour compatible.

12. That the proposed Library provision will be insufficient to cater for student requirements within five years and therefore a planned extension to provide a comprehensive Resource Centre is of immediate concern.

13. That there will be a demand for in-service training and use of College facilities to help established teachers and curriculum development groups.

14. That by 1975/76 the student population may number 1800, of whom 1000 may be three-year diploma students.

A working definition of educational technology was taken to be 'a systematic approach to learning and not solely the use of software and hardware'.

The aim for the implementation of the techniques of educational technology was that all students would eventually work for about one-fifth of their time with self-instructional units, but that an all out effort would be made to enable one-tenth of all students' time to be so occupied. For a College of sixteen hundred students with a timetabled working week of twenty-five hours and an academic year of twenty weeks (excluding teaching practice and examinations) even the latter aim requires the production of eighty thousand hours of self-instructional material for each year, a figure which gives some idea of the immensity of the task. Clearly, many units will be used by large groups of students and one hour's self-instructional time may in reality be only forty minutes, considerations which will give a more realistic figure, but to produce and maintain a balance between production on the one hand and availability and access on the other is a highly complex procedure.

PRODUCTION FACILITIES

Production requirements can be deduced from the initial premises. There will be four main provisions:

1. a printing capability
2. the production of audio tapes
3. the production of photographic stills
4. the production of motion pictures

PRINTING

The printing facility had to be capable of the production of a wide range of aids at an economical rate both in terms of materials and staff time. The general needs of the College, eg administration, also had to be taken into account, hence the equipment had to be versatile and each item justifiable in economic terms.

The following seemed to be the likely production runs for the printing unit:

1. small numbers (ten to fifteen) of multi-page booklets and programs;
2. large numbers (three hundred to two thousand) of general handouts;
3. large numbers (three hundred to four thousand) of information bulletins;
4. very large numbers (two thousand to ten thousand) of trial materials for Curriculum Development Centres attached to the College.

(each of the quantities above refers to any one item)

The printing process was to be offset and lack of space in our printing room ruled out any but console machines which require little floor space. The main requirement clearly was for presses which could be in more or less continuous action throughout the year. Reliability was a main criteria, cost secondary to this. After much investigation we purchased two Rotaprint machines, an RA4 and an RA4/QC, the latter a systems machine with automatic blanket wash, a feature which speeds the whole process of short runs of large numbers of plates.

The three plate makers were chosen with four criteria in mind; cost of machine, cost of plate, versatility of machine, and speed of production. The first machine is an electrostatic copier which is both a document copier and a paper plate maker. A range of such machines is available to educational users at prices which vary between £400 and £600. Document copies, A4 in size, can be produced for about 1.4p and paper plates for 3.25p. Each document copy or paper plate takes twelve to fifteen seconds to produce, and there is a reasonable latitude for exposure times to gain acceptable document copies. An electrostatic paper plate will produce about one hundred and fifty acceptable printed copies, the paper cost for each being one-tenth of a penny. One hundred printed copies of a document can thus be produced for about 18p including cleaning fluids etc. This figure compares very favourably with the rate for one hundred copies of any metered copying system.

This type of machine enables the production of short runs of multiple plates. So, booklets or programmes can be provided at an economic cost with a minimal demand on the time of the printing staff. We can also use it to produce short runs of any copied original, the plate taking only a few seconds to prepare at a cost of about one-third of an electro-stencil.

The second plate maker is a Rapilith and cost £650. It works on the same principle as a process camera, the plate produced being a reversed negative. This process gives up to one thousand to fifteen hundred very clean copies from each plate. The cost of each plate is approximately 8p. Thus we are able to provide handout material of a good quality for the entire College population at a very economic rate in terms of materials and time. Each plate takes about three minutes to produce by this method and it is then put onto the RA4/QC machine giving a very rapid turnover of plates.

The third plate maker is a CT (chemical transfer) machine, cost £240, with which we can produce a paper or metal plate from an original in about four minutes. Processed paper plates have been costing about 23p and metal 30p, but we are hoping to reduce each of these costs by about one-third in the near future. The paper plates will give runs in excess of two thousand, the metal upwards of ten thousand.

With these three plate makers we can cover all our needs, including the very long runs of materials required by the Curriculum Development Centres attached to the College for field trial purposes. The system is both versatile, economic and (we hope) reliable. The latter is difficult to predict as we have been operational for six weeks only and in this period the operators have been both under training and trouble shooting to clear a few initial teething faults.

The two printing machines cost £3,500 but to set against this initial cost we expect our throughput in the first year to exceed three million sheets of paper. On the other hand, the offset process can be installed for about one-third of this cost if demands to be made on the unit are not at this level. Two table-top machines, at a cost of about £650 each could give a reliable service and could be operated by office staff as all the setting up procedures are automatic.

I had hoped that a printer and trainee, with the occasional assistance of two of the office staff, would be able to keep going a flow of work. This has not been possible as our office staff are already fully occupied and so we will be taking on two additional trinees so that all three will be able to take advantage of the ten weeks in the year of block release during which they can continue their education and their training.

Type setting

The quality of any printing plate is entirely dependent on the standard of type on the original. Layout, clarity of characters and choice of type faces all contribute to the presentation and to achieve a high standard for all our learning resource material we use an IBM composing machine and consultative practices among the graphics, composing and printing staff. In the near future we hope to appoint a Production Manager whose task will be to supervise all aspects of production and assembly of finished units. He will also have the responsibility for ensuring that all print matter achieves the high standard we seek.

AUDIO TAPE

Many, if not most, of the learning units we are to produce will have an audio tape as one element. Production of these must be speedy and require little if any skilled technical attention, so a high speed dubbing machine has been purchased. The master will be produced by a lecturer on spool to spool tape and this will be dubbed onto compact cassettes. The machine we have ordered will dub four cassettes at a time, either four taking two half tracks or four taking two outside quarter tracks so that it will be possible to transfer simultaneously the commentary and synchronizing pulses for tape/slide units. The cost of the dubbing machine, a rewind machine (for dubbing machines cannot rewind also) and a demagnetizing unit was about £1,900.

STILL PHOTOGRAPHY

At present our main requirement for still photographs is for thirty-five millimetre transparencies. However, in the absence of much research evidence on the relative values of the different stills media, we will be experimenting with a variety of presentations of the same learning units in an endeavour to discover student preferences and the most effective formats.

To speed the production of visuals in close association with textual material, we have installed a process camera. This will give us screened prints which can be quickly pasted-up to form originals which can be copied by any of the plate makers. The production of programs made up of text, audio tape and slides will thus be quickly paralleled by the same units consisting of text with photographs and audio tapes. These will be produced readily in large numbers by this method, a procedure which would be much more difficult to set up if single prints had to be hand mounted onto each page.

However, one aspect of stills, colour, cannot readily be reproduced economically by the printing process so colour slides will remain an important element in all our work. Duplication of slides is done using a Bowens copier but if large numbers of copies are required we employ commercial services.

MOTION PICTURES

The need for motion pictures brought about a consideration of all the aspects of non-still visuals as a general problem. The main variables to be considered for motion pictures are:

1. Film
2. If (1), which format — super 8mm or 16mm?
3. If (1), which mode of projection — spool to spool, loop, cartridge loaded, tele-cine?
4. CCTV
5. If (4), which format — 2 inch, 1 inch, $\frac{1}{2}$ inch?
6. If (4), which mode of display — live, spool to spool, video cassette?
7. If (4), which method of distribution — distribution centre to group viewing areas, mass audience, small groups, possibly within a Department requiring talkback to a central control, small group, individual?
8. If (1) or (4), is there a colour requirement?
9. If (1), is sound required?
10. If (9) is yes, is this lip-sync?
11. If (1) or (4), does the finished product form part of a package?

To achieve an effective and economic result in any one case, I believed that the production needed to be scripted carefully from the outset. A film director was therefore appointed and his experience in both film and television work is proving extremely valuable. As our main requirements would be for short films, either cine or television, the need for a mobile unit was inescapable, but that such a unit should be highly sophisticated and, hence, highly expensive did not seem to follow. More important, I believed, were portability and simplicity. The requirement was for a production unit which could be taken anywhere, either in College or outside, and particularly into schools, and able to be controlled by one director. Two cameras should provide adequate coverage with a highly directional sound facility sufficient to record the important track on location, background tracks being mixed in in the static studio. If colour was an important aspect of production, film would be used and the result distributed eventually via tele-cine. Thus I hope to provide a comprehensive motion picture facility. The static studio mainly will be used to produce composite programs, most being dubbed onto one inch video tapes or half inch cassettes.

Distribution and access

The production unit will provide materials both for general lectures and for self-instruction. In the new College, the former in motion picture form will be made available via a video distribution system which will be fed by a number of video tape recorders housed in a central control room. Mobile video cassette recorders will also serve the same purpose, the balance between the two being established as a result of experience.

Self-instruction will need to be under individual control and carrels, designed and tested within the College, will be housed in some Departments and in the Resource Centre. Twelve versions of the prototype have been made and we now seek critical comments from the students on both their general design and the installation of the different types of equipment (Figure 1).

The basic design of the carrel is that of a working surface contained within three walls. A large proportion of the two hundred and fifty eventually to be placed in the Resource Centre will be as shown in the illustration. The compartment on the left houses the projection equipment, either Kodak Carousel or a hand loaded and operated slide/film strip projector. One section of the table top lifts to raise the screen and another to give access to the projector compartment. The shelf will carry the television monitor and video cassette recorder for those which are to be equipped with the Philips model. The Ampex model we hope will fit into the projection compartment.

All the carrels are still very much at the experimental stage. Throughout the coming year we will be trying different switching systems and means of housing projectors and displaying slide pictures.

Audio replay units also are being tested, five different versions at present being fitted into different carrels. For many programs we will require

Figure 1. Student seated at prototype of Dundee Carrel

LECTURER:	REFERENCE NO.

DESCRIPTION OF WORK:

IS COPYRIGHT CLEARANCE REQUIRED?   YES........ NO........

NO. OF SIDES TO ORIGINAL	NO. OF COPIES REQUIRED ....

Typing Instructions:– Spacing Single .... One and a Half .... Double ....   Could this work be required again YES .... NO ....

PRINTING INSTRUCTIONS:– Single Side........... Double Side..........

SPECIAL INSTRUCTIONS:–

DATE REQUIRED:–	AUTHORISATION:–

TICK (✔) AS REQUIRED

FOR OFFICE USE:–

TYPED BY ....   CHECKED BY:– ....

COST RATE:–   NO. OF PLATES USED ....   TYPE OF PLATES USED ....

TYPE OF PAPER:–   AMOUNT OF PAPER USED:–

TIME	Compositor	Graphics	Printer	Audio Tape	Photographer	Television	TOTAL COST:–

Figure 2. Form used to originate Learning Resources at Dundee College of Education

synchronized slide projection and automatic stop of the replay unit. We await
delivery of two prototypes with these provisions.

Production Control

The production units are spread throughout the present building and even in
the new building the position will not be greatly improved. It is essential,
therefore, that a method of control is devised which will speed production
and allow the costing of each exercise with a minimum of effort. The form
shown above has been designed to do this (Figure 2). Pads of these forms
are supplied to all Departments and one form accompanies each original or
request for the production of a learning unit. To initiate the production of
such a unit, I arrange a meeting with the lecturer who is in charge of the project. When the general aim, specific objectives and the media have been
decided, I issue action slips to the technicians involved and a more general
meeting is called to discuss procedures. Production can then go ahead, the
action slips being returned to my administration control with the finished
product(s) to allow costing and delivery of the unit(s) to the lecturer. Only
experience will give us the balance required for the administration. To over-
administer could prove to be very costly, to under-administer could be disastrous, creating ill-will among the academic staff and a cynical attitude
towards the development of educational technology.

The Use of CCTV in Schools.
An Account of Leicestershire
Experimentation since 1964
J LEEDHAM

INTRODUCTION

The use of closed circuit television in schools is customarily dismissed as
too expensive, except for large urban authorities. Thus, cities such as
London and Glasgow install large networks linking their schools to central
studios and make a case for use of the installations on various grounds, sometimes implying that such situations can save teachers and help with shortages.
With a more plentiful teacher supply this is not now necessarily a firm case.
Moreover, the use of such systems of replay or creation appear to be denied
to the County Rural Authorities whose schools are widespread and cannot be
linked by closed systems. Such considerations were those which exercised
the Leicestershire Authority as early as 1964 and the account which follows
represents coverage of the experiments which have been undertaken.

EARLY APPROACHES

A committee under the chairmanship of Andrew Fairbairn, now County Director, met to consider the implications of setting up closed circuit television in
schools. The committee visited the installation which operated in the Engineering School at the Leicester University. This was a very early simple
installation laid in by Thorn Electronics which permitted cameras and monitors to operate within a building on each of its four floors. The Leicestershire
Authority invited the County High Schools to submit requests and reasons for
installing such a system in their own buildings. From the applications they
elected to put closed circuit systems into two of the schools, each on a
developing campus. In Leicestershire, school campuses often consist of
High Schools which contribute to an Upper School on the same site. One of
such sites is at Birstall and another at Oadby. At each site in 1965 one High
School was fitted with CCTV. Hindsight suggests that the wiring system employed was too complex and thus too little used to enable any real conclusion
to be drawn about these first stages and experiences. It is perhaps fair to
say that a good deal of keen anticipation was blunted because of apparatus

which proved difficult to link up, and to be of doubtful serviceability.

In 1966, the author moved to Loughborough College, with a grant from the Rank Organization which was applied to the investigation of CCTV land links. Landlines were laid around the College by private contract and also to a neighbouring school. It is noteworthy that the cost of the landlines which have remained constantly reliable were done by private tender at one-fifth of the GPO quotation. Transmissions on the landlines used an RF system (10.66 MHz) with sound superimposed so that normal RF monitors could be used. With the purchase of a small Bedford van it was possible to set up cameras, modulator and to broadcast satisfactorily given time (one hour) and two technicians. The County Authority then matched this situation by paying for the installation of similar landlines and connections on three other campuses; but no further landline connections were made with the College, although this was planned. Meanwhile the experience mounted that the setting-up of apparatus was time consuming and that teachers had not the necessary time. Moreover, even a very successful broadcast was soon over and its repeat involved the same amount of work again.

The Authority and the Research grant together bought an early type Peto Scott 1" video tape recorder and the facility of record and replay, even with this somewhat cumbersome machine, eased the position. It was at once decided to cancel the plan for further landline link-up and to concentrate on the purchase of $\frac{1}{2}$" vtr's. In 1968 this was a very considerable decision because it was then firmly stated by most authorities that the standard of replay was too low for educational use. However, the purchase of two Nivico $\frac{1}{2}$" recorders seemed to disprove this, since the programmes that were recorded or made from the cameras that the schools held, were well received and the quality deemed acceptable. Such programmes are available for viewing on the accompanying video tape.

SCHOOL USE OF CCTV

With the decision to install simple CCTV systems which linked laboratories, rooms or halls on a loop into which off-air or video tape could be fed, there arose the call to make the camera, monitor and video tape recorder mobile within the school. The apparatus was bought in terms of economy, so that the Monitor served the dual purposes of an off-air receiver and a video monitor. Thus the costing of such a situation, on today's price, runs:

Camera with 4 to 1 zoom and wide angle lenses	£240
VTR	300
Monitor and leads	90
Tripod and head	50
	£680

It is customary to anticipate about a further £100 to wire in separate sound and vision to four other points, but this usually can include the relay of BBC/ITV as well. Thus the costs in question for a school appear to be within the £850 mark. To this needs to be added the cost of a trolley on which to transport the equipment. Such a trolley, specially devised, was developed at Loughborough. There are several of these now in various schools. The monitor will sit on the trolley itself if needed, but it is usually moved separately.

Twelve such systems were made available in 1969 and 1970 to a variety of schools. Three primary schools were included since it was required to know to what extent such CCTV was relevant there. One special installation was at the Loughborough College School which functions as an Upper School in the Leicestershire Scheme. Here, the Southern Television Authority fitted up a studio and control console at a more advanced level, so that productions could be more expertly made, and also to enable a CSE and GCE course to be mounted for the pupils in the use and purpose of CCTV. Some point is made of this later.

Assessment of school use of CCTV

Schools were given a very broad brief and the reviews which were made of their progress were at first centred on central displays of the programmes which various schools had made. This sometimes took place in the County Hall itself and it became apparent that schools differed very widely in the use to which the installations were put. At the outset the County advisers had been keen to influence the 'creative use' of the systems; the researcher was rather more reticent, realizing that the features which might make CCTV useful could lie in the more traditional fields of replaying programmes, amplifying meetings, magnifying experiments and so on. It was later decided to ask schools to reply to a fairly detailed questionnaire in order to determine a forward policy. A sample survey indicated that the replies would be better compiled by visits and an abbreviated questionnaire. Accordingly the enquiry listed below was made.

Alternative uses of CCTV, serviceability, teachers' attitudes

It was recognized that three features would make significant alterations in the use of CCTV in a school:

1. Did the school use the equipment for recording, relay or magnification more than it used it for making its own programmes?

2. Was the equipment serviceable over the period?

3. Were teachers prepared to use the equipment or did it stand idle?

Table I

School		Equipment Use					Equipment Reliability					Ratio of Use Off Air/Camera or Relay	
		100%	75%	50%	25%	less	100%	75%	50%	25%	less		or Relay
Junior	A					✓	✓					1	3
	B			✓			✓					2	1
	C			✓				✓				1	4
Secondary	A		✓				✓					100	1
	B				✓		✓					1	2
	C			✓					✓			6	1
	D				✓					✓		1	1
	E				✓			✓				3	2
	F		✓					✓				9	1
	G			✓				✓				9	1
	H				✓				✓			1	4
	K			✓				✓				20	1

Table II

School		Limitation of Use			Additional Points
		Shortage of Tapes	No suitable Staff	Staff not inclined	
Junior	A	✓			
	B	✓			
	C	✓			
Secondary	A				Too many staff want it at once
	B			✓	Much after school preparation needed
	C		✓	✓	
	D		✓	✓	Staff changes affected use
	E		✓		No technical help. Building levels interfere with trolley
	F		✓		No technical help, limits camera work
	G				No space
	H		✓		No technical assistance. Equipment not developed enough
	K	✓			Need trolley and camera

A sample of twelve schools, nine secondary (all Leicestershire Comprehensive) and three primary, was reviewed to determine: (i) percentage of school day equipment in use; (ii) percentage of school day equipment serviceable; (iii) ratio of use: camera composition/Off air or relay; (iv) teacher attitude. Additionally, information was sought in explanation of exceptional or adverse features. The results are set out in Table I. Table II represents the same schools and an analysis of their reasons for not employing the apparatus 100% of the time.

DISCUSSION

Table I shows that the equipment was often used for less than 50% of the school day, and that this was not, in general, explained by technical failure. It is to be appreciated that the use of such equipment 100% of the school day would be unusual; one could consider the use of a film projector in the same light. Nevertheless the equipment is costly, programmes are available and reason was sought in Table II for any degree of under-employment.

Table II suggests that the primary schools attributed their lack of recording tape as a reason for the CCTV system being under used in any way. It is certainly a point that the preservation of excellent programmes often denies the making of other ones. Some progress has been made in this respect by the provision of smaller duration tapes, and by supplying more tapes at a lower price. Nevertheless it is certainly a considerable point that a stock of about ten tapes appears to be a minimum for regular recording purposes. It is interesting to notice that in Table I, two of the schools used the apparatus much more for making programmes than for recording them.

The Secondary schools indicate that the apparatus had a fairly good level of technical reliability and only one attributes under use to lack of tape. In their cases the lack of suitable staff, ie a permanent technician for the job, and staff disinclination were the most significant reasons advanced. It had been foreseen that technical assistance would be claimed, but the equipment had been provided with the facility for teacher/pupil operation in the first cases. In-service teacher training courses in the use of the equipment and its simple maintenance, were provided at the College, but the courses were of short duration and much was left to the schools.

The discussion and tables show quite accurately what the state of affairs was at the time of the enquiry, but it is apparent that the results could be looked at in quite another way if one took examples of the sort of curriculum change and innovation which the apparatus often engendered. Moreover one could also suggest that the apparatus was 'on average' in use for one-third of school time, and in some schools for three-quarters of the time. On the point of curriculum change the course at the College school for the instruction of fifth and sixth form pupils in studio management and the principle of television was linked into a precise syllabus for the CSE. Many of the pupils are well informed and able practitioners.

In the other schools an inspection of the accompanying video tape which contains random representative sampling could well convince the viewer that a very great deal had been gained. Nevertheless, certain very definite

165

lessons have been learned following the last two years' trial. It appears that the type of equipment, subject to the comments of the final paragraph, is acceptable and adequate if it is more portable; it should be linked to an off-air point and an internal broadcasting system of a simple nature, so that control and movement are facilitated. A storage room, capable of doubling as a simple studio is needed, of minimum size, some 400 square feet. This can be dispensed with, but it means that the equipment is far less used, because it has to be taken down and put up each time. There should be assistance, not necessarily technical, to help with programme making. With these provisions schools can make productive and innovative use of such installations.

THE FUTURE

The conduct of the enquiry has produced several side benefits, not the least of which is the production of a very adequate schools receiver and CCTV monitor at a very economical price and of high performance. Because of this the possibility of colour installation has been brought definitely within range. It is fully understood by the research unit that the possession of colour sets does not imply a superior learning situation; but with the advent, in 1972, of the CCTV colour cassette recorder, the matching and integration of the units will give colour capability, a much more portable system and, allowing for an initial settling down period, equipment which is much easier for the teacher to employ.

REFERENCES

Leedham, J. F. (1967 & 1969) 'Programmed learning on CCTV'.
  Visual Education, March 1967; March 1969
Leedham, J. F. (1969) 'Use of programmed closed circuit television at
  Loughborough'. In 'Aspects of Educational Technology III'
  (Ed) A. P. Mann and C. K. Brunstrom. Page 206. Pitman, London
Leedham, J. F., Blackadder, E. and Willmore, F. (1971) 'Educational
  technology and teacher training'. In 'Aspects of Educational Technology
  V'. (Ed) D. Packham, A. Cleary and T. Mayes. Page 236.
  Pitman, London

Method of presentation: 16mm Film and videotape (Nivico $\frac{1}{2}$")

Programmed Team Problem Solving

A ŠATÁNEK and M J ADAMS

Programmed Team Problem Solving in the clinical and medical setting offers
a means of utilizing the small group as an effective teaching tool. It offers
the possibility of receiving adequate feed-back from each person in the group
which the large lecture session cannot offer. Yet it is less time consuming
and more economically efficient than individual instruction.

In programmed team problem solving (TPS) five to ten persons constitute a learning group which has certain structure and inner life. Different
aspects of the group which are of importance include: size, heterogeneity,
polarization, degree of interaction and duration of the group's existence.

Consideration should be given to the size of the groups. It seems quite
logical that if the number of the group members is too large, the solution of
the problem becomes more difficult. With an unlimited number of group
members the group deteriorates into smaller parts and various conflicts,
frustrations, aggression and other phenomena appear which impair the
quality of the performance. According to our experiences, a group of five
to ten members seems to be most suitable. A group smaller than five
becomes less stimulating and less economically efficient.

The group is heterogeneous in that the members are of different ages
and sex and have different interests. The group is homogeneous only in that
the members are of a common profession.

The polarization of the group concerns whether all group members are
aimed at one goal. In the case of team programmed problem-solving the
group is strongly polarized as the final goal is not only clearly set down but
accepted by the group as well as by each member.

In situations of team problem-solving the phenomenon of social facilita-
tion assumes special importance. It is quite obvious that the presence of
other members, their co-operation and competition influence the individual's
work and outcome. Interaction among the members in the group is facilitated
by their strong need to express somehow their own feelings and experiences
gathered during their training. At the same time, they accept their colleagues' experiences, and each parcel of new information is individually

167

classified, assimilated and evaluated. A sine qua non is for the members to be able to communicate continually. If this condition cannot be provided, we cannot talk about team work but instead about work performed in the presence of other individuals. It is expedient for everybody who participates in the discussion to adopt independent views and not to adopt uncritically everything which a colleague asserts. The discussions are very valuable only if the participants exchange ideas. Then each participant gains new experiences from which he may assimilate information. In the discussion the participant's ideas and opinions become integrated and more comprehensive.

From the group duration point of view we speak about a temporary group for it exists for a relatively short time period. In spite of this, during the course of problem-solving the group creates or accepts rules which help to remove interferences and which maximize the chances of success. The acceptance of these rules by each individual becomes a strong motivating force for learning.

The team approach used differs from usual methods of programmed instruction in that initial information is presented by a teacher, who makes an effort to create favourable conditions for each candidate's learning activities. He explains the objectives, shows different phases through which they will pass and points out the close relationships between the curriculum and the candidates' goals. Before the training is started, the candidates should be acquainted with the problem to be discussed.

GENERAL INFORMATION (SYNOPSIS)

General information might be presented in a lecture, graphically, by means of slides, by tape recorder, film-shots etc. After being given the prerequisite factual information the candidates are capable of incorporating new information more actively with more deliberation.

PRESENTATION OF THE PROBLEM

New information presented to the candidates is comprised in a proposition which usually is of broader extent than are the propositions in the common linear programs (the average extent of an individual item in Skinner's programs does not exceed two sentences!). In programmed team problem-solving we use items or propositions consisting of one or two short paragraphs with somewhat detailed information and rather complicated relations. The suggestion for a number of possible solutions follows. If the candidate is to select the right solution with full responsibility, he must engage himself in complicated thinking processes.

Solution of the problem in the group

(1) In team programmed instruction the problem to be solved by the group

is presented in the form of a proposition or plausible problem.

(2) The problem is being structured by means of cognitive abilities and co-operative forces of group members.

(3) Forces accelerating the problem-solving immediately form in the group.

(4) Under some circumstances opposite forces mobilize which have negative influences on the solution of a problem.

(5) In special situations a teacher's intervention is necessary for he can positively influence the solution of a problem using his knowledge and abilities.

Integrating and supplementary process

One of the greatest assets of this process is that utilizing the experiences of the whole group the individual member broadens his knowledge. In addition, certain individuals' marginal opinions are corrected and the standpoints of the individual members are integrated (therefore, the term of 'integrating process'). If the group becomes convinced that the solution is right, it usually accepts it. However a situation might occur in which several sub-groups are formed and each of them insists on its own standpoint which might be well grounded and none wants to give it up. Then it is necessary to accept more solutions (therefore, the 'supplementary process').

Professional trainer's interaction

If the subject matter is too complicated and we foresee difficulties, it would be expedient to add to the team a professional trainer who would help the candidates: sometimes with a mere hint, or by presenting easier cases or subsidiary information. In this way the candidates are not discouraged by their unproductive efforts and do not lose interest.

The professional's task is to keep bringing the group to situations where decision is inevitable. However, the interaction between the professional and the candidates should not deprive the members of the group of their autonomy. If the professional wants to be successful, his role must be such that it facilitates decisions which represent the desires of the whole group. The interaction among the individual, the group and the professional is characterized by the process of mutual influencing and encouraging change in other members' behaviour. A relevant type of interaction between the professional and the members is a working interaction resulting in the solution of a problem. The main task of a professional trainer in the group is to ensure effectiveness of the learning and to keep a balance among various group interactions. He should help to establish a co-operative relationship among the candidates and try to reduce competition. Undoubtedly the influence of the professional trainer is important in the team effort. He can retard it or create a situation such that the group loses interest in the team work.

Realization of the answer

The answer (or answers) to a question is presented on the one hand by the whole group in the form of a collective answer (or answers), and on the other hand by each member of the group. The advantages of these combined answers are as follows: each individual has the right not to accept the collective decision; the candidate does not need to be controlled by the collective so that a feeling of injustice does not appear and conflicts do not occur; further it is possible to register the results of each individual and on this basis to work out a final complex analysis as well as to watch each member's learning process. Collective and individual answers are registered and evaluated.

Verification, arguments, references

Each candidate may evaluate his performance by comparisons with the control answer which is always grounded by solid arguments so that there are no doubts about its unambiguity. The control answer usually contains the references to the available medical sources. This is the final part and after its completion another problem starts and the whole procedure is repeated.

CONCLUSION

A programmed team problem-solving model has been developed and used to encourage motivation and active participation of each individual in the learning process. Psychological factors underlying group dynamics contribute to the process.

The programmed team problem-solving method presents information in the form of a proposition and includes an integrating and supplementary process. In this process the candidates can discuss problems widely and thus enlarge their knowledge by the knowledge and experiences of the whole group. In addition, team programmed problem-solving provides an individual with collective feed-back and each candidate can verify his answer by comparing it with the control one which is supported by arguments and references.

The team programmed problem-solving method augments the number of presently used instructional forms and with continued use should provide increasing evidence of its utility.

The Construction and Evaluation of a Guided Oral Language Situation
S GILMORE

INTRODUCTION

Until recently the teaching of oral language skills has received little emphasis in the language arts programme of the primary school. Though highly structured schemes are available for reading and writing, teachers tend to rely upon the 'improvement by accident' approach in the teaching of oral language skills. This lack of concern for formal and systematic instruction in oral language may contribute to the persistent failure of many pupils, especially those working class pupils from culturally disadvantaged homes, to gain mastery over their language resources.

Basil Bernstein (1958) postulated two distinct forms or codes which are culturally determined: these codes were later designated **restricted** and **elaborated** respectively. Each code exhibited different lexical, syntactic and socio-psychological features. The **restricted** code users, mainly drawn from the working classes, tended to employ a less diverse lexical selection and syntactical variety and organization compared with **elaborated** code users who were generally drawn from the middle classes. As the culturally disadvantaged pupil is more likely to employ the **restricted** code in a given oral language situation and at the same time is more likely to fail at school, irrespective of intelligence, a link, in a general sense, could be established between language failure and educational failure.

If, as Halliday (1969) points out "The limitations of a child's linguistic experience may be ultimately ascribed — though not in any simple or obvious way — to features of the social background, the problem as it faces the teachers is essentially a linguistic problem", then it would seem desirable that the language arts programme in the primary school should include a strong element of oral language instruction. Moreover, if as a recent major survey of children's language indicates "Competence in the spoken language appears to be basic for competence in reading and writing" (Loban, 1963), then the need for instruction in oral language skills becomes compelling.

171

In spite of the fact that oral language skills are elusive and difficult for direct instruction, some attempt must be made to evolve teaching techniques which achieve their desired teaching objectives. A point of view reflected, for example, in a statement by Sinclair (1971) which could be taken as representative "The acquisition of a command of a language requires technique, and techniques are not highly valued in English teaching today. They smack of old-style lessons remembered with contempt because of their failure to achieve their purpose".

This paper presents a case-study involving four pupils who took part in an investigation into the possibilities of providing a teaching technique whereby the oral performance in one feature, namely fluency, may be improved.

SUBJECTS

Four boys, including one set of non-identical twins, each aged $8\frac{1}{2}$ years from the same class and from similar working-class and culturally disadvantaged backgrounds were chosen and matched in pairs from scores derived from the Sleight Non-Verbal Intelligence Test. Their IQs were in the 104-108 range. Two boys were assigned to the non-guided groups; the other two boys to the guided group. Each group contained one of the set of twins.

THE TASKS

Each pupil was given five oral language tasks designed to elicit narrative speech. The stimulus material consisted of three comic strip cartoons from a popular children's comic from which the captions had been obliterated. Each cartoon strip contained 8-9 frames depicting the adventures of a well-known comic character. The cartoon strips were presented to the pupils in the following sequence:

NON-GUIDED PUPILS	GUIDED PUPILS
1. Comic Strip No. 1	1. Comic Strip No. 1
2. Comic Strip No. 1 (repeated)	2. Guidance Session
3. Comic Strip No. 2	3. Comic Strip No. 1 (repeated)
4. Comic Strip No. 2 (repeated)	4. Comic Strip No. 2
5. Comic Strip No. 3	5. Guidance Session
	6. Comic Strip No. 2 (repeated)
	7. Comic Strip No. 3

In the first guidance session the guided pupils were instructed to consider three points in the narrative:

a) **Where** did the action take place?
b) **Who** were the characters involved in the action?
c) **What** happened to the characters in the story?

172

In the second guidance session the instructions given during the first session were repeated and a further point to be considered given:

d) Why did the main character behave in a particular way?

The oral responses of the pupils were tape-recorded and transcribed.

LINGUISTIC ANALYSIS

The transcribed speech for each pupil for each task was segmented into communication units, a unit being defined as a grammatically independent prediction. This method of segmenting speech closely followed that employed by Loban (1963) in his survey. An oral language usually contains omissions and redundancies which arrest the smooth flow of information being conveyed to the listener, those features were isolated and withdrawn from the final estimation of the fluency feature of the pupil's oral performance.

RESULTS

NON-GUIDED PUPILS

Subject	Task Number	Communication Units	Words	Omissions and Redundancies
A1	1	9	62	6
	2	10	55	3
	3	10	60	4
	4	10	65	3
	5	10	66	3
A2	1	12	76	3
	2	12	76	5
	3	13	77	5
	4	15	93	10
	5	15	84	6

GUIDED PUPILS

Subject	Task Number	Communication Units	Words	Omissions and Redundancies
B1	1	10	65	4
	2	16	117	2
	3	16	119	4
	4	17	113	8
	5	21	129	5
B2	1	11	76	4
	2	13	91	2
	3	12	83	2
	4	23	155	5
	5	10	92	4

DISCUSSION

One index of fluency is the amount of language uttered by the pupils. On this index alone the 'guided' pupils produced more language both in respect of the number of communication units and the average number of words in each unit after task No.1 than did the 'non-guided' pupils. This increased production of language resulted in an increase in the amount of information on the comic strip narrative communicated. Fluency, however, unaccompanied by organization and coherence cannot be regarded as a desirable objective in oral language instruction. The choice of cartoon strips as stimulus material ensured that the pupils were compelled to relate the narratives in logical and temporal sequence so that digressions and irrelevancies were reduced to a tolerable minimum for all the pupils.

De Lawter and Eash (1969) identify six basic errors in oral communication as "a failure to focus, poor organization of ideas, lack of supporting ideas, inadequate descriptions, lack of subordination, and stereotyped vocabulary": all characteristics of the **restricted** code.

The use of cartoon strip material along with guidance goes some way to eliminate the first two of the errors listed, ie failure to focus and poor organization of ideas.

The research of Hawkins (1969) into the nominal group revealed the fact that working class pupils tended to use more third-person pronouns with consequent restriction of modification and qualification than did middle class pupils who favoured the greater use of nominals as 'head' words of the nominal group.

If this is true, then the next stage would seem to be in the provision of such stimulus material and guidance which would encourage pupils to exploit the possibilities of elaborating the nominal group within the communication unit in order to combat the errors of inadequacies of description and stereotyped vocabulary.

REFERENCES

Bernstein, B. (1958) British Journal of Sociology, **9**, 159
Bernstein, B. (1962) Language and Speech, **5**, 221
De Lawter, J. A. and Eash, M. J. (1966) Elementary English, **43**, 880
Halliday, M. A. K. (1969) Educational Review, **22**, 26
Hawkins, P. R. (1969) Language and Speech, **12**, 125
Loban, W. D. (1963) The Language of Elementary School Children: NCTE
  Research Report No.1 Champaign, Illinois
Sinclair, J. McH. (1971) Educational Review, **23**, 220

Method of presentation: Videotape Ampex 1"

Ulster in Your Hands
J McCORMICK

This tape illustrates a simulation which has been used with Sixth Form pupils
in a grammar school in Northern Ireland. The purpose of the simulation is
to involve pupils in studying the present Ulster Problem, and to demonstrate
to the participants the influences which affect decision-making in government.
It is also intended to provide the students with a working knowledge and understanding of the main political elements in the Ulster situation. The long term
aim is to help them acquire a more mature appreciation of politics.

The videotape illustrates the action which takes place within the simulation and shows that it is an essentially simple exercise to operate since the
main activity is through the medium of Press Statements. The participants
take the roles of the Northern Ireland Government, the Home Secretary of the
Westminster Government, the main opposition groups in the province, including factions of the Unionist opposition. Police and the Army are also introduced into the simulation. The participants do not have scripts, only a set of
guiding principles upon which to base their decisions. The situation develops
solely as a result of the interaction of the different groups within the simulation. When the exercise is terminated the actions which took place are then
compared with the principles upon which each group of participants operated.

The simulation on this videotape was not rehearsed. The participants
came from two schools and did not meet until just before the exercise began.
They had previously been supplied with the participants' instructions but they
were only allocated their respective roles before the simulation began. The
videotape is therefore a record of how the simulation operated with a random
selection of pupils.

Mode of presentation: Videotape 1" IVC

An Application of Programmed Learning to Physical Training
G HUBERT-WHITE

THE HUMAN PROBLEM

In this modern world human beings are compelled to live in a way which does not allow physical development or fitness for life (Streicher, 1970). This sedentary living **impairs** the locomotor function, that is, the capacity to walk and to perform ordinary movements generally (Gardiner, 1963).

In schools, there is no health education, so children do not understand the need for hygiene, nutrition, movement and rest, care of the body (Department of Education, 1968).

In schools, training has been deleted from Physical Education, causing widespread and increasing postural defects and physical under-development among young people aged 11-19 years. No survey or means of survey exists whereby the extent of such cases may be ascertained, but I have found such cases are commonplace in every school visited.

This problem has implications for adults who may suffer breakdowns at an important stage of their career.

Because every part of the body stimulates a particular area of the brain any physical lapse, ie excessive back curvatures, causes fatigue (Colson, 1968).

This fatigue (chemical substances) intrudes into the cells of the nervous systems, blocks impulses to the brain, neutralizes the information carried, and reduces stimulation of the mentality. This prompts irrational behaviour: thus by fatigue a physical defect may impair learning.

REMEDY

The human body was evolved in an environment where its fitness was self-perpetuating. As society changed into its present form, the use of the body has lessened, but no methods have been adopted to ensure continuity or physical fitness.

Instead, substitute activities — games and sports — were loosely inserted into the education curricula and social life. There was no recognition of the unique quality of the individual.

Up to the period 1920, elementary schools had drill, but this method could not shape specific physical fitness for individuals. So, today, no attempt is made to prepare the body for these substitute-activities — that is children are put into an activity without assessment of ability, or physical preparation.

Table I. Record of boys sent to me for training

	Midland School 1966	London Track NW 1967/8	London Track W 1969/70	London Track NW 1971/2
Age range - years	11-16	14-16	14-15	14-21
Number of persons	35	16	12	9
a. fit to train	5	2	2	2
b. left/right sides - uneven development	6	3	2	1
c. posture - back curves excessive	14	6	5	4
d. flat feet	4	3	2	-
e. weak - minor ailments	6	2	1	2

This is in spite of the facts shown in Table I, which corroborates the views of Dr Griffith Pugh (National Institute of Medical Research) whose work shows also that physical training to pre-condition the body for fitness is necessary **before** taking part in physical activities, **and that it is insufficient to practise the respective disciplines** (Goldberger, 1970).

Training for fitness by physical exercises may be done by the application of programmed instruction, because this allows the individual and diverse problems to be solved within a correct framework. Because every person is an individual — physically as well as mentally — group drill is inefficient and irrelevant.

To train boys aged 13-18 for physical fitness before entering physical activities, a program has been developed during the years 1956 to date (Hubert-White, 1971) by the application of the concepts to:
1. stretch the body
2. contract/strengthen muscles
3. loosen joints and sustain posture to all body parts:
    (i) head-neck-trunk;
    (ii) arms-hands
    (iii) legs-feet

APPLICATION OF PROGRAMMED LEARNING

This Program for Training is not easily acceptable in physical education, because there is no taxonomy of objectives — as for cognitive and affective domains (Davies, 1971), and there is no known criterion for fitness.

My criterion for the practical work of programming is:

Fitness is the foundation for efficient movements

To train for movements, which replicate to change and form lines of adaptive behaviour

Each concept is related to one or all, and are present to a degree in each movement, but for instruction one concept is presented for an exercise — to the trainee

This is an abstracted system of variables (Ashby, 1960) to cope with a learning situation for display of information, which allows the trainee to teach his body the movements for acquirement, then accomplishment of fitness. The state of the system (the human body) at any instant, should be a set of numerical values, but there is no known formula for this.

TO PROGRAM

Exercises to train the body for fitness are analyzed to get the sequence:

Start position: to teach/learn posture

Movements: lead-in   key   recovery

What to do: set in easy-to-see movements

How to do: given by verbal instruction and simple line diagrams (Davies, 1963)

Benefit: specified by verbal stimuli in theory — mediating for understanding (Gilbert, 1969) — the exercise is recalled, and the benefit is expressed by a self-score.

This recall and this value provide the confirmation, and enables the trainee to satisfy his need to verbalize his physical activity. In addition, evidence of the trainee's movements during the training by program, may be provided by photography.

PRINCIPLES

For the trainee to respond completely the program enables him to perform the movements in that sequence, conforming to the laws of anatomy and kinesiology. The complete response is on four levels:

1.   physical   verbal instruction
2.   mental   overt recording; covert valuing
3.   neuro-endocrine   theory-diagram
4.   personal relevance   transfer into recreation, employment/career

When the trainee has read the verbal instruction n-times (for the PT

Program this is six times) he should not require to continue this form of instruction. But, it is necessary to continue exercising to maintain fitness, and to avoid disuse atrophy, and an algorithm-form is provided.

PROGRAM PRESENTATION

A check list is necessary to secure overt responding, also to reinforce the trainee's confidence and retention of skill (Gilbert, 1969). Unless the trainee does record, though he may read, he may not receive the instruction — that is he glances over the words.

The recording does make the trainee pause and consider what he is doing, increasing the probability that he may follow the instruction.

Because the idea of training is contrary to the common thought of the present-day culture, prior motivation is given by an introduction to the instruction, explaining the method of exercising.

Direction to medical attention is essential to counter misuse of the program by persons physically unsound.

Direction is necessary to elementary health practice such as hygiene, food, rest.

TRANSFER

If the body is trained to stretch, strengthen, and loosen in all parts and as a whole, by exercises which stimulate correct movements, and when by repetition these movements feel right, the individual will know fitness.

By constant recall how his movements are performed and their value, the individual will become skilled at giving accurate values for his movements in any activity and gain confidence. This provides a foundation for skills in the activity, which he has selected, and also for his employment when adult.

The activity is analyzed to isolate the movements and actions and play of the game or sport. The exercises are shown as the basis for the activity and how these may be done to match the moves/action. After the practice game the trainee considers his moves in turn, then he concentrates on the exercises for that move, feeling how his movements may help his play.

This enhances bodily fitness and efficiency, develops specific mental awareness, and builds up self-confidence. This is a considerable basis for recreation, employment, and everyday living. In this way the benefits of exercising to train the body will transfer into, and back-up the physical activity.

By this procedure it is possible to explore activities to find coordinations/ common cores, whose use will aid the individual, for example:

Spring up   foot + body upstretch - common in tennis, long jump, football-header, swim-dive

Spring off   foot + body drive - common in sprint, run, rugby

Manual handling	football goal + hands-to-ball tennis drive
Thrust out	shot-putt, rugby tackle

In Physical Education, these coordinations could be initiated to give relevance.

REFERENCES

Ashby, W. R. (1960) Design for a Brain. Chapman and Hall
Colson, J. H. C . (1968) Postural and Relaxation Training. Heinemann
Davies, I. K. (1971) The Management of Learning. McGraw-Hill
Education, Department of (1968) Handbook of Health Education. HMSO
Gardiner, M. D. (1963) The Principles of Exercise Therapy. G Bell & Sons
Gilbert, T. F. (1962) Mathetics. Recall - Longmac
Goldberger, M. (1970) The Times Education Supplement, 31.7.70
Hubert-White, G. (1971) Physical Training for Fitness. Program of exercises
Streicher, M. (1970) Reshaping Physical Education. Manchester University
    Press

Self- and Programmed-Instruction in Engineering Laboratory Classes

D J BUCKINGHAM

A common problem in the applied sciences is one of synchronizing the laboratory schedule with the lecture schedule. Any laboratory experiment which
has to be decoupled from related course material may conveniently be treated
as a self-contained teaching unit — a subset of the mainstream course. To
support the student who is faced with such an experiment a self-instruction
technique can be a valuable alternative to the heavy supervision normally required. It is vital that any audio-visual or programmed-instruction technique
used for self-instruction be chosen on the basis of 'suitability' to the purpose
(Buckingham & Jones, 1971), but this 'suitability' criterion is too subjective
to define rigorously. The author illustrates his own interpretation of this
criterion by an example from his laboratory program — an example chosen
because it offers several facets to each of which it is relatively easy to
assign a particularly suitable technique of presentation.

The major teaching divisions of the experiment may be summarized as
follows:

PRE-EXPERIMENTAL INSTRUCTION

Objective: Motivation and overall view of the experiment, excluding
detailed instruction.

Technique: Videotape

ASSISTANCE WITH EXPERIMENTAL PROCEDURE

Objective: Detailed instruction at student's own pace with visual identification of instrumentation

Technique: Tapeslide. This tapeslide machine allows immediate recall
of audio instructions with automatic slide re-indexing.

GUIDANCE IN DEVELOPMENT OF THEORETICAL BACKGROUND

Objective: Active student participation in development of theory (fluid
mechanics) associated with processing of experimental results
(computer program).

Technique: Programmed instruction. The programs are multiple-choice answers and are computer controlled. Successful completion of each program automatically loads the relevant data processing computer program.

EVALUATION

Objective: Testing acquisition of major experimental objectives.
Technique: Discussion between student and supervisor of computer printout and of student's response to specific (printed) questions.

Continuous evaluation of the presentation techniques employed in this experiment has resulted in two major annual updatings, leaving the format described above for the session 1971-72.

In other experiments tapeslide sequences alone are used for pre-experimental instruction, for 'help' application during the experiment, and for assistance with evaluation of experimental results, but the effectiveness of the latter application is severely restricted by the medium. A computer-linked combination of tapeslide, programmed-instruction, and graphic display is being developed to offer a wide format of presentation and response that will allow student-controlled self-assessment while fostering the art of self-criticism.

REFERENCE

Buckingham, D. J. and Jones, M. H. (1971) British Journal of Educational Technology, **2**, 48

Method of presentation: Videotape 1" Ampex

The Application of a Systematic Approach to an Electrical Engineering Course

Q V DAVIS and P J HILLS

INTRODUCTION

The background to this project, which began in April 1969 and is financed in part by the Leverhulme Trust Fund, is described in a paper which was presented to the Annual Conference of the Association for Programmed Learning and Educational Technology, held at the University of Newcastle upon Tyne in 1971 (Hills, 1971). Some of the results emerging from this work are further described in a paper published in Physics Education (Elton, Hills & O'Connell, 1971).

In the first year the project was mainly concerned in investigating the traditional university system of lectures, tutorials and practical work in relation to various forms of self-teaching. During the second year a systematic approach to a first year undergraduate course on electricity was developed and a revised version of this has been used during the current session.

This paper describes from two points of view, that of the subject matter specialist and that of the educational technologist, the application of a systematic approach to the course.

THE COURSE

The lecture course which has been the centre of study in the present investigation is a first course in Electric Circuits. Its aims are to introduce the student to a study of three problems:

1. How do electric circuits behave?
2. How can methods of analysis be refined to enable one to cope with complicated circuit systems?
3. How can electrical circuits be used to perform to a required specification?

The course consists of fifteen lecture periods and is backed by tutorials given in small groups, typically containing four students to a group. The lectures themselves are given to an audience of up to 150 students. It is a somewhat unusual course in that it is one of a group of lecture courses given in the first term at the University of Surrey as a common course for all students of the Departments of Electronic and Electrical Engineering, Physics, Metallurgy and Chemical Physics. Consequently it presents the lecturer with a number of problems.

The special problems arise from the fact that the audience is a mixed one, the various constituents having mixed needs and backgrounds. On the one hand there are electrical engineering students for whom the course is absolutely basic. It forms the foundation for a large part of their future studies and it is essential that they gain a thorough knowledge of the whole course and plenty of problem-solving practice. For them more is to come in later terms so the requirement is not for a comprehensive course but for one which is thorough as far as it goes. Furthermore the choice of topics must be such as to lead on to the more advanced techniques for solving electric circuit problems that they will learn in later years.

On the other hand there are the physics students who also require a sound foundation but who are not expected to specialize in circuit design and will not progress later to the very much more advanced techniques met by electrical engineers. Then there are the other groups whose needs are quite different again. These groups want to learn the principles of electric circuits, but are not much concerned with detail and will learn little more in later years.

Because the needs of the students differ, their motivations also differ and the amount of time they are prepared to devote to the subject varies widely from group to group.

Again, their backgrounds vary widely, a few students have already studied the subject to some depth, others have perhaps only a weak A-level in Physics not necessarily with much emphasis on electricity. In addition the size of the class imposes its well-known problems.

The choice of topics having been made, an exceptional amount of care is needed with presentation to interest all the class and to take them to the depth to be required of them. From the lecturer's point of view feedback becomes vital. The lecturer needs to know the state of progress not only across the spectrum of student ability ranges but also across the spectrum of differing needs and interests in this large class.

A SYSTEMATIC APPROACH TO THE COURSE

The approach to this course has been to decide the overall syllabus and depth of treatment and to select the starting level as a compromise between the varying student backgrounds and the time available, and then to apply a systematic approach which takes account of both the needs of the student and those of the lecturer.

The important factors in this course thus seem to be:

a) the differing background and needs of the students
b) class size (of the order of 150 students)
c) the need for feedback to students, lecturer and tutors

The students are aware of the aims of the course and its scope at the outset through the printed notes for the course which can be purchased through the University bookshop, and the objectives, the testable outcomes are clarified by the development of sets of test questions described below. In addition, copies of old examination papers are available.

The systematic approach to the course is thus based on aims and objectives specified and is intended to meet the needs given above, so that it:

1) exposes deficiencies in student background at the outset of the course
2) makes students aware of their own difficulties as they arise throughout the course
3) provides library based material which may help with these difficulties
4) makes students aware of the need to consult more than one reference book to obtain a balanced picture of the course
5) helps them to realize the importance of tutorials
6) involves them actively in the course
7) feeds back information to the lecturer and tutors in a general way so that they are kept informed on student progress and main areas of difficulty

THE SYSTEM

At the beginning of the course the student completes a pre-knowledge test for which he is given an answer sheet enabling him to mark the test immediately and to look up areas of knowledge in which he is deficient. Self-tests are given at intervals throughout the course so that the student is able to assess his own performance, and, by reference to library based reference material which is keyed in to the answers to the tests, he is able to remedy any lack of knowledge or expand any area of work he wishes.

The components of this system are further described on the tape/slide presentation associated with this paper and details can be found in the paper previously mentioned (Hills, 1971).

Additional materials associated with the course are in three main forms: books, tape recordings with associated printed notes, and tape/slide presentations. These materials are available from the University Library at any time during its hours of opening, which is thus taking on the role of a resources centre for both book and other material.

A short extract from one of the tape/slide presentations, designed as a recorded tutorial to explain one of the problems associated with the self-tests is given in the tape/slide presentation associated with this paper.

One problem has been to provide a facility so that if students lose the thread of a lecture, they can return to it again at a later stage. This facility has been provided in the form of a cassette tape recording of the actual lecture with printed notes containing the relevant diagrams and mathematical formulae. To refer to these the student borrows the tape, associated notes, a recorder and earphones from the Library.

If a student has problems which he cannot fully solve with the Library based material then he is free to raise them in tutorial sessions in the usual way. A copy of self-test answers is also handed in by the student, this is computer processed and summarized information on general areas of difficulty circulated to course tutors on the day after each self-test.

ADDITIONAL INVOLVEMENT BY THE LECTURER

In addition to normal involvement with the course, the action required of the lecturer has been firstly the preparation of self-test questions which:

a) define the testable outcomes (objectives) of the course
b) help the student to monitor his own progress
c) help the lecturer and tutors to be aware of general progress

Question areas were chosen initially by the lecturer and then looked at by other members of staff concerned with the course, for additions, amendments etc. These areas were then revised and final questions composed. Questions were initially open-ended in the first trial to show up the range of student answers and provide feedback for revision of the material in the second trial. As a result the questions were revised and cast into multiple choice form for a second trial in the Autumn term 1972.

Secondly, a selection was made of 'self-help' material mainly in the form of specific page references in books and seventeen tape/slide presentations were also prepared. The tape/slide presentations were designed to perform two functions. Some consisted of 'mini-lectures' like the extract shown in the supporting tape/slide presentation to this paper, covering certain limited areas in which difficulty was expected, while others set out to solve fairly typical tutorial problems taken from past examination papers.

ADDITIONAL TIME INVOLVEMENT OF STAFF
AND COST OF THE COURSE

In addition to normal lecturer and tutors' involvement in preparing and giving lectures and tutorials, the additional time and costs involved were:

Lecturer and other academic staff time

a) definition of intended outcomes of the course and problem areas by lecturer
b) lecturer and other staff definition of suitable book references and areas for tape/slide presentations
c) setting questions for self-tests by lecturer

d) other staff checking and advising on the material

e) analysis of results of self-tests and preparation of summarized information for tutors by lecturer

f) staff involvement in preparing, recording and checking tape/slide presentations.

Technical staff time

a) technical and library staff time in making recordings of lectures and placing them in the library

b) administering self-tests and processing results for computer

c) recording and preparing tape/slide presentations.

Cost of materials

a) cost of cassette tapes for lectures and associated notes

b) cost of printing, collating and stapling test materials

c) cost of computing facilities

d) cost of tapes and slides for tape/slide material

Cost of the system

The estimates given below are based on figures for the first trial of this approach in 1970-71 and the revised version 1971-72. Cost figures for staff are based on average salary figures.

Cost in initiating the system		
	Academic staff salary only	= £115
	Technical staff salary only	= £ 44
	Materials	= £174
	Total	= £333

Cost of maintaining the system (Allowing for periodic revision of a proportion of the materials)		
	Academic staff salary only	= £ 15
	Technical staff salary only	= £ 24
	Materials	= £ 77
	Total	= £116

If we assume that the course is for 150 students with a total course contact time of 20 hours (lectures and tutorials) then the total cost/student/hour of course time is as follows:

Cost/student/hour of contact time	
For the initial course	= 11p
For maintaining the course	= 4p

Thus there is a non-recurrent cost of 7p per student in initiating the course and hence the estimated cost for any course with s students would be £ $(12+0.03 s)$ per hour for its initiation and 3p per student per hour run-on costs. This excludes the cost of capital equipment, cassette players and tape/ slide equipment used in the library, as this could be common to several courses.

It should also be noted that in this example the approach has been applied to an existing course. If it had been applied to a new course the extra cost would have been smaller as some of the tasks would be necessary for any new course, conventional or otherwise.

EVALUATION IN TERMS OF THE FINAL EXAMINATION RESULTS

There are many ways of evaluating innovations in education, subjectively by the opinions of both staff and students, in terms of the inevitable increase in staff time and cost of materials and in terms of the effectiveness of the course as judged by examination results. In many cases the disadvantages of extra time involvement for staff and the extra cost of materials hardly appear justified as the evaluatory procedures usually indicate that no significant difference can be found between conventional methods and the new method. Evaluation of this kind is usually based on the conventional examination results or some form of them which means either that the research worker is using the wrong criteria, or the differences in performance of the learners in the new situation are so slight as to be masked by a number of other factors.

Although a number of evaluation procedures are being applied to the results emerging from the application of this approach to a first year undergraduate course, it was felt necessary to examine the results of the end of course examination to see what differences, if any, could be seen. In this we were fortunate that in the years 1969-70 and 1970-71, two electricity courses, Electricity 1 and Electricity 2 were taken by the students. Each course was given by the same lecturer and examination results were marked in the Electronic and Electrical Engineering Department. For the purposes of the following preliminary comparison, each paper in the two years was judged to be of equivalent difficulty.

In order to look at the results, they were divided into three categories, pass, borderline and fail:

pass	=	those scoring 40% and over (≥ 40)
borderline	=	those scoring between 31-39% (31-39)
fail	=	those scoring 30% and below (≤ 30)

The marks used are those of the end of course examination (pass mark = 40%) the raw scores having been normalized to a mean of 50 for the whole set of examinations.

'Graph' lines have been added to the diagrams to emphasize the relative positions of the points.

The percentage of students in each category for the two examinations over the two years is shown in Figure 1.

The percentage of students in the pass, borderline and failure categories differ little over the two years, both in the Electricity 1 course and in the Electricity 2 course. This appears to support the assumption that the examinations for these two subjects are equivalent over the two years and that the effectiveness of the courses as measured on these examinations are similar. It seems that more students fail Electricity 2 and that more students pass Electricity 1, indicating perhaps that Electricity 2 is the more difficult of the two courses.

188

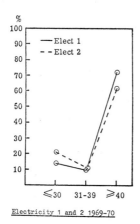 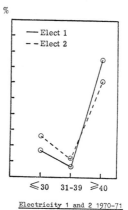

Electricity 1 and 2 1969-70   Electricity 1 and 2 1970-71

Figure 1

When we remember that the systematic approach described was only applied to Electricity 2 in the year 1970-71 and not in 1969-70 we observe the usual similarities in performance between the two methods, ie conventional lectures and tutorials in 1969-70 and systematic approach in 1970-71.

Further investigation reveals, however, that of the 112 students who took the examination, only 49 of the students in 1970-71 took all, or all but one, of the tests.

If we designate these 49 students 'Users' of the system and the others 'Nonusers' and work out the percentage of each type of student in each category for Electricity 2 in 1970-71 we get the results shown in Figure 2.

It is tempting to conclude that more users of the system passed than non users and fewer failed. Certainly there is a difference in the two categories of student, but perhaps we are only identifying hardworking students as opposed to those who do not work in such conventional ways. However, if this

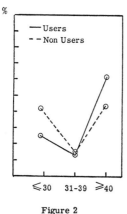 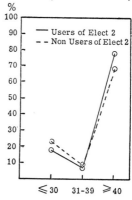

Figure 2   Figure 3

were so, then by using the results of the Electricity 1 examination taken in the same year by the same students and working out the results in terms of 'users' of the Electricity 2 system and 'nonusers' of the system, then the same sort of pattern should appear, as the students' 'study habits' should be the same for both examinations. The results are shown in Figure 3.

Whereas the previous set of results show a statistically significant difference in mean scores for users compared with non users at the 0.01 level, the comparison of users and non users of the Electricity 2 system for results of Electricity 1 show no such difference. It is obvious, therefore, that something is causing some students to perform more effectively in the Electricity 2 examination than in the Electricity 1 examination.

This tentative result emerging from the conventional end-of-course examinations is only part of the total evaluation being applied to this project. It is however important to set any evaluation in a realistic context and since one sixth of the total available lecture time on the course has been devoted to the self-tests one must enquire very seriously whether or not they should be persevered with.

Seven members of the academic staff of the Department of Electronic and Electrical Engineering were consulted for their opinions, gained as a result of taking small group tutorials. The almost unanimous view, as so often in this type of situation, was that little or no evidence was available of the efficacy of the system as evidenced in tutorials. The lecturer himself has found the breakdown of results of the self-tests useful feedback, but in general it has only tended to confirm his preformed opinions.

In a questionnaire answered by 100 of the students at the end of the current course, 90% of the students thought that the self-tests were useful, mainly saying that the tests showed them what they actually knew. Clearly the system must be judged by its effect on the performance of the students themselves, aside from their interaction with the lecturer and with members of staff, and effectiveness must be balanced against factors of cost and time.

ACKNOWLEDGMENTS

Our thanks are due to Drs G Brown and B W Ward, for help in production of the tape/slide material, Mr P J McVey for assistance with self-test questions, and Professor D R Chick and Professor L R B Elton for providing general facilities.

REFERENCES

Elton, L.R.B., Hills, P.J. and O'Connell, S. (1971) Physics Education, 6, 95
Hills, P.J. (1971) in 'Aspects of Educational Technology V'. (Ed) D. Packham, A. Cleary, T. Mayes. Pitman, London

Method of presentation: Tape/slide

The design of a 'compensatory' learning system to overcome problems of spatial visualization of Zambian children

T DRAISMA

INTRODUCTION

Rural African children, who constitute the vast majority of the continent child population, are known to share several characteristics with so-called culturally disadvantaged children in technologically more 'advanced' societies.

One such characteristic is the comparative inability to internalize spatial operations and to manipulate abstract concepts related to the perception of space. This problem is familiar to most secondary school teachers of subjects such as mathematics, the sciences, geography and art, and has been reported in many articles.

The secondary teacher, often on short contract, is tempted to shirk his responsibility in this area because, first of all, any long-term solution lies in the provision of a more stimulating environment in the homes of the very young (age 0-5), and secondly, medium-term answers must be provided by drastic reform of both content and methods of the primary school curriculum.

The teacher of mathematics and his students find themselves confronted with the problems of spatial visualization when dealing with the relationships between similar figures and between similar solids. Why is it that when an object is enlarged by a certain factor, areas are multiplied by the square, and volumes by the cube of that factor? The problem is aggravated by the fact that the traditional textbooks imported from Britain delay the treatment of this subject to the final school years (see Durell and Shannon & McLeish-Smith).

Professional bodies are partly responsible. The Incorporated Association of Assistant Masters in Secondary Schools (1957) scantily touches upon the subject in its proposed teaching syllabus for the fourth year. Thus the imported tradition of maths teaching discourages the teacher from using a developmental approach over a number of years, beginning in Form I.

In terms of Piaget's model of the phases in the development of thinking, this is what happens: the traditional syllabus demands the acquisition of abstract mathematical concepts and operations without ensuring that proficiency at more concrete levels has been established. Or, in Basil Bernstein's terminology, the imported school system, based on a 'universalistic interpretation' of reality, does not take into account the African child's 'context bound, particularist' approach to the environment (Bernstein, 1970).

For the teacher, important material on this subject can be found in Lovell and Butterworth (1966) and Flavell (1963).

This paper is not meant to contribute anything new to the ideas and theories of eminent social scientists such as Piaget and Bernstein. Rather, it describes how their concepts led to the design of a practical learning system on a specific topic for a specific student population with its own, but in no way inferior characteristics, after the dismal failure of a traditional approach.

A NOTE ON TERMINOLOGY

At this point I would like to state my position on a number of terms often used in the above context. Labels such as 'culturally disadvantaged', 'linguistically deprived', 'compensatory education' and 'less developed society' are, in my view, ideologically biased and imply derogatory value judgements. During a recent two-year spell with Africa 2000, a Zambïan-based conscientization project on Southern Africa, I have learnt to reappraise the western civilization of which I am a product. To people in Zambia the industrialized world's language appears horrifyingly simple. It is largely a language of power, paternalism and exploitation. This limited vocabulary will convince no Zambian of his linguistic deprivation. Nor will he accept as technologically advanced a society whose fruits rain down on neighbouring Angola and Mozambique in the form of napalm and defoliants. We teachers from the West do not know how prejudiced we are! (See Nyerere, 1967; Goldberg, 1969; Bernstein, 1970 and Meijer, 1971).

OVERVIEW OF THE DESIGN

The learning system on similar figures and solids was developed over the four-year period 1966-1969, and is based on the characteristics of the Zambian students, Piaget's stages of development, modern teaching methods and learning aids, and the syllabus requirements.

1. Student characteristics

Any learning system must be tailor-made to suit a specific learner population. As teachers we are usually interested in characteristics such as age, sex, command of English, ability to do maths, previously acquired mathematical behaviours, and others. In the case of spatial concept formation, the overriding characteristic for Zambian students is the degree of spatial visualization. In this context I define spatial visualization as the ability to internalize spatial operations on concrete objects, ie to imagine such operations to be carried out and the result predicted in mathematical terms.

The noticeable difficulty of many of our students to internalize spatial operations can be traced back partly to the fact that they grow up in a pre-technological society that provides opportunities for concrete operations on only a limited range of objects. Language development is also a factor in that 'context-bound' language behaviours developed in one culture are likely to hinder more abstract thinking as imposed by another culture.

Because of these two factors, any learning system on similar figures and solids must be designed as an activity programme in order to at least partially redress the pupils' lack of sufficient concrete experiences earlier on in life which are relevant to the subject. Before any theorizing takes place students must be enabled to handle concrete objects, carry out operations on them, and gradually move from specific and concrete operations to more generalized and abstract ones.

2. Piaget's contribution

In the context described in (1), Piaget's model of the stages of intellectual activity is relevant. The previous paragraph is in line with this model. A brief overview of Piaget's developmental psychology is given by Borger and Seaborne (1966). A very detailed account and evaluation is Flavell (1963). Two observations of Piaget's stages must be made here. First, the intellectual structures developed during any stage are not the automatic result of a maturational development, but are the result of a learning process taking place at this stage, based on previous learning in the context of simpler, more concrete and less generalized structures.

Secondly, stages cannot be skipped without doing harm — learning at any stage is severely hampered by incomplete development at previous, simpler levels. The earlier deficiencies are attempted to be rectified, the better the chances for success. Hence the tendency to bring 'compensation' and 'intervention' programmes down to as young an age as possible.

3. Modern teaching methods and learning aids

From 1966 onwards, as the learning system developed, I gained insight into the problems and guidelines described so far. With it came the realization that only a complete learning system, incorporating modern methods and providing a large amount of concrete practical work, would produce results.

4. Syllabus requirements

Examination syllabuses do not usually spell out expected student behaviour. They are merely checklists of mathematical topics. Syllabuses can be made operational by collecting past examination problems on any one topic, followed by stating as the criterion behaviour that students be able to solve these and similar problems. Here is a typical example (Cambridge GCE Examinations, Overseas Centres, November 1967):

OF A SCHOOL HALL AN EXACT MODEL IS MADE.

THE FLOOR AREA OF THE MODEL IS $\frac{1}{144}$ OF

THE REAL FLOOR. FIND THE RATIO OF THE

VOLUMES OF THE MODEL AND THE REAL HALL.

The solution of this problem requires behaviour at the level of formal operations (Piaget). There are relationships between corresponding lengths, between corresponding areas and between corresponding volumes of the hall and its model. And the solution of the problem requires manipulation of relationships between these relationships. Such complex behaviours can only be acquired by building on simpler and more concrete behaviours. To manage the learning situation at a more concrete level means to draw up new criterion behaviours at that simpler level. Working backwards from the examination syllabus and the Form IV textbooks, I landed up with the most basic and concrete behaviours relative to the subject of study. In the final learning system which emerged, it was these basic behaviours students had to acquire first, before proceeding to more abstract operations.

THREE LEARNING SYSTEMS

The following is a description of three distinct learning systems on similar figures and solids, together with a comment on their relation to the factors described in the previous section.

System 1: the Traditional System

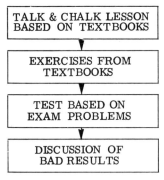

Figure 1

Texts used: Certificate Mathematics, Volume 3, exercise 65 (Durell), and General Mathematics, Book 3, Chapter 6 (Shannon & McLeish-Smith). Students: Form IV, aged 20+. Student characteristics: not taken into account under this approach. Methods: too formal, too little activity by students, emphasis on formal, ie abstract operations. Only when discussing the post-results were visual aids and models used!

Comment The worst possible method. When as a beginning teacher in 1965 I approached things this way, the results were disastrous. Students simply could not solve problems of the kind mentioned on the previous page (Syllabus requirements) and so I began to receive some glimpses of the problems involved. This led to the development of some of the demonstration materials that are still a feature of the present learning system. Here follows an example:

Apparatus: one dozen identical cardboard boxes of a sufficiently large size to be used as demonstration material (eg Persil boxes).

Method: show one box to class and ask 'How many boxes are needed to build a solid which is twice as long, twice as high and twice as wide as this one?'

Usually the following answers are given (in that order): 2, 4, 6 (often skipped), 8. The answer is found by building in one's mind the required solid (spatial visualization). The answer '8' would not be clear to all and so the teacher would ask a student to come forward and actually build the solid. Once this has been done it can be used for further questions, such as: 'By what factor is the original volume multiplied? And the base area? What is the ratio of the heights? Of the front faces? of the volumes?'

System 2: the incorporation of a Linear Programme

The next year, when similar classes had to learn about the same concepts, the sequence started with the demonstration and discussion periods, during which students were required to respond actively by answering questions, doing small calculations and writing down answers. This discovery-type of lesson led to the formulation of the mathematical model involved. This was followed up by a programmed lesson using a linear programme (Draisma, 1966), a discussion, textbook exercises and a post-test (Figure 2).

Use of concrete objects, both plane figures and solids. Also: O/H transparencies. During these lessons classes developed tables like the ones given in Appendix 1, but with numerical examples. From these a general mathematical model was induced ('The Theory'). The linear programme with the pre-post test was revised three times. The 50 frames contain a large number of drawings, and proceed from 'concrete' to 'abstract'. A brief report on the use of the programme is given in Draisma (1967).

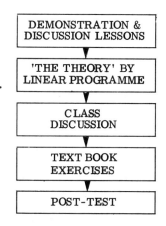

Figure 2

Comment This is a much more satisfactory system as it starts at a more concrete level. This I found was essential, regardless of whether the class was Form II, III, IV or V. The emphasis has shifted from teaching to learning, and the system is much more pupil-centred. However, from the student responses I realized that 'the theory' lends itself easily to rote learning. All that is required is to square or cube certain factors and ratios, or perform the inverse operations. Rote learning was detected when students failed to solve simple 'concrete' problems, requiring insight rather than the mechanical application of 'the theory'.

While refining the programme, additional concrete materials were developed for demonstration and discussion, in order to bring out the physical basis of the relationships between similar figures and between similar solids. One, a kind of slide rule, is described below.

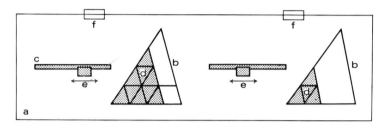

Figure 3

Key: a. cardboard rule permitting slides to move inside between front and back panels
      b. congruent triangular windows cut out in front face of rule
      c. slots in front face
      d. movable slides with identical triangular pattern, each 'unit triangle' being similar to windows b
      e. flaps glued to the slides in order to move them
      f. klemmboy holders, for attaching the rule to the blackboard

The main uses of the slide rule are:

i)   using one slide only, it can be demonstrated that 'area' grows differently from 'length' when plane figures are enlarged. This is a matter of observing what happens as the slide is moved to the right. This physical reality can then be formalized by careful questioning, eg in window b, show triangle with base of one unit. Ask student to shift the slide in such a way that the base gets multiplied by factors 2, 3 and 4 respectively. What happens to the area in these cases? Suppose we introduce an area multiplication factor of 9, what is the linear magnification? All answers can be found or verified by counting the number of unit triangles involved. Repeat by using a triangle of base 2 units as the starting point.

ii) use both slides simultaneously to create several sets of similar triangles, and study linear magnification in relation to the multi-

196

plication of areas. Repeat by using ratios. Summarize results in table form.

System 3: an Integrated Learning System

In view of the comment made in System 2 one major improvement was added, namely a 'mathematics practical', to be inserted into the learning sequence immediately after the introductory lessons (Figure 4).

The practical takes up four to six periods. During these, students use a wide range of concrete materials with a set of work cards requiring students to progress from concrete handling of objects to performing abstract operations on relationships between these objects.

Comment The teacher has now passed from being a transmitter of information (System 1) and a bad one at that when we consider reception, to a designer of a learning environment constructed to suit a particular student population, and making use of a variety of learning

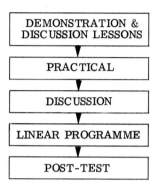

Figure 4

aids and teaching methods. The system is flexible and can easily be adapted to suit the needs of different classes. For instance by varying the number and level of the demonstration and discussion periods, by adding or removing sets of objects with their work cards, by varying individual's paths through the sequence of tasks during the practical sessions, etc. I have had good results with this final system with classes ranging from Form II to Form V. Students in Form V did no better on the practical than students from Form II, nor did they show greater skill in using the mathematical model. This would seem to support the assumption that these students share a common characteristic, namely that they have had insufficient concrete experience with materials relevant to this specific field, when they were still very young.

ACKNOWLEDGMENT

I am indebted to Mr David Grubb, then PCE student at the University of Zambia, for making an inventory of objects and work-cards used, for suggesting improvements to them, and for relating the system to 'new maths' textbooks which have now been introduced in Zambia (Grubb, 1971).

REFERENCES

Bernstein, B. (1970) A critique of the concept of compensatory education. In 'Education for Democracy' (Ed) D. Rubenstein and C. Stoneman. Penguin Books
Borger, R. and Seaborne, A. E. M. (1966) 'The Psychology of Learning'. Penguin Books

Draisma, T. (1966) 'Similar figures and solids, a Linear Programme'. In-house publication, revised three times in subsequent years

Draisma, T. (1967) 'An experiment with programmed learning'. In-house report, Munali Secondary School, Lusaka, Zambia

Draisma, T. (1971) 'Spatial Visualization, comments around a teacher designed learning system'. Report to MAZ annual conference, Lusaka, Zambia

Durell, C. V. 'Certificate Mathematics' Volume III. Bell, England

Flavell, J. H. (1963) 'The Developmental Psychology of Jean Piaget'. Chapter 10. Van Nostrand Reinhold Company, London

Goldberg, S. (1969) 'The relationships of curriculum development to teaching and learning in Zambia'. Mathematics Zambia, Volume 2, No.5, 13-17

Grubb, D. (1971) 'Special Project on Similar Figures and Solids'. Science Education Centre, University of Zambia

Incorporated Association of Assistant Masters in Secondary Schools (1957) 'The Teaching of Mathematics'. Cambridge University Press

Lovell, K. and Butterworth, I. B. (1966) 'Abilities underlying the understanding of proportionality'. Mathematics Teaching, No.37, Winter 1966, 5-9

Meijer, O. (1971) Waarom ik wil meewerken aan het ontwikkelen van een aktiveringsprogramma voor kinderen wit handarbeidersmilieus. Sil, Leiden

Nyerere, J. K. (1967) 'Education for self-reliance'. Dar-Es-Salaam: Tanzania Information Services. Also in Nyerere (1968) 'Freedom and Socialism'. A collection of speeches published by Oxford University Press, Dar-Es-Salaam

Shannon and McLeish-Smith. 'General Mathematics' Book III, Longmans, England

APPENDIX 1: SUBJECT MATTER ANALYSIS

1 Outline for junior forms (see Draisma, 1971).

2 Outline for senior forms.

2.1 **Definition** of similarity, including recognition and generation of examples
and non-examples of similarity.

2.2 **Multiplication Factors**

    a. Linear magnification, 1

    b. Area multiplication factor, a

    c. Volume multiplication factor, v

    d. Operations

FACTOR	OPERATION	FACTOR
1	square	a
Specific) 1	cube	v
numerical) a	take sq. rt.	1
examples) v	?	a
only) :	:	:

    e. The cases 1 one, 1 = one, 1 one

    f. Algebraic examples (simple plane figures and solids).

    g. Scales, ratio of corresponding lengths, ratio of corresponding
areas, of corresponding volumes, when given similar plane
figures and similar solids respectively. Relationships
between these ratios.

    h. Generalization to less defined shapes.

    (2.1 and 2.2 are largely revision of what should be taught in the
junior forms.)

2.3 Verification of 2.2d using more complex formulae: parallelogram,
trapezium, sphere, cone, pyramid

2.4 **Ratios**

    a. ratio of corresponding lengths, $1_1 : 1_2$

    b. ratio of corresponding areas, $A_1 : A_2$

    c. ratio of corresponding volumes, $V_1 : V_2$

    d. relationships between ratios under a, b and c on the one
hand, and factors 1, a, and v listed under 2.2 on the other

    e. relationships between ratios listed under a, a, b, c

RATIO	OPERATION(S)	RATIO
$1_1 : 1_2$	square	$A_1 : A_2$
$1_1 : 1_2$	cube	$V_1 : V_2$
$V_1 : V_2$	take cube root	$1_1 : 1_2$
$A_1 : A_2$	?	$V_1 : V_2$
:	:	:

APPENDIX 2: SAMPLE WORKCARDS

The 'P' Series refers to plane figures, the 'S' Series to solids

---

P1. Apparatus: Two circles glued on a piece of board
  1. Are they similar figures?
  2. Measure the diameters to the nearest tenth of an inch
  3. Calculate the following ratios:
     - (i) small diameter : long diameter = —— : ——
     - (ii) small radius : long radius = —— : ——
     - (iii) small circumf. : long circumf. = —— : ——
     - (iv) small area : large area = —— : ——

P.S. In case you think you need formulae, here they are
$$c = 2\pi r \qquad\qquad A = \pi r^2$$

P5. Apparatus: Pegboard, pegs, elastic bands
  1. Use the elastic bands to make two rectangles, one 2 by 3 units, and one of 6 by 9 units.
  2. Are these rectangles similar?
  3. In what ratio are their lengths?
  4. In what ratio are their widths?
  5. Also state the ratio of their perimeters.
  6. What is the ratio of their areas

S1. Apparatus: Two camping Gaz cylinders, one twice the height of the other
  1. Are they similar in the mathematical sense of the word?
  2. Explain your answer

S5. Apparatus: Similar rectangular blocks built from 'Lego' blocks the colours are Blue (B), Red (R), White (W).
  1. For the solids B, R and W (in that order), the lengths are in the ratio —— : —— : ——
  2. Find the ratio of their base areas. Record the answer in the same way as for question 1.
  3. What is the ratio of their volumes?
  4. Suppose we wanted to build a solid similar to B, R and W of 5 bricks long. How many bricks would be needed?

frame 4.   A photograph is $3\frac{1}{2}$ in. long and $2\frac{1}{2}$ in. wide. A magnifier is used to enlarge the photograph.

Q.   4.   If the length of the enlargement is 7 in., the width will be ———".

The linear magnification (l.m.) in this case is ——— .

This means that all lines in the original photograph will be ——— as long on the enlargement.

Note: l.m. is short for l ——————— m ———————

frame 13.   The following table was drawn up for four different line segments, enlarged by a certain factor (l.m.)

original length (in.)	new length (in.)	l.m.	orig. leng. : new leng.	
5	30	———	——— : ———	
3	———	4	——— : ———	
7	———	———	1 : 2	
———	18	———	1	3

Q.   13.   Complete the above table.

Note that the second number in column 4 is the same as the number in the third column.

frame 22.

l.m. = 2
ratio of areas = $1:2^2$

We have found that if we enlarge a square or a rectangle using a linear magnification of n the ratio of corresponding sides is 1 : n and the ratio of the two areas $1 : n^2$.

Q.   22.   Of two similar rectangles the ratio of the corresponding sides is 1 : 5 .

The ratio of the areas is 1 : ———

If the area of the first rectangle is 12 sq.in., then the area of the second rectangle is ——— x 12 sq.in. = ——— sq.in.

Hint: use the ratio of areas you've just found.

*Answers to questions were attached to the programme in the form of an answer sheet

The Educational Game as a Group Learning Program

ALAN MACKIE

The team game has for a long time been highly rated in our educational tradition as a means of developing acceptable social behaviour. Certainly, games in general reflect the social order of things: there are winners and losers; the common goal of personal advancement; and most important, a set of rules which are commonly observed.

The work described in this paper is concerned with the **educational** game which can have some, at least, of the essential characteristics of a learning program:

1) it exists in physical form
2) it has specific instructional objectives, the attainment of which is measurable
3) it is designed having special regard to the motivation of the student/player

However, the educational game considered here differs from a typical learning program in that:

1) it is not self-instructional in the usual sense
2) whereas a program is used by a student normally just once, the game can be run through any number of times — as many times as the players care to have a game

(though perhaps because of this the playing of educational games has more in common with the repetitive operant conditioning routines used on animals than does using the typical learning programs to which human beings are commonly subjected.)

GROUP LEARNING

But perhaps the most significant point is that the game provides a group learning situation where any player can be (and generally will be) corrected by other players when in error. The fact that a student can, in this situation, give out of what he has learnt, and not merely absorb information, may have an important bearing on his retention, and puts the concept of active learning in yet another light.

Now it may be objected that in the classroom the teacher will not only have to teach or consolidate the educational content of the game, but will also have to teach its rules. However, a common way, if not the best way of learning a game, is by playing it with more experienced players. This suggests a method of working in a class (in which group learning is the norm) where one group is instructed how to play the game, and subsequently by rotation is instrumental in teaching all the other members of the class.

This paper describes an attempt to teach basic set theory using this method, and the evaluation of the game by traditional program learning pre- and post-testing techniques.

THE OBJECTIVES OF THE GAME "Get Set"

The mathematical content of Get Set is at two levels, corresponding to two main objectives somewhat loosely described as:

1) given a Venn Diagram framework with three well defined sets A, B and C, the student will be able to place elements of certain specified universal sets in their correct position on the Venn Diagram;

2) given the symbols for various combinations of sets A, B and C (eg the union, intersection, complement of the union etc) to identify the corresponding region on the Venn Diagram; or given the regions, to identify the correct symbols.

Now it is arguable that in order to play Get Set the student must already have the ability stated in objective 1, since playing the game first consists in placing elements in their correct positions on a Venn Diagram framework. Clearly though there are degrees of confidence and speed at which this is done. The game is intended to provide the practice and consolidation towards increasing this confidence.

But if to play the game properly the player must have the mathematical skill stated in objective 1, then conversely the student who can play the game competently must have this mathematical ability. It follows that if a new player, who is also new to the mathematics of sets at level 1, is taught by his peers how to play the game proficiently, he will in the course of this have acquired the mathematical skill denoted by the first objective.

Regarding objective 2, the difference between the Get Set game which needs to be used repetitively, and the normal program is very apparent — since it is only by repeatedly playing the game that the student necessarily becomes personally involved with the information he is required to learn to attain objective 2. This is rather like the situation in 'Monopoly' where players come to learn the contents of the Community Chest cards after playing the game a number of times. And perhaps the proper area of investigation here is to determine the number of times the game must be played for objective 2 to be realized for each player, assuming that there is such a number. Even so, whether or not this objective is realized, playing this game just a few times does on analysis still seem to be a good educational strategy moving the student in the direction of the second objective.

THE GAME

The board for Get Set is a Venn Diagram framework for 3 sets having the 3 overlapping circles A, B and C (Figure 1).

There are two basic games which are equivalent in that the rules are the same for each game, but they are played with different universal sets.

For the 'people' game the elements consist of 49 people denoted by faces printed on counters. This is the introductory game where just by looking at a face a player can determine if that element belongs to a given set or not. The second more advanced game uses the set of numbers from 1 to 49. There are 5 'set naming' cards for each game. The players define the sets A, B and C by choosing 3 out of the 5 for a particular game. The three cards are then placed on the board beside A, B and C. In this case (Figure 1) A is the set of people wearing glasses; B is the set of people with a beard and C is the set of people wearing a hat. The selection of 3 out of 5 possible sets provides for a variety of games within the basic game; and implicit in this is the idea that a mathematician can define 'set A' for example, one way on one

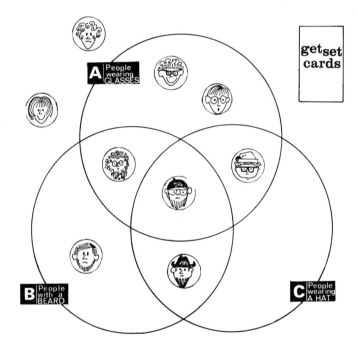

Figure 1

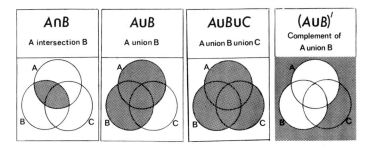

Figure 2

occasion, and a different way on another occasion.

The space marked Get Set cards in Figure 1 is for a pack of 12 cards, 4 of which are shown in Figure 2. They each denote combined sets. For example the first one in Figure 2 is for A intersection B. This is stated verbally and symbolically, and the appropriate region is shaded on the Venn Diagram below.

The cards deal with the union, intersection and complement of the union of any 2 of the 3 sets. There are also 3 cards giving some combinations of all 3 sets (eg the third card in Figure 2).

To play the game the counters (or elements) are faced downwards off the board. Each player picks up an element in turn and places it in its correct position on the Venn Diagram.

Should an element fall in the intersection of 2 sets the player is entitled to turn over a Get Set card. He can then pick up all the elements falling in the shaded region (set combination) indicated on the card. Elements not belonging to A, B or C are placed outside the circles and can be acquired by a player should he turn a card denoting the complement of a set combination.

A player who picks an element falling into the intersection of all 3 sets (eg the bearded, hatted, be-spectacled element in the centre region in Figure 2) is entitled to turn a Get Set card and to have another go.

The winner is the one who has most elements when all 49 have been played. Misplaced elements can be acquired by anyone who spots them.

In the people game the players can determine the membership of an element by inspection. (No previous knowledge is required.)

For the number game the player needs to know, for example, that 21 is a multiple of 3, or at least what is meant by multiple of 3. (Players will argue out particular cases.)

TWO INVESTIGATIONS

Two independent investigations were carried out on the use of this game as a teaching vehicle. The two experiments were not for comparison purposes; they were merely to investigate two lines of approach.

The first was concerned with the Rotational Group Learning technique

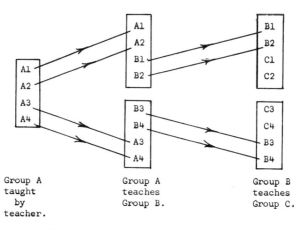

Group A	Group A	Group B
taught	teaches	teaches
by	Group B.	Group C.
teacher.		

Figure 3. Group shown in each box played one of each of two games

already mentioned, and the second with the use of the game as a teaching aid in the normal classroom situation in which the class is supervised and instructed by a teacher. In both cases the learning tasks and the pre- and post-tests were carried out in one session lasting from $1\frac{1}{4}$ to 2 hours.

Rotational group learning

Twelve ten year old children from Yatton Junior School volunteered to assist with the work on a Saturday morning and subsequently learnt they would be paid 10p an hour for this. After completing the pre-test, 4 of these were chosen at random, and are denoted by A1, A2, A3 and A4 in Figure 3.

This group was taught how to play each of the two games by a teacher, and then split into two pairs. Four more novices (B1, B2, B3, B4) joined them to form two groups in which the A group taught the B group, playing one each of the two games. Then the A group dropped out and the B group went on to teach four more novices C1, C2, C3 and C4, playing one of each game. The net result is that Group A played four games, two instructed by the teacher and two in which they acted as teachers. B group also played four games: two instructed by A group (and not by the teacher) and two where they taught group C. Group C only played two games, instructed by B group and did not have the opportunity to teach the game.

Group A were not instructed in the significance of the symbols on the Get Set cards — they were merely taught how to play the game.

THE RESULTS

First investigation

Average pre- and post-test scores and relative gains are recorded in Table I as percentages, for objective 1 and objective 2.

	OBJECTIVE 1 (Placing elements correctly on a Venn Diagram)			OBJECTIVE 2 (Interpreting symbols and identifying regions)		
Rotational Group Learning (Total 3 x 4 = 12 pupils)	Mean pre-test score %	Mean post-test score %	Mean relative gain %	Mean pre-test score %	Mean post-test score %	Mean relative gain %
GROUP A	36	97	96	16	31	19
GROUP B	33	86	81	31	47	23
GROUP C	30	75	64	31	44	18
Normal classroom teaching	46	80	63	26	52	36

All groups performed well with respect to objective 1. Group C predictably did not achieve as high scores as groups A or B and is not really comparable with them having played only half the number of games.

Group A achieved slightly better results than B, but with a mean post-test score of 86% and a relative gain of 81% the B group had clearly learnt a a great deal. Regarding objective 2 the results are similar for all groups and tend to confirm that four games are not sufficient to achieve high scores.

However, a review of the test items revealed that questions contributing a possible 20% of the marks were somewhat beyond stated objectives requiring performance at a 'construction' level (eg writing symbols) rather than at the recognition level of the objective (identifying the correct symbols).

Normal classroom instruction

In the second investigation a class of 35 top juniors (10 years of age) at Almondsbury C of E Primary School were instructed as a class and allowed to play two or three games. Again the results for objective 1 were satisfactory.

The results for objective 2 are better than in investigation 1 and presumably reflect the benefit of the teacher's instruction.

CONCLUSIONS

From the results of both experiments it would appear that the game can be used to advantage either way, particularly with regard to objective 1. It is worth noting that many teachers would not attempt to teach set symbolism to 10 year olds and certainly not in the same session as the pupils first introduction to sets. On these grounds the results can be considered good.

Method of presentation: tape/slide

Selection of a Method of Presentation to Aid the Learning of Manipulatory Skills

JANET SMITH

Aseptic technique is fundamental to the study of laboratory cultures of micro-organisms. The student beginning microbiology must learn a number of techniques for inoculating culture media efficiently and with safety.

In the initial stages of selecting a method of presentation it was assumed that:

(i)   the presentation should be visual

(ii) the visuals should be photographs rather than line drawings

(iii) all shots should be taken from 'over the shoulder'

Since the techniques are learned in a laboratory situation, the hardware involved should be simple and flexible. For this reason the idea of linking visuals to an audio system was rejected.

One technique 'The transfer of organisms from one broth culture to another broth' was presented to a group of 6th form students by:

(a)   a series of 35mm colour slides paced by remote control (19 slides)

(b)   an 8mm colour filmloop (1 min 45 sec)

Each student was given a statement of the objectives, the conditions and the level of performance expected, and told to view the whole presentation before attempting the technique.

Little quantitative data was collected in these early stages, but observations were made with reference to a number of criteria including:

1. **Student learning time**
    Students were allowed to practise and when they felt ready, perform a 'test run'. The mean learning time for students learning from the film-loop was approximately one third of that for the students learning from the slides.

2. **Student performance**
    During both practice and 'test run' it was observed that students learning from slides had difficulty in anticipating the next action and conse-

quently made errors such as placing test tube caps on the bench.

Students learning from the filmloop did not make these errors and their movements were more fluent.

3. **Laboratory convenience**

There was little to choose between the two systems with regard to space, number of power points, leads etc.

This particular type of subject matter requires the student to have his hands free to practise. The loop system was easier to operate. The slide system could be supplemented by an automatic timer, but these are expensive.

Back reference was easy as the filmloop was short. The frame stop on the loop projector allowed the student to study any frame more closely, thus incorporating the main advantage of the slide system.

Some of the characteristics of skilled performance were identified as: (a) ease; (b) fluency of movement; (c) lack of hesitation, and (d) unhurriedness, and the loop system was selected on the grounds that it conveyed these characteristics, and also provided the student with a 'master performance' against which he could judge his own efforts.

A number of further points were then identified to be taken into consideration in developing the system further:

1. Single concept filmloops should be as short as possible. The film used in the developmental testing has been reshot and now runs for less than a minute.

2. No cues are presented on the filmloop — the loop is intended to focus the attention of the learner on the sequence and fluency of the movements and to facilitate translation from stimulus to action.

3. No provision is made in the filmloop for identifying faults in the technique or the end product, or for suggesting remedial action.

4. No provision is made in the loop for developing 'readiness' for coping with accidents such as spilled cultures.

It was therefore necessary to select a method of presentation to complement the filmloop. A worksheet seemed to be a flexible system, and, by increasing the element of self instruction freed the lecturer to observe individuals and comment on their performance. The worksheet also gives the student a permanent record. A worksheet was designed which incorporates the following:

1. A statement of the overall objectives and a brief description of the applications of the technique.

2. A description of the materials required.

3. A statement of the contamination hazards both to handler and culture.

4. Detailed line drawings and written instructions for each stage in the technique.

5. Instructions for labelling and incubating cultures.

6. A guide for checking the end product against reference criteria and questions on:
   (a) remedial action in the event of an inadequate end product
   (b) dealing with accidents

In further trials it was found to be of the greatest importance to guide the student in implementing the filmloop-worksheet system. The student is recommended to:

1. Read through the entire worksheet
2. Sit in a position where he can see the filmloop clearly and assemble the materials
3. BEFORE PRACTICE, view the loop several times and stop the loop if he wishes to study a frame more closely
4. Practise the technique
5. Label and incubate cultures
6. Check the end product and answer the questions

Several techniques have been presented and the system is currently being evaluated.

REFERENCES

Borger, R. and Seabourne, A. E. M. (1970) 'The Psychology of Learning'. Penguin
Dwyer, F. M. (1970) AVCR, **18**, No.3, 235

Method of presentation: Videotape, half inch, Shibaden

Arithmetic and Visual Aids

A SORBIER and R BROWAEYS

INTRODUCTION

This investigation is an approach to the study of relations between pedagogical aids and process learning.

For the last few years we have worked on students' difficulties through the tasks they have to do. The analysis we use is that of errors. The results are that the most important kind of error is explained by a bad attainment of automatism. Often we used programmed learning, but if the students learn the rules, and answer correctly the validation tests (internal and external ones) they still make some of the same mistakes in a more complex task.

For example, our students, who are technicians in building, misread scales (32% of all errors) and miscount powers of ten (33% of all errors), after being taught traditionally.

This was the reason for producing programmed learning chapters 'Scale reading' and 'Arithmetic: powers of ten' in our slide rule course.

Another group of our students worked with this programmed learning and we found an external validity of 4% (numbers of errors/numbers of response) for scales reading and 2% for powers of ten.

But when they have to use the slide rule for calculating products and quotients we found the errors rose to 7% in misreading and 13% in miscounting.

These results give us a hypothesis for introducing a constraint in exercise training, eg an imposed rhythm for giving response.

We began with the chapter which seemed the most easy to treat, viz 'Scales reading'. Then after some experiments we would be able to work on the training powers of ten.

SCALES READING

Errors analysis

Errors analysis shows the distribution of those who misread through the sectors of the slide rule (defined by the module of graduations) and the second significant figure of the number read on the scale (Table I).

Table I. Distribution for misreading the scale

Module of graduations	Second significant figure of the number read on the scales is:		Total
	Zero	Other than zero	
1.10^{-2}	0.11	0.05	0.16
2.10^{-2}	0.36	0.19	0.55
5.10^{-2}	0.19	0.10	0.29
	0.66	0.34	1.00

Experimental design

Training exercises were built on film loops as described. Each exercise presents three pictures:

a) a sector of the scale with the principal line of the cursor on it, during a controlled time (which varies through the experiment);
b) a text in which invitation is given to the student to find the number attached to the position of the line on the scale and to write it on a response sheet. This picture stays for 4 seconds;
c) the correct response is given after 4 seconds.

Each film loop holds six exercises. Twelve film loops set up a group called 'ordinate group' or 'blue group' (Table II). The film loops are on standard 8mm Technicolor cassettes.

Table II. Ordinate group or blue group

The first picture stays during	SECTORS OF THE SCALES			
	(1)	(2)	(3)	(4)
5 secs. (A)	A_1:6 exercises	A_2:6 exercises	A_3:6 exercises	A_4:6 exercises
3 secs. (B)	B_1:6 exercises	B_2:6 exercises	B_3:6 exercises	B_4:6 exercises
2 secs. (C)	C_1:6 exercises	C_2:6 exercises	C_3:6 exercises	C_4:6 exercises

Sectors of scales are defined as:

(1) Between the figures of the scales (1 - 2)
(2) Between the figures of the scales (2.0 - 2.1)
(3) Between the figures of the scales (2.1 - 4.0)
(4) Between the figures of the scales (4 - 10)

Each film loop is fixed by the time during which the picture stays and the sector of the scale. For example (A_3) is the loop where the first picture stays for 4 seconds and belongs to the third sector of the scale. The instructions to the group could read 'Find three film loops labelled with a blue ribbon marked A_1, B_2, C_3,' (the ones which are underlined in Table II).

Another group called 'random group' or 'red group' is set up with twelve new film loops. Four of them set up a sub-group fixed only by the time of presentation of the first picture. Each exercise in a loop is chosen in random order (Table III).

Table III. Random group or red group

The first picture stays during	Sub-groups
4 seconds	(A_1, A_2, A_3, A_4) : 24 exercises $= A_R$
3 seconds	(B_1, B_2, B_3, B_4) : 24 exercises $= B_R$
2 seconds	(C_1, C_2, C_3, C_4) : 24 exercises $= C_R$

Their instructions could be 'Find three film loops labelled with a red ribbon marked A_2, B_2, C_3.'

Results

The film loops present the advantage of many experimental designs in order to find, for example, the optimal number of exercises in automatism training; order of items; rhythm of presentation, and so on.

From statistical analysis, actually we are able only to say that:

1. The best order of items for our students is to learn for half the time by this way:

first morning	ordinate group	A_1 B_1 C_1
first afternoon	ordinate group	A_2 B_2 C_2
second morning	ordinate group	A_3 B_3 C_3
second afternoon	ordinate group	A_4 B_4 C_4
third morning	random group	A_R
third afternoon	random group	B_R
fourth morning	random group	C_R

Instead of:　first morning　ordinate group A_1　A_2　A_3　A_4
　　　　　　first afternoon　ordinate group B_1　B_2　B_3　B_4
　　　　　　second morning　ordinate group C_1　C_2　C_3　C_4

The second half is better by the sequence used by the random group.

2.　Programmed learning and speed training on scales reading give no better results than programmed learning only.

3.　A booklet in which contents are given in a classical way, followed by the whole training exercises on reading scales gives the best results. In a complex task the frequency of misread is less than 1%.

A great deal of other experiments should be looked into, for example comparative study with booklets, with which the pupils can learn to their own rhythm. But we are not in a Research Centre — we are in an industrial training Centre. We have to take the best results we have found as rapidly as possible. We will try in future, if it is possible, to explain why these results are good or not and find in experimental design the factors which interfere with the efficiency of the program.

We will try now to decrease the frequency of errors upon powers of ten.

POWERS OF TEN

Errors analysis and work analysis

We have two main types of errors: the one is explained by misknowledge of the rules, the other by miscount in algebra (even if the pupils know very well the rules about powers of ten).

Among the second group, two principal work situations can be used:

a)　the exercise is given as a whole: this situation exists in training and in the work situations. Then it is possible to simplify the expression before the calculation.

For example
$$\frac{10^{-3} \times 10^2}{10^5 \times 10^{-3}} \quad \text{becomes} \quad \frac{10^2}{10^5}$$

b)　the exercise is given by factors one after the other building up to the whole expression. This situation exists only in building yards when the workers give the supervisor numbers, in verbal form, one after the other for immediate calculations.

Experimental design

The degree of difficulty could be defined (a) with the factors which set the numerator and the denominator, and (b) with the sign of each power.

It was set up in the experimental design shown in Table IV. Each square is an exercise defined by a number. For example, the exercise No. 29 is

Table IV. Experimental design for powers of ten

NUMERATOR

	Sign of powers	1 factor		2 factors			3 factors			
		+	-	++	+-	--	+++	++-	+--	---
D	1 factor +	1								
E	-									
N										
O	2 factors ++			21	22	23				
M	+-			27	28	29				
I	--			24	25	26				
N	3 factors +++									
A	++-									
T	+--									
O	---									81
R										

(DENOMINATOR reading down the left column)

set up by an expression with 2 factors on the numerator and two factors on the denominator. The numerator has two negative signs and the denominator one positive and one negative sign.

For this experimental design three kinds of media are used:

1. A booklet which contains the 81 exercises with immediate response. Through this media the pupil is able to work in free strategy of resolution and on his own rhythm. We say here that training is of free strategy and rhythm.

2. We have 81 series of slides. Each series presents three slides. We can read on the first one the whole expression during three seconds, by factors which compose it. Example: the first slide of the series No. 21 stays for 12 seconds.

The pupils use the strategy they want before giving the result (simplifying first the numerator, then the denominator, before calculating the two partial results). But they have to do it in a fixed time. We say the students are trained in free strategy and imposed rhythm.

The second slide stays for 4 seconds and during this time the students write their own results on a response sheet.

The third slide stays for 4 seconds to read the correct result.

3. **Film loop** Film loops are used for training on imposed strategy and
    rhythm. The exercise is given fact by fact up to the whole expression.
    The students are obliged to work in order of the presentation. The time
    for writing their own results and for reading the correct response is the
    same as for series of slides (4 seconds).

Results

We are not able to give statistical results because our groups are too small
for significant comparisons. We observe only some tendencies, as:

1. If our students have left school for more than three years, they give
    good results in training on the forty first exercises with booklets, and
    one week after on the slide series from five factors to the six factors
    expression.

    We observe that after fifty exercises on booklets, the students feel
    satiated, but if we began with slides they are frightened by the speed
    constraint.

2. If the building technician students come directly from school to our
    Centre, the results are a little better with only the slide series than
    with film loops, and they are not good at all with booklets.

3. We did an exercise with students in book-keeping and found that the
    results were better with film loops than with slides.

    We would not attempt to explain this result, for a variety of reasons.
    The first is that they are not statistical results; the second is that we do
    not know the optimal way of using each media before doing comparisons
    between them; finally we do not know what other work has been done in this
    area.

CONCLUSIONS

We wanted to treat this study as we might do in a psychological experimental
design. It is too long and many difficulties arise when we do not work in a
Research Centre.

As was said before, we are in an industrial training centre and we have
to find the best way of education as rapidly as possible. It is not easy because:

1. Many media are available on the market and they seem at first sight
    to be equally useful.

2. Each media is the best in a certain context of training. But the factors
    of this context are not well known.

3. The pupils are rapidly satiated by a media when we use it for too long
    or with great frequency.

It seemed that a previous analysis before using a media should be available. The analysis would be centred on the relations between the population processes of resolution and the technical characteristics of the media. Our hypothesis is that if we have the best matching between the processes of resolution and the style of presentation given by the media, we will be as near as possible to optimum efficiency in knowledge, memory and use of training.

Ergonomic studies in training situations could help teachers in finding media most appropriate to the context they work in at the moment; experimental studies would find further pedagogical rules in context and time.

REFERENCES

Crossman, E. R. F. W. (1957) Ergonomics, **2**, 153
Fitts, P. M. (1966) Journal of Experimental Psychology, **71**, 849
Leplat, J., Enard, C. and Weil, A. (1970) 'La formation par l'apprentissage'. PUF, France
Ombredane, A. and Faverge, J. M. (1955) 'L'analyse du travail'. PUF, France
Seymour, W. D. (1966) 'Industrial Skills'. Pitman, London

Method of presentation: Film loops and slide-tape

Are Educational Technologists Sufficiently Hardware-Orientated?

GEORGE STENHOUSE and
JOHN WOMERSLEY

We would argue 'NO'. There is an important interaction between decisions on hardware and software which has implications in course design and in the selection of instructional media. When designing courses it is naive to suppose that the objectives are developed independently of the selection of the instructional media ('Instrumentation alters orientation' – Richmond, 1968).

One starts with a general aim for a course and then develops some specific objectives. These objectives will depend (1) on the situation in which the instruction is to be used (for example the lecturer with a class of 200 students will have different objectives from someone prepare a tape-slide program for individual instruction) and (2) on the types of media available for the presentation. Although the media used will be dictated to some extent by the objectives it is wrong to formulate precise objectives without reference to the system of presentation; the precise objectives should be tailored to the system being used. In other words alternative systems will have different goals, although there may be some overlap. This argument has been put forward before (Cumming & Dunn, 1969) and it is the fallacy behind most comparative studies.

The system of presentation however should not dictate the objectives, and this is a danger unless educational technologists become more hardware-orientated. Let us suppose for example that it has been decided to adopt the audio-visual method of self-instruction. Many devices for relaying synchronized audio-visual presentations do exist, some with automatic stop facilities. Nearly all are expensive, costing £200 or more, and the main reason for this is that many of the components and particularly the projection part of the system are of a quality more suitable for presentations to a large audience than to a single individual. Again, most existing machines use 35mm slides for presentation of the visual material and slides are bulky to store; they can readily get out of sequence and they can easily be displayed the wrong way up or from the wrong side. On the other hand, many filmstrips can be accommodated in a box capable of taking only a few dozen slides and a mechanism for automatic progression of filmstrips is much simpler to produce than a mechanism for moving on slides. Also filmstrip is cheaper and can easily be coded to stop movement at each frame, or to permit a response – written or by depressing a switch – to be made to a question. There are however few automatic filmstrip projectors and practically all those that do exist are half-frame, which means that it is difficult to make up filmstrip from the 35mm slides taken by enthusiastic teachers and others.

In other words, we believe that there is a need for a cheap device for the presentation of audio-visual instructional material; it should use 35mm filmstrip, have automatic synchronization and stop facilities (Holroyd, 1971), and its software should be capable of being prepared by the amateur enthusiast. Such a machine, developed at the University of Glasgow, is being exhibited here and a brief specification is appended.

In the field of computer-assisted instruction the same situation has prevailed: terminals, developed for a commercial application, are used for instruction. Educational technologists must be sufficiently hardware-orientated to develop hardware appropriate to the task in hand. They should not be bound by material already available – material which is likely to be both expensive and limited in its application.

Progress is however being made in the interaction of hardware and software ideas. Our automated group-teaching device is one result of this interaction.

Work has been going on in the University of Glasgow on:
(1) the hardware of tape-slide presentation
(2) the production of tape-slide programs
(3) feed-back devices
(4) presentation of audio-visual programs to groups of students.

Each of these lines of work contributed to the development of a group automated audio-visual device. This is an audio-visual tutor equipped with feed-back stations; it indicates to the group when there is disagreement so that ideas can be exchanged and a group decision made.

The device is designed for the automatic synchronized presentation of audio-visual material to groups of from 4 to 12 students. Questions in multiple-choice form are posed at intervals, and the commentary stops; the students then respond individually by depressing the appropriate switch on their individual response units. If there is total agreement about the response a green light appears and the device moves on to the next stage of presentation if it is the correct response but there is a red light and a corrective frame appears if the responses are all wrong. When there is disagreement about the response the machine stops to give the students the opportunity to discuss the problem and come to a group decision. The important feature is that the device lets the group know whether discussion will be worthwhile. If there is no disagreement there is obviously no point in discussion.

REFERENCES

Cumming, C. and Dunn, W. R. (1969) The application of cost-effectiveness techniques to educational technology. In 'Aspects of Educational Technology IV'. (Ed) A. C. Bajpai and J. F. Leedham. Pitman, London

Holroyd, C. (1971) Symposium: Audio-visual self-instruction in medical education. In 'Aspects of Educational Technology V'. (Ed) D. Packham, A. Cleary and T. Mayes. Pitman, London

Richmond, K. (1968) Opening Address of 1968 APLET Conference. In 'Aspects of Educational Technology II'. (Ed) W. R. Dunn and C. Holroyd. Methuen, London

Summary of Discussions in Module 2

Discussions in this module were based on specific topics or questions posed by the opening speaker, Commander Budgett, at the beginning of the module and these are used as the basis for this summary.

Research in the field of selection of methods and media

Too much attention is paid to too few results. Unfortunately experiments which fail are not reported, thus making the bias even worse. The net consequence is that for each selection general research results are used and it is then necessary to introduce a 'mini' research to test the validity of the generalizations in particular situations. The usual constraints in a system are the fact that it is a real situation and not a research situation.

Selection of methods and media based purely on behavioural analysis

It was felt that the behaviour and motivation of the students should help to determine the instructional method. The selection of media may help to achieve the objectives, but selection based purely on behavioural analysis makes the use of value judgements difficult. The media chosen can often influence the terminal behaviour and the statement of it — the process is iterative and inter-dependent. Existing classifications of objectives take little account of media or the choice of the best media for that objective.

Educational Technology should make the best use of the resources already available

There is a need to provide multi-method instruction and activity to provide variety. Is it possible to match students and methods? The selection would seem to be a subjective judgement or speculation with present data. Are Educational Technologists sufficiently problem-solving orientated to deal with the selection? The use of trial and error methods in selection and the selection of the 'best' for the particular objective was advocated. In order to carry out this process it is necessary to have cooperation between successful teachers and researchers to analyze 'success' and apply this to the selection of methods and media.

Objectives can be developed independently from the instructional medium

The concise statement of objectives tend to state the obvious and obscure the problem. The media may be used as a teaching function or as a motivational function — with the latter they may enhance success in achieving cognitive objectives — but neither can be developed independently, they are inter-related. The operational objectives can be developed independently but not the training objectives which may depend on the medium.

Other points raised

1) Language is inadequate as a method and a medium. The interpretation of questions and jargon varies from one person to another. A dictionary of terms used in educational technology is already required.

2) The uses of simulation and gaming are often directed at others than those taking part. This requires dissemination of the process and results of such techniques.

Module 3
Evaluation and assessment
Posing the Problems
G HUBBARD

Our subject is evaluation and assessment, but looking at the rest of the programme, one sees that we have a wider remit than that. For we could, I suggest, feel free to range fairly widely over the whole question of the appropriateness of systematic approaches to learning, of whether or not behavioural or other objectives can always be defined, even if by so doing there is some overlap with Module 2.

For the first point to be clear upon is that evaluation and assessment is meaningless out of context. Whether we evaluate – that is make relatively objective quantitative measurements – or assess – that is make relatively subjective qualitative judgements – we must have a standard against which to measure or to judge; we must know what we had hoped to achieve if we are to determine how far we have fallen short.

One important issue therefore is that of behavioural objectives. How far can all learning be defined in terms of behavioural objectives, or in terms of behavioural objectives which can be measured in time to have any significant effect on the learning process? How far has the emphasis on behavioural objectives tended to distort our aims? We accept those aims which can be suitably expressed as objectives; we gloss over those which cannot. If we try to educate people to be capable of dealing with the problems and difficulties of changing the type of work they do in middle life we cannot measure their behaviour in that situation for thirty years or more. So we tend to devise tests of patterns of thinking, degree of conformity and so on which we **hope** correlate with the desired behaviour.

It is nothing new to find the examinable forcing out the essential. What we can consider is how we might extend our concept of objectives to help the essential resist the examinable. For one of the contributions of programmed learning, and the systems approach derived from it, which we should cling to is the concept of making explicit the aims of the learning process, making them explicit to ourselves and to the learners. Put bluntly, if we cannot define what we hope the student will gain from the learning process, why should we expect him to co-operate? Even more bluntly, in the schools sector, the more radical element might ask "Why do we imprison children from the time they are five until they are fifteen when they have done no wrong?" There are some good reasons, but I think we have a duty to set them out.

However, if we start looking for the sort of objectives, measurable or identifiable if not strictly behavioural, that correspond to the higher level aims of education, we may have to be rather more humble than we like. In terms of skills the objectives are relatively respectable, but what can one set as an objective in terms of – to take a vexed question – attitudes on race? Perhaps only "To have ensured that the pupil has encountered liberal attitudes to race, has been given an opportunity to think about inter-racial marriage," and so on. Not very satisfying to a behaviourist, but then, like Queen Elizabeth the First, we may as well recognise that we cannot make windows into men's minds. We can give them the opportunity to think; we cannot make them think; and, most of all, getting the required answer on a test paper does not by any means imply the corresponding attitude outside the classroom. Better to be honest, and settle for a realistic, if not very grand, objective.

A further point more concerned with the total system than with evaluation and assessment as such is that evaluation and assessment is rarely justified unless some use is made of the findings – use meaning something more, one would hope, than the enhancement of the investigator's professional reputation by publication. The main uses are either to guide us in modifying the learning system to improve its efficiency or to provide a measure of re-assurance as to the effectiveness of the system, and guidance as to the learners for whom it is appropriate, to those other than the originator who might be prepared to use it. It this seems a rather naive observation it is not that I have just rediscovered formative and summative evaluation; it is that by looking again at the function of evaluation and assessment, we can be guided to measure and judge those aspects which will best serve that function, and particularly perhaps to see when we should strive for evaluation and when assessment is more appropriate.

If now, in some particular situation we attempt to evaluate or assess, we should be doing so in the context of changes we are prepared to make or of other users who desire the information we are gathering. This sets an economic framework within which the exercise must be mounted; the cost of perfection is of course unlimited, and we have to limit our activity to what its usefulness justifies. Some of the resource material gives useful indications of how to devise effective evaluation methods at acceptable cost.

One thing to be a little cautious about is the temptation to devise controlled experiments; I am here expressing a personal view rather than a necessarily accepted opinion. In the physical sciences we generally do not use controls; we have a touching faith (usually justified) in our ability to isolate variables; a copper bar kept at a constant temperature will stay effectively the same length, so we simply measure the expansion of a heated bar. In the biological sciences we frequently work with control groups and use double-blind techniques, a recognition of the complexity of the organisms and the number of influences affecting them. In the social sciences including education, the organisms are as complex as they come and the influences even more numerous and unpredictable. Indeed the outcome of most experiments, however closely controlled, can be summed up as 'no significant difference'.

Why this is so we can perhaps learn from the few major pieces of sociological investigation that have offered clear conclusions – for example, J W B Douglas's classic study. * The significant variables turn out to be such massively intractable things as social class, rather than refinements in teaching/learning method. In fact, I would suggest, all our findings of 'no significant difference' are in effect telling us that, do what we will with the factors we can control, they will fortunately always be of marginal importance compared with the factors we cannot control – the elements that go to make up a total human being, with all its heritable and environmental influences and prejudices. If we want to correct the bias Douglas discovered, it requires that we do something about our Society; we are unlikely to be able to achieve the desired effect by tinkering about with what goes on in school.

This may seem at first sight a negative view, suggesting that the problems are beyond our power to deal with. This I would not accept, though perhaps it does suggest that education should not be expected to carry the can and provide the cure for all social ills. What I think it does underline is that the controlled experiment is not likely to produce many significant results; that it is seldom really controlled, in the sense even that experiments with mice are controlled, and of course one of the most obviously uncontrolled factors is the teacher in the classroom. Given such major uncontrolled variables, the better the coverage of the experiment, the larger the sample, the more the results of our particular controlled perturbations are submerged beneath greater disturbances. The aim of the research worker may still be, perhaps must always be, to try to set up and operate such experiments at least until some more effective experimental machinery has been devised. But for the development engineer – which is the more appropriate role for the educational technologist – it would be better to leave the comparison of one learning system with another and to concern ourselves with whether particular learning systems attain their objectives.

* 'The Home and the School' by J. W. B. Douglas – A study of ability and attainment in primary schools

This indeed usually debars us from any comparative operation, at least in respect of orthodox teaching and learning, since established practice seldom offers explicit objectives. However, at this stage it is salutary to remember the importance of enabling the essential to resist the examinable, and of relating our evaluation and assessment to needs, whether formative or summative.

Finally, a word on assessment. Or rather a question or so. Have we in fact applied as well as we might the available techniques for quantifying assessment? Accepting that it is a subjective process, that it is applying the judgement of the experienced observer rather than using measures in regard to the validity of which we may have serious doubts, have we gone as far as is possible in standardizing observers and their scores?

Again some of the resource material points to the economic necessity of getting the most we can out of assessment, which can be so much less demanding on resources and often so much less of a disturbance of the learning situation.

A further question arises in relation to some of the developments which can be seen in the Module 1 resource material. We are beginning to envisage learning maps, in which certain nodal areas may be fully structured, but there are a number, perhaps an infinite number, of possible starting points, routes between the essential nodes, the core elements, and hence of possible exit points from the system. With these maps, strict evaluation is relevant to the structured areas, but cannot be applied to the total learning system, for the predictable attainments of the successful students are only a part of what he should achieve. And we cannot, at present, make any very cogent suggestions for evaluating an unpredictable outcome. What sort of evaluation/ assessment procedure is appropriate to this sort of system? What we must surely avoid is rejecting a potentially important development simply because our methodology will not cope with it.

Finally, since some of what I have said may have seemed a little less than enthusiastic, let us remember the great contribution that evaluation and assessment has made to the ferment in education today. It has made, or is making, respectable the idea that one should not only question what one is in education to do, but that one should even question whether one is actually doing it.

The Evaluation of Conferences as Educational Experiences

D E BILLING and J R PARSONAGE

The results are given of a preliminary survey of the opinions of scientists on the purposes of conferences. The most important functions appear to be of an informal variety — informal discussions and communication of ideas and experience. There is considerable failure to fulfil the most important functions, some of which cannot be adequately covered without conferences. Four activities can fulfil most of the important functions — invited lectures, submitted papers, informal discussion and formal groups. Scientific Conferences should be specific, or contain a balanced selection of specific topics.   Too little advance information is given about the aims, level and coverage of conferences.

A particular conference, on chemical education, showed slight attitude changes towards more progressive educational ideas.

AIMS OF SURVEY

There have been many complaints about the usefulness of scientific conferences (Berkovitch, 1971); perhaps they should provide for learning by, and communication between, participants. In this case, the conference might be regarded as an educational experience at post-graduate level. We decided to carry out a preliminary survey of chemists who were interested in education, to determine opinions on the purposes of conferences, what they actually achieved, and what activities were important.

SAMPLE

Accordingly, a rather large questionnaire (A) was sent out in October 1971, to persons whom we thought might be interested in a conference in December 1971 on developments in tertiary chemical education. Sixty-three were returned. The sample is very selected, and our results can therefore only be preliminary. Five-point Likert scales were used where feasible. The sample consisted of 70% chemists, 5% other scientists, 8% educationalists, 6% educational technologists, 2% administrators and 9% other non-scientists. Of these, 56% were employed in universities, 22% in polytechnics, 9% in colleges of

227

education, 5% in schools, 3% in further education, 3% in industry, and 2% in other places. Experience averaged 9.8 years in full-time employment. Eight respondents had an average of 5.4 years in part-time employment.

As expected, the respondents tended to be considerably involved with teaching (68%) but not very much with educational research (27%). A large number (29%) are minimally involved with scientific research work, but a sizeable minority (24%) are extensively involved. In spite of this lack of involvement in research, the respondents tended to be interested in the findings of scientific (56%) and educational (52%) research, and in innovations in education (63%).

FAILURE TO FULFIL FUNCTIONS

A list of 40 possible functions of conferences was provided, and respondents were asked to add to this. There were only six such additions, and these merely amplified some of those which were included. We asked respondents whether they agreed that conferences should provide these functions, and also whether they were successfully promoted. Table I gives only those results where there was a marked failure. This is very apparent for 'review of the state of the art', 'bringing together different disciplines or approaches', 'practical experience in applying new approaches', 'constructive criticism',

Table I. Failures of Conferences to fulfil their functions

Notes Figures show identical trends for Scientific and Educational Conferences, except: **Educational conferences only. Figures are given for scientific conferences, except where educational conferences show the more pronounced trend, as in *) **) figures for educational conferences (N=63)	The purpose of a conference should be to provide opportunities for this function					Most conferences successfully promote this function				
	strongly disagree				agree strongly	strongly disagree				agree strongly
	1	2	3	4	5	1	2	3	4	5
Review of the state of the art	0	3	13	8	28	4	8	16	9	9
Speculation about future developments	2	5	16	21	11	6	12	11	11	5
Bringing together different disciplines or approaches	2	3	15	16	18	11	15	13	7	4
Practical experience in applying new approaches	4	10	9	16	14	11	12	12	9	3
Initiating future activities	8	9	14	13	8	10	16	12	6	0
Constructive criticism	0	5	10	14	24	3	14	11	14	3
Identification of new problems	3	3	14	13	15	6	11	15	13	4
Solving problems	7	10	22	6	5	13	16	14	4	1
Informal discussions and meeting with experts*	1	1	7	11	28	1	5	14	9	8
Informal discussions and meeting with other contacts	0	2	8	6	32	0	3	12	15	7
Communication of ideas and experience amongst participants*	0	0	3	12	33	2	2	6	17	10
An educational experience	6	6	12	7	15	6	10	7	9	5
Learning new concepts	3	6	9	13	17	1	5	20	11	4
Examining social implications**	4	5	15	10	10	3	11	8	4	2
Dissemination of information, via participant to others	2	4	15	12	18	2	6	14	15	6
Destructive criticism	31	8	5	2	5	6	20	8	5	3

'informal discussions and meetings with experts' and 'communication of ideas and experience among participants'.

IMPORTANT FUNCTIONS

We asked respondents to list the most important ten out of the forty suggested functions. Table II gives the frequencies of those mentioned most often. For comparison a histogram is given to indicate average scores on agreement that the functions should be embraced by conferences ('strongly disagree' = -2, 'strongly agree' = +2). The trends of both frequencies and histogram are very similar. At the top is the whole area of formal discussions and communication of ideas and experience.

USEFUL ACTIVITIES

We listed 24 possible activities of conferences and asked respondents to add to the list. There were ten such additions, one (informal social functions) being mentioned nine times. We also asked for the activities most appropriate for each important function. Four activities were mentioned more than 300 times: invited lectures (446), presentation of submitted papers (436), completely informal discussions (360) and formal small-group discussions on pre-arranged topics or problems (313).

There was then a clear gap before the rest of the list followed. These four activities could, in fact, account for all of the functions rated as most important — with the exception of 'practical experience in applying new approaches', which required workshop sessions for implementation.

Table II. The most important functions of Conferences (N = 63)
Shown by frequency of inclusion in first ten choices, and by agreement
that such functions should be fulfilled by scientific conferences

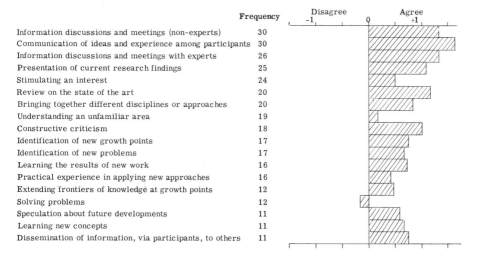

	Frequency
Information discussions and meetings (non-experts)	30
Communication of ideas and experience among participants	30
Information discussions and meetings with experts	26
Presentation of current research findings	25
Stimulating an interest	24
Review on the state of the art	20
Bringing together different disciplines or approaches	20
Understanding an unfamiliar area	19
Constructive criticism	18
Identification of new growth points	17
Identification of new problems	17
Learning the results of new work	16
Practical experience in applying new approaches	16
Extending frontiers of knowledge at growth points	12
Solving problems	12
Speculation about future developments	11
Learning new concepts	11
Dissemination of information, via participants, to others	11

SCOPE AND OTHER ASPECTS

Wide ranging conferences are not favoured, and science conferences should be on very specific topics. Informal discussions and communication of ideas were mentioned most often as the prerogative of conferences, rather than of other means of publication. Thirty-six respondents answered a question on the provision of advance information. Only one thought that all appropriate information was given about the aims, level and coverage of most conferences. The average of the suggested lengths of conferences was 2.6 days.

CHANGING OF ATTITUDES

One hundred and twenty participants in a conference on developments in tertiary chemical education were asked to complete a questionnaire before (B) and another after (C) the event. The respondents were numbered, so that pre- and post-conference questionnaires could be matched. Although 53 returned paper B and 71 completed C, only 42 returned both questionnaires. The samples were very similar in composition to the earlier group (A). In fact, by combining A and B, opinions of a sample of 101 were obtained on some of the purposes of conferences; this data confirms the results from the smaller sample (A).

Most of the participants seem to have accepted progressive views on educational methods before coming to the conference, so that there are very few changes of attitude. There were slight swings towards using objective tests, learning programmes and videotapes, specifying objectives, and especially towards using tape/slide sequences. There were slight swings away from making courses relevant to industry and against studying educational technology.

We thank Dr B S Furniss the co-organizer of the Chemical Education Conference (with DEB), and Mrs Elizabeth Billing for help in data processing.

REFERENCE

Berkovitch, I. (1971) Chemistry in Britain, 7, 341

The Evaluation of Broadcasting at the Open University

A W BATES

One of the Open University's many radical features is that it is deliberately designed as a 'self-improving system'. The ideas of setting objectives, selecting appropriate methods, feed-back, evaluation, and re-design are integral parts of the University's structure and overall teaching philosophy. Furthermore, its academics and administrators have been quick to recognise and accept the need for evaluation. This is particularly true of broadcasting. Since it is a scarce resource and yet requires a considerable investment of time and money, careful and extensive evaluation is obviously necessary.

At first sight, the University appears to be in an excellent position to carry out such an evaluation. The University is the first institution, certainly in this country and probably in the world, designed to the specifications of educational technologists. Thus in many ways, the Open University is a test-bed for educational technology. If the underlying philosophy of educational technology does not work at the Open University, then grave doubts must exist about its general viability.

With such a system in operation, it is tempting to assume that the system will automatically provide evaluation of the broadcasting. However, there are a host of problems that still need to be solved. First of all, there is the problem of the **quantity** of the information that a system such as the Open University can generate. On one foundation course, there are 6,000 students and over 300 tutors. There are 36 individual units, with up to 12 different tutor marked and 32 computer marked assignments on each course. Who is going to handle all the data that will be generated, and how? Then there is the problem of what weight to give to information from different sources. What happens when students all score high grades on an assessment, yet tutors in general feel that the unit or broadcast was dreadful?

What if students in general appear to achieve the objectives of the broadcasts, as measured by assignments, yet find the broadcasts uninteresting or not very useful? Finally, there is the most important question of all: will evaluation in terms of the 'successful' achievement of program objectives in itself be sufficient? Will it, for instance, help in making decisions about the allocation of scarce resources regarding broadcasting, or about whether to use alternative means of teaching to broadcasts? And since broadcasting is only one component of a deliberately integrated multi-media system, is it meaningful or possible to evaluate its contribution separately from that of the total instructional system?

Questions such as these force us to look very carefully at the function of evaluation. In fact, at the Open University we require evaluation of broadcasting at three distinct levels, but with overlap between these levels. Each level of evaluation requires quite different methods of approach. These levels are:

    (1) evaluation of the overall resources allocated to broadcasting, in relation to other media or methods of teaching;

    (2) evaluation of the role or function of broadcasting for a whole course;

    (3) evaluation of individual programs.

Thus the kind of questions we might ask about broadcasting can be allocated to each of the three levels. Examples are given below:

Level (1): What proportion of our total resources should we allocate to broadcasting? How many studios do we need? Should we divert resources from class tutorials to audio cassettes for courses with small numbers? How many programs should we give each course on average?

Level (2): What overall function(s) will broadcasting have for this course? Are these the most appropriate functions? Could these functions be achieved more economically/effectively in other ways?

Level (3): How could this program be improved? Were the objectives of this program appropriate to this point in the course? To what extent were the objectives achieved? Should we remake the program?

It will be seen that answers to questions at one level will depend on answers to questions at other levels.

There is also the problem of what point in time evaluation should take effect. Can we evaluate a proposal for an allocation of broadcasting re-sources in advance of the course being produced? What criteria should we use? How far can you apply evidence from one situation to a related but nevertheless new situation? For instance, a mechanics course in the Mathematics Faculty may have used broadcasting most effectively – but can you be sure that a proposed course in Computing, with different personnel and different subject matter, will use broadcasting as effectively? To make this kind of decision, it is not sufficient for evaluation to produce merely a measure of the effectiveness of existing courses or broadcasts, or even to produce creative suggestions for improving these courses or broadcasts, as difficult as both of those tasks may be. Evaluation must also lead to the identification of basic principles of course design in a multi-media system. To do this, it must look beyond the measurement of the achievement of objectives and examine ways of determining what objectives are appropriate for different components of a multi-media teaching system.

There are therefore two fundamental problems associated with evaluation of broadcasting at the Open University. The first is a practical problem: how can evaluation be organized to cope with the large number of programs and the vast amount of information about these programs that the system is capable of generating? This is primarily a **feed-back** problem, aimed at improving or assessing decisions already made. The second is – for want of a better term – a theoretical problem: how do we relate the process and results of evaluation to new design and planning decisions?

It would be a delusion to think that the University has yet solved either of these problems satisfactorily. However, certainly in the area of broadcasting, a start has been made. To tackle the first problem, a situation where there is an embarrassment of possible sources of information, the minimum requirements of a system of feed-back at the Open University need to be analysed. Next, the existing organizational and communication system already operating within the University needs to be examined, to see how this can be used, and where necessary adapted, to provide effective feed-back.

A first analysis suggests that at a minimum feed-back should be:

(a) **accurate**: it must reflect the **total** range of reaction to the material, in at least some quantitative form (eg do **all** course tutors react unfavourably?). Particularly where feed-back is summarized and passed on, bias on the part of the summarizer needs to be controlled or eliminated;

(b) **quick**: feed-back must be received and analysed quickly enough for decisions to be made which can be acted upon;

(c) **understandable**: the amount of available information must be accurately and speedily reduced, so that those who are to act on it are not swamped by an unmanageable quantity of opinion, facts, and figures;

(d) **relevant**: feed-back must concentrate on areas where decisions **can** be made – however, it is important to remember that course teams are not the **only** clients for this kind of feed-back. Other operational areas of the University (Tutorial Board, Planning Board, Marketing, etc) also have a need for feed-back on course material;

(e) **constructive**: feed-back must not only indicate areas where improvements are necessary, it should also be able to suggest **what** these improvements should be;

(f) **general**: perhaps this is not a minimum requirement, but it certainly should be possible for **general** lessons to be learned by

233

course designers which can be applied to new units or courses, and these lessons should be transmittable throughout the system, so that each new academic or producer does not repeat the same mistakes.

Each of these features of effective feed-back raises important methodological issues, but these might be better understood in the light of the existing system of feed-back at the Open University. In the first year of operation, there were two main sources, both basically **qualitative**, in that they relied on **opinion** of the broadcasts, rather than an assessment of their objectives (except in very broad terms). The most systematic of these was student-based: the course unit report form, designed by Naomi McIntosh, Senior Lecturer in Research Methods in the Institute of Educational Technology. This form was sent to a random sample of one third of the students on each foundation course. The response rate for these forms averaged about 45% per week, over a 32 week period.

The responses for the four foundation courses indicated very high proportions of students viewing and listening each week (Table I).

Table I. Viewing and listening figures
(Foundation Courses 1971)

(Source: Course Unit Report Form)

Viewed/listened (over 32 weeks)	Television				Radio			
	Arts	Soc Sc	Maths	Sc	Arts	Soc Sc	Maths	Sc
Mean	80%	85%	86%	95%	85%	78%	73%	83%
Maximum	93%	96%	97%	99%	91%	91%	85%	96%

This week by week analysis of the programs by viewing habits and the students' subjective rating of the program gives useful broad indications about the overall success or otherwise of the broadcasts, **as rated by the students.** However, feed-back of this kind cannot provide answers to many important questions. **Why** were the programs popular or unpopular? Even if a program was unpopular, or rated as not very interesting or useful by students, does it necessarily have to be remade? To what extent are students the best judges of the value or importance of broadcasts? Obviously, if a course steadily loses its viewers or listeners over a period, there is something wrong — but what? It may not be the individual broadcasts themselves, or even the role assigned to broadcasting in that course. For instance, the Mathematics foundation course radio programs were perhaps the least successful in holding their audience right through the course (although an overall attendance at lectures of 73% over 32 weeks might hardly be considered a failure!). One possible reason might be because the radio programs generally aimed at providing 'enrichment' material which, while interesting, was not crucial to the course, in that the students' assignments were not related in any obvious way to the radio programs. Basically, when it came to the crunch, students may well have felt that they could manage without broadcasts, and we already know that under a heavy pressure of work, the least essential elements of a course – at least in the students' eyes – tend to be dropped first. On the other hand, had the assignments taken more account of the radio programs, then the listening figures might well have been higher. However, this is only an assumption – there may well be other explanations, so as useful and interesting as the course unit report form figures are, in themselves they are by no means an adequate system of feed-back.

The other main source of feed-back during the first year has been the reports supplied through the regional tutorial services. From these reports, and from letters and telephone messages direct from students to the University's headquarters, and from the course team's own subjective reactions to the programs, it was possible to make decisions about which programs should be remade for this year's repeat of the foundation courses. To describe this as a satisfactory feed-back system would be misleading. Such a system might be stretched with difficulty from the four foundation courses to the 16 courses running this year, but will certainly not work for the 26 full courses being operated next year. The manpower to analyze and collate all the information that would be generated by such an informal system will not be available. The University is therefore considering for 1973 a scheme of feed-back from the part-time course tutors based on a detailed and specific pre-coded questionnaire, to be completed for each unit. This would be analysed by computer, and would allow course tutors to comment about each component of each unit. It is hoped that information collected in this way (which could be directly available to course unit authors and producers within eight weeks at the most of the transmission), together with samples of open-ended answers from the same form, will, with other less quantified information, and quantified information from other sources (eg the student-based course unit report form) provide reliable information not only about which programs or parts of programs need to be re-made, but also about possible reasons and suggestions for re-making.

Since he can see difficulties both from the University's and the students' points of view, the course tutor may well be an important source for feed-back. So too might be students' opinions of the programs. All the same, should not the University be more concerned with basing its evaluation of broadcasts on student **performance**, as measured both through continuous assessment and examinations? Surely – in the end – the main criterion against which television and radio should be measured is: has it increased the students' understanding of the subject matter?

To measure this, in fact, is peculiarly difficult in a multi-media system. The students receive their instruction from a number of sources, which are all part of an instructional package which has been very carefully designed as an integrated whole. It is therefore difficult to separate the contribution of one component from the rest. Important objectives for a unit are nearly always covered both by the correspondence text and by the television and radio programs. The following table (Table II) of the basic design structure for most units in the four foundation courses shows quite clearly that as the major objectives of the unit are all included in the correspondence text, assignment questions (both tutor and computer marked) tend to be drawn entirely from the correspondence text.

Table II. Design structure of most foundation course units

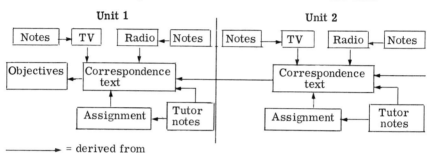

———————▶ = derived from

Indeed, since in only one of the foundation courses (Science) were students told that television was essential, it would have been unfair to many students without access to the broadcasts to have set assessments based mainly on the contents of a television or radio program. Furthermore, objectives for television and radio programs are not always measurable in assessment terms. For instance, on one second level social science course, students are asked to interview five businessmen as part of their assignment. A main objective of one of the associated television programs is to reduce the students' anxiety about the interview situation by showing other students carrying out the same exercise. Producers (and sometimes students) have mentioned the value of the broadcasts as 'pacers' in a system teaching adults at a distance. If successful, neither of these objectives would be measurable in terms of the contents of an assessment or examination paper (although of course they are susceptible to other measures), yet it would be hard to deny the validity of these objectives.

Another difficulty of basing the evaluation of broadcasting on student performance is the sheer quantity of assignments. Between 100,000 and 200,000 tutor marked assignment papers were completed across the four foundation courses last year. To analyse the content of even a very small sample of these papers to detect the influence of broadcasting would be a massive undertaking, even if a valid and reliable method of analysis could be found. This is why the reaction of the part-time course tutors to the programs is so important: they are the only people in a position to see the impact of programs on students in terms of their assignments.

Nevertheless, because of the importance attached in the Institute of Educational Technology to basing evaluation on student performance, and because of the need to obtain feed-back in a variety of forms from a variety of sources, attempts are being made in some courses to base parts of an assignment on broadcast material. However, these efforts are still in their early stages.

It is perhaps disturbing to realise that even if all these problems (and others not discussed in this paper) are overcome, an effective system of feed-back will not on its own provide an adequate system of evaluation of broadcasting at the Open University. We will have solved most of our problems at 'Level 1', but we will have hardly touched problems at Levels 2 and 3. To tackle these, we are going to have to develop other methods of evaluation and research, which there is not space to mention here in full. It is clear however that feed-back on the effectiveness of broadcasts in the narrow sense of measuring whether broadcasting assists in the achievement of the objectives set for a program, unit or course, does not take into account many of the possible advantages of broadcasting to the Open University. The availability of material that can be broadcast affects not only the material that goes into a course – and hence its objectives – but also the kind of courses that are put on, as an examination of the courses being offered by the University over the next few years clearly shows. In a very real sense, the medium does dictate the message. However, this makes an evaluation of the objectives and methods **appropriate** to a multi-media system all the more urgent (Level 2), and hopefully this in turn will lead to criteria for assessing the need of different courses for broadcasting, and a more realistic appraisal of the necessary resources required for broadcasting (Level 3). Also necessary is basic research into how students learn differentially from radio, television and reading. It may well be that efforts in these directions may prove more fruitful in the long run than too exclusive a concentration on the measurement of objectives in terms of student performance.

Strategies for the Evaluation of Curriculum Materials

MICHAEL ERAUT

WHAT EVIDENCE SHOULD EVALUATION PROVIDE?

Evaluation according to Popham and Baker (Popham & Baker, 1970) consists of five basic operations:

1. Establishing specific goals;
2. Developing a measuring device;
3. Pre-assessing students;
4. Implementing an instructional plan;
5. Measuring and interpreting evidence of student achievement.

Most people involved in programmed learning report their work in similar terms (Rowntree, 1969), though they would distinguish (Green, 1967) between developmental testing which is intended to improve a program and validation which is intended to prove its effectiveness. Both terms commonly refer to only one kind of evidence, the gain in performance by students on tests which are derived from the programmer's statement of objectives. This view of evaluation is deceptively simple, dangerously simple. Developmental testing and validation are only aspects of the evaluation processes which Scriven describes as **formative evaluation** and **summative evaluation** (Scriven, 1967). Other aspects of these processes are discussed below.

A frequent criticism in the programmed learning literature is that of the professional psychometrician berating the amateur programmer. The tests must be valid and reliable and trials must be conducted under a variety of conditions with large numbers of students. This tends to be conceived as essentially a summative procedure, although Markle has pointed out the possible implications of 'utilization testing' for formative procedures (Markle, 1967). The need for evidence which shows how effectiveness varies with different kinds of pupil and under different conditions of use is certainly important, but it can be overemphasized. If, for example, the recommendations of the Joint Committee on Programmed Instruction of the AERA, APA and DAVI were followed (AERA, 1966), one suspects that 95% of the average programmer's time would be taken up by summative evaluation. Hardly, one would think, a sensible allocation of resources. This august body also seems to assume that the only likely outcomes of a program are those anticipated by its statement of objectives. But curriculum materials in general and programs in particular are also transmitting values either explicitly or implicitly (Berlak, 1967); and developing intellectual skills which are not easy to measure and are probably acquired at a rate that is undetectable over relatively short periods of time. Does this mean that we should ignore these unspecified outcomes when we evaluate our programs? Or do we have to rely on people's judgement?

More fundamental still is the question, totally ignored by Popham, as to whether the objectives of a program are worthwhile (White, 1971). This question demands a value judgement which is perhaps why empirically-minded programs so often avoid it (Stake, 1969). The most common avoidance tactic is to state that all objectives can be logically derived from a mythical entity called the 'job'. This is clearly relevant in industrial training, professional training or the armed services but makes little sense in an education system in which curriculum decision making is becoming increasing decentralized and aims are becoming more and more complex. Even in industry many aspects of the job are not at all clearly defined, eg motivation, human relations; and in a period of increasingly rapid change judgements have to be made about training for flexibility or for future jobs which cannot easily be empirically validated. The problems of evaluation in industrial training have been nicely summarized by Martin (Martin, 1968), but his analysis cannot readily be transferred to education. Nothing in education outside the area of professional training corresponds to Martin's concept of 'external validation'. There is no empirical escape route from the debate about which educational objectives are of most worth. Nor, unless a program is intended for private use only, is there any escape from judgements on this issue by many groups of people other than its author. These judgements are a necessary aspect of summative evaluation; and we argue below that they should also be included in formative evaluation.

One further aspect of the evaluation of curriculum materials concerns their practicality. This includes such factors as what happens to them in the ordinary classroom, how much they cost, their requirements in terms of equipment, space, teacher time, etc, and how they are received by teachers considering their use. Only rarely is information on practicability published by an author; even information about cost can be difficult to obtain. Clearly practicability is an important aspect of summative evaluation, but what is its rate in formative evaluation? However irrational or frustrating teacher discussions about new materials appear to be, the author ignores them at his peril!

But let us now return to consider developmental testing, which was being

239

used by programmers (Lysaught & Williams, 1962) even before Cronbach's important article on 'evaluation for course improvement' was published (Cronbach, 1963). Two aspects of it are especially significant: the idea of approaching an effective learning sequence by successive approximations; and the use of the intensive study of a few students as the main source of information for program revisions. Although developmental testing is a powerful and still undervalued technique its limitations need to be discussed. Firstly it is a closed system approach to formative evaluation which tends to reveal mistakes in the fine structure of programs but to ignore their more fundamental messages (Connors, 1972). When results are disasterous some radical rethinking may occur, but developmental testing will not of itself suggest alternatives, either more desirable alternatives with more valued objectives or even more effective alternatives which achieve the same objectives more efficiently by adopting different teaching strategies. Secondly, developmental testing gives little information about outcomes not anticipated in the statement of objectives. Since unspecified outcomes cannot be ignored in summative evaluation, can they be ignored in formative evaluation? Then thirdly, developmental testing involves such a strong interaction between tester and student that major difficulties in student motivation may remain undetected. Not a situation we can be satisfied with when everyone is discussing the problems of the school leaving age.

How then can we broaden the scope of formative evaluation so that some of these limitations can be met? Two possibilities suggest themselves. The first is trying out some material away from the author's influence at a very early stage, either with a 'neutral' observer present or with subsequent interviewing of teacher and students. The second is the use of other people to 'evaluate' material by inspection at a very early stage. They would be asked to criticize the subject matter or the teaching strategy, to predict possible unintended outcomes and to suggest alternative objectives and teaching strategies. Our own experience is that advice of this kind can be at least as useful as the information gained from developmental testing.

HOW CAN EVIDENCE BE OBTAINED?

There are five main sources of evidence that the developer or evaluator of educational materials can draw upon:

1. Students
2. Teachers
3. Classes
4. Institutions
5. Experts

It might be expected that all five would normally be used though probably in varying proportions. But as far as it is possible to deduce the evaluation strategies actually used by program or curriculum development projects this has not in fact been the case. With a few exceptions a narrowly based evaluation has been adopted and some of these models are set out below, together with additional models that have been advocated in the literature but rarely used in practice. They have been classified according to the main source of evidence.

EVIDENCE FROM STUDENTS

1. The Tutorial or Clinical Model. The intensive study of a few individual students as they interact with the materials. This model is most commonly used by programmers (Markle, 1967); and also, incidentally used by psychological researchers such as Piaget and Skinner.

2. The Agricultural Botany Model. The study of large numbers of students, usually through batteries of tests and questionnaires. It requires resources and expertise in statistical analysis and educational research. Associated in the UK with the work of NFER (Williams, 1968), but little used by British curriculum projects.

EVIDENCE FROM TEACHERS

3. The Anthology Model. Much favoured in the UK this model is a collection of all the best "Little Johnny" stories. Though useful in indicating the kind of effect that materials can have, it is unreliable, incapable of being generalized and highly susceptible to bias. It has been the main source of evidence on the effects of such innovations as 'the integrated day'.

4. The Teacher Opinion Model. This model involves the trial of materials in large numbers of schools and the collection of teachers' opinions either by questionnaires or by feed-back meetings. It was used by the Nuffield Science Projects and the School Mathematics Project in their formative stages. Its main danger is that the information tends not to be gathered in a usable form which readily suggests how revisions can be made. Thus it can easily become a disguised dissemination rather than an evaluation exercise and is often treated as such by those in authority.

EVIDENCE FROM CLASSES

5. The Interaction Model. This model is based on direct observation of interaction in the classroom and must be distinguished from models 3 and 4 in which teachers report their views of what happened. Thus it avoids the danger of bias and of retrospective rationalization. It requires the use of 'neutral observers' or of videotape recorders and is therefore expensive. Its first use on any scale in the UK has been by the Schools Council Humanities Project (Macdonald, 1971).

241

6. **The Environmental Model.** This model uses **direct** evidence from visits about the classroom environment, its layout, furniture, equipment, etc, and also notes the integration of the materials with the other aspects of the student's curriculum. It has played an important role in the evaluation strategy of the Schools Council Science 5 - 13 Project (Harlen, 1971).

EVIDENCE FROM INSTITUTIONS

This kind of evidence has only rarely been used by projects themselves (Macdonald, 1971), but has always been the concern of potential adopters (Brickell, 1969). Though mainly associated with the writers of 'project obituaries' and with studies of the diffusion and adoption of educational innovations, it is rightly considered as an aspect of both summative evaluation and formative evaluation.

7. **The Cost-Benefit Model.** The predicted or observed benefits are balanced against expenditure and effort. This model is rarely used in the UK except to set cost-ceilings. It is difficult though important to assess all the benefits and existing accounting procedures make it almost as difficult to assess the real costs. Nevertheless, if used as a guide rather than a recipe its use can lead to a more genuine consideration of alternatives than normally occurs (Taylor, 1970).

8. **The Political Model.** Who adopts the materials and why? Is the teacher more likely to get promotion? Did the schools adopt Nuffield Science to get the extra money that went with it or to attract better qualified staff? What are the political implications of subject integration within a school? Does an innovation enhance a head's image with his LEA or his parents?

9. **The Anthropologists Model.** The 'neutral' observer assesses how an innovation changes the structure and value systems of the institution as a whole (Parlett, 1972). This method gets evidence not easily obtained in other ways but can be dangerously subjective. In one sense it is a more intensive longer term version of model 6. These three models become even more important when a project includes a 'dissemination' or 'in-service' role, which itself needs to be evaluated (Howson & Eraut, 1969).

EVIDENCE FROM EXPERTS

The term 'expert' is not meant to imply a high place in the educational hierarchy but a person whose judgement is considered likely to be of value. Such people include experienced teachers, curriculum specialists or educational technologists, subject matter experts, psychologists, sociologists and philosophers. As the earlier part of this paper implied, this source of evidence is not used in formative evaluation as much as it could be.

10. **Desirability Model.** Are the likely outcomes desirable and of sufficient

priority? This is clearly a question on which a wide spread of opinion should be sought, and not only at the level of global aims before a project begins. Opinions about desirable alternatives should be sought.

11. Feasibility Model. Are the intended outcomes likely to be achieved by the teaching strategy suggested? Are unintended outcomes likely? What alternative strategies should be considered?

SELECTING AN EVALUATION STRATEGY

It is probably desirable to use elements from all the evaluation models outlined above, but it is rarely feasible. The two main limitations are the total manpower resources available; and the nature of the resources. A project may not have people with the skills needed to implement some of the models but advice can usually be bought in or even obtained for free. So it is useful to consider the problem of selecting an evaluation strategy as being primarily one of resource allocation. Firstly, what proportion of a project's total resources should be assigned to evaluation activities (Hemphill, 1969); and secondly how should the 'evaluation resources' be distributed? For each evaluation activity under consideration three factors have to be taken into account:

1. the anticipated usefulness of the evidence gained for guiding decision-making both during (formative) and after (summative) the development of the materials;
2. whether the activity is pursued at a professional (and probably more expensive level) or at an amateur level; and
3. the scale on which the activity is planned.

Unfortunately there is very little guidance available on how to make these decisions. Though curriculum products are available for inspection and openly criticized, curriculum processes are rarely described and thus unavailable for criticism. Moreover, like criticizing someone's teaching, criticizing a project's procedures is often taken as a personal attack rather than an attempt to open a discussion of the issues and advance the state of the art.

A CASE STUDY: THE SUSSEX COMPONENT OF THE INTER-UNIVERSITY BIOLOGY PROJECT

This project has been described earlier in this conference (Tribe, 1972) and the materials being developed are on view in the members' exhibition. The developmental process is summarized in Figure 1.

The evaluation strategy emphasized evidence from students and teachers (on the left side) and evidence from experts (on the right side). Further information on the way in which the project has used some of the eleven

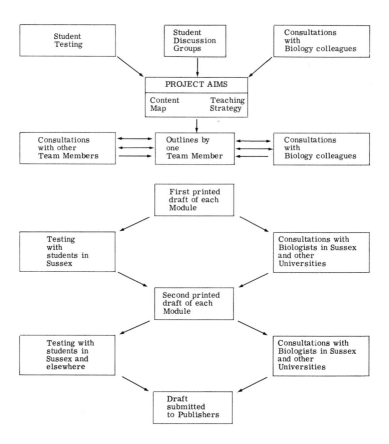

Figure 1. The developmental process at Sussex

evaluation models described above is set out below (models 3, 5 and 6 are not being used at all).

1. **The Tutorial Model.** Extensive use. Several small batches of Sussex students have worked through the material in the presence of the project team and discussed their difficulties and opinions.

2. **The Agricultural Botany Model.** Moderate use. There are about 12 trial institutions and 300 copies of the first draft have been printed. Pre-tests and post-tests measure changes in the understanding of concepts and principles. But there is no attempt to test the project's aim of developing scientific thinking. This is thought to be impractical as the course only lasts one term and many other things are happening to students in their first year at university. The extent to which the materials are likely to achieve this aim is, however, submitted to the judgement of independent experts (see below).

4. **The Teacher Opinion Model.** Moderate use, given only 12 trial institutions. Teachers are, however, used as experts (see below).

7, 8, 9. Evidence from Institutions. Used to a small extent. Cost is considered very carefully. The modular nature of the material is meant to facilitate adoption, and information about possible uses in other institutions does affect some of the content decisions and the way in which the modular boundaries are drawn. Reactions are very carefully studied and will affect the way in which the teacher's manual is written.

10, 11. Evidence from Experts. Used extensively at every stage. The pay-off to the project has been enormous and many drafts have been radically revised as a result of consultation (some even before the first printed draft stage).

Obviously the project would have liked to have done more evaluation than it has, but resources have been very limited. We have not yet come to the view that our resource allocation decisions were seriously mistaken; and, as far as formative evaluation is concerned, all the evaluation activities have fully justified themselves in cost-benefit terms.

POSTSCRIPT

"There is no single 'process' of curriculum evaluation: there are many different forms of it. All (or most) of them can and should play a part in assessing whether or not a new curriculum is any good, whether or not it is worth teachers' while adopting it. This, I take it, is the ultimate point of all curriculum evaluation. A curriculum has not been positively evaluated in this full sense until it has been shown to have clear objectives and appropriate means to achieve them; to have objectives which have been proved against all comers to be educationally respectable; to connect with the abilities of those pupils for whom it is designed; and to be more efficient than rivals in the field. Only then can it get its tick." (White, 1971)

"Although it may not be possible to have too much experience, it is possible to emphasize 'knowing the classroom' so much that no attention is given to putting experience into order. An evaluation plan may fail because it deals only with vague, personal impressions.

Although it may not be possible to be too reasonable, it is possible to emphasize rationality so much that encounters with reality are unduly delayed or narrowly conceived. An evaluation plan may fail because it squanders its resources on organization, on instrument development, and on delimitation of the problem." (Stake, 1969)

REFERENCES

AERA/APA/DAVI (1966) Joint Committee on Programmed Instruction and Teaching Machines. 'Recommendations for Reporting the Effectiveness of Programmed Instruction Materials'. AV Communication Review **14**, 1. Supplements in **14**, 2

Berlak, H. and Shaver, P. (1967) 'Why Choosing Materials Means Choosing Values'. EPIE Forum **1**

Brickell, Henry M. (1969) 'Appraising the Effects and Innovations in Local Schools'. In 'Educational Evaluation: New Roles, New Means'. (Ed) R. W. Tyler. Yearbook of the National Society for the Study of Education 1969. University of Chicago Press

Connors, Brendan (1972) 'Testing Innovations in Course Design'. British Journal of Educational Technology **3**, 1

Cronbach, Lee J. (1963) 'Evaluation for Course Improvement'. Teacher's College Record, **64**, 672

Green, E. J. (1967) The Process of Instructional Programming. In 'Programmed Instruction'. (Ed) P. Lange. 66th NSSE Yearbook, University of Chicago Press

Harlen, Wynne (1971) 'Report for Teachers on the Evaluation of the First Set and Units'. Science 5-13 Project, Schools Council Publications

Hemphill, John K. (1969) The Relationships between Research and Evaluation Studies. In 'Educational Evaluation: New Roles, New Means'. (Ed) R. W. Tyler. Yearbook of the National Society for the Study of Education 1969. University of Chicago Press

Howson, G. and Eraut, M. R. (1969) 'Continuing Mathematics'. NCET Working Paper 2, Councils and Education Press

Lysaught, J. P. and Williams, C. M. (1963) 'A Guide to Programmed Instruction'. Wiley

Macdonald, Barry (1971) 'The Evaluation of the Humanities Curriculum Project. A Holistic Approach'. Theory into Practice, **10**, 3

Markle, Susan M. (1967) Empirical Testing and Programs. In 'Programmed Instruction'. (Ed) P. Lange. 66th NSSE Yearbook, University of Chicago Press

Martin, A. O. (1968) 'Assessing Training Effectiveness'. Department of Employment and Productivity

Parlett, Malcolm (1972) Evaluating Innovations in Teaching. In 'Contemporary Problems in Higher Education'. (Ed) H. J. Butcher and E. Rudd. McGraw Hill. In press

Popham, W. J. and Baker, E. L. (1970) 'Systematic Instruction'. Prentice-Hall

Rowntree, Derek (1969) The Systems Approach to Educational Technology. In 'Yearbook of Educational and Instructional Technology (1969/70 incorporating Programmes in Print'. (Ed) P. Cavanagh and C. Jones. Cornmarket

Scriven, M. (1967) The Methology of Evaluation. In 'Perspectives of Curriculum Evaluation'. (Ed) R. W. Tyler, R. M. Gagne and M. Scriven. Rand McNally

Taylor, G. (Ed) (1970) 'The Teacher as Manager. A Symposium'. National Council for Educational Technology, Councils and Education Press

Tribe, M. A. (1972) 'Designing an introductory programmed course in biology for undergraduates' – this Volume

White, J. P. (1971) 'The Concept of Curriculum Evaluation'. Journal of Curriculum Studies, **3**, 2

Williams, J. D. (1968) The Curriculum: Some Patterns of Development and Designs for Evaluation. In 'Educational Research in Britain'. (Ed) H. J. Butcher. University of London Press

The Hansel Training Machine:
A New Aid to (Over) Learning
D V MOSELEY and D SOWTER

This electronic training machine has great potential at all levels of education. Its special features include the immediate correction of errors, the automatic introduction of practice-routines to eliminate errors, and the capacity to accept serial and multiple responses. The machine was first exhibited at the 1971 APLET conference, and was described by Hansel (1971). A new memory feature has now been incorporated, whereby the machine can be programmed by pressing the correct answer buttons. There is now no practical limitation on the length of a response sequence. A tape-slide program has been made to show how the machine was used in one adult training centre in Newham.

As the machine was available for only one month, it was decided to involve as many trainees as possible, and to include a wide range of programs. In all, 266 sessions were completed by a total of 55 trainees. Eight types of program were devised, as shown in Table I. A high level of correct response was obtained, as can be seen from the table. The percentage shown cannot be taken as a direct index of the order of difficulty, as different groups of trainees were involved. However, nearly all the adults attending the centre had sessions on the machine, and the degree of overlearning was certainly high. Most trainees made 36 responses per session, plus two more for every error. They repeated a program from session to session until they

Table I. Details of programs and response accuracy

Type of program	No. of programs	Correct responses (%)
Matching clock faces	2	97
Paired associates (Pictures)	1	96
Matching pictures and shapes	4	95
Coin recognition	2	93
Gas cooker positions	1	87
Size of screws	1	81
Counting	3	79
Prices of 6 items	1	(Insufficient data)

reached a criterion level of 24 successive correct responses. This criterion was adopted after pilot work in another training centre had shown that it was realistic. On matching and counting programs, 10 out of 11 trainees reached this level, even though initial performance had been as low as 50% correct responses.

Every question stimulus called for a single-button response in these programs. The number of response items on the keyboard was varied between three and six. It will be noted that the facility of serial and multiple responses was not used. This was because it was thought desirable to use the simplest possible programs when introducing trainees to the machine.

The mentally handicapped, as well as individuals with specific learning difficulties are very often deficient in the sequential processing of symbols. Unsuccessful attempts have been made to develop sequencing skills in severely subnormal trainees by Bradley et al (1966) and by Moseley (1971). Smith (1962) found that educationally subnormal children improved least of all in sequencing skills in response to an intensive language development program. Conventional instruction emphasizes single-item responses and makes extensive use of the multiple-choice format. It is possible that insufficient attention is given to serial and multiple response training. We do not know, for example, whether trainees can learn to count more efficiently by means of multiple responses to a single button, rather than by single responses to one of several buttons. More research is needed in this area.

No definitive statement can yet be made about learning and retention after training with the Hansel machine, but results to date have been most encouraging. Informal pre- and post-tests were given by the teachers concerned in the Newham project. These showed that six trainees learned to tell the time to the half-hour, while seven made real progress in coin-recognition and three in learning to count. Follow-up testing of the complete sample was carried out two months after the machine was withdrawn, and the high progress group was tested again at three months. The majority were found to have maintained their progress, and among the high progress group there was only one clear case of regression. Although there had been no systematic teaching of telling the time in the intervening period, there was no loss of skill, and one girl had progressed to quarters of the hour. A more thorough six-month evaluation project has now been planned.

REFERENCES

Bradley, B.H., Mauer, R. and Hundziag, M. (1966) Exceptional Children, **33**, 143
Hansel, C.E.M. (1971) in 'Aspects of Educational Technology V'.
    (Ed) D. Packham, A. Cleary, T. Mayes. Pitman, London. Page 367
Moseley, D.V. (1971) in 'Aspects of Educational Technology V'.
    (Ed) D. Packham, A. Cleary, T. Mayes. Pitman, London. Page 348
Smith, J.O. (1962) Exceptional Children, **29**, 95
Method of presentation: Tape-slide

The Kent Mathematics Project—Mode 3 Assessment Procedure

BERTRAM BANKS

The Kent Mathematics Project, in its 6th year of development, is now a major Kent Curriculum Development Project and is involving nearly 10,000 children in Kent schools. It is being used outside Kent (for instance in the ILEA), but it is not known to what extent. It is believed that some schools are also using the scheme in Birmingham.

Forty-five students in Ridgewaye School, Southborough, Kent, the 'lead' school in the Project, are now in their 5th Year after using the scheme since they entered the school and they will be needing a CSE assessment in the summer of 1972.

The Project offers a unique course in Mathematics for each student between 9 and 16 years and uses a material-bank of programmed booklets, tapes and worksheets organized into attainment levels and mathematical areas.

Table I. KMP attainment levels framework

Type of Student		Attainment Levels							
		1	2	3	4	5	6	7	8
Primary	Medium	3rd	4th						
	Fast		3rd	4th ——►					
Secondary	Backward	◄1st ———			— 5th►				
	Slow		◄1st ———			5th►			
Modern	Medium			1st	2nd	3rd	4th	5th	6th
	Fast				1st	2nd	3rd	4th	5th
Secondary Tech/Gram	Medium				1st	2nd	3rd	4th	5th
	Fast					1st	2nd	3rd	4th

1st = 1st Year; 6th = 6th Year

The attainment levels, which were created five years ago (Table I), have been developed from what would be expected from typical children in the Tripartite system, with reference to what is well-known to teachers as 'fast', 'medium' and 'slow' children. Level 1 contains material dealing with concepts that an average 9 year old Primary child could master and level 8 is what would be expected at CSE Grade 1, or an average 'O' level pass, and it works out that an attainment level is approximately equal to one year's conceptual development. Level 8 assumes that 'O' level standard can be attained by fast grammar students in their 4th year whilst fast students in the secondary modern school will reach this standard in their 5th year. Medium secondary modern students reach level 8 in their 6th year. This framework is used only to help teachers identify the attainment levels and all references to typical students in the Tripartite system are dropped when teachers become used to thinking in terms of levels.

The 'fast', 'medium' and 'slow' definitions relate to the presentation of the tasks, and describe the verbal ability of the student and pace of presentation.

Obviously, the grammar school student can handle verbiage and a fast pace through the task, and the presentation of a concept needs to be different for a fast grammar school 1st year student than that suitable for a 5th year slow secondary modern student, although each is ready to learn that particular mathematical concept.

Table II.

Average Student Years	Levels	Mathematical Areas									
		NS	NC	GP	GS	GR	AL	SG	TO	ST	CT
16	8										
15	7										
14	6										
13	5										
12	4										
11	3										
10	2										
9	1										

As Table II shows, the material is organized horizontally into attainment levels and vertically into the mathematical areas of Number Calculating, Number Structure, Geometry Plane, Geometry Solid, Graphical, Algebraic, Sets and Groups, Topology, Statistics, and Computer Technology, each task being allocated into these areas for the main conceptual development identified in the objective. A combination of attainment level, mathematical area, and fast, medium or slow suitability thus provides a coding system which quickly summarizes for the teacher the suitability of each task for a particular student. For instance, Area 1 – Leaves, GP. 1. 30 MS, is work on Geometry, Plane, designed for level 1 for medium and slow children. The '30' is merely a catalogue number.

The 'Cancelling' task, NS. 4. 20 FMS, is a programmed booklet dealing with a Number Structure concept in level 4, suitable for fast, medium and slow students.

Each student enters the scheme by taking a diagnostic test. The test result is not expressed as a mark but as the appropriate levels for the student in three mathematical areas – Number, Geometry and General, and a suitable matrix of 12 tasks from the appropriate levels is provided. In fact, the General level result is used to monitor the other two levels and we have available 14 different entry matrices, already made up and printed.

Table III.

				MATRIX K 3/4
NAME ——————————				GROUP————
	1 Char. of Nos. NS.3.20 Tape	2 Desk Cal. 1 NC.3.30 Page 9	3 Base Four C NS.3.35 Page 33	4 Hexaflexagons GP.3.20 Page 18
Date				
T/In				
	5 Triangle 2 GP.4.10 Page 8	6 Volumes 1 GS.4.40 Page 20	7 Angles & Bear. 1 GP.4.00 P/Book	8 Octahedron GS.4.20 Page 18
Date				
T/In				
	9 Polyhedra 1 GS.3.00 Page 23	10 3 Coin Prob. CT.4.01 Page 34	11 Intro. to Sets SG.4.00 Page 24	Free Choice
Date				
T/In				

For instance, Entry Matrix K is designed for students who, from the results of the diagnostic entry test, have shown their Number level to be 3 and their Geometry level 4. This matrix also gives information about page numbers in the worksheet booklets, whether the presentation is in tape or programmed booklet form, and the codes. The twelfth task is a Free Choice which serves the twin purpose of developing open-ended work in pursuit of a special interest and at the same time keeping the student busy whilst the teacher is making up the next matrix.

After working through the entry matrix, with help and guidance from the teacher where necessary, the student takes a test on the material in the matrix, extracting his test from the Test Booklet, and from the results of this test, another matrix is made up. The student thus proceeds through his own individual course designed by the teacher to strengthen weaknesses and satisfy special interests.

The material-bank is being built up along conceptual lines and the teacher uses a flow diagram when making up new matrices from matrix test results. If a student does not master a particular task, he is reinforced with more material on the same concept until he does. If he masters a task, then this learning becomes the entry behaviour for the next step on that particular concept line and retention is required for subsequent success. Retention tests are therefore redundant. If a student is so fast that the teacher considers he is wasting time on trivial work, he is looped forward until he reaches his own ceiling, and if any vital learning is contained in a task missed out, this is quickly taken in his stride.

Each task is validated in terms of mathematical content, success as learning material and identification of attainment level and it is not unusual for an attainment level to be modified after try-out in several schools. Because the validation system is operated through regular teachers' meetings, with representatives from all types of schools, the attainment levels are moderated over a large school population.

Each student's matrix is recorded on a continuous record card and the attainment levels for each matrix are averaged, and it is interesting that most of the students concern themselves with how this attainment level mean is improving from matrix to matrix. We do not find children comparing their prowess with others as much as being interested in their own improvement, and it would be very difficult, if not impossible, to produce a rank order list for a particular group which had any meaning, in view of the children pursuing their own individual courses.

We do, however, believe that our attainment levels have meaning in terms of assessing mathematical ability, and are probably more objective than the use of the results of a timed examination. With the forty-five 5th year students at Ridgewaye School expecting a CSE assessment in the Summer of 1972, we approached the South Eastern Regional CSE Examinations Board with an application for a Mode 3 assessment based on attainment levels, and to reinforce our claim that the KMP levels were meaningful, three tests were designed and correlated with the students' attainment levels. The tests were designed to match the usual CSE type examination questions and were each of 40 minutes duration, taken under examination conditions.

Separate correlations for boys and girls showed no significant difference over all the tests and the final correlation for total marks and attainment levels was 0.69.

We believe, because of the type of work the students are doing, that much of the learning cannot be measured by a written test. For instance,

Table IV. Correlations − Test results and attainment levels

	Test 1	Test 2	Test 3	Tests 1, 2 & 3
Boys	0.39	0.59	0.63	−
Girls	0.47	0.38	0.76	−
All	0.40	0.56	0.68	0.69

many of our objectives lie in Bloom's Psycho-motor and Affective Domains and would be extremely difficult to test with a written paper. We are therefore happy with the correlation result of 0.69 which shows significantly that our attainment levels are related to mathematical ability. In any case, with a very high correlation with test results, we would have a situation in which there would be no point in not using a written examination procedure. The Board moderator has accepted our application and agrees that we can considerably reduce the normal weighting of 50% for the written examination in a Mode 3 Mathematics assessment and that the main assessment should be made on attainment levels.

The scheme started with material adapted from a normal secondary modern mathematics syllabus designed to lead to CSE and 'O' level, and to meet the requirements of current philosophies of modern content and approach. The material-bank is nearly half completed and, when finished, will provide material which will cater for the topics of a CSE syllabus as well as special interest topics such as Computer Technology, Modern Mathematics at 'O' level, Mathematics for Technicians, Statistics, and so on. The fact that there is no fixed syllabus through which every student must work, creates a flexibility which is exciting in its implications because if the actual working on a task forms part of the assessment procedure, we can open up mathematical areas which could not be easily tested by a formal examination. For instance, one of the exercises in level 3 is to play noughts and crosses on a three-dimensional model and the task finishes with the calculation of the total possible rows. In level 8, there is a task which asks the student to find the relationship between the total possible rows in a three-layered three by three model, a four-layered four by four model and a five-layered five by five model and so on, and the whole point of this exercise is the fascination of working out the problem and the discovery of the relationship, something which does not lend itself to formal testing. Similarly, there is a worksheet in level 9 (we have had to create this new post-'O' level for three new tasks), which simply reads that there must be a rule governing the dimensions of the cards used in a string icosahedron (the making of such a model is a task in level 1) to produce equilateral triangular faces, so find this rule. This is a most fascinating problem with a surprising (and beautiful) answer needing quite a body of mathematical knowledge and skills to find. Again, this would be extremely difficult to set in a formal examination. I need hardly point out to mathematics teachers the range of statistical projects which could be tackled under this philosophy, sometimes in the realms of pure research.

POSTSCRIPT

In March, 1972, the 5th form students at Ridgewaye School were tested with a 2-paper mock CSE examination. January/February attainment levels were correlated with the 2-paper totals and produced a result of 0.65 (with 34 students).

These January/February attainment levels were then corrected because they do not, as calculated to date, take into consideration the matrix test result of each student. An arbitrary correcting system, which has to be simple for teacher-operation, was designed in which the difference between the matrix test result and 100% is expressed as a decimal and subtracted from the attainment level mean for the matrix. The corrected attainment levels produced a correlation of 0.71 (34 students).

March attainment levels, which could not be corrected because the students had not yet taken matrix tests, produced a correlation with the 2-paper totals of 0.63 (34 students).

For reasons of curiosity, Paper 1 and Paper 2 test results were correlated and produced a result of 0.65.

All correlations were calculated by the product-moment method, and the battery of correlations this year have reinforced our belief that our attainment level system can be as an objective for assessment purposes as the usual examination system, and that a correction technique such as that employed for one of the correlations should be developed.

SUMMARY

	r	s
October tests and October attainment levels	0.69	45
March tests and Jan/Feb attainment levels (uncorrected)	0.65	34
March tests and corrected Jan/Feb attainment levels	0.71	34
March tests and March attainment levels (uncorrected)	0.63	34
March Paper 1 and Paper 2	0.65	34

REFERENCES

Banks, B. (1967) Problems and Methods in 'Programmed Learning , 1, 21
Banks, B. (1968) In 'Aspects of Educational Technology II'. (Ed) W. R. Dunn and C. Holroyd. Methuen, London. 221
Banks, B. (1969) In 'Aspects of Educational Technology III'. (Ed) A. P. Mann and C. P. Brunstrom. Pitman, London. 175
Banks, B. (1970) In 'Aspects of Educational Technology IV'. (Ed) A. C. Bajpai and J. F. Leedham. Pitman, London. 502
Gilligan, J., Hazelton, W. and Kaye, W. (1971) In 'Aspects of Educational Technology V'. (Ed) D. Packham, A. Cleary and T. Mayes. Pitman, London. 161

Method of presentation: Tape slide

Effectiveness of Learning in General Science using Programmed Learning and the Traditional Method

KAMAL YOUSEF ISKANDER

There is no doubt that the world in which we live nowadays urges us to act rapidly for the development of our educational system, in such a way that we may be enabled to face the challenges of scientific progress in the various fields of knowledge. We require such an educational development to realise the hopes of our people, and to bring about good citizens capable of undertaking the burdens laid on their shoulders in a rapidly developing world.

THE PROBLEM AND ITS DIMENSIONS

As a result of this unprecedented rapid development in the various fields of scientific research as well as technological progress, educators have come face to face with a set of problems and a class of challenges in Economics, Psychology and Education. The most outstanding of these are: the problem of increasing knowledge to the extent of outburst; the problem of the loser of education; the problem of resorting to teaching rather than learning; the problem of employing negative reinforcements which govern the behaviour of students; the problem of the magnitude of the time interval between the occurrence of behaviour and its reinforcement with students; the problem of the impossibility of providing every individual student in the classroom with the necessary amount of reinforcement, and finally the problem of confronting the individual differences of students.

THE TOPIC AND NEED FOR RESEARCH

Seeing that the technology of education and training is still unable to keep pace with the technological progress itself, in our society, the researcher cannot but think that it is of utmost importance that we should turn our interest to the faith that the solution of problems created by technology lies in technology itself, and the extent of our success in its use in education. This is only possible if learning becomes a science.

The contemporary behaviourist and psychologist Professor B F Skinner, could, after undertaking a series of researches and studies, reach a means to improve the methods of teaching and of controlling it to be more effective and more efficient, namely the method of 'Programmed Instruction'.

In developed countries, educators have found in Programmed Instruction a first trial of applying knowledge acquired by learning, through experimentation in Psychological laboratories, to the art of teaching and training as well as to human behaviour.

But although Programmed Instruction has proved to be successful in many countries, yet we cannot but assert that successful means in one country might prove a failure in another country; and since there are not many Egyptian researches save that of Badran and El Deeb, and Faragg, the researcher sees that it is urgent that unswerving investigation should be done to test whether the method applies in our society with its language constituents as to frame of education, environmental circumstances and educational systems. In other words, experimentation should be done to test if programmed instruction leads to a more effective learning than with traditional methods, as to solve the problems of private coaching and the poor quality of our text books for instance. Yet the trial of the method might lead to an increased supply of new knowledge for researchers, and consequently to great progress in the theory of learning and the art of programming.

THE ORIGIN AND EVOLUTION OF PROGRAMMED INSTRUCTION

The origin and evolution of programmed instruction was the result of laboratory experiments on human and animal learning based on Skinner's theory of operant conditioning, yet it is not entirely new, and its roots extend back to Socrates, and it was even rooted in ancient theories of education, specially in Comenius' theory which asserts that the effectiveness of learning is increased through diminishing teaching and increasing learning through small steps. Moreover, it is rooted in the theories and laws that explain the psychology of learning, specially 'the law of effect' according to Thorndike. The historical progress in the production of teaching devices and machines began from the first machine invented by English in 1918, to Sidney Pressy, Skinner and James Holland in 1958. After 1958, there is a rapid development in writing programs, designing machines, and employing computers.

AN ACCOUNT OF VARIOUS STUDIES AND RESEARCHES

It is divided into two classes:

1. Researches concerned with the effectiveness of programmed instruction alone, compared with that of other ordinary methods.

2. Researches concerned with the effectiveness of programmed instruction integrated by ordinary or traditional methods of teaching.

Each of those two classes has been dealt with from three points of view, namely:

(a) The result of researches concerned,

(b) The experimental design adopted, and

(c) The opinions, attitudes and impressions of the students towards programmed instruction.

The researcher has concluded, after an analytic study of these two classes, that students actually learn more material through programmed instruction in a smaller time and with a smaller ratio of forgetfulness. He has also found that programmed instruction was surely accepted at all levels with many study subjects in all educational stages, especially the university stage and that integrated teaching may be accepted as a certain means of teaching to save the time of the teacher and to allow him to provide the student with experiences restricted to the teacher only. Throughout the research several things were taken into consideration, the most important are: the size of sample, the quality of sample, the educational stage, the period of training or study, the subject of learning (the nature of programmed subject matter), and the novelty of the method as well as several other variables.

The following four main points have been treated:

1. Questions to be answered by the research.
2. Selecting the sample and its sources.
3. Selecting the tools employed in the research.
4. Experimental design of the research.

As for the first point, the researcher has raised the following questions:

1. Can pupils learn through the method of Programmed Instruction only, or by both programmed and traditional method combined, in our preparatory schools under our educational system?
2. Is there any difference in the percentage of the modified gain in pupils' achievement between the traditional method of teaching, programmed teaching and the integrated one?
3. Is there a difference between the study time of pupils learning by using the traditional method and those who learn by using programmed instruction or those who use the two methods alternately?
4. Is there any difference in the amount of remembering information on the students' part after the elapse of a long period (about six months) among the three methods?
5. What are the pupils' opinions and impressions concerning the programmed instruction method alone or when integrated with the traditional method?

The sample and its sources

Concerning selecting the sample and its sources, six groups from some of the students of four boys' preparatory schools governed by the Cairo Eastern

Educational Zone have been chosen for carrying out the experiment, homogenity of age, IQ, social standing, and educational level having been taken into consideration.

The researcher selected the following instruments to be used in the research:

(a) The illustrated intelligence test by Professor Ahmed Zakisaleh,

(b) an achievement essay test to cover the first half of the assigned course,

(c) an objective achievement test to cover most of the assigned course, (The researcher has calculated the coefficient of objectivity in the essay test, compared with the correlation coefficient with another examiner and found it to be comparatively high, being 0.82. The objective test coefficient, on the basis of splitting it into two parts, namely odd numbered questions and even ones, by the use of the general Getman Equation, was an average of about 0.52.)

(d) preparing an ordinary school text book, namely a booklet on the selected course, 'Fire and Fire Prevention'. This was done after showing it to professional experts,

(e) preparing a school programmed booklet (this was done after the linear type of Skinner, the contents being identical with the contents of the usual school textbook),

(f) a questionnaire was made to measure the extent of the impressions and opinions of students towards the program.

The experimental design

The researcher has formed two main groups from the six sub-groups. One of the two was composed of three adjacent sub-groups from the same school and the other was composed of the other three distant sub-groups from three different schools. The researcher has selected from each of the two groups, either adjacent or distant groups, a control group (taught by employing the traditional method), an experimental group (taught by using the programmed instruction method) and another experimental group (taught by using the two methods alternately).

In the distant groups the researcher himself was the teacher, but for the adjacent groups the researcher selected an efficient demonstrator to teach the subjects to be taught by the traditional method in the group which learns by using the two methods alternately, and for the group which learns by using the traditional method alone.

The researcher has specified (nine) lessons for teaching the chosen subjects by using the traditional method or the methods integrated, with the addition of some lessons in the case of programmed instruction, whenever necessary for some pupils.

The researcher has discussed the psychological foundations of programmed instruction from the standpoint of view of Skinner's theory and its relation to human learning and programmed instruction, and studied the fundamental elements and units of programmed instruction, and fundamental constituents of the behaviour unit in the program (frame), namely: stimuli, constructed and overt responses, immediate reinforcement and feed-back.

PREPARING THE PROGRAM

It has been devoted to the treatment of the general foundations related to writing a program, that is: the length of the program, the period of the lesson, the length of the frame, the time of work, the number of blanks, the nature of the subject matter to be programmed, the time taken by the process of programming, the type of programmer and his characteristics.

As for the rules and conditions to be taken into consideration when writing a program, the researcher has summarized them in the items: using small units of information, obliging the student to recall the desired response closely related with the learnt subject matter by way of appropriate prompts, cues, clues and hints, ordered sequences, training on generalization and discrimination, style of repetition which should not be tedious owing to variation in prompts and content, and attracting the attention of the student by making the program interesting, diminishing the error rate, active response, immediate knowledge of responsive results, a good grasp of the subject matter to be programmed, teaching versus lecturing, and the non-presumption of an extra knowledge of the student, reluctance to present two facts in one frame, and so on.

An exposition of three types of psychological bonds, namely final (S - R) bonds, primary (S - R) bonds and transitory (S - R) bonds, has been made; and the development in the gradual transition of the bonds has been indicated.

Steps in writing the program consisted of job analysis, writing frames, and making internal evaluation of it.

The external evaluation of the program, and statistical analysis of the research

A mention of the purpose of the research and the requirement of evaluations particularly achievement tests, (post- and pre-tests) was made. Methods of measuring the effectiveness of learning by using programmed instruction such as the amount of achievement, the time of study, the time of relearning and measuring the retention ratio, have been mentioned. Analysis of variance and critical ratio and (T - Test) for testing statistical significance of the difference between the average achievement of each of the two experimental groups taught by the researcher by programmed and traditional methods, have been used.

RESULTS OF THE RESEARCH

The researcher has reached answers to the previous questions concerning the learning of the students selected for this purpose, as follows:

Question 1. The students of the experimental group have assuredly learnt the subject of 'Fire and Fire Prevention' by the linear programmed booklet as efficiently and effectively as when they learnt it by the traditional method.

Question 2. There was found in some cases a significant statistical difference at the level of more than 0.05 between the average percentage of modified gain in the achievement of the pupils of some groups taught by using programmed instruction alone, and some groups which were taught by the traditional method alone, on the side of programmed instruction.

But in most cases it was found that there were no significant statistical differences at the level of 0.05 between the groups taught by programmed instruction alone and by traditional methods of teaching alone. Results of comparison of effectiveness of programmed instruction versus programmed and traditional methods combined showed: a) there were no significant statistical differences at the level of 0.05 between these groups, and b) the differences, if any, were in favour of programmed instruction at the level of 0.05.

Results of comparison of traditional method alone with both methods combined showed the absence of differences statistically significant at the level of 0.05, except two cases in favour of the traditional method at a level above 0.01.

Question 3. Results showed the absence of any significant differences in the time of study between the experimental groups and the control group at the level (0.05).

Question 4. No significant differences at the level of 0.05 were found between the experimental groups and the control group concerning the retention ratio.

Question 5. Most of the pupils who learned by using programmed instruction in the form of a programmed booklet were perfectly satisfied with this new method of instruction, they liked it and were enthusiastic about it; they were also proud of learning and studying alone, independently of their teachers. In spite of the fact that some of them were unwilling to accept the programmed textbook as a substitute for the teacher, they rather preferred the programmed textbook to the non-programmed (traditional) text with the presence of the teacher.

Analysis of results

The researcher has analysed the results and explained them. He considered several factors which might have affected the explanation of results, specially concerning question 2, namely: the small motivation of students towards studies, difference of time of study of the two groups, differences in teachers, the possibility that programmed instruction or non-programmed treatment was not pure in neighbouring groups. The possibility of differences in the results owing to differences in types of tests, the absence of competition in distant groups and finally the standard of the efficiency of the program used might not have ensured the desired standard.

THE EDUCATIONAL APPLICATIONS

The researcher sees that the method of programmed instruction could contribute to the solution of some of the problems we suffer, such as: shortage of teachers, teaching by correspondence, helping the citizen to continue learning for his lifetime outside the school, consideration and treatment of individual differences, overcoming some difficulties, training of teachers and qualifying them educationally and professionally, using it as teaching aids, and research work.

The researcher has commended at the end of his research, the following suggestions: training teachers for a skilful use and preparation of programmed instruction, forming an organization of specialists in producing educational programmers, caution during the use of some foreign programs as they are, or after translating them into Arabic, and constructing better ways of communication among different countries or peoples who are interested in programmed instruction.

REFERENCES

Ellis, C. H. (1964) Judging the Teaching Effectiveness of Programs. In 'Trends in Programmed Instruction'. (Ed) G. D. Offush and W. C. Meicsherry. Department of Audio-visual Instruction, Northern Educational Association and North Society for Programmed Instruction, Washington
Espick, J. and Williams, B. (1967) Developing Programmed Instructional Materials. A handbook for Program Writers. Fearn Publishers, Inc, San Francisco
Farrag, L. O. (1968) The Development, Utilization and Effectiveness of Programmed Materials in Teaching Mental Health. In Journal of Modern Education, 4th Issue, April 1968, American University in Cairo
Iskander, Y. K. (1971) Some Research Activity in the Field of Programmed Instruction in the United Arab Republic. In Magazine of Visual Education, October 1971, London
Hartley, J. (1966) Summary of Research Results on Programmed Instruction. Journal of New Education
Larue, A. M. and Donelson, F. E. (1964) An Evaluation of Programmed Instruction and Conventional Classroom Techniques. In 'Trends in Programmed Instruction'. (Ed) G. D. Offush and W. C. Meicsherry. Department of Audio-visual Instruction, Northern Educational Association and North Society for Programmed Instruction, Washington
Pilep, T. R. (1967) Current Research on Programmed Texts and Self Instructional Learning in Mathematics. A. V. Communication Review, Vol. 15, No. 2
Roe, A. (1962) Research in Programmed Instruction. In 'Programmed Learning and Computer-based Instruction'. (Ed) E. J. Coulson. Wiley, New York
Schramm, W. (1964) The Research on Programmed Instruction. US Department of Health, Education and Welfare, Washington

An Experimental Evaluation of the Effects of Microteaching on Teaching Performance

R J BRITTON and G O M LEITH

Microteaching is the name given to a form of training in teaching skills. It starts from the position that teaching is a complex set of capabilities which students of teaching do not at first have. Hence, the development of these skills is better carried out if each one is identified, practised, initially apart from the others, and later combined with them when each has been mastered.

Learning how to teach is also complicated by the problems involved in dealing, from the start, with large groups of children. Consequently, in microteaching not only are the tasks simplified, but the classes are made small and the length of lessons is short.

A third problem is that the first lessons, at the outset of teaching practice, may not go well for a student-teacher. Nevertheless, he must continue to struggle with the class which has suffered his mistakes. In microteaching, the miniature class is changed so that another try can be made without the problems of recovery from errors in teaching.

Furthermore, the teacher is usually given opportunity to witness his own performance by means of videotape-playback and receives an appraisal of his performance (Allen & Ryan, 1969).

There are a number of approaches to microteaching all of which involve: analysis of teaching skills; reduction in complexity of tasks, in size of class and in duration of teaching; and feed-back and critique of performance before further practice with a new microclass (Cooper & Allen, 1969).

The experiment described in this report was undertaken not only to make an evaluation of microteaching but to test how far particular economies could be made and to appraise the contribution of different components of the microteaching system. In particular, the experiment attempted, with a minimum of reorganization, to carry out the training within the normal context of college teaching. It sought to discover if microteaching could be effective without the use of children as pupils. In addition, the contribution of individual practice with television feed-back and critique of performance was assessed in comparison with the teaching performance of students who received other aspects of the course – but omitted the practice and feed-back components – and with students receiving the normal preparation for teaching practice.

EXPERIMENTAL DESIGN

Fifty-six students from two classes in the first year of a college of education course were employed in the experiment. The classes were randomly divided into two sets to form an experimental and a control group so that the influence of the two class tutors would not be a disturbing factor. A group consisting of twenty-eight students was given a course of microteaching, the remaining twenty-eight students continuing with their normal studies. (Britton & Leith, 1971)

A period of twenty hours was allotted for the experimental teaching, four of these hours being devoted to seminar discussions on the principles of microteaching. The aim of these seminars was to present and, as far as possible, to elicit from students, the categories of teaching skills and criteria of teaching performance, through guided discussion. Two skills were examined in detail in the seminars – set induction (which is to do with starting off a lesson, focusing attention, clarifying aims, reviving pre-requisite knowledge, arousing interest, etc) and reinforcement.

In fact, set induction was the only skill practised in the microteaching situation in the time available. Unlike many microteaching systems no use was made of model performances. Practice was carried out in the television studio of the college in a space arranged like a classroom, containing a table, seats for learners and a chalkboard. The 'teacher' prepared a five minute topic as introduction to a lesson. He taught a group of four, fellow students at their own level. No attempt was made to simulate children or to engage in role play. The students completed a diagnostic schedule of the teaching performance which was recorded on videotape. In the second part of the session (or, sometimes, in a later session a few days or a week later) the 'teacher' viewed the videotape recording, on a 21 inch monitor, in private, together with the supervisor. Use was made of the students' rating schedules to develop a constructive appraisal of the performance. At the end of the critique the 'teacher' had a second, five minute lesson, with a different group of four students, in which he gave the same instruction.

All of the students in the experimental group participated as students in the micro-classes. Fifteen of the twenty-eight were able to practise teaching, receive feed-back and make another try. The remainder did not perform as 'teachers'.

The television recordings were made on half-inch videotape by means of two tripod-mounted vidicon cameras. One of these was set to give a wide-angle shot of the teacher and pupils. The other focused on the chalkboard.

A director controlled the cameras and selected the shots from the control room. This arrangement presented no problems of selection and allowed a maximum amount of spontaneity during the lesson segments.

Evaluation sessions (Critiques) were conducted so as to elicit self-appraisal from the student-teacher. In most cases perception of his performance brought spontaneous comments. Typically, the student realised that he had addressed only one of the pupils, or that, in using the chalkboard, he lost contact with the class, or that there were faults in speaking (not clearly enough, too loudly, etc).

It should be pointed out that every student in the experimental group had taken part in discussion about the types of performance which fulfill criteria of good teaching or which deviate from effective practice.

EVALUATION OF TEACHING

The microteaching practice was done in the Spring term. After the vacation there was a short period of warming-up before the whole of the first year entered its first, continuous teaching-practice in schools. Apart from a few visits to schools this was their first opportunity to engage in realistic teaching. The period of school apprenticeships lasted for three and a half weeks during which time the students took over regular series of lessons under the guidance of the school staff and supervision by a college tutor. The evaluation of their teaching performance (marked on a 15 point scale) was a product of the supervisors' impressions and those of the school. The college tutors each supervised a number of students whose range included individuals from the experimental and control groups. None of the tutors had been informed about the experiment and they did not know which of their students had undertaken microteaching. In short no bias entered into the assessments of teaching performance since the tutors neither knew which students had received special training nor that there was to be a comparative evaluation.

Tutors of the fifty-six students concerned were asked to give a further evaluation after making their assessment. This additional evaluation was completed by means of a rating instrument describing categories of teaching and using a seven point scale for each category.

RESULTS AND ANALYSIS

To give a perspective of the findings, the categories of teaching practice marks which are conventionally used to summarize results are tabulated below (Table I). The category 'Good' contains marks of B- or higher; 'Average' includes C+ and C; while 'Poor' (which may signify 'at risk') contains marks of C- and below. An earlier document referred in particular to the purpose of helping weaker students (Leith, 1970).

The table indicates that microteaching (M_2) had the effect of reducing

264

Table I. Proportions of students, given microteaching practice (M_2), micro-class participation (M_1) and no microteaching (M_0), achieving good, average and poor grades on teaching practice (supervisors' ratings)

	Good		Average		Poor	
	Proportion	Number	Proportion	Number	Proportion	Number
M_2	.53	(8)	.40	(6)	.07	(1)
M_1	.31	(4)	.54	(7)	.15	(2)
M_0	.21	(6)	.50	(14)	.29	(8)

Table II. Mean scores of students given microteaching (M_2), microclass participation (M_1) or no microteaching (M_0) on two teaching evaluation scales

	(a) Supervisors' Ratings				(b) Teaching Evaluation Instrument		
	M_2	M_1	M_0		M_2	M_1	M_0
$\bar{x}$	7.53	7.00	6.43	$\bar{x}$	24.40	21.00	18.75
s	1.30	1.29	1.08	s	6.51	5.85	5.38
n	15	13	28	n	15	13	28

the number of students at risk and increasing the proportion achieving a 'good' grade. Participation in microclasses (with seminars) shows a less marked trend in the same direction in comparison with students who had no microteaching. This mode of tabulating the data locates whereabouts on the scale the majority of scores fall. For the purpose of statistical analysis, however, the mean scores of the groups were compared. These are shown for the Supervisors' Ratings and for the Evaluation Instrument Scores in Table II.

Both sets of ratings show that students who practised in the microteaching situation achieved higher scores than those without such experience. They also show that the students who had partial training (seminars and participation in microclasses) obtained a mean score intermediate between the other two groups.

To test the significance of the findings analyses of variance were carried out, the results being summarized in Table III.

Table III. Analyses of variance

(a) Supervisors' Ratings						(b) Teaching Evaluation Instrument					
Source	SS	df	MS	F	P	Source	SS	df	MS	F	P
Between	12.27	2	6.14	3.51	.05	Between	312.58	2	106.29	3.45	.05
Within	92.59	53	1.75			Within	1694.85	53	30.82		
Total	104.86	55				Total	2007.43	55			

Table IV. Significance of differences between
means (one-tailed tests)

	Comparison	Difference	t	p
Supervisors')	$M_2+M_1-M_0$	.86	2.43	<.01
Ratings)	M_2-M_1	.53	1.06	N.S.
T. Eval.)	$M_2+M_1-M_0$	4.07	2.70	<.005
Instrument)	M_2-M_1	3.40	1.61	N.S.

In both analyses there is an F ratio which is significant at less than the
.05 level. Further tests, however, are called for in which the main hypothesis – that microteaching improves teaching practice performance (and
also how far the two microteaching groups differ) is examined. Since there
are two degrees of freedom available for follow-up tests and since the main
hypothesis contrasts microteaching with the control group, the two microteaching groups were pooled. The only additional test which is legitimate is
that between microteaching groups. The results of the t-tests are set out in
Table IV. The superiority in teaching performance of the microteaching
groups is very unlikely, therefore, to be a chance finding.

DISCUSSION AND CONCLUSIONS

The experimental project set out to discover if microteaching would have a
significant effect on the teaching performance of first-year students in their
first, continuous school-practice. The results leave no doubt that these
students were helped to start off well and to maintain their standard of teaching over the practice. From their spontaneous comments it is clear that
they gained in self-confidence as well as in skill as a result of the experimental teaching. What is more, the data suggest that partial experience together
with knowledge of principles is also helpful. Those students who did **not** have
the opportunity for teaching before the cameras, self-appraisal and further
teaching, but who took part in the seminars and acted as students (and judges
of performance), achieved mean scores which were midway between those of
the other two groups.

The project also aimed to find if economies could be made in time and in
the use of children. Indeed, it was a condition of the work that the regular
programme and organization of the college should not be disturbed. The total
length of time provided for the experimental teaching was twenty hours – four
of these being used for seminars. In the remaining sixteen hours, 15 students
were given practice and feed-back. Furthermore, since students were used
rather than children in microclasses, this aspect of the system became part
of the learning experience for students. Indeed, one reason for using students
as pupils was the belief that if learners are involved in the development or

formulation of principles and criteria and actively employ them then they are likely to incorporate the standards and practices into their own behaviour. (Leith, 1971). The constraints of the experiment did not, however, permit variation of these factors. It seems likely, however, that the microclass students through their applications of the criteria of judgement were able to set up an internal model of effective teaching, though they would probably have profited still more by the opportunity to make and eradicate faults.

This is in contrast to the findings of an experiment on the acquisition of kinaesthetic responses when vicarious experience (watching, not doing) and application of the standards (measuring another's responses and giving feed-back) had no influence on learning (Leith, 1968). On the other hand one of the lessons of this experiment is worth stating even though simple motor responses are different in kind from the complex skills of teaching. It is that subjects who were given no feed-back about the correctness of their responses nevertheless learned something, viz, to make exactly the same response again, however far away it was from the response required. In other words, without external feed-back, the learner developed idiosyncratic responses which deviated from what was required.

The positive findings of the present experiment suggest that it would be worth-while to carry out further work to develop more precise knowledge of the techniques of microteaching. For example, we need to ask how much or how little practice is necessary for optimal results and how many and which skills should be taught? Other questions relate to the mode of teaching. Is it really the case that deriving and applying rules incorporates them more certainly into practice than receiving them from an instructor? Are the categories of skills the most aptly chosen? Does it matter in which order the skills are learned? Do all students benefit from microteaching or are there some who are less able to profit? Is it useful to show model teaching performances? If so should they be perfect or contain faults? What kinds of feed-back are best? Should the sessions be spaced?

Reactions to microteaching vary. Some teacher-educators are ready to welcome the new set of tools. Others, however, react in a hostile way. They point to dangers of methods modelled on industrial training systems. They assert that such training is inappropriate for the art of teaching that every-thing is too cut-and-dried, that stereotyped performances will result. Again, the point is raised that, at the moment when classroom-teaching techniques are being abandoned (in favour of team approaches, group activities, etc), microteaching may reinforce the tendency to **teach lessons.**

It should be said that much of the hostility is unwarranted. Even though the methods have every hallmark of Behavioural Technology, there is a great deal which is familiar to college of education teachers. The idea of reducing the load for first-year students by giving them remedial groups of three or four children has been practised for years. Similarly the idea of feed-back, for example, through pupils' progress on diagnostic tests, is of long-standing. Some colleges have used a method of group-teaching in which first-year students as a group, teach a class. The group involvement is extended to criticism of each other's teaching, in an informal atmosphere.

There is, indeed, no justification for many of the counter arguments. If microteaching is administered in a stereotyped way it may result in inflexible patterns of teaching – but there is no reason to assume it must be given rigidly.

In the same way, if lecturing techniques are all that is provided in microteaching, then didactic methods may be reinforced. There is, however, no reason why formal instruction only should be taught – the method is just as open to active, learner-centred methods. As well as this it may be pointed out that, by analogy with the Marion Richardson method of teaching writing, the provision of basic forms can be the basis for individual variation and personal style.

In recent years there has been a rapid development in knowledge of learning processes and means of facilitating learning (Gagne, 1965; Leith, 1966, 1970). What we also need are investigations which focus on parallel, instructional processes to establish taxonomies of teaching. In other words we need to find what is involved on the teacher's side in setting up learning situations, steering and guiding, giving direction, stimulating curiosity and adapting to individual differences as well as presenting. Such studies will help to provide a basis for the practical as well as the theoretical aspects of teacher training and will serve to refine our methods of evaluation in teaching. The authors wish to thank their colleagues who helped in carrying out the experiment, in particular Mr L A Creswick, Director of Audio-Visual Centre and CCTV and his staff.

REFERENCES

Allen, D. and Ryan, K. (1969) Microteaching. Addison-Wesley Publishing Co., Reading, Mass

Britton, R.J. and Leith, G.O.M. (1971) in 'Aspects of Educational Technology V'. (Ed) D. Packham, A. Cleary and T. Mayes. Pitman, London

Cooper, J. M. and Allen, D. W. (1969) Microteaching: History and Present Status. (Mimeo) School of Education, University of Massachusetts

Gagné, R. M. (1965) The Conditions of Learning. Holt, Rinehart and Winston, New York

Leith, G. O. M. (1966) The Improvement of learning. In 'Programmed Learning: A Symposium'. National Centre for Programmed Learning, National Committee for Audio-Visual Aids in Education, London

Leith, G. O. M. (1968) The influence of vicarious practice and feed-back on performance on a kinaesthetic learning task. Atlantic Psychologist. Fall

Leith, G.O.M. (1970) Journal of Educational Technology, 1, 116-128

Leith, G. O. M. (1970) An Empirical Assessment of Microteaching Systems in Teacher Training (Preliminary Document). University of Sussex

Leith, G. O. M. (1971) Working Papers on Instructional Design and Evaluation, I Educational Objectives, II Analysis of Objectives and Tasks, III Sequence and Structure. World Health Organization, Geneva

Testing Oral Production in the Language Laboratory

G A B MOORE and GILBERT TAGGART

Dr Gilbert Taggart, at Sir George Williams University, Montreal, has been developing and evaluating methods for teaching and assessment of French as a second language. These include: an experimental study into audio-visual stimuli in second language learning; tape-slide presentations; a complete course consisting of 52 thirty-minute television programmes, audio exercise, student work book and marking guide; aural-visual-oral tests. The course is being used successfully in the University's own facilities, over one of Montreal's cable television systems and has recently been acquired by three other colleges and school systems.

AURAL-VISUAL-ORAL TESTING

The aural-visual-oral tests were developed and administered first in 1970-71. They were extensions of aural-oral testing procedures used previously, which allowed for mass testing of 1200 students enrolled in the second level course offered by the University. In this audio-only testing mode, students were able to register individual responses on a tape which was then graded by the instructor and his assistants.

Taggart (1969) investigated a system of dividing the stimuli presented to students in the teaching and practice mode, between aural and visual cues. In audio-only exercises all stimuli required by the student to formulate a response are contained in the aural channel. In Taggart's system the student received the usual aural stimuli, which, however, contained ambiguity as to gender, number, person and tense of verbs etc. The information required to remove the ambiguity was supplied through a visual channel — slide, picture, or videotape. From this Taggart was moved to develop situational materials using controlled structures, vocabulary and rate of presentation, but in simulated life-related contexts (Taggart, 1970). The aural-visual-oral testing procedures were then developed to provide students with a situationally-simulated context in which they were tested.

The aural-visual-oral tests are administered each term to 1200 students in the second level French course offered by the University. Students are tested by groups scheduled into a 21 position cassette audio-active-compare laboratory, by Cybervox, also used for drill and practice.

TEST MATERIALS

The test consists of a half-hour videotape presentation designed by Taggart and produced by the University's Centre for Instructional Technology.

The test material has been carefully constructed to simulate living situations. These have included job interviews, a visit to an art gallery, a family looking at slides and an old picture album, an office conversation, and students discussing the test.

The format used to produce the videotape test material provided a spacing between questions of 24 syllables of verbal material followed by a signal 'attention, écoutez, dites-moi' etc to alert the student to the upcoming test question which consists of approximately 12 syllables. This is followed by a pause sufficient to allow a student response of twice the syllabic count in the question. It is only during this period that the student machine is operative to register the response. Test questions have been ordered in an ascending scale of difficulty giving cut-off points for weaker students during the tests. Students with stronger language proficiency are able to complete all the questions.

Each 30-minute test is subdivided into three parts with each part containing 15 to 20 questions for a total of 50 in the entire test.

ADMINISTRATION PROCEDURE

While the University has a central television distribution system, in the administration of these tests a videotape playback unit is assigned to the laboratory and operated by the teaching assistant.

Each student position is assigned a carrel which is equipped with a virgin cassette identified with the student's name and registration number. These cassettes are collected following the test for grading. All student controls are gathered at the instructor's console enabling central control of the record mechanisms throughout the administration of the test.

The test is administered by playing the videotape program through 2 large monitors within a viewing pattern accessible to all students.

The student machines remain at rest while the test material is presented. The test administrator activates the student machines just prior to the response sequence. The machines are then in operation only during the interval in which the students make their oral response. Following each response the machines are stopped and the procedure is repeated for the next sequence.

The test material on the videotape is of 30 minutes duration but the above procedure designed to record only student responses results in a student cassette of approximately 5 minutes duration. Since the student cassettes must be listened to individually, by native-speaking markers in real time, the contraction of time becomes substantial across the total student population involved.

Suitability of this testing technique

1. Standardized objective questions are used.
2. Native-speaking markers are employed to score the student response as opposed to academic staff in a traditional oral test situation.
3. The procedure is efficient where large numbers of students are involved.
4. The marking time of 5 minutes per student yields substantial time savings when compared with individual orals of a traditional nature.
5. Initial indications suggest a reduction of student anxiety usually associated with tests and examinations.
6. Student response to the procedure has not shown any concern with de-personalization.
7. The procedure is most suitable for grammatical manipulation but does not assess individual creative speech nor vocabulary growth.

REFERENCES

Boyd, G. M. (1971) The Language Laboratory at the University Level: The Learning Centre, in Chatagnier and Taggart, 145
Broughton, G. (1971) Language Teaching by Film. Educational Media International, 4, 12
Hocking, E. (1964) Language Laboratory and Language Learning, Monograph 2. Department of Audiovisual Instruction
Stack, E. M. (1960) The Language Laboratory and Modern Language Teaching. Oxford University Press
Taggart, G. (1969) Etude experimentale de certains stimulus auditifs et visual dans l'acquisition d'une langue seconde. Universite de Montréal (unpublished doctoral dissertation)
Taggart, G. (1970) Cours audiovisuel de francais, langue seconde. Multi-media Course, Sir George Williams University
Young, C. W. and Choquette, C. A. (1963) An Experimental Study of the Effectiveness of Four Systems of Language Laboratory Equipment in Teaching French Pronunciation. Colgate University

Student Reaction to the Use of Detailed Objectives

JOHN COWAN

INTRODUCTION

It seems a logical, simple and attractive idea to base a course of instruction on carefully prepared objectives. Converts to the principles of Educational Technology usually tackle this task with enthusiasm, despite the initial difficulty which confronts them when they attempt to prepare precise definitions of their objectives. The teacher finds the exercise worthwhile and believes, not unreasonably, that the inevitable restructuring of his course must surely represent an improvement in his teaching. In subsequent reviews of his courses he may lose sight of the fact that he has now accepted the use of objectives as part of his normal work pattern.

But how do his students react when faced with this system for the first time? It is not established in **their** minds as the 'obvious' mode of procedure, nor is it an approach likely to be followed by the majority of their lecturers.

This brief paper sets out the results of questionnaire returned by two classes of university undergraduates after a term in which, for the first time, complete detailed objectives had been made available to them for one of their courses. The intent was to ascertain undergraduate reaction to an innovation which was introduced as unobtrusively as possible.

DESCRIPTION OF COURSES

The students were civil engineering undergraduates at Heriot-Watt University, following a four year course leading to the BSc degree. In a lecture class on Structural Design (for third year students, N = 91), a complete set of objectives was issued without comment at the beginning of the session in place of a syllabus. In the lecturer's opinion, (which is possibly biased!), there was a strict relationship between the objectives and the lecture and tutorial content, even with regard to order of presentation. An example of the list for a typical lecture is given in Table I. The course consisted of 18 such lectures and 9 audio-tutorials per term and was mathematical rather than descriptive in content.

Table I. Lecture objectives: Lecture 11

At the end of this lecture, you should be able to:

1. Describe the appearance of a reinforced concrete beam specimen during a flexural test to destruction, and classify the types of failure which might be observed.
2. State the test conclusions reached by Hognestad, Hanson and McHenry.
3. Explain the theoretical suggestions made by these workers with regard to the nature of the failure stress block.
4. Show how a method of strength prediction can then be derived on this basis.

The other class comprised 95 first year students following an introductory course in Materials and Design. This was of one term's duration, and the 60-hour program depended heavily on group-based instruction. This was made possible by virtually eliminating the conventional lecture and depending on CCTV (Cowan, 1969), tape/slide instruction, seminars, self-tuition, visits and practical work. The teaching content was mainly descriptive or practical, and the learner-directed situations (Cowan et al, 1970) were strange to the majority of students. For each activity, objectives were set out and these lists were issued to the class at appropriate occasions during the term (Table II).

Table II. Laboratory objectives: Concrete Lab Day 1

At the conclusion of this laboratory period, you should be able to:

1. **Describe:** the manufacture of standard concrete cubes from given concrete
   the testing of these cubes in a compression machine
   the appearance of a crushed cube during and after testing
   the appearance of a crushed timber cube during and after testing
   the appearance of a 'split cylinder' after testing
2. **Cast:** a cube in a standard mould and assist in the casting of a small beam, compacting on a vibrating table
3. **Examine:** crushed specimens of concrete and timber and identify evidence, where present, of the mode of failure
4. **Record:** for your own purposes all that you have learnt, using the correct terms and vocabulary

In both classes the students were given the objective lists as an **aid** to study. It was hoped that they would learn to use them as early in the learning process as possible, since they should study more effectively if they bore in mind what they were trying to learn. They were left to discover the value of the objectives for themselves, without direction to that end.

QUESTIONNAIRE

At the end of the term, prior to the class examinations, a questionnaire was issued to both classes. The questions which were asked were intended to cover:

    (a) The amount of **use** made of the printed objectives.
    (b) The clarity of **expression** of the objectives.
    (c) The **effect**, if any, of the use of objectives on study methods.
    (d) The **reaction** to this form of course management.

Some of the questions were not applicable to the third year course, since it contained no labs. All were answered by marking a cross on a five point scale, and the forms were returned anonymously.

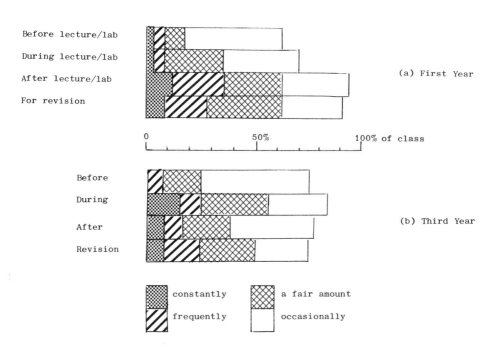

Figure 1. Use of objectives

RESULTS

(a) **Use:** Figure 1 shows the use made of the objective lists before, during and after teaching sessions, and for revision. The first year students seem to have relied on the objectives rather more than the third year students. In each case a significant proportion made more than occasional use of the objectives.

(b) **Expression of Objectives:** The students' opinions are set out in Table III, and indicate a slight weakness in the formulation of objectives for practical work for first year students. Otherwise the students were satisfied.

Table III. Expression of objectives

	Never	Sometimes	Satisfactorily	Fairly Well	Very Well	Year
Do you understand the objectives as listed?	1%	6%	43%	41%	9%	I
	0%	15%	35%	42%	8%	III
Can you relate them to the teaching content?	1%	6%	33%	46%	14%	I
	0%	0%	33%	50%	17%	III
Can you relate them to the practical content?	0%	34%	30%	33%	3%	I

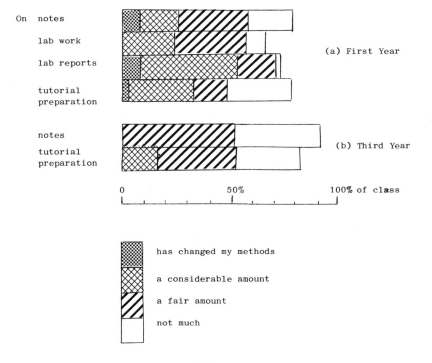

Figure 2. Effect of use

(c) **Effect on Study Methods:** Figure 2 shows diagrammatically the influence of printed objectives on notetaking, preparing for tutorials, and (for the first year only) on carrying out and writing up labs. The impact of the treatment has been considerable.

(d) **Reaction:** The results in Table IV suggest a fairly strong preference for the publication and use of objectives, although the minority support in the first year for a brief syllabus is rather surprising.

Table IV. Reaction

	Strongly Agree	Agree	Neutral	Disagree	Strongly Disagree	Year
I like the subdivision of lectures into smaller, well-defined sections	31% 50%	52% 42%	11% 8%	3% 0%	3% 0%	I III
The objectives will be useful when it comes to preparing for exams	34% 18%	55% 50%	4% 32%	4% 0%	3% 0%	I III
A brief syllabus would be more useful than detailed objectives	11% 0%	9% 0%	28% 22%	38% 60%	14% 18%	I III

COMMENTS

The survey appears to have confirmed that it is worthwhile to issue lists of detailed behavioural objectives to students. It has also revealed that a notable proportion of students claimed to make regular use of these lists and that a significant minority of first year students felt that their study methods had been appreciably altered as a result of the arrangement.

REFERENCES

Cowan, J. (1969) 'CCTV Group Study'. March, Technical Education **10**, 3
Cowan, J., McConnell, S. G. M. and Bolton, A. (1970) Learner-directed group work for large classes. In 'Aspects of Educational Technology IV'. (Ed) A. C. Bajpai and J. F. Leedham. Pitman, London

Method of presentation: Tape slide, wall chart and summary

A Preliminary Investigation into the Effects of a Curriculum on Intellectual Abilities

B BOLTON

This paper describes the results of an investigation into the effectiveness of part of an undergraduate curriculum in electrical engineering. It is shown that tests of cognitive abilities can be used as instruments of curriculum evaluation, particularly for diagnostic purposes. The results of the investigation indicate that the examinations taken in the early stages of the curriculum are not making any significant measurement of higher cognitive abilities. The results also show that students who score well on a test of ability to Analyse are less likely to show improvement, as measured by examinations, through the earlier stages of the curriculum than are students who score badly on such a test.

INTRODUCTION

The effectiveness of the undergraduate electrical engineering curriculum at the University of Bath is at present under investigation. The criterion by which effectiveness is to be measured is the extent to which general intellectual abilities are fostered by the curriculum. To measure changes in these abilities two types of test have been developed; the first measures the abilities to Comprehend and Analyse – as defined by Bloom (1956); the second measures the preferences which students show for activities at the various levels of cognitive behaviour. The first test was given to a sample of students in 1970 as a validation exercise and the results of this exercise were published at the last APLET conference (Bolton 1971). Since the first application of the test in 1970 more information has been collected on the performance of the particular sample of students on the undergraduate course, and the purpose of this paper is to discuss the correlation between the results obtained by students on the cognitive abilities test and the results obtained by students in their course examinations.

ANALYSIS OF RESULTS

The results available for each student consisted of scores for Comprehension and Analysis; four examination marks for subjects examined at the end of the first academic stage; five examination marks for subjects examined at the end of the second academic stage; and one mark obtained on an open-ended type of examination taken at the end of the first academic stage. The open-ended examination was an experimental paper which set out to measure the extent to which students could handle the more divergent problems of engineering synthesis (Hewlett & Bolton, 1970). One further score was made use of. This was a score which was derived from the average scores of a student in the first and second stage examinations. It was arrived at by converting the average scores to z-scores and then subtracting the first stage average from the second stage average. The resultant score was called the Gain in Average Score (GAS). Because it is a derived score it needs to be handled with care when comparisons are drawn and when correlations are calculated, but it does provide a useful point of reference in the following discussion.

The method of analysis used was the Factor Analysis technique. A principal-component factor analysis was carried out on the variables and the resulting factors were then rotated using the Varimax technique. To allow for variations in the reliabilities of the tests the diagonal element of the input correlation matrix was replaced by the maximum absolute row correlation coefficient and an iteration process was used to calculate the communalities. In the following discussion only the final Varimax factors are quoted, and only factors having a percentage variance in excess of 10 are included. The number of observations in each case was 48 and the 1.0% and 5.0% levels of significance occur at factor loadings of 0.37 and 0.28 respectively.

COMMON FACTORS IN THE COURSE EXAMINATIONS

Table I shows that there are only two significant factors which are common to all course examinations, and of the two the first factor is clearly the most significant. One can conclude, therefore, that the examinations are all measuring much the same ability. This ability reflects a competence in mathematics and a competence in the more applied engineering subjects. The second factor is bi-polar. That is, it contains both positive and negative components. Only two factor loadings are significant at the 1% level – 1st stage mathematics and 2nd stage electrical machines – and only three of the remaining subjects produce a factor loading significant above 5%. At first sight the obvious difference between the positive and negative loadings comes from their position in the course, positive loadings in first-stage and negative loadings in the second-stage, but if we are concerned with the nature of the ability represented by the second factor we have to look more closely at the abilities which the particular courses demand, and even more particularly at the differences between the courses. The two first-stage courses with loadings in factor II are both mathematical in content and both are

Table I. Rotated factor loadings for course examinations

Tests	Rotated Factor Loadings		Communality
	I	II	
Electrical Science (open-ended)	.43		.24
Electrical Science (1st stage)	.63	.29*	.49
Mathematics (1st stage)	.70	.45	.69
Engineering Physics (1st stage)	.66		.46
Electrical Science (2nd stage)	.79		.62
Electronics (2nd stage)	.78	-.35*	.74
Electrical Machines (2nd stage)	.76	-.37	.72
Mathematics (2nd stage)	.61		.39
Mechanical Science (2nd stage)	.69	-.36*	.60
Percentage Variance	78.68	14.60	93.28

'academic' in the sense that they are concerned with basic mathematical and scientific ideas. In contrast the second-stage courses with loadings in factor II are 'applied' courses. It could therefore be argued that the second factor is reflecting an ability in analytical techniques, and, furthermore, that students who have this ability at a high level are likely to find it a handicap when it comes to handling more applied subjects. To throw more light on this problem the results of the Cognitive Abilities Test were included with the examination scores and a new set of Varimax factors were obtained.

FACTORS COMMON TO THE COGNITIVE ABILITIES TEST AND THE COURSE EXAMINATIONS

From Table II it can be seen that there are, once again, two factors of significance. The first factor has changed very little. There is more emphasis on the engineering subjects and less on the mathematical subjects, but in essence the nature of the factor remains constant. The change in the second factor is more noticeable. The factor has swung towards Analysis, and in so doing it has moved closer to the first-stage scores in electrical science and mathematics, and further away from the second-stage scores. This tends to confirm the argument put forward previously that the two first-stage subjects appearing in the second factor are more analytical in nature than the other subjects.

Without doubt the most disturbing point to emerge from Table II is the absence of Comprehension and Analysis from the first factor. Whatever ability is being measured by the Cognitive Abilities Test it most certainly is not being measured by six of the course examinations. If we assume that the abilities defined by Bloom (1956) are hierarchical in nature so that performance at any level depends upon performance at lower levels, and there

Table II. Rotated factor loadings for cognitive-abilities test and course examinations

Tests	Rotated Factor Loadings I	II	Communality
Comprehension		.30*	.09
Analysis		.60	.36
Electrical Science (open-ended)	.39	.28*	.23
Electrical Science (1st stage)	.57	.43	.51
Mathematics (1st stage)	.60	.54	.65
Engineering Physics (1st stage)	.62		.45
Electrical Science (2nd stage)	.78		.62
Electronics (2nd stage)	.85		.76
Electrical Machines (2nd stage)	.80		.66
Mathematics (2nd stage)	.57		.39
Mechanical Science (2nd stage)	.74		.59
Percentage Variance	70.72	19.33	90.05

is some evidence to support this view (Kropp & Stoker, 1966), then the absence of Analysis in the first factor must imply that higher abilities such as Synthesis and Evaluation will also have no contribution to make to the first factor. The first factor is therefore most likely to represent a low-level intellectual ability. It obviously is not in the nature of Comprehension and the conclusion drawn is that the examinations are relying to a very large extent on recognition and recall.

Table III. Rotated factor loadings for gain in average score and course examinations

Tests	Rotated Factor Loadings I	II	Communality
Electrical Science (open-ended)	.48		.25
Electrical Science (1st stage)	.67		.49
Mathematics (1st stage)	.81		.68
Engineering Physics (1st stage)	.67		.52
Electrical Science (2nd stage)	.55	.57	.63
Electronics (2nd stage)	.36*	.77	.73
Electrical Machines (2nd stage)	.33*	.77	.70
Mathematics (2nd stage)	.48	.37	.37
Mechanical Science (2nd stage)	.29*	.71	.58
Gain in Average Score	-.62	.86	1.11
Percentage Variance	64.18	28.67	92.85

THE EFFECT OF GAIN IN AVERAGE SCORE ON
THE FACTOR LOADINGS

In this case the Comprehension and Analysis scores were left out of the factor analysis and the Gain in Average score was included. The results are shown in Table III. One can see by comparing Table I and Table III that the factors in Table III are different in nature to the factors in Table I. The splitting of the GAS into positive and negative factor loadings is of considerable interest. It implies that there is an ability, represented by factor I, which could prove to be a handicap to students taking the course examinations. However, as was pointed out earlier, the GAS is a derived mark. It is obtained by subtracting the first-stage average from the second-stage average and there is therefore an inbuilt negative correlation between GAS and the first-stage examination marks as well as an inbuilt positive correlation between GAS and the second-stage examination marks. This could by itself account for the signs of the GAS factor loadings, but closer examination of Table III indicates that there is more to this sign split than just these inbuilt effects. For example, the second-stage electrical science score makes equal contributions to each of the factors. It is therefore as likely to be a predictor of positive gain as of negative gain. The second-stage mathematics score is also split between the factors and contributes more to the factor containing negative gain than to the factor containing positive gain, and this is almost

Table IV. Rotated factor loadings for all tests
and course examinations

Tests	Rotated Factor Loadings I	II	III	Communality
Comprehension				.06
Analysis		-.52		.28
Electrical Science (open-ended)	.43			.25
Electrical Science (1st stage)	.62	-.33*		.51
Mathematics (1st stage)	.70	-.45		.70
Engineering Physics (1st stage)	.68			.57
Electrical Science (2nd stage)	.78			.62
Electronics (2nd stage)	.80	.37		.78
Electrical Machines (2nd stage)	.76	.33*		.69
Mathematics (2nd stage)	.60			.39
Mechanical Science (2nd stage)	.70	.32*	.37	.72
Gain in Average Score		.98		.98
English (1st stage)			.78	.63
Percentage Variance	53.26	26.40	10.74	90.40

281

opposite to what would be expected from the inbuilt correlations. One can conclude from these observations that the sign difference of the GAS factor loadings is caused partly by the inbuilt correlations between GAS and other scores and partly by other effects which still have to be identified.

Considering the remaining factor loadings in Table III, one trend can be identified as a possible effect. The scores which load heavily on the first factor are first-stage scores in non-applied subjects; the scores which load heavily on the second factor are second-stage scores in applied subjects. It follows, therefore, that the second possible effect is the nature of the course, ie applied as against non-applied. Additional support for this argument comes from the presence in factor I of a loading from the open-ended electrical science examination. This is the only score in Table III which was not included when the average mark was determined. It is not, therefore, directly related to the Gain in Average Score, nor is it a score based on an applied course. Examination of Tables I and II will show that this score does not have a great deal in common with the examination scores, the loading on the first factor is always low, and, from Table II, it would appear to have something in common with Analysis. So here again there is an apparent link between ability in a non-applied area and negative gain.

FACTORS COMMON TO ALL TESTS AND COURSE EXAMINATIONS

The rotated factor loadings for all tests and course examinations are shown in Table IV. Included for the first time is the score on the first-stage English examination. This gives rise to a third factor which could be identified as ability in the use of English. The second factor has a very high loading from the Gain in Average Score and might be called Capacity for Improvement in the Course Examinations. As might be expected from Table III, the factor is independent of second-stage mathematics and electrical science. It still shows a positive loading from the applied subjects and a negative loading from the non-applied subjects, but now, in addition, it has a negative loading from Analysis. This could, of course, reflect the connection between Analysis and first-stage electrical science and mathematics shown in Table II, but a straight correlation between Analysis and Gain in Average Score gives a product-moment correlation coefficient of -0.44, which is significant beyond the 1% level, and this leads one to believe that the connection between Analysis and Gain in Average Score is an absolute one.

DISCUSSION

The results quoted enable certain tentative conclusions to be drawn. To begin with, on the assumption that the Cognitive Abilities Test is giving reliable and valid measures of the abilities to Comprehend and Analyse, it can be concluded that the course examinations do not measure these abilities. This has an important consequence for the curriculum because the nature of the final examination will inevitably affect the way in which a student approaches the course, and if as in this case the examination apparently places emphasis on the lower intellectual abilities then students will concentrate on developing these to the exclusion of other abilities.

A second conclusion to be drawn from the results is that students who have a greater capability in Analysis are less likely to show improvement as measured by the course examinations than are students who are less capable in this area. It must be remembered, however, that the examination scores used were obtained in the first two stages of a four stage course, and as yet there is no evidence that this effect also occurs in the examinations taken in later stages of the course. The impact of this effect on the effectiveness of the curriculum could be significant because students who are more competent at the higher intellectual levels may lose some motivation as a result of this negative interaction between ability and measured progress.

On the evidence of these results it would be impossible to claim that the Cognitive Abilities Test could be used as a predictor of the progress a student will make on the course, but then it was not intended as a reliable measure of an individual's ability. Where the importance of a test such as this lies is in its ability to point out trends in the abilities of large groups of students. Some such trends have been observed in the results given above. The investigation reported here was a preliminary to a larger scale investigation of the effectiveness of a complete undergraduate course. It has shown that the developed test of cognitive abilities can be used as an instrument of curriculum evaluation, particularly for diagnostic purposes. In a sense one cannot ask for much more from a test such as this because a total curriculum contains so many variables that it may never be possible to quantify all the effects or relate with any certainty effects to causes, but by isolating particular undesirable trends within a curriculum it indicates where improvements need to be made.

In an investigation such as this it is impossible to work without the co-operation and goodwill of the students who take the tests, and the author would like to acknowledge the assistance of those students at the University of Bath who made this investigation possible. The author also wishes to acknowledge his debt to Professor A J Eales of the School of Electrical Engineering at Bath, who gave the author permission to probe into the workings of the curriculum and to publish the findings.

REFERENCES

Bloom, B. S. (1956) Taxonomy of Educational Objectives. Longmans Green, London

Bolton, B. (1971) 'Aspects of Educational Technology V', (Ed) D. Packham, A. Cleary and T. Mayes, Pitman, London. 136

Hewlett, G. H. K. and Bolton, B. (1970) 'Aspects of Educational Technology IV'. (Ed) A. C. Bajpai and J. F. Leedham, Pitman, London. 322

Kropp, P. R. and Stoker, H. W. (1966) Co-operative Research Project No 2117, Florida State University

An Experiment to Evaluate a Multi-Media Course in Mathematics

N D C HARRIS

THE COURSE

Entry requirements and objectives

The entry requirements were stated as 'We assume you passed GCE 'O' level or School Certificate Mathematics'. No test was included by the course designers to check this level, but it was further stated 'We are not assuming you have studied the subject since or that you know any "modern mathematics" '. No objectives were stated.

Duration and division of content

There were three terms. The work covered was:

TERM 1   (a) Functions, sequences and series
           (b) Statistics
TERM 2   Calculus
TERM 3   Matrices

The work was provided in two unequal parts for each term with a television programme discussing students' problems in the 6th week of each term (Figure 1).

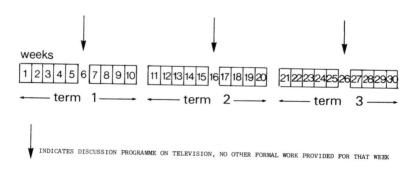

weeks

INDICATES DISCUSSION PROGRAMME ON TELEVISION, NO OTHER FORMAL WORK PROVIDED FOR THAT WEEK

Figure 1. Division of time during the course

284

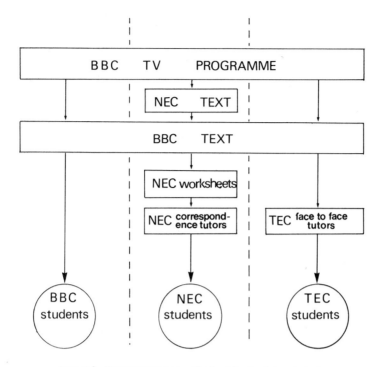

Figure 2. Presentation and methods of feedback for students

Presentations and methods of feedback for students

There were three groups of students:

1) Students who followed the BBC TV programme and the BBC text, but who worked on their own without formal contacts with a tutor (Figure 2). These students are designated BBC.

2) Students who registered with the National Extension College. These students watched the BBC TV programme, then used the text provided by the National Extension College (Figure 2), this text referred them to the BBC text and supplemented or elaborated the content. At intervals the student completed a worksheet from the College which was sent to a tutor. Comments were made based on the students' performances. These students are designated NEC.

3) Students who registered at their local Technical College. They watched the BBC programme and used the BBC text with help and advice from a tutor (Figure 2). These students are designated TEC.

EVALUATION REQUIREMENTS AND CONSTRAINTS

The evaluation was carried out at the instigation of the Open University. The course was considered to provide a useful model of an Open University course. The detailed information required was:

a)   starting mathematics of students taking the course

b)   the gains shown by students as they progressed through the course

c)   the effectiveness of the presentations, or combination of the presentations

d)   comparison of the three types of student

e)   a) to d) carried out for various levels of understanding

To these requirements should be added the constraints inherent in the system:

a)   four independent organizations working together (BBC, Open University, National Extension College and Bath University

b)   course materials (ie BBC texts and NEC texts) were usually not available until about four weeks before the tests had to be printed. (The BBC television programmes were ready well in advance.)

c)   the evaluation was a part-time exercise

EVALUATION PROCEDURE

The constraints on time required a simple method of analysis related to the minimum number of levels of understanding (even Bloom's six main categories were found to be too many). The tests, for a sample whose size was unknown until the course was actually in progress, had to be computer marked to allow for large numbers. Multiple choice and true/false items were selected for this purpose. With the limited time available trials were possible for tests, but not to allow normal item discrimination procedures to be carried out. Criterion items relating to a specific aspect of the course were used, even though this provided difficulties for any statistical analysis. Content validity was considered to be an essential element for this design. A simple coding and cross referencing system was used to identify items. The test results were transferred by hand to punched cards. The data from the cards and the basic matrix relating the test items to the parts of the course and levels of understanding were filed on the computer at Bath. The file can be consulted in relation to questions posed to provide information under the evaluation requirements a) to e).

LEVELS OF UNDERSTANDING

Three levels of understanding were used:

Vocabulary (V) New words which are introduced and used, but which do not necessarily involve a deep abstraction.

Techniques (T) Manipulations which are introduced and used, but do not need a deep understanding. (See Rosenstein's 'tools'.)

Concepts (C) Words and abstractions which it is necessary to fully comprehend in order to be able to apply them in a new situation.

These were selected after consideration of various works (Bloom, Ebel,
Nedelsky, Rosenstein) and attempting to simplify these systems for use within the time constraint. Most difficulty occurred in discriminating between
vocabulary and concept. The three levels were designated by the letters
indicated above.

ANALYSIS SYSTEM AND TEST CONSTRUCTION

The analysis system used for all presentations was to extract the vocabulary,
technique and concepts presented. For each the reference was noted and also
whether it occurred in other means of presentation. An example is shown in

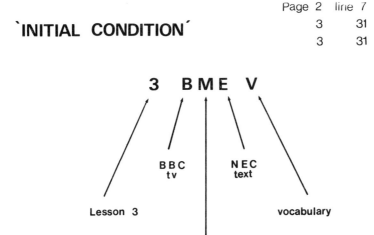

Figure 3. Designation of item to be tested

Figure 3. From the data extracted for each part of each term, possible open
ended questions were devised. When time allowed, these were used to produce multiple choice or true/false items by giving the questions to students
and selecting the range of answers. These multiple choice or true/false
items were used with a sample of students from a local College of Education.
Items which obviously failed to discriminate were eliminated, but a balance
was maintained between the levels of understanding in proportion to the analysis balance (for example test ratios 15V 10T 5C compared with analysis
ratios 29V 18T 10C).

In addition analysis was carried out to locate assumptions made in the course. From these assumptions further items were designed to measure the starting mathematics of the students in relation to the course.

The tests were designed to be used at the points indicated in Figure 4

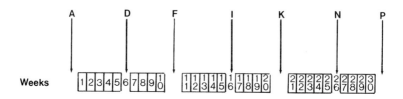

Figure 4. Location of tests during course

(the letters are not sequential as National Extension College worksheets used the intermediate letters). Each test contained two kinds of items as indicated in Figure 5. Test A was put together by using a table of random numbers so that the two types of item were mixed. Test D was produced by substituting

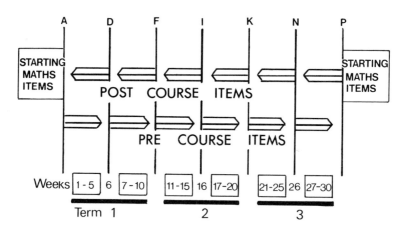

Figure 5. Content of each test

new items of the appropriate length (in lines) in place of previous items. This procedure was continued for the remainder of the tests.

A matrix (Figure 6) was then made to locate items in relation to factors being considered in the evaluation procedure. This information allowed easy access to the tests after construction.

288

LESSON	11	12	13	•
LEVEL OF UNDERSTANDING V	$35_{am}\ 46_{a}\ 54_{bme}$ 61_{m}			
T	$22_{E}\ 24_{bm}\ 49_{bme}$ 53_{ma}			
C	$4_{bm}\ 18_{bme}\ 32_{m}$		EXAMPLE OF PART OF	
METHOD OF PRESENTATION B	46_{v}		REFERENCE MATRIX	
M	$61_{v}\ 32_{c}$			
E	22_{T}			
BM	$35_{v}\ 24_{T}\ 4_{c}$			
BE				
ME	53_{T}			
BME	$54_{v}\ 49_{T}\ 18_{c}$			

Figure 6

USE OF TESTS

The tests were used by all NEC students (the sample is shown in Figure 7), by volunteers from the BBC students (Figure 8), and by the Technical Colleges who were willing to cooperate (Figure 9). The tests were posted to NEC students as one of their worksheets by the College, and to other students by the Open University. Students were given a date by which the tests should be returned.

In order to reduce guessing the following statement was included on the front of each test: "If you do not know the answer, please leave the box **blank** and move on to the next question. This will be more helpful to your tutor than an answer which you have guessed". Students were warned that some questions related to next term's work and that the questions were in no special order, so they should look at all questions. (The layout of a specimen question is shown in Figure 10).

The question papers were not returned to the students, so identical questions were used for pre-course and post-course items.

INITIAL RESULTS

There is some evidence that guessing did not take place, for example on pre-

(a) $\begin{pmatrix} \dfrac{1}{2} & -\dfrac{\sqrt{3}}{2} \\[2mm] -\dfrac{\sqrt{3}}{2} & \dfrac{1}{2} \end{pmatrix}$ (b) $\begin{pmatrix} \dfrac{1}{2} & -\dfrac{\sqrt{3}}{2} \\[2mm] \dfrac{\sqrt{3}}{2} & \dfrac{1}{2} \end{pmatrix}$

(c) $\begin{pmatrix} \dfrac{\sqrt{3}}{2} & -\dfrac{1}{2} \\[2mm] \dfrac{1}{2} & \dfrac{\sqrt{3}}{2} \end{pmatrix}$ (d) $\begin{pmatrix} -\dfrac{\sqrt{3}}{2} & -\dfrac{1}{2} \\[2mm] \dfrac{1}{2} & \dfrac{\sqrt{3}}{2} \end{pmatrix}$

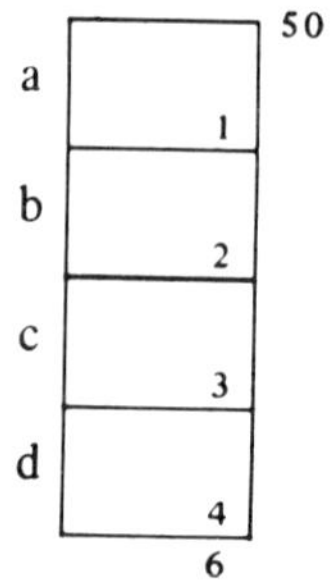

Figure 10. Specimen question

course items see the data in Table I, items D38, F5, K20 being true/false items. There is also evidence that students did complete the tests — see Table II. The items shown are the first and last of a similar type (ie either pre-course items, or post-course items).

Table I. Examples of responses on pre-course items

	← ALTERNATIVES →					
Question	A	B	C	D	E	No answer
A55	17	176	60	58	33	819
A63	30	3	552	93	31	454
D62	48	14	13	20	23	992
D38	612	340	-	-	-	157
F5	299	243	-	-	-	458
K20	83	16	-	-	-	528

Table II. Examples of responses to first and last items in tests

Question	Students attempting	No answer	Total
A1	1165	0	1165
A93	1163	2	1165
D1	601	508	1109
D59	609	500	1109
F2	686	314	1000
F65	815	185	1000
⋮			
P1	348	240	588
P80	285	303	588

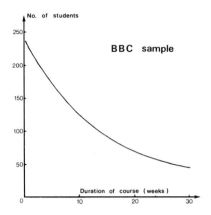

Figure 7

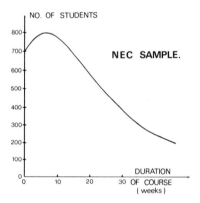

Figure 8

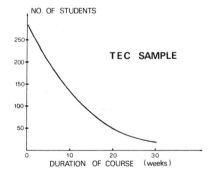

Figure 9

291

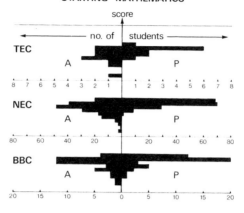

STARTING MATHEMATICS

Figure 11

The starting mathematics of the students is shown in the lefthand side of Figure 11. The righthand side shows these questions repeated at the end of the course. There seems to be some evidence to suggest that tutors have helped the students with low starting mathematics.

The scores in the tests before and after the course for the remainder of the course are shown in Figures 12, 13 and 14.

APPARENT IMPLICATIONS
With a systematic approach there appears to be some evidence that it is

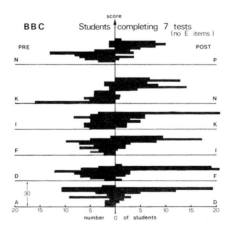

Figure 12

292

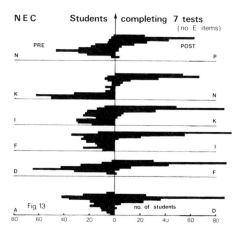

Figure 13

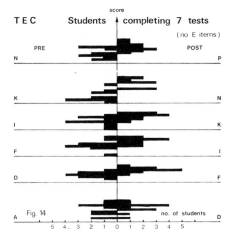

Figure 14

possible to evaluate a multi-media course using criterion referenced tests. From the information on individual items it is also possible to pinpoint possible weaknesses in the course, and from groups of items for parts of a course (see Figure 12 test A to test D where a confusion element seems to show with some **decrease** in scores at the higher end).

ACKNOWLEDGMENTS

Professor K Austwick and Mr P N Richards of the School of Education at Bath University who collaborated in devising the tests; Mr P Carr of the School of Mathematics at Bath University who maintained communication been man and computer; Mrs N McIntosh and Dr A W Bates of the Institute of Educational Technology at the Open University who instigated the project and ensured that the tests were printed, checked and circulated; they also gave every assistance to ensure the success of the experiment. Without the cooperation of the British Broadcasting Corporation and the National Extension College the project could not have proceeded.

REFERENCES

Bloom, B. S. et al (1956) 'Taxonomy of educational objectives'. Handbook 1: Cognitive domain. Longmans, London

Campbell, D. T . and Stanley, J. C. (1970) 'Experimental and quasi experimental designs for research'. Rand McNally

Ebel, R. L. (1969) 'Encyclopaedia of educational research'. Collier-Macmillan

Garrett, H. E. (1958) 'Statistics in psychology and education'. Longmans

Nedelsky, L. (1965) 'Science teaching and testing'. Harcourt, Brace and World

Rosenstein, A. B. (1968) A study of a profession and professional education. Publication EDP 7-68, Reports Group, School of Engineering and Applied Science, University of California, Los Angeles

Siegel, S. (1956) 'Nonparametric statistics for the behavioural sciences'. McGraw-Hill

Tyler, R., Gagne, R. M. and Scriven, M. (1967) 'Perspectives of curriculum evaluation'. Rand McNally, Chicago

The Case for an O & M Investigation of University Teaching
G M MILLS

INTRODUCTION

Conventionally, Organization and Methods is used as a technique for investigating non-manual work in large organizations in which the hierarchical structure contains manager, supervisor and worker, and the end product is usually a service. In a university, the lecturer in charge of a discipline or course is, in effect, the manager. The supervisor could be either the lecturer or a demonstrator or technician. The worker is the student and the end product is student learning which is a service to the whole community. One definition (Sherman, 1969) of O & M is 'a group of investigatory techniques used in the systematic examination and study of work for the purpose of advising on ways to improve efficiency'. It includes work measurement, method study and may use systems analysis and operational research.

If O & M results in significant improvement in efficiency, this may lead to manpower economy but it is not an economy drive. If economies are to be found, O & M properly carried out will find them, but its main purpose is to improve productivity.

There is no valid reason why O & M cannot be applied to university teaching, particularly with laboratory assignments and programmed learning, although, for example, work measurement may be difficult to implement for other teaching methodologies such as lectures and private study.

OBJECTIVES AND PROCEDURES

On assignment to the major part of two first year undergraduate courses in Civil Engineering, viz, Strength of Materials and Theory of Structures, the author decided to undertake a method study and work measurement over a complete year to evaluate potential improvements in the organization and presentation of learning material, the use of staff time, the use of student time, and the quantity and quality of student learning. Teaching programs were available for both courses and a preliminary analysis, based on previous experience of both the author and other colleagues, indicated the

295

possibility of a number of useful organizational changes. For example, the two courses had previously always been taught by different lecturers which resulted in overlapping of certain topics. This could now be eliminated. More radical changes were instituted in the organization of laboratory periods, programmed work sessions and assessment procedures.

ORGANIZATION OF LABORATORY WORK

In previous years, each student attended seven laboratory periods for six formal experiments and a demonstration. Experience had shown that the optimum number of students in each group was three, and they were encouraged to work out results and plot graphs as the experiments proceeded. However, some disadvantages of this system were: (i) the demonstration required a lecturer and technician for a minimum of one hour for 24 periods per year during which 48 specimens were tested to destruction, (ii) as laboratory periods were timetabled at regular intervals throughout the session, the theoretical background to the first few experiments was not given prior to their performance, and (iii) although several sheets of laboratory instructions were provided for each student, the six experiments required a minimum of three staff. Even so, there were queues for a supervisor at the start of a laboratory period. To try and eliminate these disadvantages, alternative methods for satisfying the objectives of each experiment were considered.

For example, economy in staff time and materials was achieved by videotaping the demonstration. The videotaped recording was then included in the appropriate lecture on this topic. Also, class periods were rescheduled to give more programmed work sessions in the first term so that all the laboratory periods occurred in the second term.

As experiment A was relatively simple in concept and the principles were also covered by experiment D, it was decided to use the former as a class demonstration during which the nature of experimental techniques, reasons for error, and precautions necessary to obtain accurate results could be discussed and the students questioned, using the feed-back classroom, on their understanding of experimental principles. As the equipment required for experiments B, C, D and E could not be readily duplicated, these were run simultaneously. Experiment B was relatively straightforward and could be controlled by a technician with a minimum of academic supervision. The instructions required for experiments C and D were presented in a semi-programmed form by means of slide-tape. At the end of each section of the instructions, a slide appeared requesting the students to stop the tape recorder and perform certain actions. This left the supervisor free to concentrate on experiment E which was the least suitable for slide-tape instructions.

At this stage of the course, the object of experiment F could only be to try and achieve Robbins (1963) second aim for higher education, ie, 'to promote the general power of the mind' since this dealt with a complex topic which was only fully covered in the theoretical work of the following year. To schedule this as a formal experiment hardly seemed likely to satisfy this objective. Therefore, relevant parts of this experiment were incorporated in a 20 minute videotape which discussed the topic in general terms. The recording was presented to students instead of a laboratory exercise and followed up by a discussion. Evaluation of the learning was achieved by immediately setting the students a coursework essay.

ORGANIZATION OF PROGRAMMED WORK SESSIONS

Previous experience had indicated that, ideally, programmed work sessions should last for at least two hours with students encouraged to have a short break at the midway stage. The majority of these sessions were of this form and the remainder were of 90 minutes without a break. Each session was controlled continually by at least one supervisor who normally gave assistance only when requested, although students who were spending appreciably longer than average on one frame were often given unsolicited help. The complete year of 72 students was usually divided into two groups for these sessions although timetabling dictated four groups during some periods in the first term.

The course was divided into 43 teaching units each covering a particular topic in programmed form. One teaching program was issued at the start of each period. Students were not expected to leave until they had completed the main part of the program.

WORK MEASUREMENT IN PROGRAMMED SESSIONS

Two types of measurement were undertaken. First, the average times taken by students to complete the teaching program were estimated by noting the page number on which each student was working at five or ten minute intervals. Secondly, the times taken by supervisors in helping students with problems were recorded using a stop watch.

The objectives of the first measurements were to determine the average learning time for each teaching program and for each frame in the program, and to identify potential improvements in the programs. The information obtained is contributing to a current research program on learning efficiency (Mills, 1971).

The main objective of the second measurements was to find the most efficient relationship between the number of supervisors and the number of students in a programmed session. Using queuing theory, the average waiting time of a student in need of assistance could be estimated for any size of student group and any number of supervisors.

LECTURE PERIODS AND ASSESSMENT PROCEDURES

A feed-back classroom was used during a nominal one hour period per week for both informal lecturing and for assessing student progress. Prepared transparencies on an overhead projector summarized the main teaching points and also presented multiple choice questions to the students. The latter were only infrequently required to take notes as the topics covered general principles or expounded relationships between teaching points which were presented in more detail in the parallel programmed work sessions.

Use of the feed-back classroom promoted student participation and criticism. In a typical lecture period, students would be required to respond on five or six occasions to questions of varying difficulty with an answer time averaging about one minute. Occasionally, the system was used to give the students an informal objective test with a large number of questions which were then self-marked. The average mark for the whole group was estimated from the control panel readings and announced at the end of the test so that each student could compare his performance with that of the group.

ANALYSIS OF THE LEARNING MATERIAL

The topics taught were subject to constraints imposed by the necessity of logically ordering the learning sets in hierarchical order. A full task analysis for the material is now being undertaken using the same basic principles suggested for teaching Fortran (Mills, 1970) but selecting optimum knowledge blocks so that the average student should complete them within a working session. The average measured time for each teaching program varied from 55 to 170 minutes with a mean of 105 minutes. This implies a reasonable total learning content but very uneven distribution.

It was noted that a relatively small number of teaching points, frequently those involving visualization in three dimensions, required more help from supervisors and took longer times for students to grasp than might have been expected.

DISCUSSION AND FUTURE DEVELOPMENTS

An O & M study of a university course will require first a preliminary study, then implementation of proposals combined with an evaluation of the work of students and staff, and finally further suggestions for improvements which can be put into operation for succeeding student groups. The last stage could perhaps be considered as successfully completed when no more major improvements appear possible, although new developments in any subject may require periodical re-assessments.

For the courses described in this paper, proposals for the third stage include; (a) re-organization of the course timetable to enable students to attend programmed work sessions in a single group (the analysis indicated that one senior staff and an assistant can deal more than adequately with 72 students), (b) re-allocation of learning material between teaching programs to reduce variance in the average learning time, and (c) the manufacture of a small number of simple models to be distributed round the workroom to help with certain difficult topics. Completion of the study on the above lines should result in a saving of about 50% in senior staff time plus significant reductions in student learning times.

Experience in large organizations has indicated a number of reasons for implementing an O & M survey. These include, for example, increased volume and/or complexity of work causing or thought to cause pressure on the staff, the existence of problems which cross departmental barriers and which require the mediation of an impartial agency, and new equipment or techniques becoming available which have an obvious and significant impact on work performance. All these have great significance for universities who will soon be facing a second student bulge with worsening staff/student ratios, greater development of inter-disciplinary courses, and who will have at their disposal all the newly developed resources of educational technology. For substantial benefits to be obtained from O & M, any investigatory staff should be experienced in university teaching and possess the ability to be impartial, inquisitive, realistic and determined. If such staff can be found, there is a very strong case for each university to set up its own O & M unit to supplement such other valuable service units as Computing and Audio-Visual Aids.

REFERENCES

Sherman, T. P. (1969) O & M in Local Government. Pergamon, London
Report on Higher Education (1963) Chairman Lord Robbins. HMSO
Mills, G. M. (1971) Criteria for assessing the optimum efficiency of teaching programs. In 'Aspects of Educational Technology V'. (Ed) D. Packham, A. Cleary and T. Mayes. Pitman, London
Mills, G. M. (1970) Strategies for teaching Fortran with particular reference to self-instructional methods. In 'Aspects of Educational Technology IV.' (Ed) A. C. Bajpai and J. F. Leedham. Pitman, London

Method of presentation: Tape/slide

A Comparative Study of Two Methods of Tape Slide Presentation for Pharmaceutical Representatives

R CLEMENTS

The purpose of the experiment was to compare the effectiveness of two methods of tape/slide presentation used in the training of product knowledge to groups of representatives in S E Asia. The target population was mixed groups of representatives responsible for the sales of ethical medical, consumer and laboratory diagnostic products to hospitals, laboratories, general practitioners and shopkeepers. Their lengths of service with the company, ranged from one week to twelve years. The experiment took place in September-October 1971.

Two versions of a tape/slide presentation were prepared. The original version made use of the usual techniques of programmed learning. The commentator asked frequent questions; many of the visuals re-iterated the question. The tape-recorder was stopped whilst trainees made written responses and on restarting, the commentator gave correct answers. A second version was produced for continuous presentation. All questions, pauses and answers were deleted from the sound track and several of the visuals were taken out. Trainees were not asked to make active responses. Both versions were used in conjunction with the same pre- and post-test.

The continuous version was shown to a group in Bangkok and a group in Manila; a total of 36 trainees. In Hong Kong and Singapore the programmed version was shown to 42 trainees.

THE RESULTS

	Pre-test	Post-test	Gain
Group 1 (without pauses)	47%	86%	39 percentage points
Group 2 (programmed version)	35%	82%	47 percentage points

When the gain is expressed as a percentage of the possible gain (ie the difference between pre-test score and 100%) Group 1 scored 73% and Group 2 72%.

Statistical tests showed that the average gain for the groups (calculated from individual scores) was 8.97 and 10.64 points respectively. When judged by Students 't' test the difference between the two means was shown to have no statistical significance. Examination showed that the gain was negatively correlated with the initial score. A further analysis using the analysis of covariance technique compared the adjusted gains with the effect of the initial scores removed. The analysis failed to demonstrate any difference between the two methods of presentation.

THE CONCLUSION

As far as this study was concerned, the two presentations were of equal teaching value. However, it was observed that during each showing of the unprogrammed version, trainees busily engaged themselves in writing pertinent items of information. This unsolicited participation may have resulted from the knowledge that a post-test was to follow. Further research of a more controlled nature may show different results.

Method of presentation: Videotape 1" Ampex

Validation of 'A Seaman's Guide to the Rule of the Road'

G C HYDE

One of the prerequisites for any program before its use is that it be validated. In the majority of cases a comparatively simple validation proves that the program meets its objectives or shows up areas of the program which require amendment, at the same time indicating what these amendments should be.

In the case of 'A Seaman's Guide to the Rule of the Road' the validation was far more complex. The objective of the program was to teach Cadets the International Regulations for preventing collisions at sea – a series of 31 rules and an annex governing seamanship in international waters. The rules themselves are complex with many sub-sections and constant cross-references from one sub-section to another. The programmed text set out to explain these rules and to show the trainees how they are interpreted in given situations.

Different criteria were set by the sponsors of the program – the Royal Navy and the Seafarers' Education Service – for various rules according to the degree of importance which they attached to the rules. In order to prove that the program had achieved its overall objective and also to meet the individual criteria set for each rule it was necessary to carry out two validations on groups of Cadets from both the Merchant Navy and the Royal Navy. Since the program examined each situation as seen from the bridge of a ship it was obviously necessary that the post-test should follow the same pattern: since each situation could be the subject of more than one rule it was necessary to carry out a complex analysis of both questions and answers in order to relate the exact part of any one question to the relevant rule and hence to the criteria set for that rule.

We will illustrate how the answer to a question can be broken down into its constituent parts, how each of these parts can be weighted according to its degree of importance and how this can then be related to the rule concerned. We will also show how a careful analysis of an answer paper can show the amendment necessary in a program in order that at its second validation it will achieve a very high criterion – in this case a criterion of 100% for a number of rules.

Method of presentation: Tape/slide

Summary of Discussions in Module 3

Discussion in this module was again based on topics proposed by the opening speaker.

A recurring problem was the discrimination between the words 'assess' and 'evaluate'. The need for a glossary of terms was suggested. The suggestions made were (1) that evaluation is related to specific objectives whilst assessment is a subjective measure; (2) that evaluation is used for courses and is a comparison of performance with explicit criteria whilst assessment is used for individuals who are assigned numbers related to hidden or unspecified standards.

Effectiveness of available techniques

There are not, at present, adequate techniques for quantifying performance. Concern was expressed at the tendency to normalize all results even for skew distributions when the tests were designed to give skew distributions. The suggestion was put forward that often present techniques are not doing what we think and that incorrect conclusions are drawn from numerical results based on false premises. The present tools are very blunt but it was felt that any tool is better than none. Some disquiet was felt at the emphasis on quantifying cognitive performance and psycho-motor performance, whilst the affective performance was often ignored. When it is economically feasible numerical indicators should be used and the information should be fed back to the students. This must not lead to the elimination of objectives simply because they are not examinable.

Problems were raised for hybrid systems in use at various levels of education. The need was for quantitative and qualitative data. Is it possible to evaluate the effectiveness of media presentations?

Individual assessment may move away from the lumping together of a variety of assessments to an attempt to provide an assessment profile across a wide range of techniques.

The development of microteaching techniques, whilst being welcomed, raised some doubts about methods of evaluating its success. The data available was mainly of a subjective type and it was suggested that it should be possible to use a quantitative measure of the performances of the student groups for this purpose.

Evaluation in industrial training

It was suggested that cost-effectiveness of training schemes was a useful idea, but that measures of costing benefits of any training were very difficult or impossible at present. Obviously training must be related to organizational benefits. The area of management training and the problems involved in this area with a high affective content were also raised. Delegates who used more systematized techniques for management evaluation maintained that measurement was feasible in this area.

Module 4
Dissemination and training
Posing the Problems
G H WACE

Some months ago, when Professor Austwick was explaining how this conference was to be organized, I remember asking him whether posing problems
was necessarily the right way to start each module. Did there have to be
problems? Couldn't we enter into discussion on various points without calling
them problems? It now seems to me, having heard a good deal of this conference, that he was quite right, and that there are a series of problems
which affect all the areas or modules which we are going to cover or have
covered.

I have got the impression that the way that objectives and analytical
methods have been used in industrial and service training is being questioned
by some of those in education, that the problem of acceptability of educational
technology methods and materials in schools is occupying many people, and
that the role of the educational technologist is also a problem. I think that in
one way or another all these problems will appear in this module.

We also have, as chairmen for discussion groups, people distinguished
in various fields of the technology who are acquainted with problems specific
to their own field. I will not attempt to discuss these, but I will, as my talk
progresses, raise what I think might be points that people would wish to consider who are not connected with these more specific problems.

What I propose to do is to look at the subjects of this module — 'Dissemination' and 'Training' — from the point of view of the commercial firm. I do
intend to be brief — to allow as much time as possible to look at the media
presentation and papers.

Those of you who have followed the fortunes — and misfortunes — of
firms in this industry will recognize that the progress of the survivors has
been largely based on work in the industrial and commercial training sector.
Although this is now changing and we are becoming more and more involved
in education, both in the hardware and software fields, nonetheless I shall be
speaking mainly from the viewpoint of training technology rather than educational technology — whether or not you believe, as I do, that to some extent
the two are different.

I am going to take the words 'dissemination' and 'training' as meaning dissemination of materials produced by educational technology methods and the training of educational technologists or those engaged in some way in the field. This may be rather a narrow interpretation, but apart from the fact that if I interpret them in any other way we should all be exchanging Easter eggs before we had covered the field, I think that the main points of interest and concern may lie in these areas I have mentioned.

To take dissemination first. In order to describe what the problems are for us, I would like to consider briefly the kind of situation that we might find ourselves in.

Our activities are, of course, controlled by the amount of income that each activity generates. If it doesn't generate enough then we have to stop it. The amount of income depends largely upon whether teachers or industrial trainers find that what we provide is cost effective.

By 'what we provide' I refer to the software — which should do its job of teaching, and to the hardware which carries it, which should be reliable: the two, if properly conceived, forming an effective system.

And cost-effective? I am not sure that this may not prove to be this year's OK word in education — the criterion for an OK word being that one has heard it so often that one no longer dares to ask what it actually means. I will attempt the task of defining the word. It is often used in the sense of spending less money, but does not mean this. I would consider something cost effective if:

1. It enables you to teach or train to the same standard as by any other method but more cheaply.

2. It enables you to teach or train to a brighter standard than before, but with no increase in cost.

3. It enables you to do something in teaching or training that you couldn't do before, at a reasonable cost.

It is fairly difficult to quantify the first two points, and it is very difficult to quantify the last one. However, like a lot of techniques in educational technology itself, if it does not provide the answer, at least it gives you a systematic way of thinking about the problem.

With that preamble, let me give as an example, a task of the kind that we might be involved in.

In industrial training, it is a fairly typical thing to find a training problem arising quite quickly and on a fairly large scale. For instance, say we take the case of a training officer in a business concerned with the large scale renting of equipment, who, as a result of a merger, finds himself faced with the necessity to train several hundred maintenance engineers to a higher standard in a comparatively short time.

Faced with this situation the training officer seeks an answer to a specific problem at a specific cost, and may well turn to an organization such as

306

ours to provide it. Clearly, he does not just seek a technique that will train his engineers in the most effective way in the shortest time, he seeks a solution to his whole problem, which has administrative and people aspects to it as well as training ones.

The problem, therefore, is not only to provide training, but to provide it in a form which will be usable in the circumstances of his own company. For instance it is likely that the most economical way will be to structure the training and to provide it in a package, one for each man, or for a few men. Hence, if there are a lot of men, the package has to be in a form which is easily reproducible and cheap.

Where is the material to be studied? Does it have to go through the post? And so on: the answer to these questions will determine the presentation and physical format of the material. In other words, its suitability. Most people here no doubt have some experience of this.

However, there are other aspects of the training officer's problem – he has to be able to control the training in some way, and most important of all, if there is to be another person involved in the training as a teacher or as a supervisor, that person must understand how to use the system and must accept it. If this last point is not achieved, we may have brought a bottle of Chateau Lafitte 1947 to the table, but haven't remembered to get a corkscrew – we could have saved ourselves the trip to the cellar.

These then are very important aspects of the dissemination of educational technology materials, namely suitability and acceptance. It is no good having the best possible cataloguing and physical distribution arrangements if these two criteria are not met.

I am absolutely certain that it is necessary to take what steps are feasible to obtain acceptance before the material is produced. I have quoted an example of training in one company, but this is equally the case if materials are to reach a wider market.

In many cases in industry we may not be dealing with skilled and experienced training officers but, even so, giving training, in however humble a way, is a very personal matter, and no-one will wholeheartedly use structured materials produced by someone else unless he accepts both the system and the content of the package. If this is true of industrial training, and I am sure that it is, how much more true is it of education?

The best way – possibly the only way – to gain acceptance, is to tackle it at the analysis and planning stage, by careful consultation, if not with every person engaged in the training, then at least with a representative group.

If the material is educational, and is to be disseminated widely in education then consultation with teachers at every stage – and especially the early ones – and not just with one or two teachers, however talented, but with as

307

wide a cross section as is feasible, is absolutely essential. However, it is our experience that, even then, acceptance is usually far from complete, and indeed strong antagonism is often apparent, particularly where the material is almost completely self-instructional.

In distributing educational technology materials we have to be far more careful to ensure that they are acceptable, than if we were distributing, say, textbooks, because we must never forget that in structuring materials, we are, in however small a way, restricting the teacher's or trainer's freedom of manoeuvre in that area of the subject. In other words, it may be that difficulty in obtaining acceptance is in proportion to the degree of structuring of the material (assuming, of course, that it is acceptable anyway as course material). If, as I have said, the criterion by which the commercial company is judged is cost effectiveness, then this criterion cannot be applied until the scheme has been distributed, installed and proved to work in the actual situation.

To the commercial company, therefore, the question of dissemination, if in that word we include the suitability and acceptance of materials, is a very important one. I believe that this situation applies in some degree to anyone distributing structured materials.

If one is distributing structured materials into a general market, such as is now being done quite widely in medicine and has been done for some years in our own industry, then the problem also arises of description.

It is not sufficient just to describe the technical content, but a way must be found of describing the teaching effectiveness and value of the lesson so that the potential user can decide whether it is what he wants.

There is an interesting paper in this module which discusses the British Medical Association's problems in this area.

For discussion in this area I would like to put a point on these lines: does the structuring of materials automatically preclude the wide acceptance of any one group of materials in education or industry?

There are at the moment schemes for producing resource materials or learning packages in the educational field which I understand will probably provide suitable subjects for discussion.

Now on training. If, in the commercial field the educational technologist has to cope with such a problem as I have described, what sort of person should he be? What skills should he have?

What one does need, however, is people with an analytical turn of mind, who are intelligent in the verbal field (ie could do well in a test such as the Watson-Glaser Critical Thinking and Appraisal) who can write clearly, who are persistent and not easily discouraged, but are patient and tactful in dealing with people, especially when questioning or interviewing. In addition, if they are to write **educational** material they should be practising teachers, in order to be able to understand and discuss teachers' problems with them.

Having got this kind of person, our training then primarily concentrates on the analytical aspects of their task, not only in the analysis of material, but also in the analysis of the training system. The training also covers the writing and presentation of material, in any form except for the specialized ones of moving film and TV. The form of the training is, as far as possible, problem-solving, as this is largely the field in which we work.

The aim is to give the person a way of looking at and thinking about training problems; but it is also clear that he is being trained to do a fairly specific task or tasks.

This seems to me to be reasonably close to the situation in the services. RAF Upwood have contributed a paper that describes a course for Education Officers based on a close analysis of the task. This approach appears to be very different from a course for graduate educational technologists set up at the Sir George Williams University. The services approach is clearly in terms of goals, while the Montreal approach seems to be considering roles. I think this difference may be the appearance in another form of the discussion concerning behavioural objectives — whether the same techniques apply in both education and industrial training.

In this area, therefore, I would like to put forward a suggestion that a point for discussion might be whether objectives and task analysis could be used as the basis for course design for educational technologists?

Finally, I would like to advert to a section of this module which is quite separate from the rest, but which is to me intensely interesting. This is the section on journals and the mass media, and in particular two papers concerning the influence of the mass media on children's attitudes. Dr Coldevin's paper presents some research in this field, showing the great influence that the mass media have on forming children's attitudes in knowledge of foreign affairs, and by the same token the slight influence of school and home. Richard Edwards, of my own organization, who actually edits and produces a current affairs newsheet for children, discusses the need to provide balanced background material for teacher's use when discussing news items.

It is perhaps arguable whether the activity of providing such a newsheet comes strictly under the heading of educational technology, but, if properly presented, it is doing what everyone is doing who is providing structured materials in education, whether commercially or not — namely providing lesson materials for teachers who do not, on the whole, have the time or the facilities to provide such materials for themselves.

Finally, therefore, let me suggest that discussion here might centre on the point whether structured materials can help the teacher to compete with the mass media in forming attitudes.

The Teachers' Resistance to Educational Technology—
Can a Systems Approach Help?

JOSEPH BLACK

To those of us who have become interested and involved in educational technology it presents such a fascinating array of intellectual and physical activities and challenges that we find it hard to understand the apparent indifference of so many of our colleagues. We may even find our ideas received with hostility which we tend to dismiss as confirmation of the traditional outlook of the old-fashioned teacher who believes unquestioningly in the teaching methods that he himself learnt by, or takes a Luddite view of what he believes to be the encroachment of machines and a mechanistic approach, bent on destroying the cherished personal link between teacher and pupil. There is a danger that both sides are taking up attitudes which are too extreme, and neither will lead us to the common objective of improving teaching and learning over the whole field of education and training. If we are convinced that our concepts of a technology of education are correct, then surely it is our responsibility to include the teachers with their whole range of attitudes in our total system with as much concern as we show for the learners, including if need be compromises and modifications to what we might consider a better 'educational technology' solution. Lord Butler called his biography 'The Art of the Possible' – this could be an appropriate slogan for us at the present stage of acceptance of our methods.

Looking at ourselves first, we must realize that we have built up a whole range of ideas and means which become familiar very rapidly – so long as you have been actively engaged in the problems over the past few years. We have also, perhaps, unfortunately but inevitably, built up a jargon which to the initiated is useful as a concise form of expression, to be interpreted with some flexibility depending on the circumstances. But to the teacher being presented with these ideas for the first time some terms of the art can appear much more significant than, in fact, they are, and carry implications of serious consequences. To take only one example – a professor of law, not at all opposed to educational technology, objected to 'validation' of a course on the basis that to him this implied the issue of an external certificate confirming that the course was acceptable in standard.

Looking at ourselves from the teachers' point of view, we must not appear to be usurping him, or offering a completely new educational process which threatens to make him redundant. Whilst we are quite clear amongst ourselves that what we propose will, in fact, enhance the opportunities for the dedicated teacher to make the most of his abilities, talent and flair, we must admit that often our uncritical enthusiasm for the new approaches and methods can be self-defeating; was it Bismarck who observed that if you think you are a leader it is a good idea occasionally to glance behind you and see if anyone is following? Perhaps we have not thought enough about the means of involving many of our colleagues who, while favourably disposed to innovation, do not, or cannot, devote the time and effort that we have done to the application of educational technology to their particular problems. What we must avoid at all costs is to drive them back into the ranks of the traditionalists, for example, by threatening them, as Trotter put it so well, with the wrath of a technological Jehovah if they did not use the latest electronic devices!

How then can we plan a course of action which will lead to a much wider acceptance and at least a trial of our concepts and methods? In a recent talk to librarians at a meeting of SCONUL on the implications of increasing use of non-print material for the university library, I came to the conclusion that in order to make the situation clear to librarians, who had not themselves been involved in thinking about or preparing such material, I should attempt to present a total picture of the whole teacher-learner relationship. This enabled me to relate the library, and the librarians, to both the teacher and learner, as a major learning resource, and not merely an information store and custodian. The favourable response to this presentation, which, in fact, is a straightforward pictorial representation of educational technology principles, suggested to me that perhaps we have been taking too much for granted, in assuming that because the teacher whom we have been seeking to influence have been involved in teaching for many years they fully comprehend how they fit into the whole system, and are also familiar with the areas in which the new techniques and method could be most usefully employed.

My aim therefore in the remainder of this paper is to describe in simple terms a systems analysis of a learning process, with the emphasis on the part to be taken by the teacher, in the hope that it might aid the educational technologist to convince the recalcitrant teacher that we are united in our objective of presenting the optimum learning situation to the learner. There will be nothing new to the APLET members – but if when presented to the teacher seeking guidance it makes him realize, like Moliere's 'Bourgeois Gentilhomme' excited to find he has been talking prose, that if he has been a good teacher then he has in one form or another been practising 'educational technology' all his life, it may persuade him to take a more professional interest in what it has to offer before rejecting or ignoring it, and it may also allay his animosity and fears.

THE SYSTEM

Let us look first at the 'teaching' situation as conventionally accepted in higher education (for convenience I will use 'teacher' and 'learner' in this context only, but the system is generally applicable). (Figure 1)

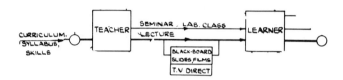

Figure 1

Even the most traditionally based course starts with an agreed 'input' * of some section of curriculum, or syllabus, or skill, and the teachers are agreed that at the end of the course or some 'terminal' stage the pupil or learner will have to demonstrate by means of an exam or test that he has acquired some acceptable level of performance or knowledge – this is the 'output'. The teacher talks to the class or group, usually basing the level of presentation and the standard of work on his personally-determined 'model' learner, in the hope that the group cluster round this assumed level of ability. As listening to lectures is largely a passive activity, the learner must be made to take an active role by means of personal efforts such as essay-writing, laboratory work, problem-solving, and design classes. These produce a feed-back signal to the teacher or tutor which can rapidly affect the discussion in the more informal seminar, laboratory class or small group class, but rarely the lecture material. Closing of this feed-back loop to the learner enables him to assess his progress: hence it must be fast.

The most direct contribution therefore that the teacher can make to the individual learner is within this fast feed-back loop provided by the inspection of the learner's work, and the consequent line-of-action which follows it. Given enough teachers and tutors to maintain this feed-back signal to every student would be acceptable as an ideal situation.

The teacher will usually use a blackboard to help his communication (though often his writing will be too small to be seen from the back of the room). The simplest service an educational technologist can do is to

---

* A more strictly correct systems analysis would consider the pupil as the 'input' to the system, and the 'output' the same pupil with his newly acquired learning, but this does not reveal the role of the teacher so clearly.

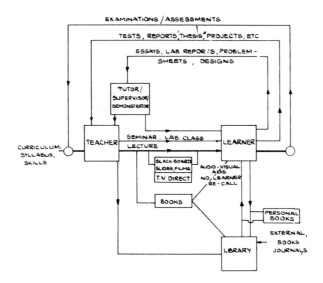

Figure 2

photograph the filled-up board from the back and present it to the teacher and if he is really enlightened he will use slides, film, overhead projector and even television to enhance his presentation. He will justifiably boast that he uses these new methods – but they are at the best 'audio-visual **teachers**' aids' in that they and the material displayed have been selected by the teacher, and once used by him the material is not usually available for recall by the learner, apart from hastily written notes.

The teacher also uses both 'set' books and reference books. He may be unaware of just how significant this is, in that it is 'learner recall' material and brings the library as a learning resource into the system; the teacher, incidentally, takes for granted that not all the printed material he requires is prepared within his own institution, and he expects and indeed demands that the library will seek out and bring him in books, journals and papers written externally. An obvious statement – but what a contrasting reaction we will find in our 'new' system when we dare to propose non-print material from external sources!

THE NEW TECHNIQUES

Instead of confronting the teacher with what may appear to be completely new ways of teaching and learning we should build up on the system with which he is already familiar. Thus to the scheme in Figure 2 we can add in Figure 3 the considerably enlarged potentialities of 'learner recall' material made available through hand-outs, audio and video tapes, cassettes and slide-tape

313

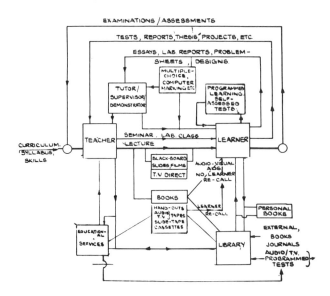

Figure 3

facilities. As such they represent extensions to course material based on textbook and other printed matter; because of its self-instructional nature it lends itself to storage and display by library methods, which again maintains the teacher in a familiar and compatible relationship. Like books and journals as before some of this material will come from external sources, and this only poses problems of selection and incorporation into the overall course presentation. But once the teacher becomes aware of the far-reaching scope of the new techniques he will realise the need to generate the new material within the institution in the context he desires.

Once he has done so he will soon recognize the complexity, both in concept and technical execution, which the new means of communication demand, and the necessity therefore for the establishment of a specialized professional service unit within his institution. Only by seeing the educational services as an essential partner in providing the best possible learning opportunities will the teacher's natural suspicions be allayed; he will also cease to think that the 'educational technology units' are setting themselves up to provide an alternative means of learning at the expense of more teachers.

Education technology has other contributions to make to the system, probably unfamiliar to most teachers. These are largely concerned with more self-instruction and improvement of feed-back to the learner. Here again the teacher may find these new techniques more acceptable if the educational technologist presents them as **additions** to the academically respectable and well-proved methods, rather than giving the impression that the acceptance of the new automatically implies rejection of the old.

Thus we are all agreed on the value of the feed-back loops through the personal tutors, but even with the most generous staff/student ratio economically possible there are bound to be limitations on the effectiveness of this loop, and techniques which allow the learner to study on his own and carry out self-assessment have a valuable contribution to make. Hence in Figure 3 there are two additional loops shown; programmed learning texts and self-assessed tests, and multiple-choice tests with computer marking; computer-aided instruction could provide yet another loop here.

Far from being replaced, the teacher should see clearly from this scheme that he is heavily involved in two respects. Primarily, it is his job to construct the course, devise the teaching and learning strategy, select the material and write it, in association with his educational technology colleagues Secondly, when the material is in use the learner will look to the teacher much more as his tutor or supervisor rather than merely his source of information in the lecture room. In advocating the adoption of self-instruction techniques the educational technologist should stress that paradoxical as it might appear such apparently 'mechanical' methods should, in fact, enhance the opportunities for the personal 'Socratic dialogue' between tutor and pupil, rather than replacing it.

EXCHANGE OF MATERIAL

Much valuable program material of a high academic standard has been produced in many institutions for all types and levels of courses, involving joint teams of teachers and educational technologists. As the new techniques were developed and facilities became generally available there arose the inspiring prospect that a widespread interchange of teaching and learning material would be bound to follow. The benefits of being able to see and hear the outstanding authorities in their subjects or the best actors and performers, to follow programmed texts written by the masters of the techniques, or to share by video-tape experimental facilities with fellow students more fortunate in the equipment and apparatus they had available appeared so overwhelming an advantage that exchange of material and incorporation into new courses appeared inevitable. There would also be the added advantage that the increased utilization would considerably reduce the cost of the heavy investment of staff time and production expenses which any good program requires.

While there have been some notable examples of the incorporation of sections of externally produced material in particular cases, we must admit that compared with the wealth available the actual exchange and construction of new courses built up on educational technology bases has been negligible.

There are, of course, many operational and economic reasons for this neglect of the opportunities to innovate which could be overcome, but the will to do so must come from the teachers. Even the teacher favourably inclined to the aspects of our 'system' already described seems to be reluctant to take this final step to the acceptance of what appears to him to be the intrusion of an external 'teacher', competing with him for the interest and approval of his students.

If, however, this facility for drawing on an external store of learning material is presented to him as a vast extension of the external book and journal information he already uses extensively through the services of the library, rather than as a 'take-over' of his lectures, or a teacher-replacement he may at least consider its potentialities. Only by this combined activity of the teacher, the librarian, and the educational services will the best use of the powerful resources and techniques now available be made.

CURRICULUM REFORM AND ASSESSMENT METHODS

Even when we have convinced the teacher about simple audio-visual aids and means of self-instruction, there remains another aspect of the work of the educational technologist which appears to the teacher to be unrelated. This covers such topics as curriculum development, aims and objectives, evaluation of courses, and student assessment. If, however, we have convinced him about the system so far, we can now ask him to go back to

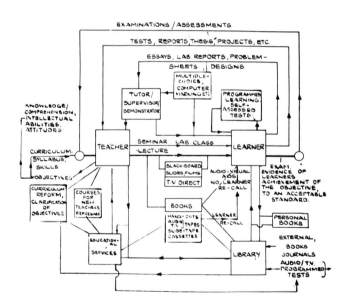

Figure 4

the opening of our discussion where we introduced the idea of a systems analysis with the statement that 'even the most traditionally based course starts with an agreed 'input' of some section of a curriculum'. (Figure 4) Once we have succeeded in making him recognize the inter-relationships involved between lectures, seminars, classes, tutorials, books, learner self-instruction, the library and the educational services, surely it must be accepted by all but the most die-hard of teachers that some systematic thought has got to be given to the clarification of the objectives of a course, or curriculum, or even as simple a matter as the transmission of a skill, before all that enormous and costly effort is put into a misdirected program, or worse still, a series of events with no clearly defined aim, so that neither teacher nor learner can determine whether they have arrived at a desired state of knowledge or ability or performance.

This poses another dilemma for the educational technologist; because he is aware of the importance of defining objectives as the basis of all his subsequent methods and techniques to meet selected needs he becomes deeply involved in the considerable research and development of ideas connected with educational theories, with psychology, with human behaviour, with statistical analysis – with any activity which can contribute to an improvement in the learning process. The teacher, on the other hand, because of his normal teaching duties, and the pressure of all the associated activities, may not be in a position to take such a professional interest in these new results; consequently, when he finds himself preparing a new course he is likely to base his judgements and procedure largely on his personal experience. This may be an excellent base, but the teacher who boasts that he knows what to do as he has been teaching his subject 25 years may in effect have only been teaching one year twenty-five times! There is a strong temptation therefore for the educational technologist to enthusiastically insist that the teacher must use all the new ideas and techniques available for establishing suitable objectives and how to achieve them. But this is difficult to carry out in the abstract, and as soon as he begins to advise on the particular course under review, the teacher may react unfavourably and quite unjustifiably, but humanly, suspect that he, the master of the subject matter, is being usurped by a theorist who knows nothing about the subject, and indeed is implying criticism of the teacher's earlier efforts.

Apart from the obvious need for skilled diplomacy in tackling such delicately based relationships, we might allay these suspicions by making our organizational role clear-cut. The majority of teachers want to improve the presentation of their teaching material, but no one expects them to become expert in printing, or graphics, or designers of laboratory equipment. While there is a great need for many more of them to become active and committed to educational technology, there is an even greater need for most

317

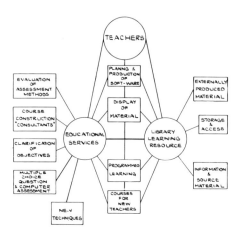

Figure 5

of them to learn to accept the expert guidance and collaboration available so that they can concentrate on the actual job of producing the 'soft-ware' of their new courses, which the educational technologist cannot do. Thus, in Figure 5 they can be assured that the whole course and subject matter must stem from them, and they must be closely associated with all aspects of its production and subsequent use and testing. A worthwhile educational technology service will work with them providing 'course consultants' whose professional knowledge and skills will save the teacher much effort, and at the same time give some assurance that the finished course is available in its most effective form. Once the course is in operation the same service can carry out all the evaluation procedures and analysis which can lead to the rapid improvement of the course as it responds to the feed-back from the students.

While it is natural for us to want to tackle the challenge of a completely new complete approach to a learning situation planned in every detail from the definition of objectives right through the hardware and software evaluation to the student testing and subsequent re-writing and re-assessment, in the real world of the innately conservative teacher, who has seen so many apparently good innovations pass into oblivion leaving no trace it may pay us to be more modest in our ambitions. Thus by demonstrating the contribution of a well-written one-hour program, or a ten-minute slide-tape instruction to a sceptical teacher a grudging acceptance of its value will rapidly turn into an enthusiasm to go further; it will be through the demands of the teacher, and not from our thrusting intervention that we will find ourselves in the fruitful close partnership we have been seeking.

The Dissemination of Learning Materials

JILL ROGERS

All producers of audio-visual aids for medical education are concerned with the problems of production and planning of learning materials, the classification of these materials so they may be quickly and easily retrieved, and the dissemination of the materials both within their own institution and to other institutions. Unless some effort is made to coordinate the work being done in different parts of the country, there is bound to be duplication of effort. Is it not time for a rationalization of the organization of learning materials to help avoid the development of mutually incompatible schemes for production, classification and dissemination?

This paper discusses the fundamental criteria necessary for the establishment of a coordinated scheme, discusses the present situation, and this unit's experimental schemes for improvement, and goes on to conclude that a final solution may lie in the acceptance of an overall administrative system which would operate on the basis of the fundamental criteria.

Audio-visual aids are used in medical education in a variety of formats. They may, for example, be planned and produced as a complete learning program, as a film, a video tape, or an audio tape. Alternatively individual transparencies and film sequences may be used as part of a learning program. At the same time, learning aids may be designed for a group of students or for individual learning.

If the rapidly increasing numbers of audio-visual aids are to be used for their optimum educational effectiveness, it is essential to establish the fundamental criteria for the production and selection of materials.

The educational effectiveness of learning materials must depend on the specification of learning objectives — what the student is expected to do in order to demonstrate that he has successfully learned from the program. In order to make these objectives clear, each program must incorporate a statement of the primary audience for which it is intended and the learning objectives which the audience should fulfil.

There are certain problems unique to audio-visual materials which make the provision of critical data an essential requirement. Audio-visual aids cannot be rapidly scanned for content and selection and there are in general, few copies of the materials available. Therefore comprehensive and critical information about the material is necessary if maximum use is to be made of learning materials. The essential requirement for the critical assessment must be: does the material achieve its stated objective, for the defined audience?

Two schemes have been initiated by the Department of Audio Visual Communication in order to obtain critical data on materials.

Subjective assessment of films and audio tapes is carried out by independent panels of subject experts. The Department acts as a neutral agent to organize the reviews. Reviews of those films and audio tapes which have reached the minimum standard of educational effectiveness are published in 'Information', the bi-monthly bulletin of the Department.

The second method of experimental assessment is an objective assessment. A series of individual learning materials, consisting of audio tapes and illustrated note books have been produced with the collaboration of medical schools and postgraduate institutions. Pre- and post-testing was carried out and students' attitudes and performances evaluated.

Both these methods are effective. The question may be raised that the subjective review may give the view of a panel which represents a controversial academic point of view. This is a valid criticism. It may, however, be said that academics concerned with the subject area will be aware of the arguments surrounding a particular subject. Until all materials can be evaluated objectively, the subjective assessment is inevitably open to criticism.

The provision of critical data is essential if the materials available for dissemination are to be educationally useful. It will also aid the effective distribution of materials if the numbers are confined to those found to be educationally effective. If critical data is not included there is a very real danger that medical teachers will use valuable time experimenting with materials which are not educationally useful.

At the present time, there are a number of methods of distribution being employed. To enumerate briefly:

1. **Commercial audio-visual companies** The majority distribute on a sale basis, although a number do loan material. Information about the materials is available from catalogues issued by the companies themselves. The majority of materials have not been assessed in either of the two ways mentioned above.

2. **Publishing companies** are active in the distribution of programmed texts, audio tapes and multi-media kits. For these materials there is a well established method of distribution, but the cost of materials tends to be

high because of the overhead expenses. The adaptibility of these materials is restricted by copyright regulations.

3. **Pharmaceutical companies** Although the majority of materials relate to the products produced by the company, a number of companies are now producing non-advertising materials for medical audiences. Distribution of these materials is generally by loan, but some can only be used in the presence of their own commercial representatives. As with the previous two categories of available material, copyright is a restricting factor.

4. **Semi-commercial organizations** These include the Medical Recording Service Foundation and charitable trusts and foundations which produce materials on specific medical subject areas. The majority of these materials have not been assessed, although it must be stressed that materials from the Medical Recording Service Foundation are currently being assessed by this Department.

5. **Individual producers in medical schools and departments of Medical Illustration** A number have an actual programme of production — the Gardiner Institute and St Bartholomew's Hospital for example. These materials are frequently the most useful as they are made specifically for a defined medical audience. There are, however, problems of distribution as most individual units do not have the facilities or the resources to copy and distribute their materials.

There are common fundamental problems of distribution facing each of these groups. A variety of attempts are being made by different organizations to solve these basic problems. The solutions to these problems will in turn facilitate the establishment of a comprehensive system of distribution.

1. In order to ensure exchange of materials, and efficient retrieval of information about materials, and the materials themselves, an efficient classification scheme must exist. If more than one schedule is operational, compatibility with other schedules must be arranged.

The Department of Audio Visual Communication is financing a research librarian to work with the Wessex Regional Hospital Board to produce a classification and vocabulary system for computer storage and retrieval of audio-visual materials — both complete learning programs and individual items.

A pilot project is also envisaged with the National Science Library of Canada and the National Library of Medicine in Washington to evolve a classification for non-book materials on a world wide basis.

2. Unlike printed book materials, no copyright laws are currently applicable to non-book materials. There is a very real fear on the part of some originators of material that their work will be adapted by purchasers and

will therefore lose its identity. An experimental copyright release scheme is being used by the Department. Materials are sold at the cost of production, plus £1 per session for the originating author, in this case the collaborating medical expert. The purchasor has the right to copy both the tape and notebook as many times as necessary, to rerecord the script and change the illustrations in the notebook. This may be done, provided that the name of the originating author is stated on the reproduced materials. A questionnaire to purchasers is currently being circulated to discover how many in fact took advantage of these facilities and why.

3. One of the greatest practical hurdles facing individual producers is that of producing multiple copies of the materials. If learning materials are to be efficiently distributed sufficient copies must exist, and facilities must be available to enable purchasers and vendors to produce copies. The Department is currently investigating the possibility of establishing a slide copying centre. An audio tape duplicating service is already available to those who do not have access to another method of duplication. In the United States, the National Medical Audio Visual Centre has initiated a video tape copying service. Masters of tapes are held at the centre, purchasers send a blank video tape to the centre and the program is copied onto the tape. There is no charge for this service.

Another of the problems relating to copying material is that of incompatibility of equipment. This problem could, however, be overcome by general agreement about a specific range of formats to be used for the production of materials.

Over all these problems rests the question of how the process of distribution is to be organized. Is each producing centre to be expected to finance the distribution of its own materials and bear the cost of the inevitable extra staff? There are a number of possible solutions to this question, all of which depend on discussion and collaboration with all those concerned with the problems of distribution of audio-visual materials:

1. A National Centre could be established holding information about all existing materials, excluding those which do not reach a minimum standard of educational effectiveness. The enquirer would contact the centre and then contact the appropriate centre to obtain the actual material. These individual centres could either be medical photographic departments, if they were able to and prepared to take on the extra work, or could be local centres specifically organized to hold all regional materials.

The duplication facilities could either be on a regional basis or integrated with each local centre. The financing of such an operation would have to be organized at a national level.

2. An alternative to the above scheme would be to establish a National

Centre which held both information about all available materials, and held a master of all materials. Enquirers would then be able to contact the centre and obtain a copy of the material. For this to operate successfully each producer would need to deposit the master material with the centre, and an adequate duplicating process would have to be devised. At present there is no deposit requirement for non-book materials. It has, however, been suggested by the Paymaster General that the important national archives of non-book materials may be associated with the British Library. A similar scheme would be initiated for medical non-book materials to ensure that the collection, storage and bibliographic control of these materials may be nationally organized. Efficient distribution of materials would depend on the existence of some such system.

3. It is felt that a computerized scheme would be essential for the accurate recording of information about medical materials; it would, however, be essential to ensure efficient on-line-retrieval, and the facility to produce specialist catalogues. The unique nature of medical materials with regard to production, classification and distribution would demand a computerized system founded on user needs. The question is open to discussion but it would be essential to employ a computerized system for the National Centre, whichever form it took.

These, then, are the main problems raised by the question of distributing materials. To a number of practical problems there are practical answers which are being used experimentally.

In the long term, a national and international scheme for the collection, classification and dissemination of materials must be established, with the collaboration of all those involved in the planning, production and dissemination of audio-visual learning materials. A number of possible solutions have been put forward and discussion is welcomed.

A Synchronized Tape-Slide for Teacher Training and Science Education

JAN H RAAT

The development of education for the so-called developed countries as well as for the developing nations is one of the greatest problems of the present time.

Some aspects of this development of education are discussed here –

(a) The big increase of knowledge during the last half century hampers the design of a suitable education programme. On the one side students are to be given a greater general education and knowledge, but on the other hand there is the necessity at a certain moment to specialize.

(b) Due to a multiplicity of causes the complexity of the society increases. Maintenance and further development of the society happens for a major part by means of education. Changes in the society cause changes in educational objectives. On the other hand the possibility exists to change the society by means of particular education policies. This also has turned the attention of politicians to education far more than before.

(c) Even more people participate longer in education. As a consequence the cost of education will increase for the country. There is limited finance and in many cases the limit appears to have been reached.

For a number of reasons it is desirable that education should take place in smaller groups. Besides instruction to and social activities within greater groups, it is to be preferred, based on a number of considerations, to have education take place by means of self-instruction in smaller groups.

(a) Self-study itself has a great pedagogical and didactical value; self-study in smaller groups is, in social respects, of great importance.

(b) Education in bigger groups is difficult to lead on to any self-study within that big group.

(c) Of the great and increasing quantity of knowledge present in all fields of society and science, one can only learn a small part. Therefore it is all the more important to make oneself familiar with the chosen parts of the subject matter by self-study.

(d) Self-study is possible by studying individually. If too much attention is paid to this aspect then too little attention may be given to social development in education.

For both financial and purely educational reasons it is desirable that study in the smaller groups happens in most cases without the presence or direct help of a teacher. To some extent this method of studying has been practiced for a long time (Dewey, Montessori, Jena-plan); proportionally measured, most of the education is given to students via the class-teaching system.

Until some years ago the help of a teacher in the self-study education-system was indirectly present only in the form of books, lecture notes and so on.

Recently more aids have become available – viz the educational techno-logical aids.

Educational technology is to be used in several ways

In this particular situation we may distinguish between:

(a) A teacher can support and illustrate his lessons with audio-visual and other technical aids, and

(b) The process of learning can also take place by using educational technological aids. For that particular part of the study the technical aid replaces the teacher; education is accomplished by the technological aid and without direct assistance of the teacher.

By self-study in smaller groups a profitable use can be made of educational technology. It is incorrect to state, that self-study in such a small group would occur by means of this or that particular aid. It is preferable to use as many different aids as available. Depending on all kinds of factors, like the available tuition, size of the group, the age of the students, a choice has to be made.

The technical aids which are used, form, together with the written lesson material, (which includes often a programmed instruction and tests) a limited study package of that particular learning activity package (LAP) (Kerman Union High School, ESEA, title III, Project 67-04401; 1968).

The audio-visual aids which can be used when making up a study package, for self-study in smaller groups are to be distinguished in three sorts:

(a) television,

(b) film,

(c) synchronized tape recorder and slide projector.

Each of these AV methods and materials has, when in use, advantages as well as disadvantages. The advantages and draw-backs to partly depend on the purposes the aids are used for. In spite of that the following general remarks can be made:

(a) The great advantage of the media television and films is that they can register and reproduce moving objects.

(b) The production of films and TV tapes has the disadvantage of a non-changeable product once finished. It demands a considerable time to make changes in an existing film or TV tape. The software is too fixed.

(c) The production of films is very costly and takes a large amount of time. For the production of TV tapes one has available rather expensive and still technically vulnerable equipment.

The use of a synchronized tape recorder and slide projector has advantages and disadvantages as well. On a number of occasions – frequently occurring in practice – advantages outweigh the disadvantages.

(a) One disadvantage is obviously that with slides only standing pictures can be performed.

(b) An advantage is that a series of slides is rather easy to produce; the same applies to the matching tape.

(c) The second advantage is that changes can easily be made in an existing series: one can interchange the slides, take them out or add others. The text can easily be adapted to the series and has only to be recorded on the tape. **This software is flexible.**

Each teacher can with rather simple means produce his own software for a synchronized AV lesson which he wants to be used for self-study in small groups. For doing this, the teacher should only be able to make slides, write the matching text and record the same. It cannot be emphasized too much that the lesson should be programmed accurately beforehand.

When teaching the educational objectives should be defined accurately; investigations have to be made regarding the sequence of the instruction and finally whether the educational objectives have been achieved. This is a similar process to developing multiple choice tests or the production of programmed instruction.

Of great importance using synchronized slides is the possibility that the teacher himself can produce the software with simple means.

Equally important is the flexibility in existing software. If a certain step in the program appears to be unclear, too great or too small, then correction is feasible in a rather simple way.

The teacher's own production of software is of great importance.

One of the major drawbacks of a good functioning of the system of self-study in smaller groups is the lack of suitable material.

Generally speaking books, ordinarily used in the class-education system, are not suitable for this purpose. Writing the scripts is a task which is hard to fulfil for one teacher or a group of teachers in addition to their existing duties.

Moreover in that case no use is made of a new dimension, given by the educational technology: programming lessons and having these integrated in a simple way in synchronized picture and sound.

It is also of importance to point out that the required hardware is comparatively cheap and reliable, the latter being of equal importance.

The hardware, which is chosen to be used for the described target (selfstudy in small groups) should answer these demands.

Experience shows that when propagating the use of educational technology in education in the way as described above, questions and remarks are elicited of the following nature:

Do you think that you can replace the teacher; with this type of education you replace the central figure in education (the teacher) by a machine; horrible for the students to learn and study (all day long) in such a way.

The following answers can be given amongst others:

(a) Due to the enormous increase in salaries one **has** to look for possibilities which go to meet a constant increase in costs of education. One possibility is to consider giving the lessons to larger groups; or to consider to reduce the number of lessons per week; but it is also possible to study and investigate the use of technological aids.

(b) Lessons, given by a teacher to smaller groups, are financially speaking impossible. When a teacher instructs greater groups (for example one might already think of a group of 25 to 30 students) there is generally a small opportunity for personal contact and personal attention.

When replacing the 'normal' duties and lessons of the teacher by selfstudy by the students in smaller groups, the teacher will sooner, and on a larger scale, be able to guide the individual student or a small group (eg 3 to 6 students).

THE TEACHER'S TASK CHANGES

Apart from other specialities in teachers' tasks (as study-enlightenment, help with the choice of a future profession) the teacher becomes more the organizer of the student's curriculum. Sooner and more often he will have time and opportunity to occupy himself pedagogically with the students: individually and in smaller groups and at the very moment they need this support and help.

It might be clear, apart from this, that self-study in itself is more important than studying in a group of, for example, 25 to 30 students, in which case all students are bound to the same level and speed.

To some it seems horrifying that students should study the whole day long (at school) in this way. Against this one might suppose that it is horrible for the students (or at least 'unpedagogical') to follow courses the whole day long in the ordinary classroom situation.

In the second place, the remark has to be made that the above mentioned does not suggest that all activities for students of secondary schools should take place in small groups. Along with self-study in small groups one might think of 'instruction-lessons', lectures for larger groups, discussions in larger groups, activities by which each student works for himself but is at the same time involved in a larger group (drawing, dexterity with the hands) or acts as a group (sport, singing, dramatic art).

By introducing self-study on a large scale in smaller groups the task of the teacher changes fundamentally.

It is obvious that the future teacher must learn to handle all the available technological aids. This bears a number of different aspects in itself.

(a) The teacher is supposed to tend the hardware and be able to do simple repair work himself.

(b) The teacher has to be profoundly trained in producing the software himself.

During his training the future teacher should not only learn how to make synchronized slide-series for a certain study-unit, but also a TV lesson, for the use of students in a small group for self-study, and the making of a film for the same purpose.

(c) For the above it is essential that the teacher learns which educational technological aid he can use the best.

The teacher will have to obtain the best possible view in composing learning packages.

By self-study in smaller groups there is far more flexibility in education than ever before via the classical system.

It goes without saying that suitable learning packages ought to be present, including the educational technological aids and tests, fitted to terminate a definite learning unit.

By this flexibility education can answer the demands, rightly posed, to which the present system of classroom education cannot answer.

Because of the flexibility each student can follow his own curriculum, constantly adapted to the possibilities and needs of the individual student.

In this way there exists the possibility of a continuous progress of the student through a school with many and divergent possibilities: that means that a Continuous Progression System (CPS) becomes realizable (Continuous Progress Plans, Cogswell 1966; Individually Prescribed Instruction, Cooley & Glaser, 1968).

The final choice of the student for a certain group of professions and later of a specific one can now be delayed until a later time, when the student is better able to make his choice.

328

The Design of a Training Course for Royal Air Force Education Officers

J WALSH

DEFINITION OF THE AIM OF THE COURSE

The primary aim of the Education Officers' Orientation Course is to train new entrants to the Education Branch of the Royal Air Force in the professional skills and Service procedures required for the effective performance of their duties. A secondary aim of the course is to develop the students' professional interest in current educational philosophy, technology and practice, especially in relation to Service training.

DERIVING THE TRAINING REQUIREMENT

The technique of analysis was used to collect information about the work that education officers have to do, the standards of performance required and the conditions in which they have to operate. A frequency survey of the tasks which have to be carried out and a survey of attitudes towards various elements of the work helped to identify the training need.

SPECIFYING THE TRAINING TASK

The results of these analyses produced the information which allowed the training objectives to be formulated. It was necessary to take account of the heterogeneity of the students' backgrounds with relatively wide variations in levels of qualifications, types of experience, knowledge and ability, and a broad spectrum of different academic disciplines.

DETERMINING THE INSTRUCTIONAL SPECIFICATION

The training objectives were eventually broken down further into enabling objectives and decisions had to be made to arrive at the most effective and efficient learning sequence. The methods and techniques to be employed were also decided within the constraints of the resources available.

FEED-BACK AND MODIFICATION

After the initial design stages, the first courses were conducted before the feed-back processes could be installed to complete the system. The techniques of obtaining information and the assessment of its reliability will be described. Finally the effects of feed-back and the extent to which elements of the course have been and continue to be modified will be outlined.

Children in a Global Village

R L EDWARDS

In January 1971, ESL Bristol launched Focus, a classroom newspaper in wallchart form. Published fortnightly during term, this provides secondary schools with background information on selected items of current interest.

According to Marshall McLuhan, today's schoolchildren are taught in a 'classroom without walls', the electronic revolution having reduced the world to a 'global village'. This paper discusses, in theory and in practice, the implications of this revolution as regards the production of a school-children's newspaper.

The quality of the communications media's representation of events is open to question, especially in its impact upon children. So intense is the bombardment of news and so uneven the media's treatment, that it is confusing and difficult for the immature mind to separate the wheat of importance from the chaff of trivia.

Further, the borderline between illusion and reality is often blunted: on television, for instance, a news bulletin depicting death in Vietnam is sandwiched between a Western in which an actor is shot and an old movie glorifying war but showing none of the misery. Values may again be confused. News presentation, by its nature, is also fragmentary: it presents isolated events as they happen, only rarely discussing causes. In many cases, children (and adults) are thus denied a perspective.

The problems confronting an editor of a schoolchildren's newspaper are thus large. There are additional problems. Among the questions asked and answered in this paper are: How does one interest a child in an important issue which will affect his life but which as yet is remote from him? How, when publication is periodic, can one compete with the mass media in terms of topicality and fresh insight? What should be the balance between entertainment and material which is educationally stimulating? How impartial can one, or should one, be?

The Impact of Mass Media upon the Development of International Orientations

GARY O COLDEVIN

The social-psychological process of political socialization is generally viewed as the transfer of political behaviour from institutions, media and persons (sources of socialization) to pre-adults (Dawson & Prewitt, 1969). Easton and Dennis (1965) suggest that political socialization refers to the way in which a society transmits political orientations-knowledge-attitudes or norms and values from generation to generation. Implicit in these definitions is the notion of a communicative nexus between a societal environment and individuals maturing within that environment. Despite an increased theoretical concern, however, relatively little direct research has been conducted on this vital aspect of the socialization process. At a time when the high technology societies have purportedly developed into a global village in terms of information dissemination, this lack of research is indeed perplexing, particularly in terms of international socialization. As McLuhan (1967) contends, any understanding of social and cultural change is impossible without a knowledge of the way media work as environments.

The technological revolution has according to Toffler (1971) confronted the individual with a continuous 'informational over-choice'. This state is assumed to be a direct result of the ubiquitous nature of the television medium and the inordinate amount of time pre-adults devote to viewing. Culkin (1967) notes that today's child spends 3000 to 4000 hours in front of the television set before he starts the first grade. By the time he graduates from high school he has clocked 15,000 hours of television time as opposed to 10,800 hours of school attendance. Given these competing figures it can be readily hypothesized that the mass media as opposed to the school are the primary sources influencing political socialization.

Studies which have been conducted on the national or regional socialization process stress the importance of traditional sources such as the family (Dawson & Prewitt, 1969; Hyman, 1959; Lane, 1959; Sigel, 1965) and the school (Hess & Torney, 1967). At the international systems level the research has primarily concentrated on the acquisition of concepts of war and peace. Haavelsrud (1970) and Hollander (1970) established the dominance of mass media in general and television in particular as major sources for adolescents' perception of war. These are the only two known studies conducted with the specific purpose of isolating sources of orientations towards international issues.

The importance of research of this nature may be appreciated when one reflects upon the nearly universal demand for schools to provide students with international dimensions in their education and to help students develop less ethnocentric attitudes to cultures different from their own. The same generalizations might hold for those who control the mass media and influence its content. A pre-requisite to furthering these objectives is to evaluate the relative impact of all sources in the development of international orientations. With these perspectives in mind, the present study was undertaken to:
(i) assess the relative impact of the mass media in general and television in particular as primary sources of adolescent's international orientations;
(ii) isolate the content area of television primarily utilized as sources.

PROCEDURES
Formulation of the instrument

Essentially four variables were isolated for analysis in this study: 1) attributes associated with the term 'international'; 2) attributes for both alternatives of general international issues; 3) perceived sources for attribute enumeration, and 4) a measure of the consistency of source utility.

The questions were adapted from the Sampson and Smith (1957) Worldmindedness Scale. This scale consists of eight dimensions of a worldmindedness frame of reference each represented by four scale items: religion, immigration, education, war, government, economics, race and patriotism. Religion was excluded from the study and substituted by "What does the term 'International' suggest to you?". This question was the first in the instrument and was intended to focus the respondents' attention to the frames of reference inherent in the questions which followed. The seven modified questions eliciting a Yes or No response consisted of the following:

1. Immigration Do you feel that immigration might be controlled better by an international organization rather than by each country on its own?

2. Education Do you think that an international committee on education should be set up to control what is taught in high school social studies in all countries?

3. War Do you think that it is possible to prevent war among nations?

4. Government Do you feel that a world government might better guarantee the welfare of all nations rather than allowing each nation to control its own welfare?

5. Economics If necessary, would you be willing to support your country in lowering its standard of living in order to help poorer countries to improve their standard of living?

6. Race Do you think that your responsibility to people of different races in other countries should be the same as your responsibility to people of your own race?

7. Patriotism Do you think that it would be better to be a citizen under a world government than a citizen under the government of one country only?

Each of these basic questions were preceded by questions eliciting attributes for the international and national adoption of the alternatives. For example, the Immigration question was preceded by 'State as many reasons as you can for having immigration controlled by an international organization' and 'State as many reasons as you can for having immigration controlled by each country on its own'. A similar rationale was used for each of the succeeding dimensions. This type of questioning methodology places the respondent within his own orientation wherein the primary attributes for both alternatives are formulated before he is asked to reach a decision.

The major independent variable examined in this study was source(s) of orientations or sources for attributes mentioned. Much of the previous research was concerned with the influence of the family, school and peer group and were for the most part 'single agency' analyses. Studies that included mass media did so on a general basis. Television content for example was subsumed under the title of 'television' or 'television at home'. As the present research was concerned with the impact of all sources in general and the specific areas of television in particular, the major content areas were isolated for analysis (Figure 1). The category Other Sources was included to incorporate any other sources respondents felt were relevant (eg religion) and to convey the impression that they were not formally bound to the listed source. Subjects were asked to provide the code of the most important source for each attribute supplied to the questions.

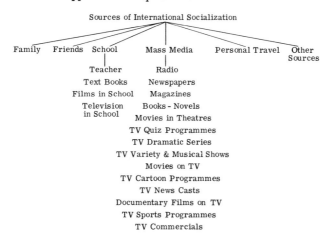

Figure 1. Sources of international socialization

333

A second task connected with source utility required subjects to rate each source on a four point (1=least used; 4=most used) rating scale as to importance in answering each basic decision question. The inclusion of these rating scales satisfies a dual purpose. First, an additional measure of source importance is probed and second, a measure of the consistency of the responses generated during the testing situation may be evaluated. Ideally, if a source was mentioned for a particular response, it should be rated high on the scale rating for that question. Through comparison of sources mentioned and scale ratings for each of the eight questions a measure of response consistency may be obtained. These measures of source utility were carried out after the subjects had answered the open-end and decision questions to ensure that attributes supplied and decision orientations would not be influenced by questions relating to source utility.

SUBJECTS

The sample was chosen deliberately from history classes in two suburban Seattle, Washington high schools. Two hundred 11th grade students were asked to complete the questionnaire during the winter of 1971. Randomization was precluded through student assignment to classes by random computer selection. In the circumstances, four intact classes were randomly drawn from each of the participating schools. In terms of socio-economic background the sample distribution approximates the shape of the normal curve with 33% coming from professional homes, 29% from white collar homes and 33% from blue collar homes. Background information on this variable was not forthcoming for 5% of the sample. The sample was composed of 52.5% males and 47.5% females. In terms of sex distribution the sample fell within 0.03% of the combined schools' 11th grade totals (414 males and 376 females) and accordingly can be considered as highly representative on this dimension.

ADMINISTRATION AND CONTENT ANALYSIS

The questionnaires were administered during normal history classes. All subjects were asked to remain anonymous to ensure a frank and thoughtful consideration of the issues. Respondents were first asked to provide attributes and decisions to the alternatives presented before undertaking the measures of source utility. A separate page was used for source listings and directions for coding the most important sources. The scale ratings on the right side of each question page were covered with an opaque half sheet. These were subsequently removed during the scale rating procedures.

A dyad coding process was employed for the attribute and most important source mentioned for the attribute. Through this type of content analysis a most important source was correlated with all attributes mentioned.

RESULTS

The attribute categories and source frequencies generated for the term

Table I. Salient sources for attributes of term 'International'

| Attribute | Source | | | | | |
	Friends	Family	School	Mass Media	Other	Total
Cooperation-Peace	4.6%	5.1%	38.5%	45.9%	5.9%	100% (371)
Between-Among (nations, races)	3.9%	2.9%	46.6%	41.7%	4.9%	100% (204)
World Problems	6.9%	2.9%	25.8%	61.5%	2.9%	100% (174)
World (news, events)	5.5%	0.7%	32.8%	57.8%	3.2%	100% (128)
World Organizations	4.2%	4.2%	27.8%	61.7%	2.1%	100% (47)

$x^2 = 37.74$ df = 16 (p < .01)

'International' are presented in Table I. Individual sources are collapsed into generic groupings for analysis simplification. The category Other incorporates personal travel and religion.

The dominant attribute associated with the term 'International', Cooperation-Peace, was mentioned by 77.5% of the sample. Between-Among (nations, races) received 62.5% response frequency, World Problems, 46% and World (news, events) 42.5%. Interestingly, World Organizations (UN, UNESCO) were mentioned by only 19% of the sample.

The data (Table I) reveal that the more specific attributes are primarily derivative of the mass media sources while the general and more traditional descriptor, Between-Among (nations, races) is primarily attributed to school based sources. Television is the dominant single medium within the mass media grouping, ranging from 45.3% for Cooperation-Peace to 58.6% for World Organizations. The vast majority of television programme content, an average of 61.5%, was given over to news casts. Documentary films were ranked secondary with an overall 19.1% response frequency.

The orientations to the basic decision questions are outlined in Table II, while in Table III are given the influential sources for the generated attributes to the international and national alternatives. It can be readily noted that the

Table II. Decision orientations to international dimensions

| Dimension | Decision Orientation (N = 200) | | | |
	International (Yes)	National (No)	Undecided	Total
Immigration	49.5% (99)	49.5% (99)	1.0% (2)	100% (200)
Education	44.0% (88)	54.5% (109)	1.5% (3)	100% (200)
War	52.0% (104)	45.5% (91)	2.5% (5)	100% (200)
Government	56.0% (112)	41.0% (82)	3.0% (6)	100% (200)
Economics	47.0% (94)	49.5% (99)	3.5% (7)	100% (200)
Race	78.5% (157)	18.5% (37)	3.0% (6)	100% (200)
Patriotism	40.0% (80)	55.0% (110)	5.0% (10)	100% (200)

Table III. Most important sources for attributes of
international and national alternatives

Dimension	Alternative	Source of Attributes						
		Friends	Family	School	Mass Media	Other	Total	
Immigration	International	5.6%	7.8%	43.3%	41.4%	1.9%*	100%	(497)
	National	6.2%	7.2%	37.3%	43.8%	5.5%	100%	(432)
Education	International	9.5%	7.2%	45.8%	32.3%	5.2%*	100%	(419)
	National	7.0%	5.0%	55.6%	28.2%	4.2%*	100%	(358)
War	International	16.1%	9.9%	27.8%	41.0%	5.2%**	100%	(442)
	National	15.4%	7.1%	19.4%	51.3%	6.8%	100%	(423)
Government	International	9.4%	10.0%	35.0%	39.9%	5.7%	100%	(442)
	National	8.1%	8.6%	34.8%	44.5%	4.0%	100%	(348)
Economics	International	11.8%	13.7%	26.6%	42.1%	5.8%	100%	(330)
	National	11.9%	16.3%	19.7%	43.7%	8.4%	100%	(295)
Race	International	24.9%	17.0%	19.4%	28.9%	9.8%**	100%	(377)
	National	17.6%	17.6%	21.7%	39.9%	3.2%	100%	(188)
Patriotism	International	13.7%	12.4%	22.3%	44.2%	7.4%	100%	(312)
	National	13.1%	11.3%	36.4%	38.1%	1.1%**	100%	(291)

* $p < 0.05$ ** $p < 0.01$

dominant pattern of source utility demonstrated in Table I is also evidenced
for attribute sources for the international and national alternatives (Table III).
The most significant discrepancy occurs in the Education dimension where
the school grouping was possibly viewed as the logical source for discussion
of alternatives. Despite attempts in recent year to produce relevant attractive textbooks, the teacher was uniformly ranked as the highest single source
within the school categories. In an era of increasing mass media influence
the teacher may be still regarded as an important source of interpersonal
communication. Textbooks assumed the secondary position with films and
television following according to priority. The logical assumption which
emerges from the low priority of the latter two sources (particularly television) is that they were rarely employed in the classroom setting.

Within the mass media grouping television repeated its ascendency as
the foremost single medium for international attributes, ranging from 51.9%
for Economics to 45.7% for Patriotism. An average of 61.8% of this television content was alloted to newscasts with documentary films assuming the
secondary role with an average frequency of 19.8%. A similar trend emerged
for attribute sources generated for the national alternatives (Table III). Cor-
respondingly, television was the primary mass medium ranging from 59% of
mass media responses for War to 40.3% for Economics. Newscasts made up
for an average of 64.5% of television content with 19.3% given over to documentary films. Newspapers and magazines were consistently ranked as the
second and third most important mass media sources for attributes to both
alternatives. Radio and movies in theatres were viewed as providing only
minor source utility for the majority of the sample.

In summary, mass media and particularly television were the primary

Table IV. Percentage of consistency between selection of
most important source and highest scale rating

	Consistency		Consistency
Friends	80%	Newspapers	90%
Family	91%	Magazines	99%
Teacher	74%	Books-Novels	97%
Text Books	84%	Television Newscasts	96%
Films in School	99%	Documentary films on Television	96%

source categories for both international and national orientation postures.
The school was rated as second in source utility with the teacher emerging
as the dominant singular source within this grouping. The peer group (friends)
was ranked third in source importance and was viewed as being particularly
influential in inducing an 'international' decision posture toward the Race dimension. Notably, this area elicited the most decisive orientation posture of
all dimensions (Table II). The role of the family was ranked fourth in overall
source utility and emerges in this study as one of decreasing importance.
Given these 'most important sources' for attribute enumeration, a parallel
counterpart of the study was concerned with the consistency of generated responses. The four point scale ratings were utilized to this end. The rationale
employed here is that if a source is mentioned for a particular response it
should be rated high on the scale ratings for that question. The most sensitive
measure would then involve the highest scale rating (number 4 or most used)
on the four point scale. Since the source selections are primarily limited to
ten sources, these are included in the consistency verification (Table IV).

The overall percentage of agreement indicates that a relatively high
degree of consistency was maintained for the primary sources mentioned
throughout the study.

DISCUSSION

The data presented in this paper to a large extent augment many of the
popularized theories of the effects of the mass media upon contemporary
youth. The importance of the family for example, traditionally accepted as
fundamental to the socialization process and which indeed has received much
of the research attention, was accorded only a tertiary role in the present
study. Reich (1971) suggests that the technologically created 'nuclear'
family functions as a grouping of parents and young children — children
cease to be a part of this family by the time they reach high school. Similarly, Toffler (1971) contends that in an era of 'future shock' and rapidly
changing norms, parents are incapable of transmitting consistent patterns
to their offspring.

The previously purported dominance of the traditional school may also
be seriously questioned. The results appear to support the McLuhan asser-

tion that the school is a part-time competitor in an 'information war', a war which in its traditional format it cannot win. Television in fact seems to present the 'real' world to today's youth and, as attested to by the present research, the foremost source of the raw material or the attributes with which to formulate decisions toward international issues.

In summary, this study brings into relief the increasing need for enrichment of the formal learning environment in harmony with developments in educational technology. The extended and sustained utilization of combined educational and mass media seem particularly warranted. If international orientations are to be considered a desirable objective for current and future generations, educational technology appears as the logical alternative toward furthering this aim.

REFERENCES

Culkin, J. M. (1967) A School Man's Guide to Marshall McLuhan. Saturday Review (March 13), 7

Dawson, R. E. and Prewitt, K. (1969) Political Socialization. Little, Brown and Co, Boston, Mass

Easton, D. and Dennis, J. (1965) The Annals of the American Academy of Political and Social Science, **361**, 40

Haavelsrud, M. (1970) Seminal Agents in the Acquisition of International Orientations Among Adolescents. Unpublished PhD thesis, University of Washington

Hess, R. D. and Torney, J. V. (1967) The Development of Political Attitudes in Children. Aldine Publishing, Chicago

Hollander, N. G. (1970) Adolescent's Perceptions of Sources of Orientations to War. Unpublished PhD thesis, University of Washington

Hyman, H. (1959) Political Socialization. The Free Press, Glencoe, Ill.

Lane, R. (1959) American Sociological Review, **24**, 502

McLuhan, M. and Fiore, Q. B. (1967) The Medium is the Massage. Bantam Books, New York

Reich, C. A. (1971) The Greening of America. Bantam Books, New York

Sampson, D. L. and Smith, H. P. (1957) The Journal of Social Psychology, **45**, 99

Sigel, R. (1965) The Annals of the American Academy of Political and Social Science, **361**, 81

Toffler, A. (1971) Future Shock. Bantam Books, New York

Changes in the Pattern of Programmed Materials Available Commercially in Britain

J W HAMER, ANNE HOWE and A J ROMISZOWSKI

INTRODUCTION

The compilation of the 1972/74 APLET Yearbook of Educational and Instructional Technology provided an opportunity to re-examine the 'State of the Industry' as far as published programmed materials are concerned. Similar analyses were carried out on the basis of data collected for the 1966 edition of 'Programmes in Print' (Cavanagh & Jones, 1966) and the 1969/70 Yearbook (Cavanagh & Jones, 1969). The first of these analyses (Basu et al, 1967) drew five conclusions concerning developing trends in published programs. The second analysis (Cavanagh & Jones, 1970) followed up these same five conclusions, confirming most of them, but noting certain changes as follows:

1. In 1966 there was an increasing number of programs being marketed by an increasing number of producers. By 1969 there was evidence that a peak had been reached and, although new publishers were still entering the market, total production was declining.

2. The 'growth areas' for programs in 1966 were mathematics, science, computer science, statistics, etc (in short the logical, factual subjects). The 1969 figures substantiated this trend.

3. British programs were still more commonly produced for use on machine, though by 1969 the production of machine programs was limited to a handful of commercial program writing firms that also had a machine to sell.

4. Linear programming was more popular than branching, though there was some evidence by 1969 of other approaches as well.

5. American programs are longer than British programs.

In this present analysis, we have investigated the first four of these conclusions further, and have attempted not only to up-date the statistics available, but have also attempted to examine any changes in the trends as previously outlined and to suggest possible reasons.

We have neglected the fifth conclusion listed. Indeed we have made no discrimination between British and American programs in our analysis.

METHODS AND LIMITATIONS OF THE ANALYSIS

Information of the following types, as supplied by publishers to the 1972/74 Yearbook editors, was analyzed: Subject taught; Mode of Presentation; Style of Programming; Year of publication. In addition, data was collected on the types of publishers engaged in program production, the numbers of programs they publish, etc. This information was compared with data contained in the 1969/70 Yearbook and in the 1970 analysis (Cavanagh & Jones, 1970).

There are several limitations to analyses of this sort. Firstly, there is no guarantee that all programs in print are listed in the respective yearbooks. The present analysis, for example, located several pre-1969 programs not previously listed. Nor is there any guarantee that those listed form an un-biased sample.

Secondly, the mere fact that a program is offered by a publisher is no guide to the use that that program is put to. There are several publishers in the present analysis, who have not added any programs to their list since 1969 and there is some doubt as to whether they have sold many in the same period. This applies particularly to some libraries of machine programs.

Thirdly, some series of programs are available from two or more pub-lishers, or in both machine and text form. Such duplication has led to the same program being listed several times in both the 1969/70 and the 1972/74 yearbooks. Whereas this improves the value of the yearbook as a reference guide, it may distort somewhat the total picture of the distribution of pro-grams among subjects. No allowance has been made in this analysis for such duplication of entries.

Fourthly, one is reliant in this analysis, almost exclusively on informa-tion supplied by the publishers of programs. Whereas basic information such as title, date of publication, whether machine or text version, can be assumed to be accurate, it was not always given in full. However, such information as programming style is open to subjective interpretation by the publisher. For example, some programs of mixed linear and branching style may have been listed as branching (and vice versa), or a program based very closely on a mathetical analysis may nevertheless appear to be linear to the publisher.

The reader should bear in mind the above mentioned limitations when considering the results reported in this survey.

THE AVAILABILITY OF PROGRAMS

Table I illustrates the range of topics for which programmed courses are currently available. The classification into 52 categories is the one adopted in the 1972/74 Yearbook. For various reasons, this is a different classifi-

Table I. Frequency of programs according to subject
Classification used in 1972/74 Yearbook

	Total listed in 1972 Yearbook	Printed 69-72
1. General Subjects	14	12
2. Business Accountancy	57	10
3. Business Clerical	6	5
4. Business Management	112	28
5. History	38	4
6. Languages, English Grammar	78	5
7. Languages, English Literature	15	1
8. Languages, English - Reading etc	100	30
9. Languages, English as a 2nd Language	14	2
10. Languages - French	15	3
11. Languages - German	6	3
12. Languages - Russian	7	4
13. Languages - Spanish	3	1
14. Languages - Other Languages	5	2
15. Librarianship	6	4
16. Logic	4	2
17. Maths - General	152	63
18. Maths - Modern	81	38
19. Maths - Arithmetic	225	47
20. Maths - Algebra	68	10
21. Maths - Mensuration	43	1
22. Maths - Graphs	9	5
23. Maths - Geometry	20	2
24. Maths - Trigonometry	19	5
25. Maths - Calculus	24	4
26. Maths - Statistics	41	15
27. Maths - Metrication	33	32
28. Medical - Dentistry/Veterinary	7	2
29. Medical - First Aid & Nutrition	22	2
30. Medical - Medical Technology	21	12
31. Medical - Nursing	48	33
32. Medical - Physiology	36	14
33. Music	4	1
34. Photography	5	1
35. Physical Education	7	7
36. P.I. Learning/Teaching	22	10
37. Religion	4	-
38. Social Studies - Civics - Politics	33	3
39. Social Studies - Economics	8	3
40. Social Studies - Geography	85	14
41. Social Studies - Psychology	17	3
42. Social Studies - Society & Environment	65	33
43. Science - General	25	15
44. Science - Biological	81	31
45. Science - Chemical	77	14
46. Science - Electrical	121	16
47. Science - Physical	82	19
48. Technology - Carpentry	7	2
49. Technology - Computers	48	9
50. Technology - Engineering	141	27
51. Technology - Industrial Safety	25	11
52. Technology - Industrial Processes	70	31
	2256	651

cation than that used in the 1969/70 Yearbook. For example, the substantial
section on Metrication in Industry did not exist at all in 1969. Similarly,
medical applications have grown to the extent that there was a need for subdivision. The major areas of application still appear to include Mathematics
(particularly Arithmetic), Science (particularly Electricity and Electronics)
and Technology (particularly Engineering). However, other major areas
are Business Management and the basic skills of English (reading, writing,
spelling etc). New areas of growth include Metrication and Medical topics.

TRENDS IN PROGRAM PRODUCTION
Altogether 651 new programs (printed 1969/72) were identified (47 of these

were previously listed in the 1969/70 Yearbook). However, the total of listed programs (2256) compared with the total listed in 1969 (2009) gives a net increase of 247. Some pre-1969 programs, not previously listed were also identified. Table II has been prepared to illustrate the changes which have taken place in program production. Broad general categories have been

Table II. Trends in program production - by broad subject groups

Categories	Programs listed in 1969 Year book	Programs listed in 1972 Year book	Net Growth	Printed 1969 onwards	Printed pre-1969 not previously included	Out-of-Print since 1969 Yearbook was printed
	(1)	(2)	(3)	(4)	(5)	(6)
General Subjects	15	14	- 1	12	-	12
Business & Management	158	175	17	43	7	34
History	34	38	4	4	-	-
English Lang. & Lit.	187	207	20	38	6	21
Foreign Languages	41	36	- 5	13	3	19
Librarianship	5	6	1	4	-	3
Logic	3	4	1	2	-	1
Mathematics	617	682	65	190	14	124
Metrication Re-training	1	33	32	32	-	-
Medical & Nursing etc	84	134	50	63	9	20
Music	5	4	- 1	1	-	2
Photography	4	5	1	1	-	-
Physical Education	1	7	6	7	-	1
P.I. & Instruction Theory	13	22	9	10	1	2
Religion	5	4	- 1	-	1	2
Social Studies/Sciences	140	208	68	56	13	1
Physical etc Sciences (Pure Sciences)	383	386	3	95	-	85
Technologies/Industry	313	291	-22	80	20	104
Totals	2009	2256	247	651	74	431

Note: Figures in Column (4) '69 Programs included in '69 Yearbook (Total 47).
Thus 2009 + (651 - 47) + 74 = 2256 + 431

adopted to enable direct comparison with the 1969/70 Yearbook data. It is clear from this table that the major areas of application and growth also have a substantial 'turnover' of programs. Large numbers of new programs have been written since 1969, but large numbers have also been withdrawn. In the case of the industrial technologies, more have gone out of print than have been written. This need not necessarily be a discouraging trend. During the early days of 1963/67 publishers were desperate for programs. Just about anything was published, whether validated or not, whether there was a real target population of appreciable size or not. It is not surprising that much of this 'dead wood' should be removed, and replaced by better material. However, another explanation is that new publishers are 'jumping on the bandwagon', not having learnt from the old hands who have burnt their fingers

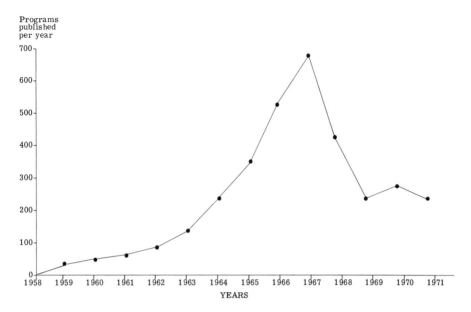

Figure 1. Annual program production (data from 1969 and 1972 Yearbooks combined)

on program publishing. This possibility is investigated later.

Table II suggests a state of dynamic equilibrium, rather than overall growth, and this is borne out by Figure 1, which graphs the annual program production of publishers with outlets in Britain.

It appears that after a period of fast, almost exponential, growth until 1967, program production has fallen to about the 200 per annum level, and appears to be fairly steady. This again is a trend to be expected in a newly developing field suffering from early over-promotion and over-enthusiasm.

The rather low level at which production seems to be steadying off is, however, rather disappointing. One should note, of course, that not all programs which are written are published. Indeed in the business, industry and technology field, only a very small fraction of programs written are ever generally published. Evidence from other sources suggests a continuing expansion of program writing activity in these fields. In the formal education sector, matters are not so clear, though again a fall in the number of program titles on the market need not necessarily mean a fall in the usage of programmed materials. Further investigation is needed on this point.

MODE OF PRESENTATION

A breakdown of programs into text, teaching machine and other methods of presentation is shown in Table III. The lefthand half of the table compares the total listings in the 1969/70 and 1972/74 Yearbooks. This indicates very

343

Table III. Mode of presentation of programs

Mode	Listed in 1969 Yearbook No. (as %)	Listed in 1972 Yearbook Total No. (as %)	Listed in 1972 Yearbook	
			Published before 1969 No. (as%)	Published 1969 onwards No. (as %)
Programmed Text	876 (43.6)	977 (42.4)	637 (38.6)	340 (52.2)
Teaching Machine	1134 (56.4)	1202 (52.2)	1000 (60.6)	202 (31.0)
Slide Tape/Film	?	123 (5.4)	14 (0.8)	109 (16.8)
Totals	2010	2302	1651	651

Notes: (1) Totals in columns add up to more than totals of programs listed in yearbooks, as some programs listed use more than one mode of presentation.

(2) Programs for special machines such as Bell & Howell Language Master, or Synchrofax, are listed as 'Teaching Machine')

little change in the previous pattern, particularly if we count programs produced on slide-tape, film and videotape as 'machine' programs. The 1969/70 Yearbook analysis makes no distinction between teaching machines of a specialist type and general-purpose presentation devices. We have done so to highlight one of the current trends — the trend towards the programming of audio-visual presentations. Obviously not all slide-tape presentations, video tapes etc can claim to be programmed. In the 1972/74 Yearbook we have attempted to list those which appear to be (ie have stated objectives, terminal tests etc).

The righthand half of Table III is perhaps more useful in illustrating the trends. By comparing currently available programs published pre-1969 with those published since, we see (a) that the growth in slide-tape programs in the last few years is quite significant, and (b) that machine programs are no longer the most popular. The programmed text is gaining ground.

Table IV. Frequency of programming styles

	1969 Yearbook	(as a % of total)	Printed 1969-72	(as a % of total)
Linear	1496	(73.5)	267	(44.9)
Branching	341	(16.8)	91	(15.3)
Mixed	122	(6.0)	114	(19.1)
Adjunctive	46	(2.3)	1	(0.2)
Audio-Visual	28	(1.3)	114	(19.1)
Mathetic	2	(0.1)	6	(1.0)
Algorithmic	-	-	2	(0.4)
Totals	2035		595	

Notes: (1) Styles only known for 595 of new programs.

(2) In some cases different styles used for different sections of program.

(3) In some cases it is difficult to differentiate (eg a linear, or a branching sequence may be the result of a mathetical analysis).

PROGRAMMING STYLES

In Table IV we compare the 1969 figures with those for new programs published since 1969. This again suggests that the previous trend towards purely linear written programs has been reversed (although this is still by far the most popular style). The gain has been for mixed linear and branching programs (including skip-linear) and for audio-visual programming (which is generally linear in progression, but is by no means 'Skinnerian'). Adjunctive programming has almost died out, whilst the figures for Mathetic and Algorithmic programs are not to be relied upon as they indicate the programmer's strategy rather than the appearance of the program from the publisher's point of view. If these are to be used as 'programming style' categories, perhaps we should also use 'Ruleg', 'Egrul', 'Hunch' etc. This particular question also required further investigation, and would involve the inspection of the programs (and the programmers' analysis?) rather than just a publisher's statement.

THE PRODUCERS OF PROGRAMMED MATERIALS

The number of producers of programs for the general market continues to grow — 73 in 1966, 92 in 1969, 142 in 1972. This growth in numbers is not matched by a similar percentage growth in programs on the market, suggesting that many newcomers have only a very small library of programs to offer.

Table V. Mobility among publishers engaged in program production

	Full time publishers	Others	Total
Ceased to offer programs since 1969 yearbook	7	8	15
Have entered this field since 1969 yearbook	25	40	65
Net Gains	18	32	50

Table V shows the overall change in the numbers of publishers in the field. We note that the major growth has been among producers who are not primarily publishers (ie training boards, trade associations, individual teachers or colleges, groups of schools or colleges who cooperate etc). This emphasises the trend towards the production of special-purpose programs primarily for use by the producers or their sponsors. Some of these programs then get published and circulated to a wider audience. There is, however, a significant increase in the number of commercially oriented producers. Some of these are accounted for by the boom in audio-visual programming, some are accounted for by the expected boom in metrication retraining (after the experience of decimalisation, when programmed learning contributed much to a smooth transition in many sectors of commerce). Others are publishing materials produced under sponsorship (for example Blandford Press are publishing much of the Nuffield project materials). Others are specialist medical publishers (another growth area).

Table VI. Change in the size of major publishers'
libraries of available programs
(A major publisher taken is one who had
10 or more titles in print in 1969 - N = 37)

Increase of over 25% in titles in print	Increase of less than 25%	No change in number of titles	Decrease of less than 25%	Decrease of more than 25%	Total withdrawal from the market
6	10	5	5	6	5

Quite another picture may be obtained from Table VI, which follows up the major pre-1969 producers (ie those who had 10 or more titles in print in 1969). There were 37 of these — 16 have increased their libraries, 16 have less to offer, 5 have made no change. On the whole the extent of the decreases are more significant than the increases. Exceptions to this are one or two established program producing firms (eg ESL Bristol have increased their library by over 100 titles and Stillit books by about 40 titles). There are, however, to balance this, some specialist program publishers (eg ITM Weighbell, Packman) who have hardly changed their libraries at all since 1969.

The overall future for the program producers preparing a range of programs for a general market does not therefore seem to be too rosy. However, producers specializing in specific areas where there is an established training need, where large target populations exist and where there is some coordination among users and (possibly) some sponsorship of training materials, continue to thrive.

CONCLUSIONS

Several trends are noticeable, some of which were identified in the 1970 analysis, some of which are new.

1. Programming effort (as far as published programs are concerned) has indeed fallen off from the peak in 1967 and now appears steady.
2. Logical and factual subjects are still the most common areas for programming effort. However, the emphasis has moved from the 'formal' subjects — maths, science and languages — to 'problem' subjects. One such a few years back was decimalisation. Currently metrication retraining and medical training seem to be the vogue.

3. Teaching machines are no longer the most common presentation medium for recently produced programs. Since 1969, the programmed text has gained popularity. Also a significant growth in the application of programmed methods to audio-visual presentations has been noted.

4. There is little real change in programming styles, although a mixture of linear/branching/etc is more common. It is probable that the techniques of analysis and preparation for programming have undergone more significant changes, but the present study cannot quantify these accurately.

5. The number of producers of programs continue to increase, but these tend to be organizations with a commitment towards education or training in a particular sphere, rather than commercially-oriented publishers. Old-established producers in the field vary from healthy increases in their commitment to programmed learning, to total withdrawal from the market.

6. In the authors' opinion the present picture, as presented here, whilst definitely indicating an end to the boom in program production of the mid-sixties, does not necessarily present a picture of abject gloom. Activity continues, though in different areas under different systems of sponsorship. Users are developing better skills for the selection of instructional materials. The early 1970s will be a time for producers to reappraise the situation and to match their production and selection skills to the needs of the market.

REFERENCES

Basu, C. K., Cavanagh, P. and Jones, C. (1967) 'Trends in programmes in print in the United Kingdom'. In 'Problems and Methods in Programmed Learning'. (Ed) M. J. Tobin. NCPL, Birmingham University

Cavanagh, P. and Jones, C. (1966) 'Programmes in Print'. APL, London

Cavanagh, P. and Jones, C. (1969) 'Yearbook of Educational and Instructional Technology 1969/70'. Cornmarket, London

Cavanagh, P. and Jones, C. (1970) 'Further Trends in Programmes in print in the United Kingdom'. Programmed Learning and Educational Technology, Vol.7, No.1. Sweet and Maxwell, London

Romiszowski, A. J. (1972) 'The APLET Yearbook of Educational and Instructional Technology - 1972/73'. For the Association for Programmed Learning and Educational Technology by Kogan Page, London

Summary of Discussions in Module 4

As in other modules, the study groups in Module 4 constantly came back to the theme of attitudes and roles. It was felt that disseminating ideas was necessary in order to influence attitudes before one could hope to develop training successfully in educational technology.

It was felt that the attitudes of teachers towards new methods and media would influence the attitudes of their pupils. There also seemed to be a general feeling that structured materials should be available in small units to permit maximum flexibility in their use — so that teachers could adapt these resources to their own ideas and work schemes.

The groups concerned with administration made the point that some teacher resistance to educational technology was caused by lack of ancillary or support technical staff. Resource centres should be learner-based rather than teacher-based in terms of their materials and facilities.

The teacher-training groups emphasized the importance of relationships within school departments between staff and staff as well as between staff and pupils. Too highly structured materials tended to be inflexible and constraining, not making sufficient allowance for differing personalities, attitudes and learning modes. Although the preparation of materials at an advanced academic level is perhaps more difficult than at elementary levels, it was felt that a greater degree of acceptance was likely at university level than in the primary school.

In industrial training and further education there was similar concern to that of administrators and school teachers — that developments in modern teaching techniques implied the need for support staff, particularly technicians.

In the case of journals and mass media, interest centred on the latter, particularly the importance of television in forming children's views and outlook. It was felt that television and other mass-media resources should be easily accessible to teachers and the software designed for and responsive to the needs of the schools.

One emphasis which appeared throughout the group discussions was on the need for matching — matching methods to materials, personalities, attitudes — matching support resources to recommended aids — matching the mass-media software to the needs of the schools.

Modules 5 and 6
Introduction
C E ENGEL

Educational technology, in its limited meaning as the application of audio-visual aids, has been applied in medical education more consistently and for a longer period of time than in any other aspect of higher education. In its wider sense, as a more systematic approach to teaching and learning, educational technology has in recent years come to play an increasingly more important role in medicine. However, the 1972 APLET Conference was the first occasion in Great Britain and, indeed, in Europe, for an international survey of concrete achievements to date.

The morning session of the one day meeting concentrated on actual examples of the specification of learning objectives for preclinical, clinical undergraduate and postgraduate subjects respectively. The afternoon session was devoted to three papers which described the design and use of systematically planned individual learning material. While most texts or audio tape recordings for self-instruction have tended to be used on an episodic basis, these papers reported on their use for entire courses of instruction. It is important to note that the learning material was fully integrated with other learning activities in all three examples.

The discussion by no means reflected an uncritical enthusiasm. While accepting the logic of specifying learning objectives as the starting and end point of all educational decision making, implementation and evaluation, participants were also interested in the wider implication of this approach. Teaching would have to be accorded much greater recognition than is the case at present, if teachers were to be given the extra time needed for the effective application of educational technology. Clearly, the enthusiasm of individual academics could not be relied upon indefinitely. Innovation by the few would have to be accepted into daily practice by the many, if educational technology were to be employed to its full potential.

Although the use of individual learning material can provide welcome relief from routine teaching responsibilities, its design and preparation is very time consuming. Collaborative production and interchange of existing

material between institutions is, therefore, a logical next step. Joint production of a course on general pathology was reported from Holland with the
participation of a number of European countries. An even more ambitious
project involving some twenty medical schools is centred on the University
of North Carolina. It is perhaps a significant coincidence that the World
Health Organization's Technical Publication No. 489 on 'Implications of Individual and Small Group Learning Systems in Medical Education' had been
published in the previous week.

A Systematic Approach Applied to Postgraduate Education (Paediatrics)
DANYA GLASER

INTRODUCTION

This study was designed to explore the practicability of applying the systems approach in postgraduate medical education. A further aim was to investigate the suitability of this approach for a trainee specialist to study educational methods while, at the same time, furthering his studies in his specialty.

The essential steps of the systems approach can be summarized as follows:

1. Specification of learning objectives
2. Suggested order of learning
3. Specification of learning situations and learning materials
4. Evaluation of learning

The subject chosen for study was 'The Detection of Health Problems in Children 5-11 years, and the Initial Subsequent Management'. The postgraduate learners were defined as 'trainee local authority doctors and trainee general practitioners'.

This task was deliberately chosen as a recognized part of medical practice. It was thought, therefore, worthy of being learnt by trainees in the field, although the contents of its practice varied, and were not wholly defined.

The author had previous paediatric experience, including the developmental assessment of young children. She was not familiar with educational methods or the systems approach. At the time of embarking on the study, the author was seeking part-time non-clinical work, relating to paediatrics.

SPECIFICATION OF LEARNING OBJECTIVES
The Task

The first part of the study has been concerned with the specification of the

---

Financed by The British Life Assurance Trust for Health Education with The British Medical Association learning objectives. Initially, this meant defining those aspects of the child which are relevant in a detecting examination, and this necessitated the clarification of the purposes of such an examination.

The detection of health problems and their initial subsequent management is based on an overall assessment of the child. It is an assessment of the state of the child at the time of the examination, in relation to his chronological age.

Broadly, this assessment poses two questions: (a) Does the child function satisfactorily for his age? (b) What is the nature of any underlying disorders of anatomy and physiology?

The detection of health problems is effected by taking the history and carrying out a clinical examination. These actions provide the means of obtaining the answers to the above two questions. The initial subsequent management follows from the assessment.

This stage of the study, provided both the opportunity and the motivations for increasing the author's knowledge of the subject.

The list of aspects to be considered, which was then constructed, permitted subdivision into several sections:

I.   Initial observation
II.   (i) History concerning function
      (ii) Examination of function
III. History and examination for underlying neurological disorders
IV.   History and examination for disorders of other systems
V.   Final overall assessment
VI.   Initial subsequent management.

The Task Analysis

Next, a detailed task analysis was constructed, by setting out the sequential steps which a doctor would take while examining a particular aspect of the child.

Where a doctor might enquire for items of history, observe the child, palpate or use instruments, these have been included in the task analysis. An attempt has been made to define the alternative findings which are likely to be encountered by the doctor and how he would proceed in each case. In each instance, the end point of his action has been defined as: No further action; For further consideration with a relevant subsection; Note for future reference; Review; or Referral. In all cases, two points apply. They are the need for explanation to the child, parent and teacher, and the importance of observing the way the child acts during the examination. These were, therefore, considered as part of the common core material.

Only the initial steps of each task analysis would be applicable to most children, since the division between normal and abnormal occurs at this early stage. In practice the whole examination would, therefore, be considerably shorter than the detailed analysis would make it appear.

Required Understanding, Knowledge and Competences

It was now possible to define the understanding, knowledge and competences required in order to carry out the task analyzed. These requirements were set out in parallel with each step of the task analysis.

This is illustrated here by two examples shown on the following pages: Task analysis of Gait, and Task analysis of Scrotum and Testes.

Much of the understanding and knowledge is concerned with definitions of what is considered as normal, with where to refer, and with outline knowledge of further management. No competences for treatment were included, since this falls outside the scope of the project.

While the trainee may have already acquired some of the necessary understanding, knowledge and competences, the remainder will form the educational subject matter to be learnt. The threshold has been set deliberately low in order to allow for the inevitable variation of baseline knowledge already held by the trainees. It is the teacher who would determine the needs of the learner according to the teacher's evaluation of what is essential or what requires most emphasis.

SUGGESTED ORDER OF LEARNING

The second part of the study was concerned with constructing a suggested order of learning.

It would be possible to apply a variety of criteria to determine the sequence in which the trainee might learn the task of detecting health problems in 5-11 year old children. We have elected to base our order on the process of overall assessment of the child. As this is intimately related to the task for which the learner is to be trained, this sequence will afford positive motivation for learning. It will also help the learner to adopt the desired set of attitudes towards the child and his assessment.

The task of detecting health problems was divided into a number of sections, and each section was subdivided into several subsections. The specification of an order of learning was attempted in three steps:

1. The sections were placed in an overall order of learning
2. Within one section, used as an example, the subsections were placed in an order of learning
3. A detailed order of the learning content of one subsection used, as an example, was determined.

(a) First, the sequence of the sections was altered to a minor extent, in order to enable learning to be based on previously acquired knowledge.

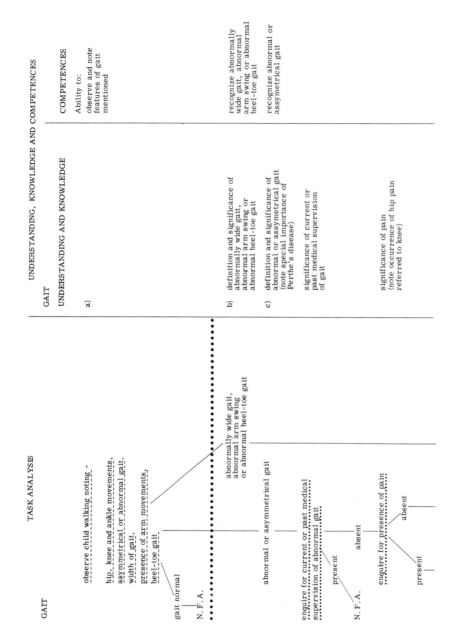

TASK ANALYSIS

UNDERSTANDING, KNOWLEDGE AND COMPETENCES

GAIT

GAIT

UNDERSTANDING AND KNOWLEDGE

COMPETENCES

a)

Ability to:
observe and note
features of gait
mentioned

observe child walking noting -

hip, knee and ankle movements,
asymmetrical or abnormal gait,
width of gait,
presence of arm movements,
heel-toe gait

gait normal

N. F. A.

abnormally wide gait,
abnormal arm swing
or abnormal heel-toe gait

b) definition and significance of
abnormally wide gait,
abnormal arm swing or
abnormal heel-toe gait

recognize abnormally
wide gait, abnormal
arm swing or abnormal
heel-toe gait

abnormal or asymmetrical gait

c) definition and significance of
abnormal or assymetrical gait
(note special importance of
Perthe's disease)

recognize abnormal or
assymetrical gait

enquire for current or past medical
supervision of abnormal gait

significance of current or
past medical supervision
of gait

present

N. F. A.   absent

enquire for presence of pain

significance of pain
(note occurrence of hip pain
referred to knee)

absent

present

354

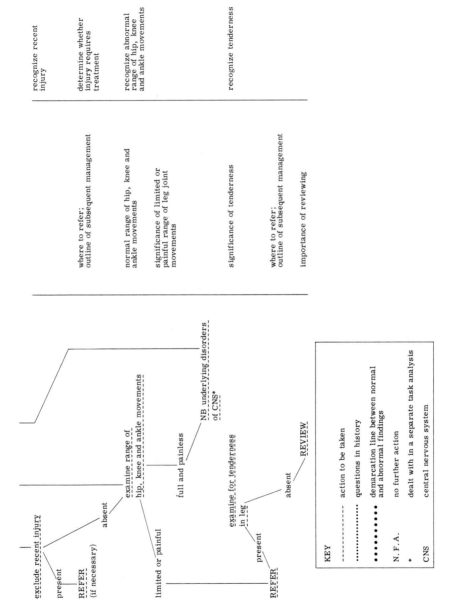

recognize recent injury

determine whether injury requires treatment

recognize abnormal range of hip, knee and ankle movements

recognize tenderness

where to refer; outline of subsequent management

normal range of hip, knee and ankle movements

significance of limited or painful range of leg joint movements

significance of tenderness

where to refer; outline of subsequent management

importance of reviewing

exclude recent injury

present

REFER (if necessary)

absent

examine range of hip, knee and ankle movements

NB underlying disorders of CNS*

full and painless

limited or painful

examine for tenderness in leg

present

REFER

absent

REVIEW

KEY

- - - - - - -	action to be taken
....	questions in history
●●●●●●●●	demarcation line between normal and abnormal findings
N.F.A.	no further action
*	dealt with in a separate task analysis
CNS	central nervous system

355

UNDERSTANDING, KNOWLEDGE AND COMPETENCES

TASK ANALYSIS

SCROTUM AND TESTES

inspect scrotum for symmetry, and presence of testes,
palpate for presence of both testes, noting –

their distance from pubic crest,
their size and consistency,
presence of other swellings

both testes situated
> 4 cm below pubic crest,
size and consistency normal,
no other swelling present

N.F.A.

consistency hard
or other swelling
present

REFER

bilaterally
enlarged testes

see abnormal and
early sexual
development *

one or both testes
situated < 4 cm below
pubic crest

(continued)

SCROTUM AND TESTES

UNDERSTANDING AND KNOWLEDGE

a) normal path, distance and age
   at descent of testes
   (full descent is to > 8 cm below
   pubic crest. Note occasional
   descent to 4-8 cm below pubic
   crest, testes often smaller in
   size, probably of no pathological
   significance)

b) definition and significance of
   hard and large testis;
   significance of other swellings
   (hydrocele)

c) where to refer;
   outline of subsequent management

d) causes for testis situated < 4 cm
   below pubic crest (failure to descend,
   retractile, ectopic)

COMPETENCES

Ability to:

recognize asymmetrical
scrotum or presence of
testis

palpate scrotum and
locate testes, noting
size

measure distance of
testes from pubic crest

determine consistency;
recognize other
swellings

recognize enlarged
testis

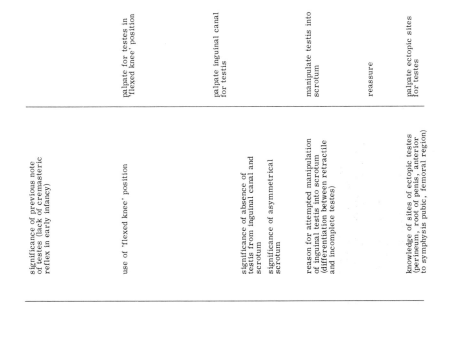

N.F.A.

enquire whether both testes previously noted by a doctor
— noted
— not noted or history not available

both testes descend to > 4 cm below pubic crest → **N.F.A.**

palpate scrotum in 'flexed knee' position

one or both do not descend

palpate inguinal canal downwards on absent side

testis absent (scrotum often smaller on affected side)

testis present

attempt manipulation into scrotum

descends to > 4 cm below pubic crest → **REASSURE**

not descending

palpate sites of ectopic testes

(continued)

---

significance of previous note of testes (lack of cremasteric reflex in early infancy)

use of 'flexed knee' position

significance of absence of testis from inguinal canal and scrotum

significance of asymmetrical scrotum

reason for attempted manipulation of inguinal testis into scrotum (differentiation between retractile and incomplete testes)

knowledge of sites of ectopic testes (perineum, root of penis, anterior to symphysis pubic, femoral region)

---

palpate for testes in 'flexed knee' position

palpate inguinal canal for testis

manipulate testis into scrotum

reassure

palpate ectopic sites for testes

where to refer;
outline of subsequent management

where to refer;
outline of subsequent management;

significance of bilateral impalpable
testes (possibility of Klinefelter's
syndrome; or hypopituitary) and
significance of genetic sexing

absent

present

REFER

REFER
(including for
genetic sexing)
if necessary

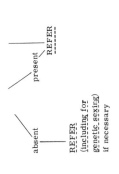

KEY

------------	action to be taken
....	questions in history
●●●●●●●●●	demarcation line between normal and abnormal findings
N.F.A.	no further action
*	dealt with in a separate task analysis

358

(b) Next, subsections of the section selected ('History and examination for disorders of other systems'), were placed in a learning order based on the systems of the body.

The task analysis was based on the order of a hypothetical clinical history and examination. However, this order is not constant for all examination situations in which regional considerations may conflict with those of the body systems.

This led to a discrepancy between the titles of individual task analyses and titles of subsections which were based on systems. Nevertheless, the content of learning within each subsection was directly derived from the relevant task analyses.

A suggested order of learning within this section is set out with an indication of the relevant task analyses (see following page).

(c) The next step entailed the amplification of the understanding, knowledge and competences required for the selected subsection of 'Testicular Descent' — and derived from the task analysis 'Scrotum and Testes'.

It was here attempted to define the precise extent of learning necessary.

SPECIFICATION OF LEARNING SITUATIONS AND LEARNING MATERIALS

Using the subsection selected for defining detailed content and order of learning (Testicular Descent), appropriate learning situations (eg individual, group, clinical), and appropriate materials (eg text, patient or model) were specified (see following pages).

EVALUATION OF LEARNING

Evaluation was here implemented in two ways:

1. Using the selected subsection as an example (Testicular Descent), test questions and problems were posed to evaluate the extent to which successful learning had been achieved. The model answers to these questions and problems constituted what has to be learnt (see following pages).

2. The trainee's ability to carry out the tasks described in the Task Analysis would demonstrate his attainment of the learning objectives.

DISCUSSION

In relation to postgraduate medical education, the approach used here appears to be a neat method of arriving at precisely what needs to be learnt and which learning situations and materials should be selected. The approach also allows an overall sequence of learning to be constructed. Because of the multi-faceted nature of the task to be learned by the trainee, a number of possible criteria may determine the choice of a specific learning sequence. As this choice

Section on HISTORY AND EXAMINATION FOR DISORDERS OF OTHER SYSTEM

Sub-Sections	Task Analysis	Understanding, knowledge and competences
Growth	Height and weight	cc. principles of growth percentile charts
		a)
		cc. positive correlation between mean parental and child's height percentiles
		b) - f)
		cc. principle of equivalent height and weight percentiles in one child in health
	Fingers	g) - k)
Sexual development		c)
Girls	Early and abnormal sexual development	a)
		cc. significance of appearance of several signs of puberty in a girl aged >8-9 years
		b) - d)
	Inguinal region.	a) - c)
Boys	Scrotum and testes	a) - c)
		(testicular descent - see detailed sequence)
	Early and abnormal sexual development	a)
		cc. significance of appearance of several signs of puberty in a boy aged >10-11 years
		b) - c)
	Scrotum and testes	b) (tumour and hydrocoele)
Inguinal region	Inguinal region	a) - b)
Blood	Colour	a)
Skin	Skin	a)
Oral cavity and teeth	Oral cavity and teeth	a) - c)
Nose	Nose	a) - b)
Throat	Throat	a) - b)
Ears	Ears	a)
Glands	Glands	a) c)
Respiratory system	Respiratory system	a) - b)
	Chest shape	a)
	Fingers	a)
Cardiovascular system	Cardiovascular system	a) - j)
	Fingers	a)
	Colour	b)
	Headache	b)
Thyroid		
Hyperthyroidism	Hyperthyroidism	a)
	Cardiovascular system	b)
	Skin	c)
Hypothyroidism		
	Height and weight	b)
Liver	Liver	a)
Spleen	Spleen	a)
Urinary tract	Urine	a)
	Enuresis	a)
	Ears (external configuration)	b)
Skeletal system and posture	Chest shape	b)
	Back	a) - b)
	Legs	a) - c)
	Feet	a) - c)

KEY: c.c. - common core

CONTENT AND SEQUENCE OF DETAILED LEARNING

SUB-SECTION ON TESTICULAR DESCENT

Questions and Problems		Learning Situation	Materials
	Normal descent of testis into scrotum	Individual	Text
When is testicular descent completed?	Descent complete by age of 6 weeks (3 months in premature babies)		
Define complete descent	Distance 8 cm below pubic crest reached by early childhood		
	Descent probably unaffected by androgenic hormones		
What is the significance of a testis lying in scrotum, but not reaching to 8 cm below pubic crest?	Note: existence of testis in scrotum 4-8 cm from pubic crest, sometimes smaller in size, often associated with inguinal hernia - probably of no pathological significance		
	Competence to -	Clinical	Patient or model
Demonstrate ability to recognize an asymmetrical scrotum or the presence of a testis in the scrotum. Demonstrate how you would palpate the scrotum for presence of testes, their distance from pubic crest, and their size	inspect scrotum and recognize assymetry and presence of testes		
	palpate scrotum for testes, noting distance from pubic crest and size		
	Causes, incidence, significance, diagnosis and management of testis/es absent from scrotum		
	Causes		
Faced by a boy with no testis palpable in the scrotum, what would be the most likely cause and what is its mechanism?	**Retractile** - commonest	Individual	Text
	Normal testis, retractile due to cremasteric reflex causing cremasteric muscle to pull testis into superficial inguinal pouch.		Live demonstration or film
	Reflex elicited by apprehension, cold, or touching medial aspect of thigh.		
	Reflex appears after age of 3 months, when testes fully descended.		Text
How would you reassure parent and child about retractile testes?	Reflex is abolished at puberty, with permanent descent of testis.		
If a testis is absent from the scrotum and not retractile, what is another possible cause, its mechanism and significance?	**Failure of, or incomplete descent**	Individual	Text
	Arrest along normal path of descent: intra-abdominally, in inguinal canal, or 4 cm below pubic crest.		
	Testis often smaller, poor spermatogenesis, risk of malignancy.		
	Failure of, or incomplete descent may be bilateral.		

(continued)

If a testis is absent from the scrotum and not retractile, what is a possible, rare cause, its mechanism and significance?		
Ectopic testis – very rare	Individual	Text
Descent through internal and external inguinal rings, then into ectopic site: perineum, root of penis, femoral region, or anterior to symphysis pubis.		
Testis often smaller, poor spermatogenesis, risk of malignancy.		Still picture
What is the significance of bilaterally impalpable testes?		
Bilaterally impalpable testes – possibility of testicular absence due to Klinefelter's syndrome (xxy, xxxy, xxxxy and mosaicism – chromosomal abnormality; infertility); or hypopituitary.		Text
Incidence	Individual	Text
What is the total incidence of unilateral and bilateral true absence of the testis from the scrotum?		
Total incidence of true absence from scrotum – 0.8%, in 10% of total absence is bilateral.		
Method of differentiating causes of absence of testis from scrotum		
Retractile		
Describe how you would verify a retractile testis, giving your reasons	Individual	Text
Suggested by history of previous note of presence of testis in scrotum, especially in infancy, after complete descent and before appearance of cremasteric reflex.		
In absence of history – use of 'flexed knee' position, with relaxation of cremasteric muscle usually leading to full descent of testis into scrotum.		
Demonstrate the 'flexed knee' position and its use for palpating for a testis	Individual	Live demonstration, film or still picture
Competence to – palpate scrotum for testes in 'flexed knee' position, (warm room and examiner's hands; child sitting in a large chair, holding knees to chest with both arms).	Clinical	Patient
If no descent occurs in 'flexed knee' position, how would you attempt to verify a retractile testis?		
No descent in 'flexed knee' position – possibility of manipulating testis from super-ficial inguinal pouch into scrotum to position of full descent.	Individual	Live demonstration, film or picture
Demonstrate how you would attempt manipulation of an inguinal testis into scrotum	Clinical	Patient or model
Competence to – attempt manipulation of inguinal testis into scrotum.		
Incomplete descent and ectopic testis		
What are the signs of incompletely or undescended, and ectopic testis?	Individual	Still picture
Scrotum often smaller on absent side.		
Testis palpable in path of descent, or in ectopic site.		
(continued)		

Demonstrate how, and where, you would attempt to locate an extra-abdominal testis, which is not lying in the scrotum

Competence to –
locate testis extra-abdominally, in path of descent, or in ectopic site.

Clinical

Individual

Patient or model

Outline the further management of a child in whom a testis is truly absent from the scrotum. What further steps may be taken if both testes are impalpable?

Management

Retractile

Reassure

Failure of, or incomplete descent; ectopic testis

Explanation to child and parent.

Refer: paediatric surgeon.

Outline of subsequent management: surgery to place testis in scrotum.

Bilateral impalpable testes – nuclear sexing to exclude Klinefelter's syndrome, possible replacement therapy with androgens.

Text

363

cannot be based on the analysis of the task, the responsibility for selecting a particular overall sequence of learning will rest with the teacher who plans the course.

The question of the efficacy of learning what has here been specified is, as yet, unanswered. The implementation of a course of learning and its evaluation in terms of the learning objectives would appear worthwhile. This would necessitate the construction of actual learning material based on the detailed learning content of several subsections.

During the study, it has been possible to gain some insight into educational methods. This ought to be of interest to any doctor who will be engaged in the planning and implementing of teaching.

The hypothesis that a systematic analysis of learning requirements would assist the author in the study of the subject of his choice has been substantiated. The project provided the incentive for a clarification of the structure of the task that had been selected. The study also provided the opportunity and the motivation to further the author's understanding and knowledge of the subject.

The systems approach, being based on the construction of a task analysis, can only be applied to a clearly defined task. This is a pre-requisite to a detailed specification of what is to be learnt. This study has substantiated the existence of areas which merit clarification, for a subject which is considered sufficiently important to be learnt by postgraduates.

ACKNOWLEDGMENT

The author would like to express her sincere thanks to Mr Charles Engel, Director of the Department of Audio Visual Communication, The British Medical Association; Professor T Oppé, St Mary's Hospital Medical School and the Members of the Consultative Committee for their help and guidance with this project.

Objectives for a Course in Physiology for Medical Students

N. NAERAA.

Owing to a serious illness, Dr Naeraa was unable to attend the conference. His paper, in the form of an audio tape with overhead projection transparencies, was presented on his behalf by his colleague, Dr C Olsen. The present paper is based on Dr Naeraa's introduction to the English edition of **Objectives for a Course on Physiology for Medical Students** prepared by the Department of Audio Visual Communication, British Medical Association and British Life Assurance Trust for Health Education, London, with the collaboration of the Education Committee of the Physiological Society.

Medical students at Aarhus normally enter the University at 18-19 years of age. During their **first** year they study chemistry, medical physics, statistics and genetics, microscopic anatomy, and medical psychology. Most of the examinations are of the open book type and the student is permitted three attempts. **Second** year work includes biochemistry and macroscopic anatomy, and the **third** year concentrates on physiology. In this paper we are concerned with a recently developed course in physiology.

In 1967 a new medical curriculum was started in Denmark. For a number of reasons the Institute of Physiology at Aarhus took the opportunity to adopt a more systematic approach to the teaching of physiology, a thorough knowledge of which is fundamental for the recognition, evaluation and treatment of pathological conditions – as the appreciation of any departure from normal function must clearly depend on a knowledge of what is normal.

The first step in the development of the course was a definition of objectives. The first edition of instructional objectives appeared in 1969 and further editions have been produced since then, the contents having been revised according to proposals from students and from four clinicians who agreed to act as reviewers. A booklet of learning objectives is given to the student at the beginning of the course, so that he has a clear picture of how he will be expected to demonstrate that he has learned successfully. This is reinforced by diagnostic tests which are set throughout the two semesters. Analysis of the diagnostic test results is designed to assist the student to develop optimal learning habits and to establish his own learning criteria. In addition, team-work is specifically encouraged through group learning and seminars.

In our planning we have worked on the basis of the following hypotheses:

(a) Learning is a private process – "We can **teach** you, but only you can **learn** for yourself".

(b) Due to the large amount and rate of growth of information, teaching must place particular emphasis on training in collecting and critically evaluating new information and on the application of knowledge, ie in problem-solving.

(c) No teaching method is ideal for all students or all teachers. Therefore we provide alternative methods to meet individual needs.

(d) A variety of opportunities for learning seems to be essential in order to help students generalize what is learned.

(e) The course only **offers** such opportunities for learning – there is no compulsion on the student to participate.

The course is spread over two semesters. It offers a total of 230 hours and is based on the concept of a spiral-curriculum: the subject is covered in three 'turns' – first a brief survey, next somewhat more thoroughly in lectures, group work and laboratory experiments related to specific organs, and finally by integration through group work, experiments and seminars in the last 14 weeks.

The course is preceded by an **introductory** week intended to make it possible for teachers and students to discuss the main teaching and learning problems using a common terminology. The course itself begins with a four-week activity, where groups of up to 20 students go through Green's book, 'An Introduction to Human Physiology' together with a teacher who may well be the senior professor. Motivation, to interest the student, is the main purpose of the **lectures**, for instance, by showing how physiology is applied in clinical situations. Lectures may therefore present experimental problems which are not directly related to examination requirements.

Group work is intended to offer opportunities for discussing problems arising from individual study and to expose the student to the advantages and difficulties of tackling a problem as a member of a small team. The primary purpose of the **laboratory experiments** is to create situations which demand the same type of problem-solving skill of the student as he will need later on, be it as a scientist or as a practising physician.

The **seminars** are intended as a forum for problems dealing with the integration of several physiological functions. Most frequently we start by presenting a number of problems within the field to be discussed.

Diagnostic tests have nothing to do with formal grading through examinations. They are not compulsory, but are anonymous and informal, providing each student with a detailed analysis of his knowledge and skills at a given time, and providing staff with a basis for the continuing evaluation and revision of their teaching.

The Rotterdam Basic Pathology Teaching System, and the Role of Teacher and Student Within it

M J de VRIES and H S VERBRUGH

The 10-week course in basic pathology for third year students introduced in 1967 at the Medical Faculty of Rotterdam (de Vries et al, 1970; Verbrugh et al, 1971) is best known for its audio-visual (slide-tape) course for individual use. Because the teaching machines are the most spectacular part of the course, visitors and other people from outside the department tend to overlook the fact that the audio-visual course is only meant as a teaching aid to a much broader educational system. For this reason an explanation and tentative evaluation of the whole programme would seem to be appropriate.

CENTRAL PHILOSOPHY

Intrinsic motivation

Effective learning in the sense of ensuring integration of knowledge into the personality structure as a whole, occurs only when a person genuinely wants to acquire knowledge in a certain field: he needs it to solve a problem or to accomplish work meaningful to him. The passing of an examination or a set of examinations required to obtain a degree is not considered to be intrinsic but extrinsic motivation.

Creative action

Effective learning in a sense similar to the above occurs only when a person handles facts, concepts and techniques appropriate to a particular field and actively follows them up. This usually means that he has made a personal — however minor — contribution to the field (evidence for this can be found in references McGeoch et al, 1952; Lahti, 1956).

GENERAL AIMS OF THE SYSTEM

Problem solving attitude

In a satisfactory educational system a person should acquire the capacity to define, analyze and solve problems both independently and as part of a team.

Ability to transmit knowledge

An efficient educational system should train people to transmit recently acquired knowledge to others (scientific communication).

THE EDUCATIONAL MODEL

To meet these general aims we have chosen as a model a system derived from some modern principles of organizational management and planned change (De Groot, 1964). This system has three phases which are successively, and preferably repeatedly, passed through by the student in various directions and within relatively short intervals (Figure 1). These phases are described below.

PHASE I. INFORMATION PHASE

Objectives

This phase corresponds to the teaching systems around which most education, in and outside the universities, usually revolve, to the exclusion of anything else: namely the learning of facts and techniques.

Contents

Lectures, books, tape-slide courses, videotape, film, programmed instruction, practical courses, etc.

Structure

Classroom or instruction group consisting of one (as in the case of the individual slide-tape course) or more students and a staff member.

Sociodynamic model of phase I

Function of staff member The teacher is an authority in the subject being taught. In the more conventional systems he is also expected to be an expert in educational method. In modern systems he is assisted by educational and audio-visual advisors.

Interactions These are unilateral between teacher and student(s) and most of the time also unidirectional, from teacher to student.

Psychological attitudes The teacher is active as a functional authority in the field. In many systems using exclusively phase I, the psychological setting is such that the teacher manoeuvres himself or is manoeuvred by his surroundings into an authoritarian attitude. This is defined as non-functional authority with regard to other fields, as for example the educational sciences.

The student's attitude is mainly passive. He is not contributing creatively through spontaneous, original and independent activity.

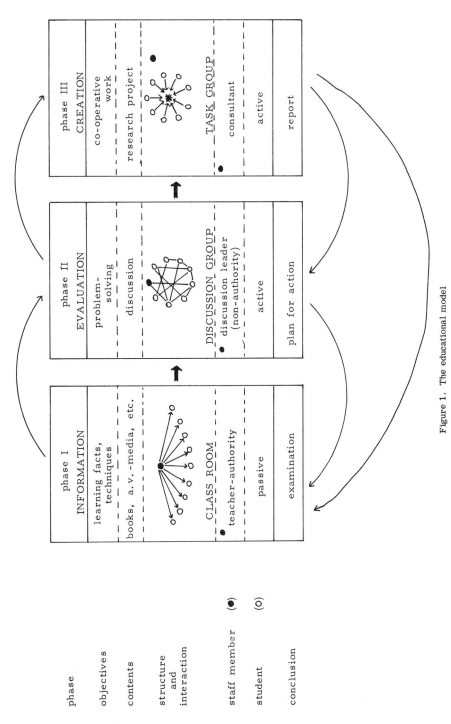

Figure 1. The educational model

phase	phase I INFORMATION	phase II EVALUATION	phase III CREATION
objectives	learning facts, techniques	problem- solving	co-operative work
contents	books, a.v.-media, etc.	discussion	research project
structure and interaction	CLASS ROOM ● teacher-authority	DISCUSSION GROUP discussion leader (non-authority)	TASK GROUP consultant
	passive	active	active
conclusion	examination	plan for action	report

staff member (●)

student (○)

369

Conclusion of activities

Individual examinations of students are conducted, preferably by objective (written) tests. A single test can be given at the end of the course or multiple tests can be distributed throughout the course. The latter system necessitates some degree of programming of the course, but assures a much more efficient feed-back to the student.

PHASE II. EVALUATION PHASE

Objectives

1. To promote assimilation and application of knowledge. This includes the integration of knowledge in the field in question with that of other fields in the curriculum.
2. To promote active participation in the learning process: to develop the student's confidence in his own intellectual capacities and powers of judgment.
3. To induce critical thinking, in the sense of appropriate selection and interpretation of data according to well defined criteria. This includes the evaluation of the relevance of such data to the scientific field under consideration, to medicine in general, social welfare and personal goals.
4. To learn when and how to consult books and resource personnel in a given field. This demands insight by the student into the limitations of his own knowledge and capabilities, and those of the various specialists.
5. To develop the ability to understand and respect the viewpoints of others. The student must also learn to recognize his own blind spots in respect to problems under discussion.

Contents

Discussion and solution of a problem presented, together with the relevant data, by one or more members of the group.

Structure

Discussion groups consisting of 7-12 students and a tutor. A pool of staff members is available to act as consultants to groups whenever the need arises for specialist information.

Sociodynamic model of phase II

Function of staff member in the group A junior scientist or a senior student acts as tutor. As such he guides the interaction and the discussion procedure in the group. He has previously been specially trained in discussion technique and group dynamics: he has a general knowledge of the subject matter acquired from following the course as a student himself. Since the major task of the tutor does not involve the contribution of specialist knowledge he does not require to be (in fact, preferably should not be) an authority in the field.

Interaction   Multilateral and multidirectional.

Psychological attitudes   The tutor is active whenever the group needs procedural guidance or when interaction between group members is non-productive. He does not actively contribute to the scientific content of the problem solving process.

The students participate actively in the procedure and in interaction during the discussion, and they contribute to its scientific content.

Conclusion of activities

The group as a whole comes to a conclusion with regard to the problem presented, which includes a summary and decisions for future activity.   This may be a return to phase I for further information, consultation with a specialist staff member, the formulation of a new problem for discussion or progression to phase III.   The latter involves the design of an experiment or any other procedure for action and the selection of the appropriate materials and methods.

PHASE III. CREATIVE PHASE

This phase concerns the actual realization of a piece of work and may take various forms (such as the carrying out of an experiment, field work, or the preparation of an essay).   Although this can be undertaken by individuals, preferably two or more members and when possible the whole group work together at the problem.   Tasks are divided between group members, each task demanding an understanding of its own specific information and techniques. In this way the group functions as a model of a multidisciplinary team.

Objectives

1.   To create possibilities for the carrying out of a piece of original work for which the student takes full responsibility.
2.   To promote the division of labour among the members of a team in relation to the central problem.   This involves the acquisition of special knowledge and technical abilities by each of the members, and leads to the development of a sense of mutual dependence together with an awareness of the unique nature of an individual's contribution.
3.   To ensure that the student learns how to cooperate and communicate with colleagues and non-academic staff who have theoretical and tech-

nical competence in fields different from his own.

4. To provide experience in the process and difficulties of research and in the practical application of its results.

5. To train the student in making effective oral or written reports on his work.

Contents

A research project or a part of such a project.

Structure

Task groups consisting of students and members of the non-academic staff (technicians, etc). A pool of staff members experienced in research is available.

Sociodynamic model

Function of staff members Scientists experienced in different fields, who act as consultants to groups or individuals from groups.

Interaction Multilateral and unidirectional, in the sense that all activities centre around the cooperative production of a piece of work.

Psychological attitudes The staff members, not being part of the task groups, are only active as consultants on request. The students and non-academic staff members are each actively contributing their part of the solution of the problem.

Conclusion of activities

A joint publication: alternatively a seminar during which the group members give an oral report of their results.

THE REALIZATION OF THE BASIC PATHOLOGY COURSE
WITHIN THE MODEL

The central philosophy underlying the pathology course is that, in today's organization of health services as well as in the modern medical curriculum, morphological pathology can no longer be viewed as a separate science. The clinical pathologist is a member of a medical team and has a service function, and his knowledge of morphology contributes towards diagnosis, prognosis and treatment of patients. In experimental pathology, research problems are as a rule solved by workers in specialties in which the pathologist has usually not acquired a working knowledge. In this field, also, the morphologist is a service man supporting work carried out by colleagues in other disciplines. For these reasons, it is considered that morphological pathology in an undergraduate curriculum should be **learned** as a service discipline.

General aims of the course

1. The basic pathology course at Rotterdam serves as a bridge between the preclinical and the clinical sciences. The early part of the course therefore attempts to link up with biochemistry, cell biology, histology and physiology. In its later parts the course increasingly centres around clinical problems.

2. It serves as an introduction to the course in clinical pathology which is given in the fourth year. The latter course consists mainly of case work and is partly integrated with the teaching of the clinical departments.

3. To promote understanding of the uses and limitations of morphologic pathology in its contribution to clinical medicine and research.

4. To develop an understanding of the pathologist's role in the medical team and his contribution to books and articles on general topics in clinical medicine and biomedical research.

PHASE I. INFORMATION PHASE

Contents

1. **Theoretical information**
    a) A tape-slide course of 54 lessons each of 15 to 20 minutes, which can be studied with the use of a simple teaching machine for individual use consisting of a tape recorder and a slide projector. The course covers the following topics:
    Introduction (position of pathology in medicine and in the medical curriculum, materials and methods in pathology); concepts of disease and pathogenesis; degeneration and biochemical lesions; cell death and necrosis; atrophy; disturbances of circulation; infections and immunopathology; inflammation; disturbances of growth.
    b) The students are also provided with the printed text of the tape together with black and white reproductions of graphs, tables and schematic illustrations. In the margin of the text are printed references to the microscopical slides and gross specimens (Verbrugh et al, 1971).

2. **Materials provided**
    a) A collection of microscopical preparations, partly illustrating individual lessons, partly related to a number of autopsy cases. The slide box is accompanied by a work book, containing clinical or experimental data, explanations and questions with reference to slides and autopsy cases. Most of the microscopical illustrations in the slide-tape course have been made from this collection.
    b) A collection of gross specimens.

Structure

During the 10-week course the student studies about six lessons per week together with the appropriate slides and gross specimens. This is done in a study room, in which 20 teaching machines are available each with bench space and a microscope. The students are entirely free to use the available teaching material in their own way. Some listen to the audiotape, others read the printed text while looking at the illustrations, a few read the printed text and use the machines only to view the microphotographs and listen to their explanations on the tape, etc.

To assist students, two tutors from the pool of senior students are continuously present during the hours that the study room is open (9am - 11pm) on a rotational schedule (see phase II below).

PHASE II. EVALUATION PHASE

Contents

In general, problems for discussions are derived from all parts of the course: slide-tape course, microscopical slides, etc. In addition a series of autopsy case studies is available, each study comprising a set of microscopical slides, the clinical history of the patient and a description of the findings at autopsy. The students are also free to bring in materials which they have collected themselves.

Structure

During the course, groups of 12-15 students meet twice weekly for one and a half hours each. The group discussions are guided by a senior tutor (a fifth year student) assisted by a junior tutor (a fourth year student) Each pair of tutors is responsible for one group of students. The students attending the course have been divided into ten groups, so that a total of 20 student tutors

Figure 2. One of the cubicles provided with a teaching machine (Philips audiovisual trainer), a microscope and a box of microscopical slides. Note the book containing the printed text of the tape together with black and white reproductions of illustrations

are contracted for each course. A group has its session in a room in which students and their tutors are seated around a table. There are facilities for ordinary slide projection and for projection of microscopical preparations.

During the first fifteen minutes of a meeting, a problem is introduced by two students, who elected to do so at the previous session. This is accompanied by a demonstration of material relevant to the problem (microscopical slides, gross specimens, clinical picture, autopsy results, experimental data, etc). The two students assisted by their group tutors usually prepare their demonstration in the days preceding the meeting. This preparation takes place in a separate room (the 'pathology club'), which is provided with ten double view microscopes, a teaching machine, books for reference, boxes of microscopical slides, a collection of gross specimens and facilities for projection.

At the later part of the meeting as discussion proceeds, the students are free to call in a consultant. The two consultants are qualified pathologists and are available on a rotational schedule.

During the course the whole teaching staff meets at the end of each week to evaluate the week's proceedings. These sessions are under the chairmanship of an educational psychologist of the faculty's teaching research department. The psychologist gives advice on the solution of problems which have arisen, the new strategies are developed to meet the following week's requirements.

Training of student tutors

Two weeks before the beginning of the course, a group of ten students, selected from students who have attended the previous course and who have applied to act as tutors, is contracted for a period of two years. During the course they act as junior tutors. After the conclusion of the course the junior tutors follow a short course in social skills, group dynamics and discussion technique, which is given by social psychologists (the training period has varied from four to six days of full time instruction. In 1971, the juniors had already received preliminary training before the onset of the course). Following this training, the students meet with the teaching staff one afternoon per week in the period intervening between two courses (summer holidays excluded). During these weekly sessions they discuss subjects in the field of pathology and further train in social skills within their own group. About a fortnight before the coming course they follow a brief refresher course in social skills (one long weekend). Thereafter they are promoted to be senior tutors in the next course.

PHASE III. CREATIVE PHASE

The third phase of the teaching model has not as yet been realized. During last year, exploration of possible ways to engage students in research projects of the department has been carried out on a small scale.

The Rotterdam curriculum provides for an elective period of five months in the third year. Six students, five of them having been appointed as student tutors have spent their elective period in the department, working on three separate research projects, together with other academic and non-academic staff members. It is hoped that the results of this trial will provide such information as is required to develop a satisfactory organization of phase III in the near future. However, a major difficulty will be to provide for a sufficient number of research projects and staff to engage all the students in a project. It has already become evident that a single department in a medical faculty will not be able to support such a programme. This, therefore, makes necessary a joint effort of several departments and almost certainly amounts to a reorganization of the whole faculty curriculum. This might render the prospects for the immediate future rather uncertain.

EVALUATION OF THE FIRST THREE YEARS OF THE PROJECT

To evaluate objectively to what extent the general aims of the course and the specific objectives of its phases have been met is a major problem. It is evident that results of examinations, however objectively they may measure factual knowledge, are far from being satisfactory to evaluate such intellectual and social faculties and attitudes as motivation, critical thinking, problem-solving, or confidence in one's own abilities. While test systems for factual knowledge have been developed to high levels of perfection, there are hardly any methods available for objective evaluation of complex educational systems.

At present only a preliminary attempt at evaluation of the Rotterdam course can be made. This is based on the results of examinations, attendance at group discussions and questionnaires.

Results of examination

Students were subjected to two examinations, one at about the middle and one at the end of the course. The examinations consisted of multiple choice and yes/no items (which included the interpretation of projected microphotographs and diagrams) and precoded essays. The total number of items varied between 80 and 120 per examination.

These examinations were evaluated in collaboration with the teaching research department, a faculty unit independent of the department of pathology. In order to make the determination of the pass rate as independent as possible from the actual results of the examination, 15-20 core items were identified by the staff before the students were submitted to examination. A core item had to satisfy the following criteria (de Groot, 1964): 1) it is a critical item in the sense that those who deserved to pass must answer it correctly; 2) it

Table I. Pass rates of examinations
in the first 3 years of the course
(in %)

	1968	1969	1970
First test	74	78	78
Second test	75	80	84

should be of average difficulty; 3) the item should cover knowledge of central relevance to the subject matter taught. The pass rate of the test was determined by the average percentage of correct answers to the total number of core items.

Although this method cannot be considered as being entirely objective, it has been preferred to procedures which determine the pass rate after the examination has been conducted. The results are given in Table I. No definite conclusions can be drawn from these data. Because of differences in student population, subject matter and methods of evaluation, it is not possible to make direct comparison of these results with those obtained at other universities. The only conclusion is that the pass rate and marks of individual students did not differ significantly from those obtained by the same group of students at other conventionally structured courses in the Rotterdam curriculum.

Attendance at group discussions

Data are available for the 1969 and 1970 courses (Table II). These have been divided into percentage attendance before and after the summer holidays. The reason for this is the experience during the 1968 course (for which no data are available), that attendance dropped considerably following the holidays. Staff members who questioned students about this phenomenon were informed that, after the first examination (before the holidays), they knew what sort of items they were expected to answer.

Attendance gradually increased in 1969, leading to a considerable im-

Table II. Attendance at group discussions in 1969 and 1970:
second and third year of the course (in %)

	1969	1970
Before summer holidays	45	80
After summer holidays	80	90

provement at the end of the course. Early in 1969 the teaching staff (at that time still academic members of the staff) followed a course in small group teaching (discussion technique, group dynamics). One is tempted to conclude that the increasing experience of the staff in small group teaching has favourably influenced student attendance. In 1970, the year that the student tutor system was introduced, attendance was still more improved. This shows that, as far as student motivation is concerned, the student tutors did at least as well as teachers much more experienced in pathology. The data, therefore, also seem to support the concept that to create a satisfactory educational system, expert knowledge and educational skills need not be combined in one and the same person. This is also the opinion of many of the students themselves (see Table III, question 4).

Table III. Some results of the questionnaire given at the end of the 1970 course (94 of 140 students answered the questionnaire)

Question	Agree	Disagree	No opinion
1. I would prefer to have formal lectures and practical courses rather than the present audio-visual course and group discussions	4	83	7
2. The group discussions contribute little to the teaching	8	76	10
3. In the course of the group discussions I have learned things that I could not have learned elsewhere	59	21	14
4. The group discussions would be more effective if they were led by a pathologist	35	46	13
5. The training in group dynamics of our discussion-leader should have been more thorough	18	44	32

The questionnaire

A few of the most significant items of the 1970 questionnaire are presented in Table III. The questionnaire was answered by 94 of a group of 140 students half way through their medical course.

It appears that the majority of the students have accepted the present educational model (question 1). Group discussions are considered to contri-

378

bute materially to the learning process (questions 2 and 3). Over half the students feel that expert knowledge of the subject is not a necessary attribute of a tutor (question 4). About the same number of students appreciated the training of their tutors in group dynamics (question 5).

Conclusion

It may be concluded that, although the methods for evaluation of the Rotterdam model have so far been far from satisfactory, the results are sufficiently encouraging to warrant further development and perfection. Both teachers and students appear to be strongly motivated by this educational system.

Development of objective criteria for evaluation of educational objectives, other than the acquisition of factual knowledge, is urgently needed. This necessitates close collaboration between teachers and educational experts.

Small group teaching appears to be a valuable asset in education, especially with regard to student motivation. Practical training of students and teachers in group dynamics should therefore become a regular part of a modern curriculum.

The experience in Rotterdam tends to support the feeling expressed by participants at the 1970 WHO congress on medical education held in Madrid, that the effective use of group discussion and the audio-visual media is one of the most important developments in medical education today.

REFERENCES

Groot, A. D. de (1964) 'De kernitemmethode voor de bepaling van de caesuur voldoende/onvoldoende'. Paedagogische Studiën, **41**, 425 (English translation not available)

Lahti, M. (1956) 'The inductive-deductive method and the physical science laboratory'. Journal of Experimental Education, **24**, 149

Lievegoed, B. C. J. (1972) 'The developing organization'. Tavistock publications, London

McGeoch, J. A. and Irion, A. L. (1952) 'The psychology of human learning'. Longmans, Green, New York

Verbrugh, H. S., Vries, M. J. de and Eastham, W. N. (1971) 'Group discussions and student tutors in a preclinical pathology course'. Lancet, **1**, 228

Vries, M. J. de., Verbrugh, H. S., Eastham, W. N., Wolff, E. D. and Gisolf, A. C. (1970) 'Audiovisual aids in medical schools'. Lancet, **11**, 981

A Package Deal for the Individual Study of Metabolism in the Preclinical Biochemistry Course

JOHN B JEPSON and A D SMITH

For some years, the Middlesex Hospital Medical School has run a fairly traditional type of preclinical course, with the teaching organized by departments using a timetable divided into lectures and practical work labelled 'anatomy', 'physiology', and 'biochemistry'; increasingly, other subjects have been added — cell biology, psychology, computing — so that every student has a crowded day, with every hour of his time from 9 am to 5 pm accounted for on the timetable. In particular, the third term of the preclinical course included fourteen one-hour lectures per week, but **no** free time that could be used for tutorials or small group study. The biochemistry course is arranged so that the topic of 'metabolic pathways and controls' is covered during this term, having been preceded in the first two terms by study of proteins, enzymes, and nucleic acids. Until three years ago, this biochemistry teaching on metabolism was by formal lecturing, about twenty one-hour lectures spread through the term.

We became increasingly aware that we ought to find a 'better' way, or at least a 'different' way, for the following reasons (some of which we see more clearly in retrospect than at the time):

a) the total number of lectures had reached the point of diminishing returns;
b) we wanted more immediate feedback on student reaction, and students themselves wanted more personal dealings with the lecturers;
c) metabolism is a topic which draws heavily on what should previously have been understood. In a lecture, a student has no opportunity of re-equipping himself with suddenly-required background information;
d) diagrams, flowsheets and some chemical formulae figure largely when studying metabolism, and cannot be copied down during a formal lecture. It is unsatisfactory to rely on textbooks which seldom emphasize the points that matter for a particular approach;
e) most current textbooks treat the materials and tissues engaged in metabolism as though they were isolated one from the other. We wanted the emphasis to be on metabolic interrelations and controls such that the

380

student could **use** this minimum knowledge to argue his way into or out of real physiological and clinical situations. All textbooks pad out their descriptions of metabolism with lots of chemistry, which is seldom required for the purpose we had in mind. On the other hand, we wanted to encourage appropriate students to pursue the topic further than the bare minimum distance;

f) metabolism is a topic of importance across departmental boundaries — physiologists, nutritionalists, endocrinologists, all want to know what is being covered by the biochemists. Cooperation and efficient utilization of resources is far easier if the objectives and boundaries of a course are set out for all to see — which can never be done with a lecture course. It also helps the department to have all its own staff conversant with objectives and coverage for parts of the course outside their own immediate responsibilities, especially if they are called upon to conduct revision groups or act as general tutors.

The outcome was to scrap our twenty lectures and replace them by a learning package including tutorials based on a metabolism Manual written by ourselves. The package is not nearly as radical as that described by Professor de Vries and did not have anything like the same intellectual analysis devoted to its construction. Nevertheless, the outcome from the two approaches, and the students' reactions, have turned out to be very similar. Our changes were introduced into a traditional timetable with minimum disturbance to other departments and disciplines, and show that the situation within which most teachers are forced to operate need not prevent experiments with the newer educational fashions.

The Metabolism Package is still under development, but currently it contains four items:

THE METABOLISM MANUAL

This is mimeographed using electronic-scanning stencil cutting, about 120 pages, covering:

(i) a statement of general objectives, though these would better be called aims for they are not behavioural objectives in the sense used by Naeraa and Olson at Aarhus University (this volume). A quotation from this statement shows what achievement is expected when the package study has been completed:

"The student should be able to interpret changes in blood levels of glucose, triglyceride, free fatty acid, lactate, ketone bodies and other related compounds in response to:

a) ingestion of carbohydrate or fat;
b) fasting;
c) muscular effort;

d) administration of insulin, cortisol, adrenaline, ACTH and growth hormone, or diminished availability of these;

e) administration of drugs such as steroids and hypoglycaemic agents;

f) specific diseases such as diabetes, arterial disease, hypertriglyceridaemia, chronic alcoholism, nutritional deficiencies, and certain inborn errors of metabolism.

"This interpretation will be in terms of the interrelationships of the pathways involved in the metabolism of these compounds, considered at the subcellular and molecular levels, and of the hormonal and other types of control mechanism affecting these interrelationships."

We think we have been successful in testing achievement of these objectives, by using problems based on research or clinical situations **novel** to the student and asking for reasoned (though not necessarily 'correct') analysis of the situation described.

(ii) **the text**, divided into sections, with an aim and summary for each section. Many diagrams and flowsheets are included, on separate sheets so that they can be studied side by side with the text. The text is interspersed with short questions, particularly in relation to points from diagrams that could otherwise escape appreciation. Some data sheets are included, not to be learnt, but to be used in tutorials.

(iii) **self-assessment** tests for each section, 14 in all. These are objective-answer questions (answers supplied) which students are expected to use before and/or after study of each section.

(iv) **bibliography** of appropriate textbooks and simple monographs, and of original papers or reviews showing 'metabolism' applied to clinical medicine.

TUTORIALS

The class of 84 students is divided up into tutorial groups of about 15 students. We wish these groups could be half the size, but conditions preclude this for the present. Each group has one tutorial period per week, at a timetable spot still labelled 'Biochemistry Lecture'. This gives each student a total of 9 tutorials during the term, three with each of three different tutors (senior members of the teaching staff). Each week the tutorial concentrates on a defined portion of the Manual, working progressively through it; students are expected to have studied the Manual in advance, and to come prepared to ask and answer questions about that week's portion. Devices such as the 'buzz group' work quite well with this number of students. Tutors take special care to involve all students present in the proceedings.

STUDY PROGRAMMES

At the level of the Manual (and most preclinical textbooks) the topic of cell metabolism is presented in a factual manner, with little indication of the experimental basis or of the intellectual turmoil which went into shaping our current beliefs. In an attempt to rectify this, we have produced two Study Programmes, one dealing with 'Glycolysis' and one with 'Terminal Oxidation' ('the citric acid cycle', though this is not included in the title because that is what the student has to work out for himself!). These programmes are separate from the Manual, but are referred to in the Manual.

The students work through the text of the Programme, which starts to put forward the problems to be solved and the paradoxes to be resolved. At intervals, an experimental approach is devised, described, and the results set out; the student is asked to answer questions; draw conclusions, and devise further experiments to test them. If he wishes, he can summon assistance by reading a parallel Comments section. In general, the experiments described are the original ones conducted by Warburg, Krebs and so on, suitably simplified. The conclusions are cumulated and modified as the Programme proceeds, and at the end the student should feel that he himself has been able to appreciate the metabolic sequences, not only at a factual level, but also at the **intellectual** level. About half our students consider these Study Programmes to be dispensible luxuries, but they are useful starting points for the tutorials, and introduce students to the analysis of **problem situations**, which is the point of the whole package.

(It must be emphasized that this is **not** 'programmed learning' in the educational technologist's sense — they were called Study Programmes because they were self-contained courses presented in an organized form.)

TAPE-SLIDE PRESENTATIONS

Because the Metabolism Manual operates at a very basic level, we are developing opportunities for students to delve deeper into certain parts which interest them. Tape-slide presentations seem ideal for this, particularly if guest speakers are involved, eg the Head of the Middlesex Hospital Diabetic Clinic talking on 'The complications of diabetes', or if a more chemical study is possible, eg 'The structure and transformations of glycogen'.

Reference to the Manual is made as appropriate. Each presentation uses work-sheets and papers that the student can retain. In time we hope to have ten tape-slide packets available for students to study if and when they feel the need.

Although the metabolism package covers the third term, some of the diagrams for it are given to the students in the second term, for use during the lecture course on enzymes. It is explained that these pages are from the Metabolism Manual which will be provided in full later. In this way, the students incorporate into their Manual pages which they have already seen and which probably bear their own added notes. Toward the end of the second term, the whole Manual is distributed, and three lecture periods are devoted to a **general** survey of metabolic pathways in relation to nutritive states.

In the fourth term, following the Metabolism package, the students use their Manual for the group study of various research papers and (last year) for playing a simple 'game'. This game sought to simulate a clinical problem in which the total information available about a patient is parcelled out amongst many people, who have to communicate accurately with each other before the problem can be resolved. In the game, students operated in groups of seven; each individual had a paper bearing the result of some biochemical investigation mainly expressed in the form of graphs — different information to each member of the group, but all referring to the same patient. The winning group was that which first found a way of pooling this information and solving the problem. The subject of the game last year was a case of Type-I glycogen storage disease, but can we use the same material again with this year's class? We doubt it, but at least there are six more types of glycogen storage disease to continue with.

Student response has been quite favourable; less than 10% wish to abandon self-study with tutorials, and return to lectures only. Quite a lot of students want the Manual and Programmes and tutorials and lectures, but do not explain where the time is coming from. One of our tasks is to find the right blend of formal lecture with informal tutorial, of organized presentation with self-study. Because of the large size of the groups and the time limitation, the tutorials are highly structured and tutor-dominated even though there is much interaction within the group. The students have accepted this, commenting on the uncertainty of student-run groups, but we would like to experiment with such methods.

The Second MB and Class Examinations have shown the students to be at least as well equipped with useful knowledge as their predecessors and probably better able to manipulate that knowledge in novel situations. They have certainly enjoyed their course more than previous classes.

A considerable investment in staff time has been required, but this is partially offset by savings in administrator's time and the ease of persuading colleagues to contribute. Plenty of paper is required, but only a minimum of hardware.

New regulations and curricula for the medical course will operate in the University of London from October 1973. The Middlesex Hospital Medical School hopes to take this opportunity to reduce drastically the student's timetable commitments, giving him more opportunity for private study and alternative learning pathways in all disciplines. Perhaps the Medical School feels confident in doing this over a wide area because we have shown that it can at least operate successfully in a limited field.

We acknowledge the joint efforts and enthusiasms of all members of the teaching staff of the Biochemistry Department, and of the classes of preclinical students, in developing and sustaining this approach.

Observations on the Writing of
Programs on Cytology and Histology
J M D HARDING

Material on exhibit will include a tape-slide presentation describing practical experience gained in the writing of cytology programs which include the use of colour photomicrographs. This will be accompanied by an example of a fully illustrated introductory program on Cervical Cytology displayed on the AutoTutor teaching machine.

It is hoped that the exhibits will stimulate discussion on such programs and the problems likely to be encountered in their production.

The commentary will cover the following points:

1.   The possibility of using high fidelity photomicrographs as illustrations in teaching programs means that on one and the same frame the student can be provided with a close simulation of what he would actually see through the microscope, accompanied by descriptive text related to the photograph, and supplemented, where necessary, by an explanatory diagram. The student is taught to recognize cells or tissues as they really appear, not as they ideally ought to appear. He is, therefore, much better equipped to deal with the practical part of his training.

2.   A description is given of the format of the introductory program on Cervical Cytology (which will be on display), in which colour photomicrographs were extensively used.

3.   Reference is made under the following headings to some of the problems inherent in writing this type of program:

   a)   achieving an efficient working relationship between the consultant, who is expert in the subject matter, but usually not in programming, and the programmer, who possesses skill in program writing, but is unlikely to have specialized knowledge of the subject matter;

   b)   deciding on how much information to include in an introductory program on a subject of vast extent;

   c)   dealing with differences of opinion between experts;

d)   finding suitable photomicrographs for use as illustrations; the
advantages and disadvantages of using ones already available
or of having a set taken specially for the program; consideration
of features which make a picture unsuitable for program use.

4.   Some suggestions are offered as to how the work of producing such a
program could be organized and on ways in which difficulties can be
minimized or overcome.

5.   Reference is made to the possibilities and limitations of extending this
type of programming to other areas in the medical and biological fields.

Method of presentation: Tape-slide and teaching machine

Editors' note:

The programme also included a paper in Module 5 by Dr J Day of King's
College, London, entitled "Learning Objectives: their definition and implementation for a series of individual learning programmes in clinical diabetes",
and one in Module 6 by Professor H U Zollinger of the University of Basel,
entitled "A programmed course in pathohistology: design and use", which
was published in "Medical and Biological Illustration", Volume 22, No. 3
(July, 1972).

A Programmed Approach to Staff and Patient Training in an Artificial Kidney Unit

S N MARSON

INTRODUCTION

In 1968 the Sheffield Area Nurse Training Committee initiated a research project to study the application of programmed instruction to the training of nurses. The project to run for a three year term, was financed by the Nuffield Hospitals Trust, the Board of Governors, United Sheffield Hospitals and the Sheffield Regional Hospital Board. A nurse tutor was appointed to carry out the research working under the direction of Professor Kay of the Department of Psychology and the Director of the Programmed Instruction Centre for Industry at Sheffield University.

THE INTRODUCTION OF PROGRAMMED INSTRUCTION INTO SCHOOLS OF NURSING

Discussions early in the project resulted in a decision to concentrate effort on introducing the use of programmed instruction into schools of nursing. Sources of programmed material published and unpublished were located and the information collected was compiled into a 'Register of Programs for Nurses' (Marson, 1970), a copy of which was distributed to all schools in the region. Nurse tutors now had access to more detailed information on sources of programmed materials than was previously available. Programs considered suitable were selected for evaluation. The studies aimed to test the teaching effectiveness of the programs in terms of the achievement of the stated objectives (not all published programs contain validation data). Students' attitudes towards programmed instruction, and constraints surrounding class administration, were also assessed. Information collected from the studies was disseminated around the region by means of regular news letters and published papers. Conferences and workshops were held in schools in the region to show programmed learning in action (Marson, 1971).

A PROGRAMMED APPROACH TO 'ON THE JOB' TRAINING

During the three year term of the project there has been a gradual increase

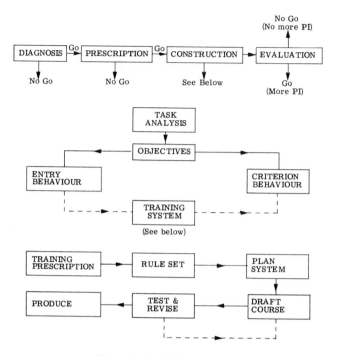

Figure 1. The Sheffield System

in the amount of programmed materials produced and used in schools of
nursing.

The programs covered mainly the knowledge content of nurse training,
in particular anatomy and physiology. The use of programmed techniques to
teach the skills required by nurses 'on the job' is as yet virtually unexplored,
yet it is on the job that the transmission of information may be at its minimum. The introduction of automation into medical care has brought its own
special problems. The use of complicated machinery to take over vital functions for the patient or to monitor his progress, means nurses working
in units containing such machines have to learn skills not included in basic
training courses. Discussion of these problems led to the proposal that an
attempt be made to improve 'on the job' training by applying the Sheffield
System of Instructional Programming (Hudson, 1969) to the teaching of skills
required by nurses and patients working in an artificial kidney unit (Figure 1).

A CO-OPERATIVE PROJECT

THE PROBLEM

Haemodialysis has gained such acceptance as an effective method of treatment
for chronic kidney disease, that the number of patients kept alive on kidney

machines has doubled over the past two years. The pressures on staff and space at the hospitals has led to the development of training patients to carry out the treatment in their own homes. In the Sheffield region alone there are 37 patients dialyzing at home, some as far as forty miles away from the nearest hospital unit. Patients and relatives must therefore be capable of dealing with any emergency that may arise, and be able to carry out simple fault finding exercises on their machines.

The recruitment of staff to work in haemodialysis units can be a problem. The skills taught in basic nursing courses do not appear relevant to the work carried out on such a unit and nurses may be called upon to make life or death decisions early in the training course. The presence of complicated machinery and an awareness that the patient may in some instances know more than the nurse, greatly adds to the feeling of insecurity experienced by many. Nurses are reluctant to come forward to work in such units: therefore staff capable of carrying out such specialized training are in short supply.

In such a situation a training scheme which enables patients and staff to acquire the basic knowledge and skills with the minimum of assistance, is clearly a desirable innovation. Such a scheme is currently being developed by the Nursing Research Officer of the Programmed Instruction Centre for Industry in co-operation with the Charge Nurse and Senior Technician of the haemodialysis unit, Lodge Moor Hospital, Sheffield.

METHODS AND MEDIA

The 'training package' developed so far consists of:

1. **A synchronized tape/slide program** 'An Introduction to Haemodialysis'. This three part program, which can be used for individual or group instruction, teaches the background knowledge necessary for safe dialysis. Part one covers the function of the natural kidney, kidney disease and its treatment, parts two and three the artificial kidney and the kidney machine. Validation trials show that the program is successful in achieving the specified objectives.

2. **An instruction manual** covering the preparation of the two types of kidney machines used on the unit. The manual consists of algorithms, flow charts and instruction sheets covering the procedural steps and decisions involved in preparing a machine for dialysis. The manual has proved easier to follow than the prose style manufacturer's manual (Gane et al, 1966). The discussions involved in its preparation brought about agreement on the correct procedures to follow and techniques are now standardized. After a short period of instruction and encouragement the trainees can prepare a machine for dialysis with minimal or no supervision, faster than with previous training methods.

3. **Skill Evaluation check lists**, covering the various practical skills required, eg building a kidney, 'putting on' or 'taking off' dialysis. In the early stages of training an experienced member of staff carries out a skilled operation while the learner observes and checks off each step on the list as it is carried out. The check lists are also used by the trained staff for assessing the degree of competence achieved at various stages of the training program. As with the instruction manual, preparation of the 'check lists' has brought about standardization of procedures.

4. **A series of fault diagnosis charts** have been prepared for the commoner clinical and technical complications that can arise. Some of the complications are life threatening, so decisions must be reached swiftly. The charts list in columns the complications, symptoms, possible causes (in order of frequency of occurrence) and remedies.

EVALUATION

Many difficulties have been encountered in developing the materials. By no means the least has been the continual interruption of continuity, caused by pressures of work on the unit. The expanding developments and constant modification of equipment within the field has meant that some of the materials produced have been out of date before coming into general use.

While there is evidence that the individual items of instruction are effective, and have stood up well to subject matter critics, the long term benefits can only be surmised.

The evaluation criteria should be that the training system has reduced training time without causing any deterioration in standards of performance. Before this can be achieved more extensive development will be required, and comparisons made between comparable units, one relying on traditional methods of training, the other using systematically developed training material.

REFERENCES

Gane, C. P. et al (1966) 'Algorithms for decision making'. Aspects of Educational Technology I (Ed) Leedham and Unwin. Methuen, London
Hudson, E. (1969) 'The Sheffield System'. Programmed Instruction Centre for Industry, Sheffield University
Marson, S. N. (1970) 'Register of Programmes for Nurses'. Programmed Instruction Centre for Industry, Sheffield University
Marson, S. N. (1971) Final Report 'Sheffield Area Nurse Training Committe's learning project'. Programmed Instruction Centre for Industry, Sheffield University

Method of presentation: A 16mm colour/sound film

Integrating Programmed Learning Techniques into Training Courses in a General Nurse Training School

E J HULL and B J ISAACS

We have found that there is considerable interest among nurse tutors in the use of learning programs, shown by a steady demand for programs produced at the Herts Centre for Programmed Learning, and by the experience of Miss S Marson of PICI in the Sheffield region, as well as by requests to ourselves for the loan of programmed texts.

However, tutors often seem to be uncertain as to how programs will fit into their curriculum as a whole. Our objective, therefore, is to show the different uses to which we have put programmed learning techniques over the past few years, and particularly how they are integrated into our whole scheme of training.

THE INTRODUCTORY COURSE

We introduce student nurses to programmed texts early on in the course, and have found that these have certain advantages, as the students often have somewhat varied educational backgrounds. For example, some have previously learned some Human Biology, and others may have done some previous nurse training. These groups often need some revision, however, and programs allow them to work faster than those to whom the material is new. As this is a new way of learning for most of them, it is also more acceptable than going over 'the same old thing' in classes and lectures. Other students may have newly arrived from abroad, and have some difficulty in following spoken English. Once accustomed to programmed learning they are grateful to be able, for some of the time, to work at their own pace from a programmed text.

Programs used during the course include several on elementary Anatomy and Physiology, one on metric system measurements, and some on more practical subjects such as cross infection and infectious precautions. All the usual teaching aids, such as models, charts, micro-slide viewers or practical equipment are available to the students, and explanations and instructions for their use is included in the texts.

We do not expect students to swallow a new method of learning uncritically. It is usually necessary to supervise the class at first, and to make sure that they write down responses etc. As adults, they also deserve some explanation of the principles of programmed learning, so we wrote a short program on programs', which amuses them and helps to 'sell' the idea. Good results and gain scores on post-tests also encourage them, and they are often quite keen to act as guinea pigs when we are trying out a new program.

We would like to emphasize that students are not working on programmed texts for more than one to one and a half hours on any one day. This activity requires a lot of concentration from them, and in any case some would feel a lack of contact with tutors and other members of the class. But doubtless the way of thinking has greatly influenced all our methods of teaching.

TEACHING PRACTICAL WORK

Film loops, film strips and tape-slides are all available commercially for teaching some practical aspects of nursing. As we have a helpful hospital photographer, we have some series of transparencies, to which we have written commentaries: basically a very similar method. The point is that any of these become much more effective teaching tools if the students are given some structured means of digesting and responding to the information given, instead of watching and listening passively. We do this in some cases by producing a booklet of questions, explanations and short tests to go with the slides and commentary. This also gives the tutor an opportunity consciously to formulate the objectives of the teaching aid.

We use **spoken** commentaries, rather than taped ones. This is because slides etc are generally shown to a whole class, and it is useful to be able to break off to answer questions and encourage class participation.

If one is teaching a practical procedure, the only appropriate form of 'post-test' is a practical one. The students should be seen to **do** the procedure to the satisfaction of a tutor or clinical instructor.

THE STUDY BLOCK TIMETABLE

We are sometimes asked how we use self-instructional, self-paced programs, when some students will get through a program more quickly than others do. What do we do with these students while the others are finishing?

Once they have confidence in programs, students themselves are perfectly capable of arranging to complete them during 'study periods' or for homework, along with notes, reading and other work. So in the study block timetables we arrange for a certain number of 'study periods', and add a list of programs and other work to be done. Students know when the post-test will be given, and arrange their work accordingly.

THE LIBRARY

A corner of the nursing staff library contains copies of all the programs which we use, with necessary apparatus, such as a small slide-viewer, X-rays, bones, etc on one shelf. There are also some other programs on subjects in which some students or trained staff might be interested. Students can use programs at any time for revision, and a separate folder is available containing all the post-tests and answer sheets. By doing a post-test and correcting it, the student can see whether or not she needs to revise a particular subject.

PREPARING STUDENTS FOR PRACTICAL EXPERIENCE

Student nurses sometimes get allocated to a special department before they have had any teaching on that specialty. This unfortunately sometimes happens because service needs of the hospital take precedence over the nurses' educational needs. Programs are sometimes useful in making the best of this situation. For example, a student allocated to the ophthalmic department can work through a programmed text on the eye, so that she has at least some of the basic knowledge which will help her to understand the work she is about to do.

Practical experience may also come too long **after** the nurse has learnt the theory, and self-instructional programs, which can be used at any time she is free, are useful for revision. A recent piece of research by Miss Eve Bendall (1971) seems to confirm one's impression that learning of theory is most effective if it is near in time to the appropriate practical experience. This supposition also underlies the 'modular' system of training recommended by the Royal College of Nurses in its 'Evidence to the Briggs Committee on Nursing'. We think that programmed texts would be of considerable use in any such system.

Again because of service needs, student nurses sometimes are faced with situations causing them much anxiety. A particular instance which we have met is that quite junior students have sometimes been made responsible for observing oscilloscopes on cardiac monitors, especially when there is a shortage of staff on night duty, when they have little idea of what they are looking for. This particular situation led to our writing a program at an elementary level on the meaning of tracings and their significance. In this, we had the advice of one of the medical registrars and of a colleague who had worked in a coronary unit. A copy of this program is supplied to each of the medical wards, as there is no separate coronary care unit in our hospital. It is often used by trained nursing staff as well as by students, as some of the former are married women who have been out of hospital work for some years and have recently returned to nursing. The program consists of a booklet of pictures and diagrams, with a text to go with it. We have a slightly different form with slides and commentary which we use during the first year study block.

POST-REGISTRATION STUDENTS

Twice a year a group of trained nurses on the Mental and Mental Subnormality parts of the Register start a shortened course to qualify for the General part.

These students have a short induction course of one week, but do not enter the Introductory Course or the first year study block. As they have had no experience in a general hospital, most of the induction course has to be spent in revising bedside nursing and aseptic techniques, applied to methods used in our hospital, and in introducing them to the wards. We find that they also need a lot of revision in **theory**. They have previously learned some of the necessary material, but as their training has been geared to different objectives, may never have applied it, so a lot has been forgotten.

We rely very much on self-instructional programs to cover revision of theory, especially of anatomy and physiology. We make a point of giving them **one** such program during the induction course, and explaining how to use it. We then give them a revision plan to cover their first few weeks in the hospital. They are responsible for completing this before they enter their first study block.

Each week, the student collects one program from the tutors' office, and works through it when he or she has time. She then collects the post-test, which she can correct herself by the answer sheet. The calls at the office are essential. They give us an opportunity to sort out any difficulties, and also to ask students how they are getting on generally. The post-registration students like this way of working. It does a good deal towards preparing them for their first study block, and also familiarizes them with the use of programs.

LANGUAGE DIFFICULTIES

We have been trying to make some programs to be used with a tape recorder, to help some of our overseas students who find it difficult to follow and take notes in lectures. This is rather experimental so far, and it is rather difficult to show results objectively.

The idea is for a student to collect a taped lecture and the recorder, with a booklet which tells her what to do. She either has to take notes, or to listen and answer questions about the sense of the lecture. She checks her work by answer pages in the book.

We have no particular qualifications for teaching a language; but it is often difficult, because of the times of duties etc to get students to proper language classes. At least we can help them with the sort of vocabulary they need and accustom them to our accents. But perhaps it is chiefly because they feel they are getting some special attention that they quite like these programs.

"DO-IT-YOURSELF" REVISION

Student nurses are only in the 'school' - Introductory Course and study blocks - for a total of 24 weeks during a training of three years. Their success, especially in theoretical work, therefore depends on their continuing to study in the intervals between 'blocks'. They also need practice in answering the 'essay-type' questions which are set in their Final examination.

We used to find it very difficult, with a smallish staff of tutors, to correct even one piece of work a month from every student. It was even harder to get hold of students to give back and discuss their work, as they might be on night duty, at an annexe the other side of the town, or for some reason not free at the same time as the tutor. It was this that led us to develop our DIY system of revision. There are three parts to the plan:

(i) planned revision, based on analysis of an examination question;
(ii) writing an answer to the question in the 35 minutes or so available in an examination;
(iii) correcting and marking the answer by a 'model answer', which is done by the student herself.

The **revision** for each set of students is posted on the noticeboards each month. They collect the **question** when they have done the revision, at any time convenient to themselves, from the tutors' office. When they have answered it, they collect the **'model answer'** and correct it.

This may not be an ideal system, but it does make it possible to keep a large number of students doing regular work when they are not in study blocks. In fact, we find we see more, not less, of them than in the days when we tried to correct all the questions ourselves, and they certainly get more 'immediate knowledge of results'. Their visits to the office provide opportunities for them to ask questions about the answers, and one can always include in the answer sheet some discussion about the way a question should be answered and reasons for the allocation of marks.

To conclude, what we are trying to do, very imperfectly, is to use programming **techniques** to meet particular needs, but also to 'programme' the curriculum as a whole.

REFERENCE

Bendall, E. (1971) 'The learning process in Student Nurses'. Nursing Times, October 28 and November 4
Method of presentation: Tape/slide

The Message, The Medium—and Post-Literate Man

K AUSTWICK

Educational Technology is a phrase which seems to upset people, especially teachers and other educationists — perhaps they fear that it will pollute the atmosphere of the schools. It has an industrial flavour, so in order to get ourselves in such a context let us start with an industrial problem. I would ask you to imagine a major national industry, with an annual expenditure of about two-and-a-half-thousand million pounds, a work force of about 400,000 and a further 100,000 trainees. The manufacturing time for each product varies between 10 and 20 years and a further ten or more years is required for evaluation afterwards. The number of items going through the system at any one time is of the order of eight million. The industry itself is very old but has been expanding rapidly during the past 100 years and seems likely to continue doing so. If you ask for a specification of any of the products of the industry you will be told that this is not available, being still under discussion! The industry has no central board of directors, but during the past 25 years has had 15 successive general managers — an average of about 20 months each!

The 'industry' which satisfies these conditions is of course the educational system of England and Wales.

Education is something which we have all experienced in one form or another. This seems to make everyone an expert or an authority on the subject.

You will recall that I mentioned a figure of about two-and-a-half thousand million pounds as the annual cost of education in England and Wales, in other words about 6% of the GNP. It has been estimated that this would need to rise to 8% of the GNP by 1980 simply to maintain the level of provision and opportunity now available. Looked at another way, we are spending at the rate of about £5,000 per minute on education. Expenditure on this scale in industry would call for some careful costing and planning as well as close inspection of the quality of the end product; whereas in education the only certain factor seems to be that the more education we provide for this generation the more will be demanded for the next.

Education is not easy to quantify and so it is difficult to decide whether or not we are getting 'value for money'. The system contains a complex of human and material resources, a lot of interrelated social considerations, no known quality control system, a lot of decision-making made on emotional grounds, and a product (the pupil) which has a mind of its own and an ability to interact with the system through which it is passing.

However, let us try to bring a little order and systematic thinking into at least one part of this industry. At the heart of the whole enterprise is the relationship between teacher and taught — or perhaps these days we should say the learner and the manipulator of the educational environment! Either way there is a communication process. In earlier days this was perhaps a little one-sided and autocratic, whereas nowadays it is a little less formal.

There are also opportunities for this communication to be much richer and more sophisticated than it was, in the light of present-day technologies. Let us take a closer look. The interaction between teacher, learner and their surrounding environment is complex and so we must again narrow down our area of discourse if we are to keep it within manageable proportions.

Let us consider a pupil or student, seeking to study an area of subject matter, with access to various aids to learning. We shall not concern ourselves here with the why's and wherefore's of whether or not he **should** be studying this particular topic at this particular time, nor the state of his relationships with the teacher, the institution — or with his current girl friend!

In other words, we will try to deal with a simple problem — **what** the student is to learn, **how** he can do this, how these two factors are inter-related, and how **he** reacts with them:

> What he learns - the subject area or **message**
> How he learns - study aids and modes, ie the **media**

and the student himself, whom we shall describe as **post-literate** man — but more of that later.

Incidentally, we should not regard this situation as static in any way. Not only do the parts influence each other, but also the situation is constantly changing with time — new and more subject matter, new learning aids — and more and more students, and in addition the student's own participation helps to determine how the situation will develop.

By way of illustration we shall refer from time to time to work involving sixth-form or first-year university students in such fields as mathematics, science, and engineering.

Many writers approach this problem with a process model for communication. In this case the sender is the teacher and the receiver is the

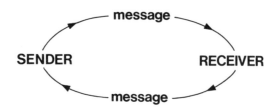

Figure 1. Communication model

learner. This model has often been applied in the teaching/learning context (although we shall in fact find it is not fully adequate for the purpose).

First of all, before any communication can take place we must determine **what** we want to talk about. What are our objectives? In school or university these can be considered at two levels — the overall study covering say a term or a year's work, and the immediate content of a lecture, lesson, or tutorial.

We are notoriously vague about this, tending to use wide generalizations, or idealistic phrases — like 'teaching students to think', 'understanding calculus', 'appreciating modern art'. We are often ambiguous, or imprecise — a point which is well made in that excellent film on programmed learning produced recently by the Royal Navy.*

Much of the film is, of course, concerned with motor skills, but the general principles apply more widely. Take the macro case. How do students know what we propose to study in a given course? Normally we give them a syllabus for the term like this, in statistics (this is **not** an extract from an actual prospectus):
Populations, samples
random variation
probability
frequency diagrams
mean and standard deviations
distributions
estimation
testing hypotheses   — a typical collection of items.

But if we go back to the principles enunciated in the Navy's film and define our objectives, in other words what can the student do and what should he know at the end, then we can work backwards from the objectives and produce a flow diagram (Figure 2) which will show how the various parts of the syllabus fit together.

Thus, referring to the diagram, we cannot talk about **estimation** until we have dealt with **distributions** — of various kinds — which in turn require some understanding of **probability**, and so on.

In this way we can produce a map or model of the syllabus and one suspects that this might be much more valuable to a student than the conventional

---

*Programmed Learning. Stewart Films Ltd.

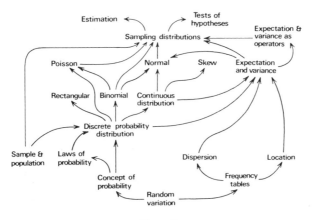

Figure 2

presentation of a list of topics, since it gives him some idea of where he is at any time and how the scheme fits together.

Similar charts have been produced by the Open University illustrating the structure of its courses. The same procedure can also be applied to individual topics from a syllabus, for instance Figure 3 shows an analysis of a 6-hour unit of work on aseptic techniques in biology. It is interesting to note how the statistics syllabus, whilst not linear in form, did at least flow generally in one direction (upwards!), whereas the biology one goes round in circles (or centrifuges perhaps).

These diagrams tell us something about the structure of the subject

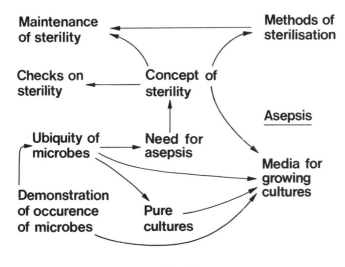

Figure 3

399

matter or message. They do not tell us how best to teach it, but they suggest that there are differences in the nature of different subjects, in the possible order of presentation of topics within one area (even if we use critical path analysis), and in the nature of topics within any one subject. For instance, going back to the statistics chart (Figure 2), we might pick out two topics: **frequency distributions** and **random variation**. The former involves a few simple techniques or procedures to be followed in summarizing and presenting data. These skills can be learnt by each student, with a little practice, and are essentially made up of steps in which the students' answers can be marked right or wrong each time. This part of the syllabus could therefore be taught by some form of individual self-instruction, like programmed learning, in which the student can monitor his own progress.

On the other hand, again referring to the statistics chart (Figure 2), the topic of **random variation** involves a general idea or principle — a concept — which can occur in a variety of situations as different as roulette, the movement of nuclear particles, and the lengths of samples of woollen threads. This suggests a method of presentation requiring movement, quick change from one illustration to another, and opportunity perhaps for discussion — for instance by a closed circuit television presentation.

(A detailed discussion of the relationship between subject matter and teaching mode in statistics appears in 'The first course in statistical methods and the use of teaching aids' - Austwick, K., Hine, J. and Wetherill, G. B. Rev. I.S.I., 39_x pages 287-306.)

We are thus moving from a consideration of the message alone to a consideration of the message and the medium and the interaction between them — and I think it is already clear that the 'communication model' which we started from is already proving incomplete, since it hardly suggested that the message and the channel would interact!

However, before we leave the message, let us pursue a little further this method of classifying different types of subject matter. We suggested that 'random variation' was a concept or idea, whereas '**frequency tables**' involved essentially a skill — which is perhaps a simpler kind of intellectual activity. There have been a number of attempts to produce a classification of these types of subject matter — or the type of thinking (or learning) which they imply, and perhaps it is worth mentioning one or two.

A system developed for engineering courses by Professor Rosenstein in the University of California uses categories like principles, laws, concepts, percepts, definitions and so on.

This is a classification of types of subject matter, whereas the well known system associated with the name of Bloom is an attempt to classify material on the basis of the activity or behaviour of the student and uses terms like comprehension, application, analysis, and so on.

Finally, a third, much simpler classification into vocabulary, skills and concepts, was used by my colleagues, D Harris and P N Richards and myself when working with the Open University on some BBC mathematics programmes called 'Square Two' which you may have seen. In addition to the TV broadcasts, students following the course were also provided with a supporting text and could in addition follow a correspondence course from the National Extension College in Cambridge. The Open University were anxious to know how effective was each mode of presentation — broadcast, text and correspondence course. In order to assess this we classified the subject matter into the three categories: vocabulary, skills and concepts. We had a preview of the broadcasts, and read the texts, and in each case classified the material under the three headings. We then developed tests to measure these types of subject matter. The data, when analyzed, may help us to determine what relationship, if any, exists between the nature of the subject matter — vocabulary, skills and concepts — and the mode of presentation — television, books or correspondence course — in terms of how much of each students learn of each from each! Some of the results were referred to by Duncan Harris in his paper in Module 3 of this conference.

We have suggested so far then, that one can map the parts of a syllabus or subject area to show the relationship between the topics, we can categorize the topics in terms of the kinds of intellectual activity they involve — and this may give us a guideline as to an appropriate method of teaching or learning. In other words, following a normal method of investigation in science we have made observations and on the basis of these proposed some tentative hypotheses which we are now trying to test.

It is also interesting to note, in relation to Bloom's taxonomy, how often the aims and objectives of courses are expressed in terms of the higher levels — synthesis, analysis, etc, whilst lectures and examinations tend to be at the lower end.

Let us now turn to transmitting the message. Teaching/learning originally was a family affair — learning by imitation or by oral instruction. Later on the more wealthy began to delegate this to professionals like the Sophists of Ancient Greece. Socrates is said to have viewed the advent of written material into teaching with concern lest it should lead to a lowering of standards! However, plays, pictures, stained glass windows and even icons played their part in education, particularly at the non-literate levels of society; written material only became a really serious component after the invention of printing — the so-called Gutenburg technology! This latter to some extent tended to ossify spelling and forms of speech, and whilst aiding the development of learning in many directions it has been suggested that it may have restricted it in others. Certainly the written word achieved a status and universality which had profound effects in education. To the academic, of course, having 'read' his discipline as an undergraduate, his ambition is to be known for his 'writing' and publications thereafter.

The extension of education to the whole population, which developed in Western Europe during the last century and which is the aim of developing countries in this, is expressed in the desire to be 'literate'. But, during the present century we have seen a development of communication systems — either in the entertainment industry or as a result of war — which have brought a new dimension — in fact a new frame of reference — into education which may take us into a new or 'post-literate' phase. Photographs, slides, films, radio, tapes, television, have increased and complicated the lines of communication to the student. In fact the **physical** science model, which regards mechanical or electronic devices as adjuncts or aids to communication in education, is rapidly being superseded by a **behavioural** science concept which sees the communication process as a function of people, subject matter and modes of communication interacting together. (If that doesn't sound too much like educational jargon!)

The aids to and methods of learning themselves can be categories in a variety of ways: for instance, they may involve individual learning, as in language laboratories and in programmed learning, they may involve small groups using slide or film projectors, blackboards and discussion modes, and teachers! Or they may involve mass media like film, television and radio. In other words, the aids and methods can be classified in terms of the size of group of students involved.

Alternatively they may be categorized in terms of the degree of involvement or abstraction on the part of the learner — from real-life situations like industrial placement and teaching practice, through simulations like laboratory work or dramatics, to sound and colour film, to slides and charts, to books, to that ultimate in abstraction — a lecture on mathematics!

Let us therefore move round our communication cycle and **look at things from the student's angle.** The most widespread method of teaching at university level is, of course, the lecture, which can be supplemented with visual or sound material. But we want to avoid an approach which suggests sticking bits on to an existing structure. In other words, instead of using an occasional aid in an ad hoc fashion, we should seek to plan the communication as a whole.

But let us start with the lecture. Recently one of my colleagues* agreed to give a demonstration lecture for us to analyze. The topic was in first-year materials science and was at a reasonably elementary level. We were told in advance the items which would be discussed and the lecture was essentially

---

*The writer is indebted to Professor C R Tottle of Bath University School of Materials Science for this demonstration and for permission to make reference to it in this paper.

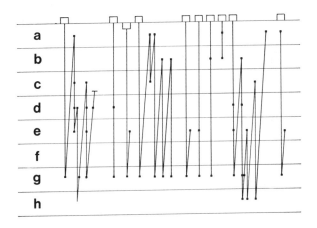

Figure 4. Level of understanding required from student Bloom levels 1 & 2

based on reference to a series of practical situations, like pouring water and other more viscous fluids, which led to discussion and description of certain physical phenomena, like shearing, viscosity, etc. The items to be covered were listed and we plotted the route followed by the lecturer as shown in Figure 4. The letters a, b, c, d ..... refer to: a Molecules; b Graphs; c Elasticity; d Stress; e Strain; f Yielding; g Viscosity; h Shear rate. The items are listed on the left, a dot indicates the item was referred to and each time a new illustration was taken up a new line starts from a space at the top. From this we got a rough and ready picture of the pattern of the lecture. Notice how the lecturer varied the density of presentation, and also how he constantly comes back to this particular item (viscosity). This item would, therefore, appear to be the main point of the lecture.

Now, you might ask, what is the point of this exercise? I think it provides some insight into the lecturing process, and it can be of value in assessing one's own lectures. It could also be that we each have a particular pattern or 'tune' which we play — one cannot resist the temptation to replace the topic list on the left by the music clef — the similarity with a piece of music is interesting. Is our particular tune dull, monotonous, striking, soothing ...... ?

This method of 'routing' was also applied to the Open University project to which I referred earlier, and here one notes a perhaps expected result as we see in Figure 5, that a 25-minute television broadcast covers a large number of topics in 'long paths', whereas the same material is covered more slowly and in shorter runs in the written text. This corresponds to our theory that film or television can cover concepts or ideas because of its rapid sweeps — as mentioned earlier. This again, I think, illustrates the interconnection between what we teach and how we teach — this time from the

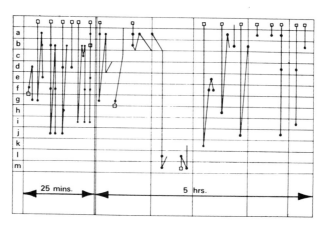

Figure 5

point of view of the learner — the message and the medium are interrelated. This also shows how we can move from considering a live lecture to a broadcast as a modification of a **system** of teaching.

These processes we have illustrated have been **analyses** of other people's work. We were able to reverse the process in the 'aseptic techniques' in biology which we mentioned earlier, by making our own synthesis.

You may recall that we had drawn up a flow chart relating the parts of the subject matter (Figure 3); we then categorized these — into vocabulary, skills, concepts (this time the skills were practical laboratory skills). We were seeking to produce a 6-hour teaching module which could be used here or in other schools or universities, perhaps overseas, and there were certain constraints to be met. The work should, if possible, fall into two 3-hour units, or preferably, smaller units which could be made up into 2 or 3-hour units. It should be possible for students to work in pairs or on their own,

	Content	Media
Unit 1	Overview of asepsis	Film Study guide Photos
Unit 2	Aseptic transfer	Study guide 5 film loops
Unit 3	Sterilisation	Study guide 2 film loops

Figure 6

with the minimum of supervision, and any equipment should be usable on congested laboratory benches.

We decided that there might be a wide range of initial student abilities and background and that a general overview of the topic was desirable first. This we achieved with a ten-minute film, made at the University and at the Bath Academy of Art. This introduced the general **concept** and some **vocabulary**. After this there was a certain amount of consolidation by work book and illustration — the latter being drawn from the film. This is summarized here in terms of 3 units (Figure 6). These materials have been developed by two of our research students — Janet Smith and Caroline Robinson — in cooperation with the School of Biological Sciences.

In addition, there were several simple laboratory techniques to be acquired which involved practice on the part of students. The laboratory skills involved not only doing operations in a given sequence but also within a given time — in other words, timing as well as accuracy was important. We decided that this could best be achieved by a short film loop demonstrating the technique, running continuously, so that, by imitation the student could teach himself (with the help of a work book). But it was important that the equipment used should not interfere with the practical work. This was achieved using a small 8 mm projector, a drawer which stood up to become a screen, and a cassetted film loop — running continuously — and the students working in pairs. The film loop takes only one minute to run through and can be repeated until the skill has been acquired.

We have thus matched subject matter, teaching aid, student need and organizational constraints. This obviously takes us from message and medium to the student. Which leads us on to our advertising gimmick — post-literate man. It is in considering the part played by the learner that the physical science model of the communication process really breaks down, because we are not only concerned that the message gets to the student and that he perhaps replies — he has to be motivated to receive it, he must be able to understand and use it (or let us know otherwise) — and the form of

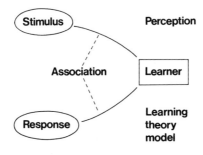

Figure 7

405

further messages will depend upon his success in coping with the current one.

Learning theory models, parallel to the communications one, have been proposed (Figure 7), but even this seems scarcely adequate, and more complex models are being developed. The process which goes on inside the student in learning is a sort of 'black box' situation. However, there do seem to be some areas of agreement, for instance, as children grow up they deal first with concrete material and gradually acquire the ability to cope with logical or abstract thinking. Similarly, at any given age it seems to be easier to deal with concrete rather than abstract problems — which has an interesting parallel with one of the ways we mentioned of categorizing teaching aids (see page   ). It also implies that where growing children are concerned there are some subject areas which involve **types** or levels of thinking which they cannot cope with below particular ages. For instance, young children cannot grasp the concept of conservation of matter — tall slim objects are 'bigger' than small fat ones.

Also, as children receive new ideas and information they may be able to assimilate them into existing patterns or schema in their minds. At other times they have to rethink and reorder concepts and schema to accommodate new ideas, rather like the stage when classical physics had to be abandoned in favour of modern physics because the data would no longer fit.

There are, however, other factors which influence learning — for instance personality factors. A common classification is into anxious/non-anxious types, and into introvert/extroverts. There is evidence* to suggest that anxious or introvert students learn more successfully on their own or with more formal teaching, whereas non-anxious or extroverts favour informal or discovery methods. But we must be careful not to identify all learning with book learning.

Ideas can often be presented more rapidly via film/television, as we saw earlier (Figure 5). Children can often understand and perform mathematical operations without being able to explain or verbalize what they are doing. It is also worth recalling Dewey's view that thinking directly in terms of colours, tones and images, is a different operation technically from thinking in words.

It has been argued that literacy as such can be inhibiting; that, for instance, it places a premium on rational logical argument or verbal reasoning — the 'if A then B' type of sequence which Kenneth Richmond has called a 'ribbon development of the brain'. I suppose literacy has never appealed greatly to the masses, and there seems to be a shift back to oracy as well

---

*G O M Leith 'The acquisition of knowledge and mental development of students'. British Journal of Educational Technology, Vol.1, No.2. May 1970. Page 116.

as a trend to picturacy with the growth of telephones, tape recorders, radio, television and so on. It seems possible that we are moving into a post-literacy phase. This does not mean the end of books but perhaps an end or reduction in their dominance.

But it might be argued that the paperback revolution brought a great increase in the number of books being read. In fact, enquiries suggest that many readers do not get beyond the first 30 pages; the same apparently is true of books borrowed from public libraries. It is worth nothing that educational services other than books, in the University, now have a budget which is equivalent to an appreciable proportion of that of the library. Again, at school level, average expenditure on books for school children is about £1.50 per annum per head, while family expenditure on television rental is about £1.50 per month. National expenditure on school books is £1.2 million. BBC expenditure on educational programmes is £4 million. If we could determine how much teenagers spend on tapes and other creations of the entertainment industry (and what they will spend if cassetted videotapes come on the market) and compare this with what they spend on written material, we should be left in little doubt where **their** priorities are going.

If we might digress for a moment to consider the effect of new media on learners: will post-literate man behave differently from us? It has been suggested that written language stresses conformity, abiding by the rules, a linear cause-and-effect type of logic, that it is socially detached, whereas the popular spoken language and the moving picture are dynamic, emotionally involving and immediate. As we suggested in categorizing teaching aids — written material is symbolic and therefore several stages removed from reality, whereas speech and the moving picture are much nearer to real life.

In the present day there is more information to process, and we have seen that it can be transmitted more rapidly by mass media like television. The impact is more rapid and — being dependent on spoken (rather than written) material and on visual images — is more emotionally involving. It may be less reliable and more prone to bias but equally it may be regarded as less authoritarian.

If you compare the impact of news coverage of accidents or tragedies by television and by newspapers it is clear how much more involved one is by the non-literate medium. Again, the fact that the electorate now seems more volatile may be a reflection of this greater involvement in the immediate. Perhaps the greater reaction to the Vietnam war than the Korean war is another example, popular television viewing having developed between these two wars.

Is the generation now growing up, nurtured on these mass, non-literate media, already showing signs of a new outlook as suggested by Marshall McLuhan which leads to an emotional involvement in the 'here and now' which makes